Pastoralism and Common Pool Resources

The grazing of animals on common land and associated property rights were the original basis of the concept of "the tragedy of the commons." Drawing on the classic work of Elinor Ostrom and the readings of political ecology, this book questions the application of exclusive property rights to mobile pastoralism and rangeland resource governance. It argues that this approach inadequately represents property relations in the context of Mongolian pastoralism.

The author presents an in-depth exploration and analysis of mobile pastoral production and resource management in Mongolia. The country is widely considered to be a prime example of successful and resilient common pool resource management, but now faces a dilemma as policy advocates attempt to adjust historical pastoralism to a modern property regime framework.

The book strengthens understanding of the complex and multilateral considerations involved in natural resource governance and management in a mobile pastoralist context. It considers the implications for common pool resource management and pastoral societies in Africa, Russia and China and includes recommendations for formulating national policy.

Sandagsuren Undargaa is a Development Researcher with 15 years of experience in environmental management and development. She recently completed her PhD at the Australian National University, Canberra, Australia.

Sandagsuren Undargaa has written an excellent book. Utilizing common pool resource theory and access theory, she has developed a conceptual framework for analyzing the institutional, legal, socio-economic and political processes shaping mobile pastoralism in Mongolia. A convincing work regarding the dynamics shaping property relations, land and resource access in Mongolia which is of wide relevance.

John F. McCarthy, *Crawford School of Public Policy,*
The Australian National University

Pastoralism and Common Pool Resources

Rangeland co-management, property rights and access in Mongolia

Sandagsuren Undargaa

First published 2016
by Routledge

2 Park Square, Milton Park, Abingdon, Oxfordshire OX14 4RN
711 Third Avenue, New York, NY 10017

Routledge is an imprint of the Taylor & Francis Group, an informa business

First issued in paperback 2018

© 2016 Sandagsuren Undargaa

The right of Sandagsuren Undargaa to be identified as author of this work has been asserted by her in accordance with sections 77 and 78 of the Copyright, Designs and Patents Act 1988.

All rights reserved. No part of this book may be reprinted or reproduced or utilized in any form or by any electronic, mechanical, or other means, now known or hereafter invented, including photocopying and recording, or in any information storage or retrieval system, without permission in writing from the publishers.

Trademark notice: Product or corporate names may be trademarks or registered trademarks, and are used only for identification and explanation without intent to infringe.

British Library Cataloguing-in-Publication Data
A catalogue record for this book is available from the British Library

Library of Congress Cataloging in Publication Data
A catalog record for this book has been requested

ISBN: 978-1-138-84748-4 (hbk)
ISBN: 978-1-138-58895-0 (pbk)

Typeset in Bembo
by Wearset Ltd, Boldon, Tyne and Wear

This book is dedicated to my parents
(Энэхүү бүтээлээ аав ээждээ зориулав)

Хэдий дээрээс алдартай
Хэрлэн Баян-Уулс минү зээ
Хэтний ган шигээ цэнхэрлээд
Яасан ч холын бараатай зээ...

Hedii deerees aldartai
Herlen Bayan Uuls minu zee
Hetnii gan shigee tsenherleed
Yasan ch hol baratai zee...

(My Mt Herlen Bayan Uuls
Famous from the ancient time
Seen from the long distance
As blue as tinder steel...)

From *Herlen Bayan-Ulaan*, (a long drawn song),
lyrics by Sh. Surenjav and music by S. Tsoodol

Contents

List of figures	viii
List of tables	x
Acknowledgments	xi
Acronyms and abbreviations	xiii

1   Mobile pastoralism, access and policy   1

2   Understanding common pool resource and rangeland management   16

3   Mobile pastoralism and the pre-collective period (*c.*1206–*c.*1921)   49

4   Mobile pastoralism and the collectivization period (1921–1991)   75

5   Pastoral production and pastureland management during transition to a market economy   106

6   Land reform in pastureland management   135

7   Community-based natural resource management   171

8   State territorial strategy for natural resource governance and pastoral production   205

9   Conclusion   235

Glossary	250
Index	253

Figures

1.1	Herlen Bayan-Ulaan, case study area, 2010	9
2.1	Kids are helping in the move to another seasonal pasture	37
3.1	HBU case area until late seventeenth century	68
3.2	Huduu Aral from the southwest: Dolood hills (right) stretch to the south from HBU Mountain (left), May 2010	69
3.3	Huduu Aral from the southeast: the Dolood hills (right), the end of the HBU Mountain, May 2010	70
4.1	Territorial boundaries in HBU case area prior to 1923	82
4.2	Territorial boundaries in HBU case area prior to 1962	83
4.3	Territorial boundaries in HBU case area 1962–1991	84
4.4	A *buuts* with rock wall, outskirt of the HBU Mountain (a). A winter *buuts* with an old wooden shelter in the mountain (b), 2010	97
5.1	Storage buildings from HBU RPA, half looted and used by other households	119
5.2	Territory of the three *bags* after 1992	121
6.1	Winter campsite, 1 ha in HBU *bag*	137
6.2	HBU *bag* participants' migration status by herd size	150
6.3	Participants' herd size by *bag*	153
6.4	Spring campsite next to the river	155
6.5	HBU (a) and elsewhere (b) in the same Herlen River terrain in July, 2010	159
7.1	At the UU *bag* meeting, herders were concerned about pollution on the salt lake	180
7.2	Local herders milking mares for their friends, who were absent (a). Siblings herd and milk only their horses jointly due to scarce pasture and livestock thievery (b)	182
7.3	Range of livestock ownership by household per *bag*	183
7.4	Everyone in the family contributes to household production	184
7.5	Occasionally some herders claim pasture around their locally recognized summer camping spot by leaving a landmark. However, they need to camp elsewhere when other seasonal herders are camping nearby	186

Figures ix

7.6	Movement frequencies by different *bag* households	187
7.7	HBU participants' movement frequency by livestock number	188
7.8	DD participants' movement frequency by livestock number	188
7.9	Ulaan Uhaa participants' movement frequency by livestock number	189
7.10	*Otor* frequencies by households in different *bags*	189
7.11	Broom grass area, where local herders spend spring in UU	190
7.12	*Bag* is also where herders gather for social and cultural events as a community	196
8.1	Map of inter-provincial RPAs in Mongolia	211
8.2	Territorial boundaries of the HBU case area after 2007	213
8.3	Spring shelter is an invaluable asset in pastoral production	217
8.4	*Otor* frequency by household in different *bags* 2000–2010	218
8.5	HBU participants' *otor* frequency by livestock number 2000–2010	218
8.6	DD participants' *otor* frequency by livestock number 2000–2010	219
8.7	Ulaan Uhaa *otor* frequencies by livestock number 2000–2010	219
8.8	Households already built their *gers* in the RPA by September 2010	223
8.9	Spring campsite tarnished and polluted with carcasses by visiting households (on the way out of the HBU Mountain) May, 2010	225

Tables

1.1	HBU case study area administrative structure	10
3.1	Pre-collective governance structure	57
4.1	Changes in the state territorial administrative units in the HBU case study areas	81
4.2	1983–1984 schedule assigned for officials from provinces on *otor* in HBU RPA approved by Party Committee, HBU *Horoo*	99
5.1	Administrative and territorial governance structure after transition	108
5.2	Migration status of herders from each *bag* since 1958	117
5.3	Changes in the territorial administrative and production management units in three *bags*	120
6.1	Inward migration status by each *bag* participant since 1991	143
6.2	Herding experience by *bag*	144
6.3	Seasonal campsites by *bag*	150
6.4	Most practically involved actors in regulating daily pasture use and satisfaction	154
6.5	Impact of legal possession of campsites on changing pasture use rules and norms	156
6.6	Seasonal mobility patterns of the local households with legal possession of campsites	157
6.7	Seasonal mobility patterns of the migrant households without campsite possession	157
6.8	The participants' perception of challenges to pursuing mobile pastoralism	158
7.1	Herder group formation by *bag*	178
8.1	Pasture use fees in the HBU RPA	212
8.2	Determining key actors in organizing *otor*	224
8.3	Satisfaction with current arrangement of *otor*	226

Acknowledgments

I would like to express my gratitude to John McCarthy for his supervision, advice and guidance during the development of my thesis on which this book is based. His continued support was invaluable to me in completing my thesis, improvising this manuscript and in making the research experience enjoyable. I also thank my panel members, Sally Sargeson, Patrick Kilby and Li Narangoa, for providing constructive comments during the final stages of my thesis. Your time and effort are greatly appreciated.

My work would not have been possible without the financial support of the Endeavour Postgraduate Scholarship of Australia. I am also grateful to the staff of the Crawford School of Public Policy, College of Asia Pacific School at the Australian National University for their on-going support of my research. Many thanks also go to my friends and colleagues at Crawford School and the Australian National University for sharing their experiences, both professional and personal, and for the support and laughter we shared throughout. Thank you to Megan Poore for academic advice and Sue Holzknecht for final copy-editing. I would also like to extend my thanks to Kay Dancey at CartoGIS, ANU for developing, producing and revising the maps in my thesis, and B. Batbayar and L. Oyunchimeg for their support. My acknowledgement also goes to my thesis examiners for their valuable insights, comments and the suggestion for this manuscript.

For their welcome, invaluable information and insights, I owe a deep debt of gratitude to my research participants for sharing their experiences. This includes herders from all backgrounds, and local *bag* and *soum* officials in Herlen Bayan-Ulaan, Dolood *bags* in Delgerhaan *soum* in Hentii *aimag* and Ulaan-Uhaa *bag* in Bayanjargalan *soum* in Tuv *aimag* as well as officials from the Department of Interprovincial Reserve Pasture Area Management at the Ministry of Food, Agriculture and Light Industry and Faculty of Earth Sciences of National University of Mongolia. I also owe appreciation to other local people not involved in my research, but who helped me during travel adventures such as being stuck in deep mud or flat tires or trail directions when lost or comfortable accommodations and warm food during extreme weather conditions throughout the summer and winter of 2010.

xii *Acknowledgments*

Finally, I thank my parents L. Sandagsuren and Sh. Tsevelmaa for their constant support and encouragement. Particularly, I appreciate my father's persistence and dedication in accompanying me during the fieldwork for my safety, and his patience waiting many long hours in extreme weather conditions regardless of his own discomfort, while I met my participants. His affection for HBU Mountain, his *nutag*, was inspiring. Also, the time my parents spent supporting the improvisation of this manuscript and their assistance with obtaining rare literatures was greatly appreciated. Lastly, my gratitude goes to my husband Mark Murphy, whose continuous support made it possible for me to pursue my PhD, despite the great distance and separation involved, and his efforts supporting the improvisation of this manuscript under limited time and financial capacity.

Acronyms and abbreviations

ADB	Asian Development Bank
BCE	Before Common Era
BZ	buffer zone
CBNRM	community-based natural resource management
CPR	common pool resources
DD	Dolood
EPL	ecologically preferable land
HBU	Herlen Bayan-Ulaan
HHNP	Han Hentii National Park
IRPA TSC	Interprovincial RPA Temporary Standing Committee
GTZ	German Technical Cooperation
MFA	Ministry of Food and Agriculture or Ministry of Food, Agriculture and Light Industry
MNET	Ministry of Nature, Environment and Tourism
MPRP	Mongolian People's Republic Party
NRM	natural resource management
NSO	National Statistical Office
PRA	Participatory Rural Appraisal
RPA	Reserve Pasture Area
SLP	Sustainable Livelihood Project supported by the World Bank
TOH	Temporary *otor* headquarters
UN	United Nations
USAID	United States Agency for International Development
UU	Ulaan-Uhaa

1 Mobile pastoralism, access and policy

> I have not tried [getting/applying for a campsite] yet. It seems strange neither to get it or not to try for it [applying for one]. We may need to get [legal possession of campsite] one. However, if we get one, then I may need to argue with someone to protect it [campsite and pasture around it] from others. If I do not argue, then others would come and use it. Also, if there is no grass or water, then we have to leave for elsewhere. So, there are troubles with it [legal possession of a campsite]...
>
> A poor migrant herder in HBU *bag*[1]

Introducing the challenges of common pool resource management in Mongolia

Upon learning of the large territory (1,564,116 sq km)[2] that Mongolia has for its comparatively small population of 2,992,908 (July 2015 est.),[3] many foreigners and even some Mongolians are often startled. The need for larger territory, even at the smallest rural administrative level, may have much to do with Mongolians' predominant culture of mobile pastoralism. Local actors, including state-based agencies and herders, have always vied for maintaining as large a territory as possible for obtaining benefits from rangeland. That is why the state territorial administration has become ever more significant for managing pastoral people and production. Since 1990, Mongolia has shifted its economic policy from a centrally planned to a market economy. This policy transition has led to dramatic modifications in mobile pastoralism and environmental management practices. This has resulted in a decline of formal pastoral institutions and possibly in customary land use practices. This decline has led to livestock overgrazing and increasing disputes over natural resource use among various actors (herders, local and national level officials from different jurisdictions) involved in resource management. These outcomes have partially contributed to rangeland degradation in Mongolia. A majority of national and international advocates and scholars have identified the underlying problem as "open access" or an absence of or poorly defined property rights to pastureland (Fernandez-Gimenez and Batbuyan, 2004; Fernandez-Gimenez et al., 2008; Griffin, 2003; Ickowitz, 2003; Mearns, 2004a, 2004b).

2 Mobile pastoralism, access and policy

They suggest that the collapse of the former *negdel* collective institution has led to an absence of legal mechanisms to control the herders' access to pastoral resources. As a consequence of such assessments, national and international development agencies have attempted to strengthen local pastoral institutions and reform pastureland management by implementing policy initiatives based on property rights and regimes, collective action and conservation-oriented community-based natural resource management (CBNRM) (Griffin, 2003; Mearns, 2004b; Upton, 2008). These policy approaches focus on introducing exclusive property rights in order to define key actors to control access to pastureland. However, these policy approaches have failed to solve the problems in pastureland management. Hitherto, pastureland management has been a contested issue in rural and environmental development. This is because mobile pastoralism and its pastoral food production depend upon exploiting common pool resources (CPR) such as rangeland, water and forests. CPR is a system of resources in which it is hard to pursue exclusion and management is costly, because the resources are large and migratory. The users' exploitation of the resources subtracts from the availability of the same resources to others, because they are shared among many actors (Feeny et al., 1990; Ostrom et al., 1999). The failure of current land management policies is based on a poor understanding of the rangeland ecosystem and the pastoral production (Miller and Sheehy, 2008, p. 191). This poor understanding is in fact rooted in questionable global perceptions of mobile pastoralism as an economically inefficient and primitive production system that causes overgrazing (Hardin, 1968; Khazanov, 1994; Sneath, 2007). As a result, sedentary colonial and modern development policies have aimed at shifting this production system to agrarianism, primarily seeking to make use of natural resources more effectively in economic terms and avoid environmental degradation (Hardin, 1968; Khazanov, 1994).

In the twentieth–twenty-first century, this negative attitude towards pastoralism has been reflected in two major policies adopted by the governments of post-socialist and post-colonial countries. First, the state nationalized the pastoral production system towards developing intensive production and took control over pastureland management in larger pastoral societies in Africa and Inner Asia. When the centralized economy failed, state control of production systems weakened. Second, some international development advocates viewed the role of the market as positive for development, but sometimes the market is constrained by the lack of capacity in governments of the developing countries. Thus, from 1970 to 1990, the World Bank introduced its Structural Adjustment Program (SAP) with the aim of shifting the economy of indebted countries from a state-controlled to a market-based economy (Razavi, 2003; Sneath, 2004). The aim of the SAP was to "'emancipate' the economy from the political structure" and allow its own nature to imbue through private property and the market (Sneath, 2003, p. 442). In the agricultural sector, landholding systems have been conventionally seen as static and inflexible in the face of changing economic conditions, because traditional community-based land tenure is considered unable to respond to these changes (Yngstrom, 2002). Thus, the World Bank also introduced land reform to achieve economic growth through increasing efficiency in agricultural land management. The World Bank introduced land titling by registering and certifying existing informal or formal rights (Griffin 1995) and advocated the titling of both agrarian and pastoral land managed under a state property regime. The interest in titling initially derived from a concern that smallholders, who are the key players of agricultural growth, did not have sufficient access to and control over land. Now, under land reform, secure tenure was to be guaranteed to individuals and "household" units through land entitlement. This interest in titling gradually became tied to the economic policy of privatization of state properties, especially of land rights, in order to restructure economic processes (Yngstrom, 2002). Rural land would be privatized as a way to restore agricultural export growth and improve rural incomes and livelihoods (Razavi, 2003). This privatization was expected to trigger the development of a market for land, and consequently provide collateral for credit and promote economic efficiency by facilitating the transfer of land to those who would make the best use of the land. It was argued that this would eventually lead to increased productivity and better land stewardship (Fernandez-Gimenez and Batbuyan, 2004; Griffin, 1995; Razavi, 2003; Yngstrom, 2002).

Ironically, in many cases these policies themselves resulted in environmental degradation;[4] changed the land use practices and limited the value of the land to cash income due to the commoditization of the land or land rights; and contributed to a growing disparity between rich and poor and exacerbated the increasing conflict between state, local communities and individual households (Devereux, 1996; Izumi, 1999). Following the commoditization of natural resources, the very allocation of rights has also become commercialized and has attracted the attention of different, non-primary users; this is seen, for example, in land grabbing by political elites, and has resulted in the appropriation of village land and resources by the state. Locally, in many cases male community leaders and household heads, who are registered for land entitlement, have gained control over a resource (Meinzen-Dick et al., 1997). More recently a growing number of scholarly works have recognized the significance of pastoralism as it provides a secure livelihood that is adjusted to the existing environmental conditions (Humphrey and Sneath, 1999; Miller and Sheehy, 2008). Since the survival of rural livelihoods hinges on natural resources in the pastoral context, natural resource management has been considered alongside agriculture as a way to prevent environmental degradation/desertification caused by the "mismanagement of pastoral lands" and improve environmental stewardship (Bruce and Mearns, 2002; Fratkin, 1997). Thus, some international development agencies have shifted their policy from state control or a market-based policy approach to a CBNRM approach (Agrawal and Gibson, 1999, Fratkin and Mearns, 2003).

4 Mobile pastoralism, access and policy

The development discourse referred to here is mainly based on narratives derived from a variety of theories on property right and regimes, community, and self-governing institutional arrangements, among others. In Mongolia, these development policy discourses led, first, to land reform (Korsun and Murrel, 1995; Nixson and Walters, 2006) regarding that herders' use of pastureland would lead to overuse (Hardin, 1968). Also, based on the notion of a state property regime, the government put in place a territorial strategy for natural resource management that expanded the protected areas system in Mongolia (Bedunah and Schmidt, 2004). Second, following the prevailing property regimes approach, Mongolian land tenure was defined as (failed) overlapping or nested state and customary management (Mearns, 2004b; Fernandez-Gimenez and Batbuyan, 2004), or de jure state or de facto common property (Upton, 2005, p. 586) or even traditional open access commons (Griffin, 2003, p. 67; Ickowitz, 2003, pp. 96, 97). Consequently, international development agencies advocated policies based on the CBNRM approach and prioritized formalizing herders' property rights by engineering nested community institutions under the arrangement of autonomous herder groups (Mearns, 2004b; Schmidt, 2004; SDC, 2010). This reflected the CPR approach of improving/mending historical local institutions or crafting new self-governing institutions (Agrawal, 2001; Agrawal and Ostrom, 2001; Ostrom et al., 1999). For this, national policy advocates re-defined local community and/or the rural socio-economic unit using the Mongolian concept of *neg nutag usniihan* (people of the same neighborhood, who share the same resources).[5] Engineering such socio-economic units, which are smaller than the existing territorial administrative units, has a broader agenda of supporting extensive and intensive livestock husbandry and eventual village-based sedentarization, and developing alternative livelihoods toward strengthening community collective action and adaptation to changing climatic conditions (Bazargur, 1998; SDC, 2010).

However, there is a gap in the literature in (a) explaining the ways in which these policy reforms have failed and contributed to altering pastoral production and pastureland management, and (b) why the theoretical approaches which embed these policies fail to explain the CPR dilemma in Mongolia. This book argues that key problems faced by policy are related to market-based land management approaches and CPR theory specifying property rights to natural resources (Undargaa and McCarthy, 2016). Market-based management attempts to use notions of exclusive individual rights. The CPR approach allows for more sophisticated approaches: building on the notion of a bundle of rights, these approaches privilege community-based natural resource management and co-management (Feeny et al., 1990; Meinzen-Dick et al., 2004). However, both approaches face several particular shortcomings. First, policies based on these theories tend to be prescriptive in nature: both attempts to present universalizing theories of property rights. As applied in Mongolia they are normative, suggesting how things ought to be organized, while inadequately providing a lens for describing how things are, or explaining the process of why things came to be. Second, the application of these property approaches raises questions of equity and legitimacy. Implementation of these approaches increases the complexity of property institutions, leading to further fuzziness. Third, they neglect the way actors make use of wider legal and extra-legal mechanisms beyond property rights to derive benefits from pastoral production. Fourth, they are built on an inadequate understanding of resource governance. Together these approaches via CPR in terms of primary production resource compartmentalize its management, whilst neglecting the management of other production components, which equally influence resource governance. Policy advocates applying such approaches readily misread how pastoralist institutions have historically adjusted their integrated framework of management of the three components (livestock, labor and land) of production to a continuum of equilibrium and disequilibrium conditions. Finally, based on assumptions embedded in CPR property regimes theory, analysts have misread the Mongolian landscape – constructing a problem of open access, which is misleading. In essence, these theoretical approaches tend to lack the conceptual acuity required to understand the dynamic contexts found in Mongolian Pastoralism. They present a "fixed" menu of property mechanisms for defining access and use of property rights and for improving management (Undargaa and McCarthy, 2016).

Mongolian Pastoralism cannot be distilled into the fixed categories of property theory. Most herders continue to rely on customary independent pastoral production and mobility as they lack access to resources to benefit from any other rural development alternatives. Policy initiatives based on these concepts are inadequate in regulating herders' complex patterns of access to pastureland during unstable market and weather conditions. As we will see later, policy makers faced difficulties in applying policies based on a property rights approach as a means of strengthening local pastoral institutions. These policies do not penetrate to the core logic of herders' flexible CPR use patterns, nor do they explain how herders gain access to pastoral resources and manage their production. In other words, they do not necessarily reflect the reality of the historical pastoral production system and the ecological conditions in Mongolia (Undargaa and McCarthy, 2016). Although many have reviewed historical patterns of resource management (Fernandez-Gimenez, 1999a; Griffin, 2003; Ickowitz, 2003; Mearns, 2004b; Sneath, 2003; Upton, 2009), few have emphasized the need for deeper understanding of customary pasture use rules and norms and property relations in pastureland (Fernandez-Gimenez et al., 2008; Humphrey and Verdery, 2004; Sneath, 2004; Upton, 2008). Therefore, the problem is related to both the adoption of inadequate theory in scoping the problem and understanding the extent of change that occurred to various aspects of historical pastoral institutions, and the poor policy practices of adjusting the complexities of customary production management in Mongolia.

6 *Mobile pastoralism, access and policy*

Engaging with emic understanding

My observations[6] have shown me that the concepts of property rights, pastureland management, community and state/public ownership need to be investigated in depth as these are much more locally contextualized than might be anticipated by applying externally derived theoretical concepts. In this book, I use the Mongolian term *ulamjlalt* (customary) to refer to pre-collective (rather than collective)[7] strategies and mechanisms of pastoral production in order to contribute to an emic[8] understanding of property relations in pastureland. This term embodies the complete context of land use practices. Some national and international scholars recognized the term as *ulamjlalt mal aj ahui* (pastoral production that is customary or passed on or inherited by) and *ulamjlalt belcheer ashiglalt* (customary pasture management) (Bazargur, 1998; Erdenetsogt, 1998; Upton, 2009). What constitutes these terms may support any herders' land rights anywhere regarding their historically dynamic migration movement due to conflict, severe weather events or changing socio-economic conditions. Claims under these terms are much stronger than "indigenous," "natives" or "traditional" claims, which are globally contested for identifying local users[9] (Fratkin, 1997; Humphrey and Verdery, 2004; Meijl, 2006). Although pastoral production can be considered as an indigenous production system (Sneath, 2003) in the face of growing urbanism, it still functions as a safety net and a dominant food production system in Mongolia (Humphrey, 1978; Mearns, 2004a).

Understanding property relations in pastureland management requires understanding customary pastoral production management. After reviewing historical (Mongolian and English) sources, contemporary literature, and referring to other scholars' individual points and concepts, I constructed a comprehensive structure of what constitutes the various aspects of historical fundamentals for customary pastoral production management and how these changed throughout history (Chapters 3–5). Historical fundamentals, which continued until transition (Humphrey and Verdery, 2004) embody two characteristics. First, globally, the pastoral production management system involves control of three main components of production: livestock, labor and pastureland (this refers to both the campsite and the pasture around it) (Bazargur, 1998; Bjorklund, 2003; Erdenetsogt, 1998). Second, the control system of these components can be dual, referring to an integrated system of formal and informal institutions (Fernandez-Gimenez, 1999a; Mearns, 2004b). These two fundamentals have been prominent in rural jurisdictions to govern production and herders, despite changes that occurred to various aspects of production management in the past. In its attempt to adjust pastoral production to a modern property regime framework, the state dismantled these historical fundamentals, causing the underlying problems in rangeland management. The changes in these fundamentals led to problems of overgrazing, disputed pasture use and even land grabs by corporations or informal mining entities in rural jurisdictions in Mongolia, regardless of its ecological condition or population. This is because both national and international development agencies overlooked the significance of the fundamentals of pastoral production management in regulating access to pastoral resources. As a result, historical state/public ownership of natural resources (Lattimore, 1932) has shifted to exclusive modern state ownership of natural resources under the notion of the state property regime. In other words, the state has shifted its historical co-management[10] approach from production-oriented land management to a conservation-oriented one (Mearns, 2004b).

Approach, setting and structure of this study

This book addresses the shortcomings of development policy discourse and theoretical concepts engaging natural resource management (NRM) by examining herders' patterns of access to pastoral resources. Employing an access approach, it explores why some benefit with or without property rights to natural resources (Ribot and Peluso, 2003). In particular, this study seeks to understand why recent changes in herders' access to pastureland have led to overgrazing and disputed use of pastureland. The aim of this study is to explore the underlying problems in rangeland management from the perspective of political ecology by examining socio-political, historical and institutional aspects of pastoral production and pastureland management in Mongolia. I address two linked research questions: Why are herders changing how they access (gain, maintain and control)[11] seasonal pasture and how do these changes affect pastoral land management? These questions are divided into more specific questions:

- How have changes in policy affected herders' access to pastoral resources?
- What conditions and factors have influenced the diversification of their access strategies?
- What mechanisms[12] are herders using to obtain access to seasonal pasture?
- How and why do these mechanisms affect herder mobility and flexibility?

Theoretically, this will contribute to our understanding of how and why CPR management succeeds or fails, particularly in the context of mobile pastoralism. This extends theories on CPR management and access regarding the rights and access to pastoral resources. Specifically, it explains the extent of change that has occurred in historical pastoral institutions and the conditions of adjusting to a market economy. The broader literature on NRM emphasizes the significance of defining property rights in managing pastureland. This analysis will reveal the extent to which different state-based actors and herders employ various mechanisms and strategies other than property rights to gain access to pastoral resources and benefit from pastoralism. Practically, it will explain why Mongolian pastoral institutions succeeded during some periods, whilst struggling in other periods, and what needs to be acknowledged when devising national laws and regulations on rangeland management.

8 *Mobile pastoralism, access and policy*

In my research, I considered the qualitative case study approach suitable for examining mechanisms, which herders employ to gain, maintain and control access to pastoral resources in conditions of depleting pastoral resources, which prevail throughout Mongolia. In particular, I focus on the complex relationship between formal and informal mechanisms and the significance of these mechanisms in pastureland management. I chose Herlen Bayan-Ulaan Reserve Pasture Area (HBU RPA) as a single case study as it offers an excellent context in which to study the phenomenon of resource access in Mongolian Pastoralism and the impact of access on pastureland management. First, RPAs were important pastoral assets to improve herder access to pastoral resources and production under unstable weather conditions during times of scarce pastoral resources (Fernandez-Gimenez et al., 2012; SDC, 2010). Herlen Bayan-Ulaan Mountain is historically well-known[13] for its rich forage and pasture, particularly in the winter months. HBU is the largest RPA in Mongolia. It has experienced a succession of management strategies and witnessed several different historical patterns of influx from visiting herders under feudal, collective and market-oriented economic production systems and in times of scarce pastoral resources. It is a risk management destination as well as an easy market access area for many herders from all over Mongolia. Second, this RPA is located within a jurisdiction or in a level of cross-boundary jurisdictions. Thus, it is significant in understanding relationships between various vertical and horizontal levels of territorial administrative units and other state-based agencies. Third, HBU RPA provides an unfolding case, where herders are developing different access arrangements in a real-life context. In response to the high demand on reserve pasture, the state re-established the HBU RPA in 2007. This increased the value of HBU RPA pasture among herders,[14] who competed to gain access using different mechanisms, particularly during the 2009/2010 *dzud*.

The HBU case involves three *bags* (rural micro-districts). First is the Herlen Bayan-Ulaan (HBU) *bag*, where the RPA was established on the territory of HBU *bag* as shown in Figure 1.1. The HBU *bag*/village is the 6th *bag* (smallest administrative unit) in Delgerhaan *soum* in Hentii *aimag*. It contains around 60 households. I also selected Dolood (DD) and Ulaan-Uhaa (UU) *bags* as part of my case study area. As shown in Figure 1.1, (a) the HBU RPA was established by taking some territory from the surrounding *bags* including DD *bag* and (b) these *bags* are the main corridor route for visiting herders to gain access to HBU RPA and herders from these two *bags* also use HBU RPA extensively for *otor*. Thus, competition over the RPA affected pastureland management in all three *bags*. These three *bags* are useful for exploring interactions between local and visiting herders who share and negotiate access to pastoral resources in the RPA. As shown in Table 1.1, these three *bags* differ in (a) their governance of the territorial administrative unit and (b) the type of resource management applied. These differences allowed me to examine the impact of HBU RPA on pasture management in the three *bags*. During my fieldwork in 2010, I carried out observations on herders' daily resource use as well as their four-season resource use patterns and negotiation processes for resource access to understand the

Mobile pastoralism, access and policy 9

micro-politics involved in local land management. I also investigated the relationship between the *ulamjlalt* mechanisms and strategies that herders employ in accessing resources, and the legal mechanisms administered by the local government. The main participants in my research were national and local level state-based agencies and local herders who had lived in the three *bags* and who had experienced differing environmental and land management policies during the collective and transition periods.

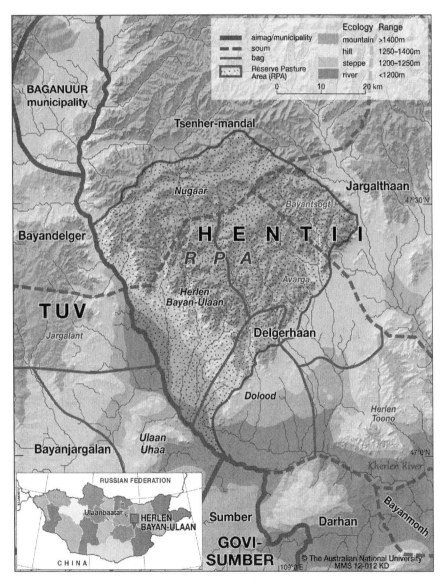

Figure 1.1 Herlen Bayan-Ulaan, case study area, 2010.

10   *Mobile pastoralism, access and policy*

Table 1.1 HBU case study area administrative structure

Key variables	HBU bag	DD bag	UU bag
Pasture	*Bag* territory RPA territory	*Bag* territory Partial RPA territory	*Bag* territory
Governance	*Bag*/village government, Delgerhaan *soum*, Hentii *aimag*	*Bag* government, Delgerhaan *soum* Hentii *aimag*	*Bag* government, Bayanjargalan *soum*, Tuv *aimag*
Purpose	Four season and *otor* pasture	Four-season pasture	Four-season pasture
Pasture use fee	The ministry charge for visiting herders	Local administration charges occasional pasture use fee for herders coming on *otor*	Local administration charges occasional pasture use fee for herders coming on *otor*

Précis

This book consists of nine chapters. Chapter 1 introduces the challenges of CPR management in Mongolia and situates the current study within the related literature. It introduces the scene for the study, describing major analytical approaches used for explaining the problems in rangeland management in Mongolia, and identifying the author's own position on the underlying problems and analytical framework adequate for understanding Mongolian Pastoralism. Chapter 2 begins with a critical review of the major theoretical concepts and frameworks to understand the underlying theoretical issues in CPR management. This chapter essentially argues for a need to investigate resource access patterns, the mechanisms and strategies that different actors employ for both accessing resources as well as for controlling the benefits derived from exploiting CPR within their historical context. Then, this chapter reviews historical changes that occurred to rangeland use practices in larger mobile pastoral societies in Africa and Inner Asia and highlights the conditions and factors that are relevant to why some succeeded whilst others failed in their CPR management. It specifically highlights the ways in which Mongolian Pastoralism relates to or is differentiated from these other contexts regarding its social, geo-political and ecological conditions and builds the background necessary to understand Mongolian Pastoralism. This chapter also justifies the approach, setting and structure of the case study to examine the problems of pastureland management in Mongolia. Chapter 3 presents a historical overview of pastureland management in Mongolia from the thirteenth to the twentieth century. Reviewing various other research works regarding the pre-collective period, it specifically explains concepts such as the fundamentals of the pastoral production management system, property rights, community, the socio-economic units and state/public ownership to understand the historical property relations in pastoral contexts. Chapter 4 reviews mobile pastoralism in the collective period (1958–1991) using various secondary and primary research data. This chapter argues that different political and economic systems can draw benefits from pastoral production, whilst maintaining rangeland conditions, as long as they maintain the fundamentals of production management. This chapter also introduces the particulars of the case study sites: the Herlen Bayan-Ulaan Reserve Pasture Area, the state enterprise, a pastoral institution parallel to collective enterprise as new material in the literature regarding an historical review of the state territorial administration and pastoral institutions.

Chapter 5 discusses the ways in which the state dismantled the fundamentals of pastoral production following the transition to a market economy. It discusses changes in herders' resource access patterns based on the wider literature on Mongolia and the findings from the case study to examine the problems in rangeland management. Overall, this chapter argues that, during privatization, open access prevailed with regard to state and collective assets rather than with pastureland, leading to the collapse of formal pastoral institutions. Customary practices are still relevant when herders access pastoral resources, particularly in dealing with reduced mobility as a pre-condition to disputed pasture use and overgrazing. Chapter 6 discusses the ways in which reduced mobility was aggravated by land reform when the state formalized herders' exclusive individual property rights to campsites. This provision essentially de-coupled campsites from pasture and articulated separate tenure arrangements for each. It changed herders' access to pastoral resources and created conflicting institutional arrangements, which led to disputes over use between local actors from different jurisdictions, and overgrazing of pastureland. The first section discusses the broader implications drawn from various case studies conducted in other parts of Mongolia. The second section examines the problems in detail in the HBU case study area. Chapter 7 discusses CBRNM and the formalization of herder groups' property rights to pastureland and collective action. Reviewing different case studies conducted in other parts of Mongolia under various different international donor projects, the first section discusses key challenges to forming herder groups and in strengthening collective actions in pasture management and collaboration with other herders, stakeholders and territorial administrations. Based on the HBU case study, the second section examines why the formation of herder groups has had limited success in strengthening local community institutions and explores existing notions of socio-economic units, community and collective action on pasture management. This chapter concludes that the policy initiative failed because it created rigid notions of these concepts, which contrasts from their historically flexible forms. Chapter 8 examines the overall implications of exclusive state ownership under the notion of a state property regime and its pursuit of territorial strategy for both territorial administrations and NRM, and its failure and impacts of applying zoning on pastoralism. This chapter argues that the state's territorial strategy over natural resources needs to acknowledge (a) the historical fundamentals of pastoral production management, (b) locally recognized

12 *Mobile pastoralism, access and policy*

resource boundaries and (c) address the interests of jurisdictional authorities over controlling access to pastoral resources. This section also discusses existing mechanisms and its adequacy for herders to express their opinions on various policies.

Chapter 9 concludes the main findings of the study and suggests ways to move forward. A lack of understanding of property relations in Mongolia led to defining the pastureland predicament as one of open access. This misconception led to the application of an alien concept of exclusive property rights, which resulted in aggravating problems of overgrazing and disputes over use of pastureland. My argument in this book affirms the idea proposed by other researchers that Mongolian Pastoralism functions with very complex property relations, which have developed historically and still persist. The system involves historical co-management with dual control over integrated management of the pastoral production components. In other words, regulating pastureland involves regulating the pastoral production components. In this case, I argue that rangeland management embodies strengthening the institutional arrangement around pastoral production and its marketing, rather than focusing only on regulating the land through market mechanisms. This book challenges the idea of national and international development policy initiatives that often promote forms of exploitation that are acting under the analytical notions of various property regimes such as state exclusive ownership under a state property regime or exclusive individual or group possession of natural resources, which could potentially diminish local and visiting herders' ability to move and reciprocate in a flexible manner according to the *ulamjlal*. Overall, it presents the difficulties in specifying property rights in pastoralism and re-explores the notion of historical state craft of state territorial and population administration for pastoral production and resources.

Notes

1 Interview 10 (Undargaa, 2013).
2 See www.cia.gov/library/publications/the-world-factbook/geos/mg.html.
3 See www.cia.gov/library/publications/the-world-factbook/geos/mg.html.
4 Degradation of pastureland is defined as "a more or less permanent decline in the rate at which land yields livestock production, although it is often impossible to determine whether declines in productivity are permanent and to what extent they result from human or natural processes" Sneath (1998, p. 1147).
5 They arguably assumed that this concept had once referred to former state-territorial and fixed socio-economic units (see Bazargur 1998).
6 This is related to my background as a Mongolian. I was born and grew up in the heart of Ulaanbaatar. Also, I have been extensively exposed to a rural herding lifestyle since my childhood, helping my grandparents for almost a decade from 1987 to 1995 and spending the past decade working with herders in different parts of Mongolia in order to understand their role in environmental management and pastoral production.
7 Collective mechanized support was an established practice, rather than pragmatic adaptation. Instead, state formalized few pre-collective *ulamjlalt* rules and norms for production and pasture use (see Chapters 3–4).

8 An emic approach highlights local people's understanding and explanation of their rules and norms. An etic approach focuses on researchers' (Kottak, 2006).

9 Some mining companies contest herders' rights to specific jurisdictional land when herders use the term "indigenous" to claim their rights to pastureland. See also http://bankwatch.org/sites/default/files/letter-EBRD-OT-15Feb2013.pdf.

10 Co-management in pastureland in Mongolia refers to pastureland management, proposing a legal lease of a particular area of pastureland to a group of herders with exclusive use rights for management in collaboration with a co-management committee composed of representatives from the herders, *bag*, *soum* and *aimag* government (Fernandez-Gimenez, 2002, p. 68). This proposal is also discussed in the SDC report (SDC, 2010).

11 Gaining access refers to the "more general process by which access is established" (Ribot and Peluso, 2003, p. 159). Maintenance of access refers to "expending resource or powers to keep a particular sort of resource access open" (Berry, 1993 cited in Ribot and Peluso, 2003, p. 159). Control of access refers to "the checking and direction of action, the function of power of directing and regulating free action" (Rangan, 1997 cited in Ribot and Peluso, 2003, p. 158).

12 Ribot and Peluso (2003) used mechanism, which refers to means, process and relations, because "means" implies agency, whereas access is not always a matter of agency. "The manifestation of mechanisms in power relations between people in other realms of social interaction may have the disciplining effects of controlling someone's access to the resources by favoring the access of others" (Foucault, 1979 and Moore, 1993 cited in Ribot and Peluso, 2003, p. 160).

13 It is famous, because Chinggis *Khaan* often used it for grazing his livestock in winter (Ulziisuren and Tsogtbaatar et al., 2010).

14 For instance, in the HBU RPA in the winter and spring of 2007–2008, there were 351 herding households present with 206,829 livestock migrating for *otor* (long distance movement) from 20 *soums* involving five provinces from central and eastern Mongolia. This increased to 422 households with 272,082 head of livestock in the winter and spring of 2008–2009. These households stayed in HBU RPA for the winter and then some of them camped throughout the neighboring three *soums* during other seasons on the way out.

References

Agrawal, A (2001) "Common property institutions and sustainable governance and resources," *World Development* 29:10, 1649–1672.

Agrawal, A and Gibson, C (1999) "Enchantment and disenchantment: the role of community in natural resource conservation," *World Development* 27:4, 629–649.

Agrawal, A and Ostrom, E (2001) "Collective action, property rights, and decentralization in resource use in India and Nepal," *Politics and Society* 29:4, 485–514.

Bazargur, D (ed.) (1998) *Geography of Pastoral Animal Husbandry*, TTC Company, Mongolian Academy of Science, Ulaanbaatar.

Bedunah, D J and Schmidt, S (2004) "Pastoralism and protected area management in Mongolia's Gobi Gurvansaikhan National Park," *Development and Change* 35:1, 167–191.

Bjorklund, I (2003) "Sami pastoral society in Northern Norway: the national integration of an indigenous management system" in David Anderson and Mark Nuttall (eds.) *Cultivating Arctic Landscapes*, Berghahn Press, New York, 124–135.

Bruce, J W and Mearns, R (2002) "Natural resource management and land policy in developing countries: lessons learned and new challenges for the World Bank," IIED, London.

14 *Mobile pastoralism, access and policy*

Devereux, S (1996) "Fuzzy entitlements and common property resources: struggles over rights to communal land in Namibia," Institute of Development Studies, University of Sussex, England.

Erdenetsogt, N (ed.) (1998) *Mongolian Nomadic Livestock*, "MMM" Association, Ulaanbaatar.

Feeny, D, Berkes, F, McCay, B J and Acheson, J M (1990) "The tragedy of the commons: twenty-two years later," *Human Ecology* 18:1.

Fernandez-Gimenez, M E (1999a) "Sustaining the steppes: a geographical history of pastoral land use in Mongolia," *The Geographical Review* 89:3, 315–336.

Fernandez-Gimenez, M E (2002) "Spatial and social boundaries and the paradox of pastoral land tenure: a case study from post-socialist Mongolia," *Human Ecology* 30:1, 49–78.

Fernandez-Gimenez, M E and Batbuyan, B (2004) "Law and disorder: local implementation of Mongolia's land law," *Development and Change* 35:1, 141–165.

Fernandez-Gimenez, M E, Batkhishig, B and Batbuyan, B (2012) "Cross-boundary and cross-level dynamics increase vulnerability to severe winter disaster (dzud) in Mongolia," *Global Environmental Change* 22, 836–851.

Fernandez-Gimenez, M E, Kamimura, A and Batbuyan, B (2008) "Implementing Mongolia's land law: progress and issues," The Center for Asian Legal Exchange (CALE), Nagoya University, Japan.

Fratkin, E (1997) "Pastoralism: governance and development issues," *Annual Review of Anthropology* 26, 235–261.

Fratkin, E and Mearns, R (2003) "Sustainability and pastoral livelihoods: lessons from East African Maasai and Mongolia," *Human Organization* 62, 112–122.

Griffin, K (1995) *Poverty and the Transition to a Market Economy in Mongolia*, St. Martin's Press, New York.

Griffin, K (ed.) (2003) "Urban-rural migration and involution in the livestock sector," *Poverty Reduction in Mongolia*, Asia Pacific Press, Canberra, 56–71.

Hardin, G (1968) "The tragedy of the commons," *Science* 162, 1243–1248.

Humphrey, C (1978) "Pastoral nomadism in Mongolia: the role of herdsmen's cooperatives in the national economy," *Development and Change* 9, 133–160.

Humphrey, C and Sneath, D (1999) *The End of Nomadism?*, Duke University Press, Durham, NC.

Humphrey, Caroline and Verdery, Katherine (2004) "Introduction: raising questions about property" in Katherine Verdery and Caroline Humphrey (eds.) *Property in Question: Value Transformation in the Global Economy*, Berg, Oxford, New York, 1–25.

Ickowitz, A (2003) "Poverty and the environment" in K Griffin (ed.) *Poverty Reduction in Mongolia*, Asia Pacific Press, Canberra, 95–112.

Izumi, Kaori (1999) "Liberalization, gender and the land question in sub-Saharan Africa" in Caroline Sweetman (ed.) *Women, Land and Agriculture*, Oxfam GB, Oxford.

Khazanov, A M (1994) *Nomads and the Outside World, second edition*, University of Wisconsin Press, Madison.

Korsun, G and Murrel, P (1995) "Politics and economics of Mongolia's privatization program," *Asian Survey* XXXV:5, 472–486.

Kottak, C (2006) *Mirror for Humanity*, McGraw-Hill, New York.

Lattimore, O (1932) *Manchuria, Cradle of Conflict*, The Macmillan Company of Canada, Toronto.

Mearns, R (2004a) "Sustaining livelihoods on Mongolia's pastoral commons: insights from a participatory poverty assessment," *Development and Change* 35:1, 107–139.

Mearns, R (2004b) "Decentralisation, rural livelihoods and pasture-land management in post socialist Mongolia," *European Journal of Development Research* 16:1, 133–152.

Meijl, T V (2006) "Who owns the fisheries? Changing views of property and its redistribution in post-colonial Maori society" in F V Benda-Beckmann, K V Benda-Beckmann and M G Wiber (eds.) *Changing Properties of Property*, Berghahn Books, New York, 170–193.

Meinzen-Dick, R S, Brown, L R, Feldstein, H S and Quisumbing, A R (1997) "Gender, property rights and natural resources," *World Development* 24:8, 1303–1315.

Meinzen-Dick, R, Pradhan, R and Grigorio, M D (2004) *Collective Action and Property Rights for Sustainable Development*, CAPRI, Washington DC.

Miller, D and Sheehy, D (2008) "The relevance of Owen Lattimore's writings for nomadic pastoralism research and development in Inner Asia," *Nomadic Peoples* 12:2, 103–115.

Nixson, F and Walters, B (2006) "Privatization, income distribution, and poverty: the Mongolian experience," *World Development* 34:9, 1557–1579.

Ostrom, E, Burger, J, Field, C B, Norgaard, R B and Policansky, D (1999) "Revisiting the commons: local lessons, global challenges," *Science* 284, 278–282.

Razavi, Sh (ed.) (2003) "Introduction: agrarian change, gender and land rights," *Agrarian Change, Gender and Land Rights*, Blackwell Publishing, Oxford, 296.

Ribot, J C and Peluso, N L (2003) "A theory of access," *Rural Sociology* 68:2, 153–181.

Schmidt, S M (2004) "Pastoral community organization, livelihoods and biodiversity conservation in Mongolia's Southern Gobi region," in *Annual Meeting of Society for Range Management*, Salt Lake City, USA.

SDC (2010) "Livelihood study of herders in Mongolia," Swiss Agency for Development and Cooperation (SDC), Ulaanbaatar.

Sneath, D (1998) "State policy and pasture degradation in Inner Asia," *Science's Compass* 281:21, 1147–1148.

Sneath, D (2003) "Land use, the environment and development in post-socialist Mongolia," *Oxford Development Studies* 31:4, 441–457.

Sneath, D (2004) "Property regimes and sociotechnical systems: rights over land in Mongolia's 'Age of the Market'" in K Verdery and C Humphrey (eds.) *Property in Question: Value Transformation in the Global Economy*, Berg, Oxford, New York, 161–182.

Sneath, D (2007) *The Headless State*, Columbia University Press, New York.

Ulziisuren, B, Tsogtbaatar, B and Shagdar, Sh (2010) *Han Hentii Tovchoon*, Beat Press, Ulaanbaatar.

Undargaa, S (2013) "Property 'owners' without rights? Exploring property relations and access in the Herlen Bayan-Ulaan Reserve Pasture Area of Mongolia," Crawford School of Public Policy, Australian National University, Canberra.

Undargaa, S and McCarthy, J F (2016) "Beyond property: co-management and pastoral resource access in Mongolia," *World Development* 77, 367–379.

Upton, C (2005) "Institutions in a pastoral society: processes of formation and transformation in post-socialist Mongolia," *Comparative Studies of South Asia, Africa and the Middle East* 25:3, 584–599.

Upton, C (2008) "Social capital, collective action and group formation: developmental trajectories in post-socialist Mongolia," *Human Ecology* 36, 175–188.

Upton, C (2009) "'Custom' and contestation: land reform in post-socialist Mongolia," *World Development* 37:8, 1400–1410.

Yngstrom, I (2002) "Women, wives and land rights in Africa: situating gender beyond the household in the debate over land policy and changing tenure systems," *Development Studies* 30, 21–40.

2 Understanding common pool resource and rangeland management

Common pool resource management

For over four decades, the idea of using property policy provided a foundational tenet of landed resource management. Hardin (1968) presumed that the uncontrolled use of natural resources would result in overexploitation, leading to a "tragedy." Therefore, clear regulations needed to be placed under a state or private property regime (Hardin, 1968). In response to Hardin's (1968) analysis, an intuitionalist reading – referred to as the 'collective action approach' or 'CPR theory' – emerged focusing on common pool resources (CPRs) that are readily overused (Johnson, 2004; Saunders, 2014). This framework opened up a new way of thinking about, and managing the problem of complex and overlapping bundles of rights (Feeny et al., 1990; Robbins, 2004). According to CPR proponents, it is critical to differentiate the nature of the resource (CPR) from the management system, which exists with or without a property regime. CPRs are resources from which it is difficult to "exclude" others and where one person's use subtracts from what others can use (Ostrom et al., 1994). Analytically, there are four recognized property regimes (state, private, common property and open access), under which CPRs are managed (Berkes, 2009; Berkes et al., 1989; Feeny et al., 1990; Ostrom, 2009). Hardin defined all situations as an open access problem as there were no specific property rights that he could discern governing the use of the resources and did not recognize existing community based natural resource management (CBNRM). Also, privatization or government control in practice has not necessarily avoided "tragedy" (Berkes et al., 1989; Feeny et al., 1990; National Research Council, 1986). Thus, key challenges for CPR management became that of ensuring exclusion and the degree of control necessary for managing the subtractability inherent in CPRs under joint use (Berkes et al., 1989). The CPR critique pointed to the existence of local actors collectively developing self-regulating capabilities to pursue exclusion and to regulate joint use under specific conditions. In studying why some communities still manage whilst others fail in management of CPRs (Berkes et al., 1989), CPR theorists focused on the effects of changing socio-political conditions on CPR management (Basurto and Ostrom, 2009; Berkes et al.,

Understanding CPR and rangeland management 17

1989; Ostrom et al., 1999). In this revisionist view central state ownership can be detrimental in so far as it breaks the self-governing capacities of community institutions and hinders their ability to exclude and avoid open access. Therefore, the answer to CPR management lay in recognizing and re-installing historical or creating self-governance by community institutions. Alternatively, co-management[1] approaches might provide a way to get co-existing management authorities to work together to govern resources held under complex bundles of rights (Agrawal and Gibson, 1999; Berkes et al., 1989; Feeny et al., 1990). This refers to state-based actors enforcing state rules and norms, and collaborating with local communities under a communal regime (Berkes et al., 1989; Feeny et al., 1990).

Here, discussion of community is critical. McCay and Jentoft (1998) argued that the CPR dilemma is not due to an absence of property rights, but is often attributed to the capacity of the community, which is vulnerable in maintaining social capital or can fail in its protection. This is due to changes in state policies or arrangements (members rely more on the state than on each other) and market-led socio-economic reforms, where economic production is not shaped by members' needs, but by the needs of the market. The authors also emphasized the significance of traditional community management, particularly customary rules and regulations, in solving conflicting uses (McCay and Acheson, 1987). Thus, it was critical to strengthen the community through "co-management institutions and inclusion of user-knowledge as a way of re-embedding management responsibilities within the local community" (McCay and Jentoft, 1998, p. 26). However, community is a fluid notion and is open to a challenge. McCay and Jentoft (1998) remained ambivalent regarding the mixed results of delivering community agenda through participatory development and devolution management schemes. This is, first, due to the misleading idea of communities, which are often seen as small units that are spatially and socially homogenous and well-integrated in terms of interests, cooperation and distribution of resources (Agrawal and Gibson, 1999; McCay and Jentoft, 1998, p. 27). Second, traditional communities should not be assumed as being protective of the environment as they have different intentions towards natural resources (Agrawal and Gibson, 1999) or have not always been able to protect nature. For instance, the extinction of certain species of wildlife in the Arctic occurred during the time of early hunters and gatherers (Lopez, 2001). Third, the possibility of community as a stakeholder assuming responsibility for resource management raises questions about power relations within the community; whether the community would serve the interests of all, or only those who seize authority and make the rules (Agrawal, 2003). For instance, feminist academics question whether customary communities can guarantee female members equal rights to benefits from resources as strengthened customary tenure is transformed into a structure in which most land rights are concentrated in the hands of a minority (Lastarria-Cornhiel, 1997). Agrawal and Gibson (1999) emphasized that communities have a heterogeneous nature in terms of social

18 *Understanding CPR and rangeland management*

composition, resource type and size of territory, which reflects their local political, resource management and broader social dynamics. Thus, community development and CBNRM needs to focus on the politics of the conservation process, which is embedded in local resource management. This process requires the acknowledgement of different actors, of their involvement in local level conservation processes and the strengthening of local resource management institutions. Strengthening weakened local institutions reconciles these different actors to the common goal of regulating power relations among the actors, who are involved in creating the institution, and structuring their interaction towards managing the resources. In this way, formal and informal institutions can function effectively, and remain free of a dominating interest (Agrawal and Gibson, 1999, p. 637).

Therefore, the focus on resource management shifted from an absence of market mechanisms to engineering a complex set of existing local or traditional property institutions into a form of durable self-governing community institution. CPR theorists emphasized that it did not matter as to whether a formalized state or unofficial local institutions maintained the rules and enforcement capacity. This is mainly based on the assumption that "Global and national environmental policy is ignorant of local and traditional knowledge … [and] … leave[s] local officials and users with insufficient autonomy and understanding to design effective institutions" (Dietz et al., 2003, p. 1907). Thus, "those who impose must be seen as effective and legitimate by resource users" (Dietz et al., 2003, p. 1909). A key question became one of fit (ecological and social-structure), enforceability and legitimacy as users are likely to comply with rules and monitoring when involved in the decision making (Ostrom and Nagendra, 2006). Since the rules and norms were very diverse in different contexts, they focused on clarifying the institutional regularities which were found in long-lasting, successful CPR management, but which were missing in some of the failed cases. Thus, the challenge became one of clarifying the circumstances that might support improved CPR management, and either mending deficiencies in the old institutional arrangements, or crafting newer and better rules using a nested approach involving different layers of enterprises and actors in a wider enabling context (Agrawal, 2001; Agrawal and Ostrom, 2001; Ostrom et al., 1999). This process of designing principles implies a redefinition of local community groups and their resource management institutions (Agrawal, 2003). Institutional theorists came up with design principles that rely on 8–36 variables that communities need to possess to ensure a successful self-governing community institution (Agrawal, 2001). This design focuses on "the power to exclude people other than members of a defined community" (Ostrom et al., 1999, p. 7). The following variables appear to be crucial to the "principle of exclusion": (a) a well-defined social and resource boundary of (b) a smaller size group with (c) all local members affected by the resource regime involved in developing or modifying the rules (Agrawal, 2001; Agrawal and Ostrom, 2001; Dietz et al., 2003; Ostrom, 2009; Schlager, 2004; Wollenberg et al., 2007). Although not

Understanding CPR and rangeland management   19

a prescription for institutional design, community self-governing institutions become an alternative to the state-led and market-oriented policies that governed CPR management (Agrawal, 2003; Marshall, 2008). However, recognizing complexity in real life, Ostrom (2009) acknowledged the importance of going "beyond a panacea," a universal design principle, and incorporating flexibility when addressing the specific social and historical aspects in various CPR governance arrangements in different contexts and tenure regimes. Thus, there is a challenge of engineering a form of durable property institution that has a capacity to cope and adapt in changing socio-political, economic and ecological conditions (Agrawal, 2010; Basurto and Ostrom, 2009; Feeny et al., 1990; Ostrom, 1990, 2009; Wollenberg et al., 2007).

This challenge is related to the fact that it is difficult to apply these variables in different contexts, where resource type and user groups are mainly diverse and dynamic (Cleaver and Franks, 2005; Schlager, 2004). First, a design principle is usually applied without recognizing the socially constructed values that shape collective action (Ruttan 2000 cited in Cleaver and Franks, 2005). Design principles highlight the responsibility of rule-making to a minority within a group, those who have the power to rule over the majority of the members (Cleaver and Franks, 2005). Also, locally made rules are problematic to enforce as these can be quite abstract in the context of shared CPRs without clarifying what types of rules are appropriate to whom and who is local among the different communities and different actors (Agrawal, 2007). Second, a design principle is problematic when it is specifically focused on exclusion by drawing clearly defined social and resource boundaries. In reality, "resource boundaries rarely match social boundaries, and resources tend to be used by competing user-groups, even within the same community" (Berkes, 2009, p. 263). CPRs are usually shared among inter and intra groups in a reciprocal way. Defining a group's social boundary without acknowledging inclusion or reciprocity between different groups is highly contested and ambiguous due to the different dimensions and effects of heterogeneity in a group's collective action (Agrawal, 2007). The resource boundary is discussed more in terms of how property rights shape the outcome of exclusion rather than acknowledging how the biophysical or ecological condition affects the outcome (Agrawal, 2007). Third, it is questionable whether design principles reflect what constitutes a historical self-governing or customary institution in each context, and to what extent the centralized states broke the self-governing capacities of community institutions or historical interactions between different actors for co-management and their complementary role in CPR management. For instance, Ostrom *et al.* (1999, p. 278) assumed that Mongolian pastoral institutions were under traditional group management without specifying what constitutes a traditional group institution or what is the role of the state in shaping local community institution. In Inner Asia, mobile pastoralists were reported to be a "society within, rather than against, the state" (Meeker 2002 cited in Sneath, 2007, p. 191). Some scholars argue that multiple actors are involved in resource management, including different community groups and local authorities (Schlager, 2004).

20 *Understanding CPR and rangeland management*

Nevertheless, more insights have been exposed that show that CPR management problems extend beyond engineering a collective action institution. First is the issue of equal access. Creating equal resource access has been an historical struggle as formal and informal rules often result in unequal access to CPRs (Sen, 1981 cited in Johnson, 2004). Second is a methodological issue in understanding the underlying problems in CPR management. Although CPR theorists emphasized nested institutions and wider enabling institutional, social and historical contexts when testing principles for a durable collective action institution (Ostrom, 1990, 2009), "ambitious attempts to merge the scientific approach with historical narratives are limited in the sense that they subvert the peculiarities of historical events to the logic of deductive reasoning" (Johnson, 2004, p. 427). Third is the dynamism and flexibility inherent in customary tenure, which make supporting specific customary tenure and devolution of resource use rights to the local community a challenging process (Fitzpatrick, 2005). In fact, the notion of customary institution has been contested as these are built on a bricolage of old rules and norms mixed unevenly with new arrangements (Cleaver, 2001) and diverse customs of different groups were re-defined for obtaining benefits (Berry, 1993). Fourth, in resource governance, the credibility or an historically proven function of an institution matters more than engineering a form of institution (Ho, 2013).

Moreover, a body of literature has emerged that demonstrates that projects applying collective action approaches have led to 'disappointing outcomes' (Saunders, 2014, p. 637). A critique of collective action approaches has emerged that suggests that it may be difficult to engineer property institutions along the lines suggested by those actually applying collective action theory (Hall et al., 2014; Johnson, 2004; Saunders, 2014). First, policy approaches derived from property theory can be prescriptive in nature, focusing "more on how property regimes should be instead of how they are" in order to promote a socio-economic agenda of equity, efficiency and sustainability (Benda-Beckmann et al., 2006, p. 2). These approaches try to formalize "individual" property rights under the assumption that formalization of property rights enforces legal empowerment for those who are stuck in an informal economy and being marginalized from market opportunity. These are limited in their effectiveness, given that processes of formalization are contingent on so many factors (Cousins, 2009). It is also difficult to develop the types of property rights prescribed in societies with ineffective government enforcement, or cultural norms, particularly those that have property relations and notions that are broader than those deployed by policy analysts that assume the virtue of secure, exclusive property rights (Sturgeon and Sikor, 2004; Verdery, 1999, 2004). In particular, the application of exclusive property rights in many developing contexts does not match that of western societies because both customary and statutory property relations have emerged through unique historical processes embedded in specific socio-political contexts. For instance, "in the category of common or communal

Understanding CPR and rangeland management 21

property, radically different mixes of rights of individuals, or smaller and larger social groups are thrown together" (Benda-Beckmann et al., 2006, p. 24). Also, in some developing contexts, "needs and aspirations of individuals and households do not easily conform to conventional property rights narratives (privates vs. collective) or the implementation of policy prescriptions that emerge from these narratives" (Marschke et al., 2012, p. 3). As concepts of property are understood in specific ways in each socio-political context, "property must be viewed in a broader context, including both legal and illegal uses of resources, because the determination of what is legal is subject to changing politics, variable perspectives, and shifting, though always unequal power relations" (Benda-Beckmann et al., 2006, p. 9). All too often this complexity eludes simple property categories, leading to interventions that struggle to accommodate meaningful socially embedded norms, values and interests (Saunders, 2014).

Second, some users may be unable to exercise property rights due to their lack of access to other means of production including labor, information, capital or assets (Berry, 1993; Cellarius, 2004). The social stratification which generates inequities of access creates a problem of legitimacy. As actors work around the state law, this can lead, in the eyes of those advocating exclusive property rights, to 'fuzzy' property rights, which 'lack clarity of borders, owners and exclusion' (Verdery, 1999, cited in Sturgeon and Sikor, 2004, p. 3). This was a common phenomenon that emerged from the process of socio-political transitions particularly in post-socialist countries, where transformation from collectivist property regimes to private property was promoted as representing the collapse of socialist regimes.[2] This created ambiguity regarding who has what sort of rights and authority over which property and resources (Sturgeon and Sikor, 2004).

Third, the narrow understanding of CPR management with the focus on property institutions and mechanism generates another challenge. A concept of property and using it as a control mechanism can be inadequate in explaining the underlying problems of resource management in some contexts. According to observations provided by Humphrey and Verdery (2004), in the western concept of property relations, "those 'persons' and 'things' are clearly bounded, have integrity, and are easily recognizable as separate kinds of entities" (p. 5). This concept has a limited application in the context where "persons and things are not seen as clearly bounded and separate but as participating in one another..." and their relations are not fixed, defined or aimed to exclude others from the things (p. 8). Even then, property rights could still be used as a simple mechanism to control resource access by creating scarcity in things, rather than scarcity as an actual condition for creating property rights (Humphrey and Verdery, 2004, p. 9). Also, access theorists questioned why some people appear to benefit from the exploitation of natural resources irrespective of their property rights (Ribot, 1998; Ribot and Peluso, 2003). From this perspective, beyond the questions of property rights, CPR management is a process of gaining, maintaining and controlling access

22   *Understanding CPR and rangeland management*

to the benefits derived from resources. In property-based approaches, the notion of access is limited to a "right to benefit." Here a right is more of a prescriptive norm or "enforceable claim, one that is acknowledged and supported by society through laws, customs or conventions" (Ribot and Peluso, 2003, p. 155). The difficulty remains that of applying property rights where fuzziness in property relations shapes the context and affects the strategies applied by different actors seeking to benefit from natural resources. Here actors use legitimate rights-based as well as relational or other structural mechanisms (wider processes, strategies and means involved in resource access) to gain, maintain and control access to derive benefits, beyond property rights (Berry, 1983; Ribot and Peluso, 2003). In other words, access refers to one's ability to benefit with or without property rights (Berry, 1989b; Ribot and Peluso, 2003). Ability in this context represents one's power based on one's capacity to influence others' actions (Weber 1978 and Lukes 1986 cited in Ribot and Peluso, 2003). This capacity refers to individuals seeking out strategies to access human, financial and material inputs, as well as the knowledge and institutional means to enable control over benefits (Berry, 1989a, 2009). Actors' ability to benefit from the exploitation of natural resources may have little relation to their formal property rights (Ribot and Peluso, 2003). Thus, it may be difficult to apply property theory or property rights approaches in cases where actors employ other mechanisms and strategies to benefit from natural resources, which bear little relation to prescriptive norms, or enforceable claims, supported by property institutions (Ribot and Peluso, 2003, p. 155). In fact, a closer look into access indicates that natural resource management is directly related to particular production management and marketing systems that need to be understood. Regardless of the contexts of crop cultivating or mobile pastoralism, production management appears to depend directly on control over the key production components; labor, land and production species (livestock or crop species) (Bazargur, 1998; Bjorklund, 2003; Peluso, 1992). Socio-political and economic changes not only affect the resource management institution, but the production management and marketing systems.[3] Different actors seek various access mechanisms to produce and market, ultimately shaping local CPR resource management. Therefore, Ribot and Peluso's (2003) access approach provided the means of rethinking CPR management problems, opening up new ways of reading changes in how actors control production and marketing beyond a focus on exclusive property rights to land.

Rangeland management in the context of pastoralism

Here we focus on rangeland management to explain why some CPR management approaches succeed, whilst others fail in regulating overuse and subtractability. To date, land degradation has been a challenging global issue for environmental management and food security. Conventional rangeland management has been rooted in the concept of environmental equilibrium, in

Understanding CPR and rangeland management 23

which rangeland use is based on calculating carrying capacity of the land or the balance between the number of livestock and the regenerative capacity of the pasture (Behnke and Scoones, 1993). However, rangelands, particularly in dry-land ecology, are fragile and inherently unstable because of large climatic variations, which affect the growth of vegetation (Swift and Mearns, 1993). Globally, more than half (60 percent) of pastureland is dry and has less capacity to regenerate due to the fact that mean annual rainfall is low for keeping pace with the total amount of evaporation back to the atmosphere. Cold climates also limit the vegetative growth of pasturelands (Reid et al., 2008a). In addition, dry-lands vary in terms of the amount of precipitation that falls seasonally and inter-annually, generating geographical variability. This complexity reduces the possibility of calculating carrying capacity for a range condition. This feature is referred to as the disequilibrium rangeland system, and results in highly variable primary production (Vetter, 2005). Thus, it is necessary in rangeland management to "reconsider dry-land ecology and what it means to derive livelihoods from an environment that is intrinsically at disequilibrium" (Behnke *et al.* cited in Fratkin, 1997, p. 114).

Mobile pastoralism is one of the major ways to derive livelihood from rangelands in disequilibrium ecology and is significant in environmental management (Miller and Sheehy, 2008). Over the last few decades, mobile pastoralism has been positioned within a new paradigm of rangeland management, 'disequilibrium ecology' (Fratkin, 1997; Fratkin and Mearns, 2003; Swift and Mearns, 1993). It is a more viable form of production in dry-land environments compared to many sedentary agricultural production systems (crop-growing and ranch-style). It is better at responding to fluctuating and patchy resources in a disequilibrium environment through high mobility for the pursuit of wide-ranging, well-coordinated and specialized production of diverse species (Fratkin, 1997; Goldstein and Beall, 1994). Although the disequilibrium condition complicates the application of exclusive property rights, particularly exclusive individual ownership of natural resources, rangelands in disequilibrium conditions have been regulated through market oriented land reform policies and practices, regardless of the ecology. Pastoralists have been facing barriers in pursuing mobility (Miller and Sheehy, 2008). Private livestock ownership in the pastoral economy dates far back in history. In contrast, application of exclusive property rights to rangeland in largely pastoral societies in Africa and Inner Asia seem to have emerged particularly during European colonization, affecting their customary management system of pastoral production and rangelands. European settlers expanded to more extensive rangelands, the impact of which differed depending on the extent of the changes in the socio-political system and the geo-political history of each pastoral society.

Colonial period

Rangeland in these regions has been a sought after natural resource for political and economic benefits. Initially, up to the twentieth century, colonial

24 *Understanding CPR and rangeland management*

policies began to force most pastoral societies into a sedentary lifestyle to some extent, changing their socio-political and resource management institutions due to the demands of commodity-based agricultural production (Khazanov, 1994a; Meredith, 2005; Reid, 2003).

In Africa during European colonization, pastoralists began losing their pastoral territories. For instance, from the 1910s, European laborers brought by the British eventually settled to farm with other African laborers on 60 percent of the territory of Maasai pastoralists with little resistance (Berry, 1993, p. 79; Fratkin, 1997, p. 243). Also, these pastoralists began witnessing change in the definition and interpretation of their customary land management institutions. Based on some rules and norms interpreted by local tribes in favorable terms to themselves at a time, colonists re-invented customary law by piecing together a "homogenous system of primordial law and culture … to serve as the basis of the colonial order" (Berry, 1993, p. 31). This was because pre-colonial communities were "neither static nor internally cohesive … [who] moved in overlapping, shifting associations … rested not on any institutionalized system of central authority" (Berry, 1993, p. 28). This created a misleading interpretation of many customary practices of resource allocation and application of community and individual property rights, which were contested within and between members of different tribal communities with dynamic boundaries and structure (Berry, 1993). Since then, farming, group ranching, commercial uses, conservation and game parks took over most of the rangelands, restricting the movements of pastoral people, livestock and wildlife to access necessary natural resources (Fratkin, 1997; Reid et al., 2008a, p. 13).

In Inner Asia, land degradation is also a problem for many steppe societies including Kazakhstan, Tuva and Buryatia in Russia, Northern Xinjiang, Tibet and Inner Mongolia in China, and Mongolia. Although these pastoral societies lost their political independence to colonial rules of Russia and the Manchu Qing Dynasty, the extent of the changes they experienced in their pastoral institution varied depending on each country (Barfield, 2011, p. 118). In China, the Manchu Qing Dynasty prohibited Chinese migration into Inner Mongolia. Later in the early twentieth century, it lifted the ban and allowed settlement of many migrant Chinese into Inner Mongolia to bolster a growing Chinese population, and strengthen the government position toward Japan, Russia and Western interests in the Far East. Chinese migrants introduced sedentary agriculture on grazing lands and created a dominant farming population next to minority ethnic groups of mobile pastoralists, who became marginalized from their land (Endicott, 2012; Lattimore, 1941; Rowe, 2009). In Xinjiang, the Qing Dynasty allowed Kazakh pastoralists to migrate to the area in the eighteenth century (Banks, 2001; Barfield, 2011). Simultaneously, it also began to settle many farmers and converted the rangeland to a Chinese-style sedentary agriculture in order to reduce the population concentration and provide a food supply for the growing demand of its military (Rowe, 2009, p. 92). The Qing Dynasty also ruled Tibet through its nominal political official (*amban*) and some trade relations until the twentieth century, but with little influence in altering Tibetan society and culture (Rowe, 2009).

In Russia, Kazakh and Kyrgyz pastoralists were free from any of these colonial rules until the expansion of Tsarist Russia. Between 1700 and 1900, Tsarist Russia was largely involved in the region to rule "lawless" Kazakh and Kyrgyz Steppes to compete against its great game rivalry, Great Britain (Hopkirk, 1994, pp. 74, 95). Specifically from 1854, the colonists officially attempted to break its cultural and social orders, by settling Russian peasants (or exiles) and declaring pastoralists' grazing land (and later the livestock) as Russian property in order to "force them off the land" (Stacey, 2007, p. ix). Russians turned pastoral land into farm fields and many Kazakh herders into farmers. They divided pastureland into administrative units, reducing herders' mobility, pasture and herd size. Meanwhile, a hybrid land management system, combined of traditional Kazakh and Russian property regimes, emerged, which Kazakhs employed for their own benefit (Endicott, 2012, p. 123). Nevertheless, they remained largely pastoral until the twentieth century (Robinson et al., 2003). Similarly, during the eighteenth–nineteenth century, Buryats began replacing their pastoral lifestyle with the Russian way of husbandry under the Tsarist government policy of discouraging pastoralism (Khazanov, 1994a; Reid, 2003, pp. 67, 68). In contrast, Tuvans remained as a part of Outer Mongolia under the political control of the Manchu Dynasty until the end of the nineteenth century. As a result of prohibition of Chinese migration, they experienced little change to their culture and lifestyle, except for paying tribute. This continued until 1914, when Tuva officially became a part of Russia, but remained nominally independent until 1944 when Soviet Russia took control (Humphrey, 1980, p. 3; Humphrey and Sneath, 1999, p. 18; Reid, 2003, p. 101). Overall, during the colonial period, these pastoral societies began to witness their identity reduced to a minority in their own territory in the presence of a majority Russian and Chinese migrant culture and sedentary agricultural system (Humphrey and Sneath, 1999).

Post-colonial or socialist period

Later in the twentieth century, modern development initiatives led by the outside world intensified the sedentarization of pastoral societies, ultimately changing their pastoral institutions (Khazanov, 1994a; Meredith, 2005). Hardin's (1968) metaphor of the "tragedy of the commons" was particularly influential for the popularity of a state or private property regimes in managing CPR resources and the population control (Eggertsson, 2009; Fratkin, 1997). Under these regimes, most of the post-colonial and socialist states transformed extensive grazing lands into agrarian farms and introduced modern property rights regimes to rangeland management. Pastoralists were alienated from their land, which was used for expanding intensive livestock husbandry, agriculture, and conservation and game parks. Mobility has been curtailed through the introduction of indigenous reservations, re-settlement and collectivization (Fratkin and Mearns, 2003).

26 *Understanding CPR and rangeland management*

In Africa, de-colonization found many countries opting for socialist modernization to break away from western capitalist exploitation and colonial rule. They were convinced that their indigenous social system had many similarities to socialist egalitarian communal ownership of resources. However, a socialist agenda was merely on paper. Many de facto pursued capitalist strategies of development; private sector and foreign investment for industrial development rather than low-productivity agricultural production (Meredith, 2005, pp. 144–146). In 1967, for instance, the Tanzanian government introduced the *"ujamaa"* (family hood), a socially engineered village community as a form of socialism. Similar to Soviet collectives, it aimed to modernize and increase production of agriculture and/or livestock, and marketing through collectivization with modern technology (Berry, 1993; Fratkin, 1997; Meredith, 2005). Among Maasai pastoralists, they used the "livestock village" for regulating pasture and water with enormous support for infrastructure development from international donors (Fratkin, 1997). Without much increase in production and marketing, these development programs led to incoming migration of farmers and forced settlement on marginal land. This resulted in the concentration of villages near water resources and land degradation as well as shortages of food, which led to dependence on international aid. The program failed because it only existed on paper. It did not have any coherent planning or meaningful enforcement, and lacked knowledge of the region, and an overestimated ability on the state to control resource allocation (Berry, 1993, p. 65; Fratkin, 1997, p. 244; Meredith, 2005, pp. 253–256). Moreover, the expansion of agriculture and the introduction of property regimes on landed resources also shifted pastoralists' focus from integrated management of all the means of production (labor, livestock and land) to only land as a primary resource. For instance, the Maasai pastoralists continued losing their territory to commercial farmers (wheat-growing and beef-producing), mainly non-Maasai migrants. Although they shared territory among community members, some influential members "sought title to individual sections of land" to be able to lease, rent and sell the land. Then in 1968, community rights were legalized under "group ranches" in order to avoid losing land to farmers, and to be able to loan and get production support (Fratkin, 1997, p. 243). However, the dramatic policy of entitling community land to individuals in the 1980s resulted in Maasai pastoralists seeking title to land more than to livestock (Galaty 1992 cited in Fratkin, 1997, p. 244). Besides, state control of land versus customary rights to land became a contradictory and contested legal mechanism to access land. For instance, the Baragaig people in Tanzania lost their struggle of reclaiming access to important pastoral and cultural sites against the state representing the public interest for agricultural development. The reason was attributed to the state's contradictory approach towards customary rights to land, and a conflicting legal interpretation of the term "natives" (Fratkin, 1997, p. 245). Overall, indigenous rangeland management and customary rules and norms based on pastoralists' production strategies largely shifted to those based on property rights to the land.

Understanding CPR and rangeland management 27

In Inner Asia, China and Russia considered pastoralism backward. However, the socialist states obtained benefits from pastoralism by exploiting pastoralists' labor. They imposed central government control over pastoralists, settling some parts of the rural population and sought to modernize the production system through collectivization (Barfield, 2011; Humphrey and Sneath, 1999; Khazanov, 1998). The state declared all productive resources as public property and took control. They imposed administrative rights along different vertical hierarchical levels, one of which was the collectives assigning managing rights to pastoralists (Sturgeon and Sikor, 2004, p. 7). Specifically, collectives assigned certain pasture to herders under use rights for grazing (Humphrey and Sneath, 1999, p. 245). Collectives introduced specialized herding of different types of livestock, and changed herding units and patterns from their pre-collective modes in order to maximize pastoral production (Barfield, 2011). They also introduced intensive livestock husbandry and foreign livestock breeds, and expanded agriculture on to the rangeland, using costly and heavy modern machinery (Humphrey, 1999, p. 46). This reduced pastoral areas, curtailed pastoralists' mobility and rotational and rehabilitative use of pasture, exacerbating rangeland degradation (Humphrey, 1999, pp. 47–53). In Xinjiang, pastoralism remained the "pre-dominant form of land use," though settlement by Han Chinese rapidly increased (Banks, 2001, p. 725). Herding of poorly adapted foreign-bred livestock, settlements, and the development of other industries such as agriculture and mining reduced pastoral areas and herders' mobility (Humphrey and Sneath, 1999, p. 241). In Tibet, the Chinese invasion in 1950 created huge socio-political and economic instability. The government confiscated land and livestock wealth from the nobles and monasteries and replaced traditional agro-pastoral husbandry and land use institutions with settled agrarian collectivization and settlement of Chinese migrants (Bauer, 2004, pp. 84–87; Hopkirk, 1995, pp. 260, 264). Until the 1970s, pastoralists were forced into working for state enterprises. Then, they were forced to join communes for herding and production in each region. Pastoralists were resettled around small production units and their mobility was reduced. Even with improved collective infrastructure and transportation, the initial reduction in livestock caused food insecurity and little improvement in livelihoods. Later when the number of livestock increased, this situation persisted due to the government's expropriation of surplus products (Bauer, 2004). In Inner Mongolia, the collectives restricted herders' seasonal movements within a territory or *brigade* – production unit – reducing herders' movements much more than their pre-collective patterns in conditions of increasing numbers of livestock (Humphrey and Sneath, 1999, pp. 253, 261). In general, collectivization of the pastoral economy presented less concern to Inner Mongolian pastoralists than the continuous expansion of Chinese farmers into their land, exacerbating the marginalization of them as a minority (Barfield, 2011).

In Russia, collectivization in Buryatia and Kazakhstan intensified rangeland degradation in a similar fashion. It largely turned pastoral lands into agrarian land

28 Understanding CPR and rangeland management

using intensive farming techniques, and reduced herders' mobility and intensified concentration of livestock (Endicott, 2012, p. 124; Humphrey and Sneath, 1999, pp. 255–257). Although they remained pastoral to some extent, pastoralists experienced famine, livestock loss, resettlement, confiscation of livestock and forced settlement in rural collective farms (Endicott, 2012, p. 124; Humphrey and Sneath, 1999, p. 19; Shayakhmetov, 2007). They were also marginalized from mainstream social and economic development. Many remained unemployed or employed only in rural sectors of pastoral or cotton production. This was unlike migrants from western parts of Russia, who as a majority took over most of the skilled positions in other development sectors such as industrial, agricultural and mining (Humphrey, 1999; Khazanov, 1994b). Only the Tuva maintained their traditional system of pasture use due to limited change in mobility and continuity of herding local breeds of livestock inherited from the pre-collective period (Humphrey and Sneath, 1999, p. 247). The survival of Tuvan pastoralism may have a lot to do with the late arrival of Russian control along with the introduction of industrial development, and modern technologies (Humphrey, 1980, p. 3). This occurred due to the hands-off approach of political control of the Manchu colony, which essentially kept its socioeconomic institutions and small population intact.

Twentieth to twenty-first century and post-socialist period

In Africa, the key environmental concern is land fragmentation, which leads to desertification, land degradation and competing land use among pastoralists, wildlife and agricultural development in a non-equilibrium environment. In East Africa, settled agro-pastoralists built fences for cultivation to protect access to forage and diversify food production. This contradicts wildlife conservation. For instance, in the Athi-Kaputiei plains in Kenya, wildlife use pastoral lands for calving during the dry season. This challenges pastoral people on whether to accept wildlife on their land or impede their economic and cultural well-being (Reid et al., 2008b). Protected areas are also important dry-season refuges for both pastoralists and wildlife. Denying pastoralists access to their customary lands in protected areas impinges their pastoral production or the pursuit of alternative livelihoods by marketing handcrafts, food products as well as providing services for tourists. For instance, the Ngorongoro Conservation Area Administration (NCAA) manages the park and limits Maasai pastoralists' benefits from the park, because it assumes that pastoralists have vague property rights. In contrast, pastoralists see NCA as their customary land and their legally recognized customary rights to the park are equated with real property rights for specific pieces of land (Galvin et al., 2008b, p. 262). Moreover, protected areas removed pastoral practices and reduced livestock grazing in different levels and zones in protected areas. Now, livestock is likely to graze in the highlands most of the year. This has resulted in changes in the population trends of wildlife, and the composition of rangeland vegetation and overgrazing (Galvin et al., 2008b).

Understanding CPR and rangeland management   29

Although various ecological factors contribute to the degradation of rangeland, it is also driven by socio-political reasons rooted under colonial and apartheid policies. For instance, in South Africa, dominantly white farmers own vast amounts of farming land for commercial farming, whereas mostly black Africans own communally held pastoral land for their livestock (Galvin et al., 2008a). This dominance of commercial farming is demarcated by fencing, which affects the mobility of livestock and wildlife. Also, pastoralists' right to land is not necessarily secured through property rights mechanisms, because they are unable to exercise their property rights to the full extent. Pastoralists' mobility is prohibited within communal rangeland allotted to individuals. For instance, in the Amboseli ecosystem in Kenya, the Maasai people's communal land is subdivided into individual parcels, which leads to sedentarization. This results in the change in wildlife habitation, extensive conflict and competition over resource use among pastoralists, declined mobility and less flexibility to respond to ecological heterogeneity (BurnSilver et al., 2008). Moreover, in the case of Namaqualand reserves in South Africa, power relations affect policy attempts to avoid overgrazing and land shortage in communal land, which allows small scale mobility (Galvin et al., 2008a). Poor members often lack funding or resources to build stock posts/campsites, movement between old and new commonages, and to overcome bureaucratic procedures governing the allocation camp. As a result, they are often excluded from the decision-making process and eventual impediment to their access to communal resources. In contrast, a few wealthier individuals are likely to impose their own rule by manipulation over these communal lands, introducing an individualized leasehold system for commercial farming. Besides, the shift from subsistence oriented herding of cattle to market oriented goat herding occurred, as in the case of Pokot pastoralists in Kenya, in order to adapt to changing market conditions. These days, goat herding is more marketable, and requires less mobility in a bushy environment, is less vulnerable to livestock raids and more of a subsistence asset to poor households (Osterle, 2008). Overall, when pastoralists' mobility and flexibility is hindered, they are likely to rely on any access mechanism to benefit from available resources and change the ways in which they manage resources.

In Inner Asia, land degradation is widespread; not only in grazing land, but also in agricultural land (Sneath, 1998). Compared to pastoral societies in Russia and China, Mongolia along with Tuva in Russia has experienced a comparatively low level of land degradation by maintaining a greater level of mobility (Humphrey and Sneath, 1999). Except for Tuva, more than 75 percent in Russia, and more than 90 percent of the rangeland (40 percent of the whole territory) in China has been degraded[4] (Banks, 2001; Humphrey and Sneath, 1999; Sneath, 1998, 2003). In China,[5] the government shifted its regulatory authority from the management of production to land only. As most of the rangeland was converted for the use of other industries, the government introduced the "Household Responsibility System" (HRS) in the

30 *Understanding CPR and rangeland management*

1980s to the remaining pastoral lands (Banks, 2003; Changqing et al., 2012). Whilst privatizing all livestock, the government leased pastoral lands to individual households in order to "give pastoralists the incentive to stock pasture within the carrying capacity and invest in pasture improvement" (Banks, 2001, p. 718). The implementation of this policy differed throughout China in its scale and timing and resulted in various social and environmental outcomes. In Xinjiang, the de-facto implementation was based on a group (a few to several hundred households) lease of pasture, since it was not feasible to draw boundaries for individual households on rangeland. This allowed traditional herding practices and mobility. Kazakhs managed to form groups due to their strong kinship ties and family relations (Banks, 2001). Although the Chinese government eventually introduced individual household leases to these communities as well as other parts of China (Banks, 2003; Changqing et al., 2012), practices of traditional mobility based on kinship ties may explain why mobile pastoralism still persists in Kazakh communities in northern Xinjiang (Barfield, 2011). In contrast, Mongol Tuvan village herders were unable to create group rights to pasture as they often consisted of both dynamic kinship relatives and neighbors (Banks, 2001). Even as in the case of the Kazakh village, kinship-based groups required flexibility on delineating the boundaries of pasture due to the different needs of pasture in each season and changing group membership (Banks, 2001, p. 731). Moreover, land management under HRS appears costly. Although some groups were able to increase their livestock numbers, pastoralist production costs are increasing as they need to supplement degraded pasture with the purchase of more fodder (Changqing et al., 2012). The government policy of providing herders with seasonal pasture created the simplistic pattern of mobility as the policy still abounds to clearly defined principles of mobility. As in the case of Gansu province, simplistic mobility and herding management overlooked the various grazing patterns, mobility and flexibility (Bedunah and Harris, 2002). Besides, Kazakh herders hire Han-Chinese, who are inexperienced in traditional ecological knowledge and extensive herding skills, and flexible, mobile strategies in different ranges and seasons that are needed for handling large numbers of livestock. These all contribute to intensifying land degradation, which are harmful for both domestic livestock and wildlife such as gazelles and wild sheep (Bedunah and Harris, 2002).

Besides land degradation, land reform in China also affects the social aspects of many traditional communities. In Tibet, the current trend of pastoral production is to increase livestock through intensive grazing management, and turn rangeland areas into agricultural plots for growing hay and other fodder. Ultimately, it affects rangeland productivity and brings herders' mobility and traditional lifestyle under threat (Miller, 2001). For instance, drawing boundaries on summer pasture led to growing disputes and violence among communities. Since the local administration is unable to solve complex boundary problems, pastoralists rely on traditional mediation to stop the conflict at least for the time (Pirie, 2006). Also, rangeland enclosures

Understanding CPR and rangeland management   31

for intensive livestock production spread fencing over seasonal pastures, leading to diminishing well-being. Fencing is seen as a social status for those who are wealthy enough to afford it for protecting their pasture. They graze their herds freely on unfenced pastures, where poor people cannot afford to fence their pasture (Bauer, 2005). Responding to these impacts, pastoralists in other parts of Tibet began to form multi-household groups (average ten households) to share pasture and cope with the inadequacy for arranging labor, production and sharing pasture and water under the HRS (Jianjun et al., 2012). Similar trends are observed in Inner Mongolia. Wealthy herders build fences that block access to water resources. Other herders have to travel around the fences, incurring petrol costs and much lost time. Some wealthy herders also graze their livestock on unfenced common grazing areas, whilst renting their own pastures to others (Xie and Li, 2008, Zhizhong and Wen, 2008). Nevertheless, herders continue to make informal arrangements to access each other's private pastures on a seasonal basis as an emergency strategy or *otor* movement to fatten their livestock and cope with these social and environmental impacts. Yet, such strategies are conditional depending on social ties and status as well as access to productive resources such as information. This makes reciprocity costly or unguaranteed for seeking access to pasture elsewhere (Xie and Li, 2008). Although land is not privatized in China, trading land use/lease rights appears popular at least in an agrarian context as the government "has privatized use rights while leaving ownership in the hands of the state" (Ho, 2013, p. 1106). Thus, it is worth examining this phenomenon in the pastoral context regarding whether certain transactions occur in transferring lease rights or at least if it's legitimate on paper.

In Russia, minority pastoral societies in Buryatia and Chita continue to experience land degradation. Following the collapse of the Soviet Union, their production was transformed into cash-based ranching with high levels of mechanization and increased production of fodder with little or no mobility (Barfield, 2011, p. 122; Humphrey and Sneath, 1999, p. 265). In Kazakhstan, small pastureland remained as state property for the few remaining herders to lease it with tax payments. In the absence of collective mechanized support, herders move less and abandon distant pastures. Herders are concentrated around village centers for the purpose of public services and the overgrazing process increases. By 1999, the use of distant pastures re-emerged, but on a much smaller scale (Endicott, 2012, pp. 125, 126). However, recent research reports that the extent of degradation was lower than widely suggested in some parts of Kazakhstan, depending on the extent of seasonal movement (Robinson et al., 2003). In contrast, rangeland degradation in Tuva is reported to be less. This was perhaps due to the fact that local authorities and herders maintained, to some extent, the patterns of production and pasture use and mobility from pre-collective and collective periods, whilst combining these with mechanized transportation and the use of a large amount of hay (Humphrey, 1999).

32 *Understanding CPR and rangeland management*

As a solution to the socio-ecological issues encountered in rangeland management, the development policy approach is shifting towards protecting pastoralists' rights as indigenous people to pursue pastoralism and/or retain custodian rights to land, strengthen community or group self-governing institutions, CBNRM and collective action, and its resilience towards changing socio-ecological conditions (Agrawal, 2010; Klein et al., 2012). Since the government's change in attitude towards grassland policy, scholars and advocates promote CBNRM (strengthen and formalize collective/cooperative or group land tenure and production marketing) and co-management initiatives in Inner Mongolia, Xinjiang and Tibetan regions over individual exclusive land use rights, top down and simplistic plans of pasture use, costly land and production management (Banks, 2003; Changqing et al., 2012; Dalintai et al., 2012; Jianjun et al., 2012). However, these policy approaches need careful reflection of the fact that the socio-economic, political and ecological changes affect the management of rangeland and pastoral production system and the local institutional arrangement around them in an integrated way, and to a different extent depending on the socio-political (state or tribal, minority or majority) structure, and geo-political locations and positions of each pastoral society. These differences could explain why some pastoral societies fare better than others in their rangeland management. These provide insights into the conceptual understanding of various conflicting, contested and changing notions – (land management and rights, property or territorial mechanisms to access land and/or production, state and/or community land ownership, equal/unequal access to pastoral resources within and between communities, customary and/or statutory rules and norms, the ability/inability of central state or local community to manage land and/or production, and the extent of indigenousness of pastoralists or pastoral production) – that are all critical for examining how CBNRM, community, collective action and (stakeholders) co-management are understood in each pastoral context before applying them as a blanket land policy approach. During different historical periods, great efforts have been made to intensify agricultural production at the expense of mobile pastoralism, by applying blanket development and modernization policies, regardless of the abovementioned differences in socio-political systems and geo-political history of each pastoral society. Some pastoral societies have still persisted in maintaining their mobility and pastoralism (Barfield, 1993; Goldstein and Beall, 1994; Humphrey, 1999; Khazanov, 1994a).

Mongolia is one of the very few remaining pastoral countries where mobile pastoralism is still a dominant food production system. As Humphrey noted:

> The pastoral economy was not merely a "traditional" sector of a national economy; it *was* the national economy. To this extent, the problems are dissimilar from those facing pastoral peoples who are integrated into larger economies; on the other hand, a discussion of the Mongol situation has the advantage of clearly outlining the critical points relevant to a pastoral economy.
>
> (1978, p. 139)

Until the end of the socialist period (Humphrey and Verdery, 2004, p. 17), the state maintained the fundamentals of the so called "sociotechnical system" of Mongolian mobile pastoralism (Sneath, 2004). During the socio-political transition from a centralized to a market economy in the 1990s, the government, de jure, broke up the fundamentals, causing dramatic changes in herders' access to pastoral resources and rangeland management in Mongolia. Although rangeland degradation is reported to be much less in Mongolia compared to other countries (Sneath, 1998), there is no consensus regarding the extent of degradation on rangeland, which account for 80 percent of the Mongolian territory (MNE, 1996, p. 20). Dramatically different estimates, ranging from 9 to 90 percent[6] have been quoted (Addison et al., 2012; Sternberg, 2008). Without necessarily explaining the specifics, some consider that Mongolia succeeded[7] in its rangeland management due to its historical retention of public ownership of land or group customary land management (Fratkin, 1997; Ostrom et al., 1999). The existing ecological, social and geopolitical location/position of the country that favored the continuity of mobile pastoralism throughout history (Lattimore, 1962; Simukov, 1931, pp. 593, 594). Mongolia has a unique and dissimilar history of geo-politics as well as the political economy of pastoralism from those facing European colonialism and modernization, influencing the resilience of its pastoral institution. On the other hand, the history of its pastoral institution can clearly present crucial insights into the issues of rangeland or overall CPR management as it shares few similarities to others' pastoralism and the changing political and economic systems. Although both equilibrium and disequilibrium continuum exists in Mongolia, herders throughout Mongolia continue to pursue pastoral production (Fernandez-Gimenez and Allen-Diaz, 1999; Fernandez-Gimenez et al., 2008). This may be due to the fact that Mongolians' pursuit of pastoralism is still "as much spiritual as ecological" (Lattimore, 1932, p. 74). Or it still remains as a nationwide safety-net for many, particularly with regard to food security, because it is an independent production system.

Analysis of access mechanisms in mobile pastoralism in the context of disequilibrium ecology can be useful for understanding rangeland management. Here, access to landed resources is strongly contested and management is complex due to the dynamic nature of social and resource boundaries, particularly when applying policy based on property mechanisms. Such analysis will fill the gaps in previous research on pastoralism, which used approaches such as property regimes and rights, CBNRM and institutional arrangements, and contribute to the understanding of why CPR management succeeds or fails in some pastoral settings. Therefore, this study aims to understand what conditions and factors led to challenges in rangeland management, whilst Mongolian Pastoralism persists as a dominant food production system. My research question is "why are herders changing how they access (gain, maintain and control) seasonal pastures and manage pastureland (disputes and overuse)"? Drawing on a qualitative case study, this research applies an access

34 Understanding CPR and rangeland management

approach to explore specific mechanisms that different actors apply in accessing pastoral resources and examine property relations in pastureland management. Overall, this study examines, theoretically and at the policy level, which historical, cultural and institutional aspects of pastoral production and pastureland management need to be addressed for regulating access to pastoral resources in the context of mobile pastoralism in Mongolia.

Mobile pastoralism in Mongolia

Understanding rangeland management needs examination of the (food) production system, which shapes the daily resource use pattern. This section briefly discusses the distinction of mobile pastoralism current in Mongolia in its unique contexts of ecology, geo-politics and socio-political history to set the background for the next chapters. This book uses the term "mobile pastoralism" due to the following reasons. First, nomadism and pastoralism are different concepts with different spheres of reference: the former refers to movement and the latter to a type of subsistence (Barfield, 1993). Regarding movement, there are two kinds of nomads: there are wandering nomads, independent of economic function; and there are nomads who practice pastoralism, which is independent of agriculture or dependent on it to a small extent (Khazanov, 1994a, p. 21; Lattimore, 1941). As a type of subsistence, pastoralism is in general defined as a food producing economy with different purposes and characteristics of mobility, which makes it different from food-extracting nomads such as hunter-gatherers (Khazanov, 1994a, p. 15). Among them, extensive pastoralists primarily derive dominant economic production from grazing in a mobility pattern of seasonal rotations and distance movements in search of pastoral resources, whereas agro-pastoralists gain small amounts of production from livestock grazing that supplements their dominant agricultural pursuits (Swift, 1988). However, the term nomadism appears to be problematic as it is an extensively broad term and there are many different types of nomadic pastoralism (Hesse and MacGregor, 2006; Khazanov, 1994a). Specifically, Humphrey and Sneath (1999) noted that this term broadly refers to old views of backward, free and egalitarian, wandering nomads with low productivity. This is analytically inadequate to explain contemporary pastoralism, because it does not necessarily define the specific techniques involved in the extensive pastoral production system. Thus, the preferred term is "mobile pastoralism" since the pastoral production is inherently based on the technique of mobility (Humphrey and Sneath, 1999). Although complex and understood to a limited extent, this technique of mobility in Mongolia is based on a well-developed "natural frequency of occurrence in movement ... repeatable and cyclical ... in spite of the diversity of the type of nomadic orbits" for accessing natural resources (Simukov, 1934, p. 717). Also, this term is "compatible with many different social and economic systems including technologically advanced and market oriented ones" (Humphrey and Sneath, 1999, p. 1). Second, Inner Asian mobile

Understanding CPR and rangeland management 35

pastoralism is a political economy as its production system has a state-centered socio-political structure and is "framed and transformed by political power" (Sneath, 2007, p. 17). In particular, Mongolian Pastoralism was "a mixture of the economic survival of the most profitable and the political survival of the fittest" (Lattimore, 1941, p. 292). Therefore, the term mobile pastoralism is more pertinent to the context of current Mongolia as herders' mobility occurs within a specific geographical territory and is adaptable to the changing socio-political and economic structure. The socio-political context of Mongolian Pastoralism owed its uniqueness to its ecological and geographical condition. First, as a food producing economy, mobile pastoralism is distinctive from each other depending on existing animals and plants. Lattimore noted:

> Nomadism cannot be uniform. If your tribe holds a more desert orbit of migration you have more camels and perhaps more goats. You are certainly not so rich in sheep, though sheep you must have, and you probably have few horses and perhaps no cows at all. Also, you live widely scattered and move often.
>
> (1941, p. 246)

These differences among mobile pastoralist societies relate to the types of livestock and grazing land available (Heather, 2010; Lattimore, 1941). In Mongolia, herders combine different types of livestock (sheep, goat, cattle, horse and camel) to exploit any available vegetation and water resources on ecologically diverse rangeland, whilst allowing less competition of resources among these types of livestock. This combination is a risk-mitigation strategy as these types of livestock have different vulnerability levels to environmental stress such as disease, harsh climate and disastrous natural phenomenon (Lattimore, 1962, p. 48). This also offers a greater range of livestock products, increasing food producing options. Nevertheless, domesticated livestock became inherently dependent on herders and became less capable to protect themselves or to breed successfully on their own (Barfield, 1993). Herders use appropriate pasture management to keep the animals healthy and reproductive for the purpose of a continual source of livestock products. For that, herders "move their animals to exploit the seasonal ebb and flow of vegetation and maximize the transfer of energy from vegetation to livestock," for which, mobility is inherent to adaptation (Goldstein and Beall, 1994). Herding mixed species (or types) of livestock in an ecologically diverse rangeland involves greater freedom of movement (Lattimore, 1941). This mobility involves a pattern of rotational grazing following seasonal migration between key pastures while avoiding the harshest climatic conditions. The sequence of rotation and mobility in general can always change depending on weather conditions (Behnke and Scoones, 1993). Depending on the geographical and climate distinctions, it varies from hundreds of miles to a few miles annually (Goldstein and Beall, 1994). Herders' mobility also allows the pasture to rehabilitate for use at another time (Humphrey and Sneath, 1999), which has

36 Understanding CPR and rangeland management

been the key to conserve environmental resources (Fratkin, 1997). Moreover, herders directly or indirectly control production and gain by manipulating the age and sexual composition of their livestock based on their preference for certain products (Spooner, 1973). Directly, they produce unprocessed (raw materials) or processed products such as dairy products, carpets and ropes made of raw livestock materials. Indirectly, they benefit through the use of markets by bartering these products for grain and other goods (Goldstein and Beall, 1994; Spooner, 1973). In addition, herding combined livestock in these geographical conditions (complex relationship between the landscape and climate) also affords a greater supply of labor, including everyone from small children to elders in a herding household or a coordination of several households or community (Fernandez-Gimenez and Swift, 2003) (Figure 2.1). Particularly, when in times of crisis, herders move beyond their usual grazing area and seek another pasture for a specific period of time. Their coordination is based on reciprocity. A visiting household or a group of households negotiates with local herders and authorities, hoping to reciprocate in the future if the host faced extreme climatic conditions in their area (Humphrey and Sneath, 1999).

Mobile pastoralism in Mongolia is an efficient economic production system regarding the combination of factors such as socio-political structure in an existing geo-political location and climatic conditions. Many scholars opposed the fact that mobile pastoralist societies have been characterized as backward, primitive, stagnant in their evolution, and inefficient for civilized socio social-economic development (Barfield, 1993; Humphrey and Sneath, 1999; Sneath, 2007; William, 1996). First of all, mobile pastoralism in Inner Asia was not primitive as it appeared later than agriculture, having emerged in the middle of the second millennium BCE, while agriculture had emerged on the Inner Asian steppe by the sixth millennium BCE (Natsagdorj, 1975; Sneath, 2007). Also, the emergence of mobile pastoralism points to a societal choice for the purpose of evading agrarian-based poverty. In Inner Asia, "where much land could not quite be used better to feed men than to feed animals, ... the less successful farmers had the largest number of animals at pasture to supplement their inadequate grain crops" (Lattimore, 1962, p. 36). This is why mobile pastoralism is described as an economy for gaining benefits from the existing ecology for political and economic power (Sneath, 2007).

Second, the concerns about the economic inefficiency of pastoralism in the modern era of economic growth (Khazanov, 1994a) seem to overlook the fact that mobile pastoralist and settled agrarian societies have deeply contrasting views on efficiency of economic production regarding the key components of production (labor, livestock/crop and land). For instance, settled Chinese people saw pastoral land as unfit for human habitation, judging it to be a waste, vast, overgrown, untamed, impoverished, and as an emptiness or an absence of domestication and civility[8] (William, 1996). They saw pastoral production as the outcome of unlabored land use in a wasteland, which should be opened up to labor oriented efficient production (William, 1996,

Understanding CPR and rangeland management 37

Figure 2.1 Kids are helping in the move to another seasonal pasture.

p. 672). This view is also reflected in the Marxist-Leninist-Maoist view that pastoral land has no intrinsic value, because it does not involve any labor effort (Natsagdorj, 1975, pp. 2, 3). This thinking strongly assumed that such land could hardly be further degraded no matter what the manner of exploitation (William, 1996). This view of backwardness and inefficiency even enforces application of property rights to rangeland management. For

38 *Understanding CPR and rangeland management*

instance, Europeans considered their exploitation of the Americas as effective, because they "would create private property in land and improve it, something the natives did not do ... and property was what distinguished 'civilized man' from the 'primitives'" (Humphrey and Verdery, 2004, p. 4). In contrast, mobile pastoralists had their own position towards pastoralism and sedentary agriculture, regarding the fragile condition of the rangelands (Lattimore, 1941, 1962). Mongolians viewed opening up the rangeland as shattering the land; they prefer instead to let the "land lie untilled and be restored to its dignity as steppe" in order to avoid "hurting the earth" (William, 1996, p. 647). Similarly, Pokot pastoralists in Kenya called agricultural activities "scratching the earth" (Osterle, 2008, p. 88). Thus, a specific production technology, shaped by its geographical and climatic conditions, also embodies a function of protection and management of the land.

Third, inefficient production technology and its crudeness are also interpreted through the lens of political structure as a pre-state tribal kinship society. This position is heavily influenced by the expansion of European colonialists, who considered indigenous societies and their political structure dramatically different from their own political governance by the state, focusing only on the differences and overlooking the similarities (Sneath, 2007). This view persists today among historians as they explain that "tribal" in this context does not necessarily refer to an image of savage barbarianism,[9] but a particular political structure, which is unable to create a complex state polity (Kradin, 2011). Several authors argued against the misconception that Inner Asian mobile pastoralists in general were perceived as traditional kinship-based tribes in their pre-state form (Natsagdorj, 1972; Sneath, 2007). Particularly, Sneath argued that nomads were misunderstood as:

> fluid, rootless, simple and without fixed points.... Free to move as they were, nomads would not support a stable hierarchy, and since they had not been fundamentally reordered by a state ... their basic organization must have remained a variety of kinship society.
>
> (2007, p. 37)

Although mobile pastoralism in Inner Asia has an economic characteristic of free-range grazing of a herd year-round, it is within specific boundaries of *nutag*, seasonal grazing territories (Grousset, 1970; Larson, 1930; Sneath, 2007; Vreeland, 1954). *Nutag*[10] is an emic term, in general, referring to someone belonging to or using a specific area or territorial base, which is mainly marked by specific geographical landmarks and bound within a specific state jurisdiction. In this book, it specifically refers to one's seasonal pasture area (*belcheeriin nutag*). Herders' freedom of movement within this territory is regulated by a pastoral institution that facilitates community access to pastoral resources. Here, community refers to a social and political organization of a group of herding households, who pursue pastoral production by sharing all-season pasture within one jurisdiction. In this regard, the community social and resource boundary was mainly defined by a jurisdiction, within which the authorities administer its residents and their production and pasture use practices. Otherwise, in Mongolia, the use of the term community (discussed in the next section) is flexible and so are its social and resource boundaries, depending on the condition of seasonal pasture and the weather.

Nevertheless, the ways in which a community uses geographically segregated territories, its pasture and other resources (water and saltlick) under state territorial administration is hardly a matter explained in western property terms. By arguing mobile pastoralism is a socio-technical system,[11] Sneath puts "property in its place":

> Mobile pastoralism techniques can be seen as part of larger socio-technical systems and require the integration of complex social and material systems ... property can be understood as part of the wider social and material networks that generate its value.
>
> (2004, p. 170)

Regarding the political structure involved in Inner Asian mobile pastoralism "the economic possibilities depend upon the nature of the property regimes that exist for resources and products and the wide political systems that frame them" (Sneath, 2007, p. 17). Lattimore (1962) also noted that the Chinese often defined "nomad" as "following grass and water" and overlooked the "technically skilled division of labor to cover a wide spread of activities, close gradation of responsibility and authority, precise legal concepts of territory – what land belongs to which tribe" (Lattimore, 1962, p. 32). Also, Heather described the function of pastoralists' mobility for political and economic benefits as:

> nomads do not usually move at random, which is punishing for both humans and animals ... as setting off into the wild blue yonder without knowledge of a potential destination's carrying capacity or, without equally important established rights to graze, would have been to invite economic disaster.
>
> (2010, p. 211)

Thus, herders must collaborate with one another within and between jurisdictions in order to take advantage of the available working power, transportation facilities, the pastoral institutions and jurisdictional authorities, which exist at any point in time in geographically convenient territory, and access available pastoral resources. This was to pursue mobile pastoralism for optimum benefits and solidify their political and economic power under existing geographical and climatic conditions[12] (Sneath, 2007). This development is essentially based on a "wide range of human experience, including the technical constraints on production imposed by an environmental externality be that conceived in spiritual or in materialistic terms" (Sneath, 2004,

40 *Understanding CPR and rangeland management*

p. 171). Thus, this form of mobile production technology adjusted to the existing geographical and climatic conditions inherently embedded in the socio-political structure for the purpose of controlling access to benefits.

In other CPR management, understanding the socio-political structure also appears critical, because the changes in socio-political structure (colonial and post-colonial and socialist and post-socialism) changes the production management, which in turn influences the management practices of landed resources. In mobile pastoralism, the ways in which changes in socio-political structure affected rangeland management have depended on geo-political locations/positions of particular pastoral societies. Particularly in Mongolia, geo-politics greatly shaped the socio-political institutions and the extent to which the state in different historical periods retained the fundamentals of the institutional framework for pastoralism to obtain political and economic benefits. Understanding these details is critical for examining current state-based pastoral production institutions. It requires the examination of the historical changes that occurred in herders' access to pastoral resources in Mongolia, and of Mongolia's socio-political structure in its own, emic, term; the ways in which the state afforded a capacity to retain the fundamentals of Mongolian Pastoralism in some period, whilst exploring the notions of private, public or state, customary ownership or land management, and the ways in which the term "indigenousness" represents herders and the pastoral production system in Mongolia. This will shed light on (a) why, in some periods, policy approaches on pastureland management (regulating overuse and subtractability) succeeded, but failed at other times and, (b) its similarities as well as differences in comparison to other countries regarding the concepts of community, collective action and the management of production components.

Notes

1 It can be defined in many different ways, but in general, it is the state partial devolution of skills and rights to local community, which receives responsibility in conserving resources (see Ballet et al. 2009, p. 55), or each state and local community play a complementary role and responsibility in managing natural resources (Baland and Platteau, 1996, pp. 346–347).

2

[F]ollowing upon nineteenth-century uses of it [property] in opposition to socialists, it became a central weapon in the Cold War and in American anti-communism. This made it especially potent in the politics around the collapse of the Soviet Empire 1989–1991.

(Humphrey and Verdery, 2004, p. 5)

3 See Peluso (1992).
4 The extent and the cause of rangeland degradation is contested (see Ho 2001).
5 Effective rangeland management in China is crucial in terms of protecting water resources for millions of people, as China accommodates the headwaters for the major rivers in Asia (Miller, 2001).
6 This is due to the use of different scales, indicators and sampling regimes, or figures cited out of context of the methods or methodological assumptions (Addison et al., 2012). It can also be due to ecological factors such as variable annual rainfall or

Understanding CPR and rangeland management 41

human actions or a combination of different variables (Sternberg 2008). Also, see Addison et al. (2012), Sternberg (2008) for explanations of these different figures. It appears that land degradation occurs in one-tenth of the total pastureland of Mongolia, three-quarters of the pastureland in Russia and more than one-third in China. Estimates for degradation in Mongolia are 9 percent, 30 percent, 70 percent, 80 percent and 90 percent of the whole pastureland (80 percent of the total territory). Mostly, 70 percent is quoted, but this is contested (The World Bank, 2003 cited in Addison et al. 2012). Also, 33.5 percent or 41.9 million ha degraded according to the Mongolian Academy of Sciences (MNE, 1996, p. 20).

7 Effective resource management refers to ecological sustainability. This does not necessarily imply resource use that is ecologically or economically optimal (Berkes et al., 1989).

8 See William (1996) for these terms in Chinese.

9 This view was expressed by Igor de Rachewiltz, a historian and philologist specializing in Mongol studies (Personal communication, November, 2012).

10 The following are the least, but not the last definitions of *nutag*. First, Sneath (2010) defined *nutag* as "local homeland" or someone's birth land. In this regard, this word is used as *tursun nutag* (birth land). The reference to the land is quite subjective: one lives in the city and refers to a certain *aimag* as one's birth land. When living in the *aimag* centre, one refers to a specific *soum* as their birth land. When living in the *soum* centre, one refers to a *bag* as one's birth land. When living within a *bag*, one refers to a specific grazing area as one's birth land. Second, *nutag* is also used as jurisdictional territory. In the past, the authorities carried out *nutag zaah*, sending someone to a different place for exile. Third, this term also used for referring to a community. It is used as *neg nutag usniihan*, a group of people linked by some common geographical residence depending on the context for social networking functions (Sneath 2007, 2010). Legrain (2009) sees it as "variable geometry, it connects dispersed places" (p. 338). This is not only a geographical concept but also used referring to a network of social relationships based on the shared experiences of people from the same administrative territory. For instance, Mongolians in settled areas network for social activities using *nutagiin holboo* (association of a community of people, who came from a same jurisdiction). Fourth, as used in this book, *nutag* refers to the use of *belcheeriin nutag*, a specific seasonal pasture area. Upton (2009) used it as one's customary pastureland in pastoralism. This term also goes beyond: *nutaglah*, someone camps seasonally in such a grazing area. Herders carry out [*shine*] *nutag songoh* (select a new camping and grazing area) when their former pasture is not good. Herders often use this term when they migrate to a new administrative territory for herding. It is also used as *khar nutag* (deserted camp and grazing area by majority) (Tsevel, 2013).

11 "A system of activity that links techniques and material objects to the social coordination of labour … technology and resources are inextricably bound up with social form" creating "efficient productive techniques" (Sneath, 2004, p. 170).

12 Lattimore (1941, 1962) and Natsagdorj (1972) also discussed the benefits of pursuing pastoralism in the existing ecological and geographical conditions for political economic benefits.

References

Addison, J, Friedel, M, Brown, C, Davies, J and Waldron, S (2012) "A critical review of degradation assumptions applied to Mongolia's Gobi Desert," *The Rangeland Journal* 34, 125–137.

Agrawal, A (2001) "Common property institutions and sustainable governance and resources," *World Development* 29:10, 1649–1672.

42 Understanding CPR and rangeland management

Agrawal, A (2003) "Sustainable governance of common-pool resources: context, methods and politics," *Annual Revenue of Anthropology* 32, 243–262.

Agrawal, A (2007) "Forests, governance, sustainability: common property theory and its contributions," *International Journal of the Commons* 1:1, 111–136.

Agrawal, A (2010) "Local institutions and adaptation to climate change" in R Mearns and A Norton (eds.) *Social Dimensions of Climate Change*, World Bank, Washington DC, 173–199.

Agrawal, A and Gibson, C (1999) "Enchantment and disenchantment: the role of community in natural resource conservation," *World Development* 27:4, 629–649.

Agrawal, A and Ostrom, E (2001) "Collective action, property rights, and decentralization in resource use in India and Nepal," *Politics and Society* 29:4, 485–514.

Baland, J-M and Platteau, J-P (1996) *Halting Degradation of Natural Resources: Is There a Role for Rural Communities?* FAO and Clarendon Press, Oxford.

Ballet, J, Koffi, K J M and Komena, K B (2009) "Co-management of natural resources in developing countries: the importance of context," *Economie Internationale* 120, 53–76.

Banks, T (2003) "Property rights reform in rangeland China: dilemmas on the road to the household ranch," *World Development* 31:12, 2129–2142.

Banks, Tony (2001) "Property rights and the environment in pastoral China: evidence from the field," *Development and Change* 32, 717–740.

Barfield, Th (2011) "Nomadic pastoralism in Mongolia and beyond" in P L W Sabloff (ed.) *Mapping Mongolia: Situating Mongolia in the World from Geologic Time to the Present*, University of Pennsylvania Museum of Archeology and Anthropology, Philadelphia, 273.

Barfield, T J (1993) *The Nomadic Alternative*, Prentice-Hall, New Jersey.

Basurto, X and Ostrom, E (2009) "The core challenges of moving beyond Garrett Hardin," *Journal of Natural Resources Policy Research* 1:3, 255–259.

Bauer, K (2004) *High Frontiers: Dolpo and the Changing World of Himalayan Pastoralists*, Columbia University Press, New York.

Bauer, Ken (2005) "Development and the enclosure movement in pastoral Tibet since the 1980s," *Nomadic Peoples* 9:1 & 2, 54–81.

Bazargur, D (ed.) (1998) *Geography of Pastoral Animal Husbandry*, TTC Company, Mongolian Academy of Science, Ulaanbaatar.

Bedunah, Donald J and Harris, Richard B (2002) "Past, present & future: rangelands in China: here we examine rangelands and changes in pastoral use in an ethnic minority region, Gansu, China," *Rangelands* 24:4, 17–22.

Behnke, G B and Scoones, I (1993) "Rethinking range ecology: implications for rangeland management in Africa" in *Range Ecology at Disequilibrium, New Models of Natural Variability and Pastoral Adaptation in African Savannas*, ODI, London.

Benda-Beckmann, F V, Benda-Beckmann, K V and Wiber, M G (2006) "The properties of property" in F V Benda-Beckmann, K V Benda-Beckmann and M G Wiber (eds.) *Changing Properties of Property*, Berghahn Books, New York, 1–40.

Berkes, F (2009) "Revisiting the commons paradigm," *Journal of Natural Resources Policy Research* 1:3, 261–264.

Berkes, F, Feeny, D, McCay, B J and Acheson, J M (1989) "The benefits of the common," *Nature* 340, 91–93.

Berry, S (1983) "Access to land: property rights as social process" in S Berry (ed.) *No Condition Is Permanent: The Social Dynamics of Agrarian Change in Sub-Saharan Africa*, University of Wisconsin Press, Wisconsin, 101–134.

Understanding CPR and rangeland management   43

Berry, S (1989a) "Access, control and use of resources in African agriculture: an introduction," *Africa* 59:1, 1–5.

Berry, S (1989b) "Social institutions and access to resources," *Africa* 59:1, 41–55.

Berry, S (1993) *No Condition is Permanent: The Social Dynamics of Agrarian Change in Sub-Saharan Africa*, University of Wisconsin Press, Madison.

Berry, S (2009) "Property, authority and citizenship: land claims, politics and the dynamics of social division in West Africa," *Development and Change* 40:1, 23–45.

Bjorklund, I (2003) "Sami pastoral society in Northern Norway: national integration of an indigenous management system" in David Anderson and Mark Nuttall (eds.) *Cultivating Arctic landscapes*, Berghahn Press, New York, 124–135.

BurnSilver, Shauna B, Worden, Jeffrey and Boone, Randall B (2008) "Process of fragmentation in the Amboseli ecosystem, Southern Kajiodo District, Kenya" in Kathleen A Galvin, Robin S Reid, Jr., Roy H Behnke and N Thompson Hobbs (eds.) *Fragmentation in Semi-Arid and Arid Landscapes: Consequences for Human and Natural Systems*, Springer, Dordrecht, 225–253.

Cellarius, B (2004) "'Without co-ops there would be no forests': historical memory and the restitution of forests in post-socialist Bulgaria," *Conservation & Society* 2:1, 51–73.

Changqing, Y, Taibazar, A, Huijuan, W, Xiangjun, Ch, Mi, Zh, Yibat, T and Hazaiz, N (2012) "Customary community-based rangeland management: a case study of Kazak nomadism and rangeland management in Xinjiang" in M E Fernandez-Gimenez, Xiaoyi Wang, B Batkhishig, Julia A Klein and Robin S Reid (eds.) *Restoring Community Connections to the Land: Building Resilience Through Community-based Rangeland Management in China and Mongolia*, CAB International, Wallingford, Cambridge, 136–149.

Cleaver, F (2001) "Institutional bricolage, conflict and cooperation in Usangu, Tanzania," *IDS Bulletin* 32, 26–35.

Cleaver, F and Franks, T (2005) "How institutions elude design: river basin management and sustainable livelihoods" Centre for International Development, University of Bradford, Bradford.

Cousins, B (2009) "Capitalism obscured: the limits of law and rights-based approaches to poverty reduction and development," *Journal of Peasant Studies* 36:4, 893–908.

Dalintai, Gauwau, N, Yanbo, L, Enkhee, J and Shurun, L (2012) "The new *otor*: risk management in a desert grassland" in M E Fernandez-Gimenez, Xiaoyi Wang, B Batkhishig, Julia A Klein and Robin S Reid (eds.) *Restoring Community Connections to the Land: Building Resilience Through Community-based Rangeland Management in China and Mongolia*, CAB International, Wallingford, Cambridge, 93–112.

Dietz, T, Ostrom, E and Stern, P C (2003) "The struggle to govern the commons," *Science* 302, 1907–1912.

Eggertsson, Th (2009) "Hardin's brilliant tragedy and a non-sequitur response," *Journal of Natural Resources Policy Research* 1:3, 265–268.

Endicott, E (2012) *A History of Land Use in Mongolia*, Palgrave Macmillan, New York.

Feeny, D, Berkes, F, McCay, B J and Acheson, J M (1990) "The tragedy of the commons: twenty-two years later," *Human Ecology* 18:1.

Fernandez-Gimenez, M E and Allen-Diaz, B (1999) "Testing a non-equilibrium model of rangeland vegetation dynamics in Mongolia," *Journal of Applied Ecology* 36, 871–885.

Fernandez-Gimenez, Maria E and Swift, David M (2003) "Strategies for sustainable grazing management in the developing world," in N Allsopp, A R Palmer, S J

44 Understanding CPR and rangeland management

Milton, K P Kirkman, G I H Kerley, C R Hurt and C J Brown, *Proceedings of the VIIth International Rangeland Congress*, Durban, South Africa, July 26–August 1, 2003, Document Transformation Technologies, 821–831.

Fernandez-Gimenez, M E, Kamimura, A and Batbuyan, B (2008) "Implementing Mongolia's land law: progress and issues," The Center for Asian Legal Exchange (CALE), Nagoya University, Japan.

Fitzpatrick, D (2005) "'Best practice' options for the legal recognition of customary tenure," *Development and Change* 36:3, 449–475.

Fratkin, E (1997) "Pastoralism: governance and development issues," *Annual Review of Anthropology* 26, 235–261.

Fratkin, E and Mearns, R (2003) "Sustainability and pastoral livelihoods: lessons from East African Maasai and Mongolia," *Human Organization* 62, 112–122.

Galvin, Kathleen A, Boone, Randall B, Thornton, Philip K and Knapp, Linda M (2008a) "North-West Province, South Africa: communal and commercial livestock systems in transition" in Kathleen A Galvin, Robin S Reid, Jr., Roy H Behnke and N Thompson Hobbs (eds.) *Fragmentation in Semi-Arid and Arid Landscapes: Consequences for Human and Natural Systems*, Springer, Dordrecht, 281–304.

Galvin, Kathleen A, Thornton, Philip K, Boone, Randall B and Knapp, Linda M (2008b) "Ngorongoro Conservation Area, Tanzania: fragmentation of a unique region of the Greater Serengeti ecosystem" in Kathleen A Galvin, Robin S Reid, Jr., Roy H Behnke and N Thompson Hobbs (eds.) *Fragmentation in Semi-Arid and Arid Landscapes: Consequences for Human and Natural Systems*, Springer, Dordrecht, 255–279.

Goldstein, M C and Beall, C M (1994) *The Changing World of Mongolia's Nomads*, Twin Age Limited, Hong Kong.

Grousset, Rene (1970) *The Empire of the Steppes: A History of Central Asia*, Rutgers, New Brunswick, New Jersey, London.

Hall, K, Cleaver, F, Franks, T and Maganga, F (2014) "Capturing critical institutionalism: a synthesis of key themes and debates," *European Journal of Development Research* 26, 71–86.

Hardin, G (1968) "The tragedy of the commons," *Science* 162, 1243–1248.

Heather, P (2010) *Empires and Barbarians: Fall of Rome and the Birth of Europe*, Oxford University Press, Oxford.

Hesse, Ced and MacGregor, James (2006) "Pastoralism: drylands' invisible asset?" IIED, Edinburgh.

Ho, P (2001) "Rangeland degradation in China revisited?," *The Journal of Development Studies* 37(3), 99–132.

Ho, P (2013) "In defense of endogenous, spontaneously ordered development: institutional functionalism and Chinese property rights," *The Journal of Peasant Studies* 40:6, 1087–1118.

Hopkirk, P (1994) *The Great Game: The Struggle for Empire in Central Asia*, Kodansha America, LLC, New York.

Hopkirk, P (1995) *Trespassers on the Roof of the World: The Secret Exploration of Tibet*, Kodansha America, Inc., New York.

Humphrey, C (1999) "Rural institutions" in David Sneath and Caroline Humphrey (eds.) *The End of Nomadism: Society, State and the Environment in Inner Asia*, Duke University Press, Durham, NC, 68–136.

Humphrey, Caroline (1980) "Introduction" in Sevyan Vainshtein, *Nomads of South Siberia*, Cambridge University Press, Cambridge, 1–33.

Understanding CPR and rangeland management 45

Humphrey, Caroline and Sneath, David (1999) *The End of Nomadism?*, Duke University Press, Durham, NC.

Humphrey, Caroline and Verdery, Katherine (2004) "Introduction: raising questions about property" in Katherine Verdery and Caroline Humphrey (eds.) *Property in Question: Value Transformation in the Global Economy*, Berg, Oxford, New York, 1–25.

Jianjun, C, Yangyang, Y and Guozhen, D (2012) "Research on the management models in pastoral areas in Qinghai-Tibet Plateau: a case study of Maqu, Gansu Province" in M E Fernandez-Gimenez, Xiaoyi Wang, B Batkhishig, Julia A Klein and Robin S Reid (eds.) *Restoring Community Connections to the Land: Building Resilience Through Community-based Rangeland Management in China and Mongolia*, CAB International, Wallingford, Cambridge, 150–165.

Johnson, G (2004) "Uncommon ground: the 'poverty of history' in common property discourse," *Development and Change* 35:3, 407–433.

Khazanov, A M (1994a) *Nomads and the Outside World, second edition*, University of Wisconsin Press, Madison.

Khazanov, A M (1994b) "Underdevelopment and ethnic relations in Central Asia" in *Central Asia in Historical Perspective*, Westview Press, CO, Oxford, 144–163.

Khazanov, A N (1998) "Pastoralists in the contemporary world: the problems of survival" in J Ginat and A M Khazanov (eds.) *Changing Nomads in a Changing World*, Sussex Academic Press, Brighton, 7–23.

Klein, J A, Fernandez-Gimenez, M E, Wei, H, Changqing, Y, Ling, D, Dorligsuren, D and Reid R S (2012) "A participatory framework for building resilient social-ecological pastoral systems" in M Fernandez-Gimenez, Xiaoyi Wang, B Batkhishig, J A Klein and R S Reid (eds.) *Restoring Community Connections to the Land: Building Resilience Through Community-based Rangeland Management in China and Mongolia*, CABI International, Oxfordshire.

Kradin, N (2011) "Heterarchy and hierarchy among the ancient Mongolian nomads," *Social Evolution & History* 10:1.

Larson, F A (1930) *Duke of Mongolia*, Little, Brown, and Company, Boston.

Lastarria-Cornhiel, S (1997) "Impact of privatization on gender and property rights in Africa," *World Development* 25:8, 1317–1333.

Lattimore, O (1932) *Manchuria, Cradle of Conflict*, The Macmillan Company of Canada, Toronto.

Lattimore, O (1941) *Mongol Journey*, Doubleday, Doran and Co, New York.

Lattimore, O (1962) *Nomads and Commissars: Mongolia Revisited*, Oxford University Press, New York.

Legrain, L (2009) "Confrontation on the River Ivd, or, how does music act in social life?," *Inner Asia* 11, 335–358.

Lopez, B (2001) *Arctic Dreams*, Vintage Books, A Division of Random House, Inc., New York.

Marschke, M, Armitage, D, An, L V, Tuyen, T V and Mallee, H (2012) "Do collective property rights make sense? Insights from central Vietnam," *International Journal of the Commons* 6:1, 1–27.

Marshall, G R (2008) "Nesting, subsidiarity, and community-based environmental governance beyond the local level," *International Journal of the Commons* 2:1, 75–97.

McCay, B J and Jentoft, S (1998) "Market or community failure? Critical perspectives on common property research," *Human Organization* 57:1, 21–29.

McCay, B J and Acheson, J M (1987) *The Questions of the Commons: The Culture and Ecology of Communal Resources*, University of Arizona, Tucson.

46 *Understanding CPR and rangeland management*

Meredith, M (2005) *The Fate of Africa: A History of Fifty Years of Independence*, Public Affairs, Perseus Book Group, New York.

Miller, D and Sheehy, D (2008) "The relevance of Owen Lattimore's writings for nomadic pastoralism research and development in Inner Asia," *Nomadic Peoples* 12:2, 103–115.

Miller, Daniel (2001) "The importance of China's nomads: the sustainable future development of China's rangelands depends on integrating nomads indigenous knowledge," *Rangelands* 24:1, 22–24.

MNE (1996) *Biodiversity Conservation Action Plan for Mongolia*, GEF/UNDP/MNE, Ulaanbaatar.

National Research Council (1986) "Proceedings of the conference on common property resource management," in National Research Council, *Common Property Resource Management*, Washington DC, National Academy Press.

Natsagdorj, Sh (1972) *Soum, khamjlaga, shavi, ard*, Academy of Science Publishing, Ulaanbaatar.

Natsagdorj, Sh (1975) "Main characters of Feudalism: the Mongolian society as an example" in *XIV International Congress of Historical Sciences*, Ulaanbaatar, San-Francisco, 1–18.

Osterle, Matthias (2008) "From cattle to goats: the transformation of East Pokot pastoralism in Kenya," *Nomadic Peoples* 12:1, 81–91.

Ostrom, E (1990) "Reflection on the commons" in Elinor Ostrom (ed.) *Governing the Commons*, Cambridge University Press, Cambridge, 1–28.

Ostrom, E (2009) "Beyond markets and states: polycentric governance of complex economic systems," Workshop in Political Theory and Policy Analysis, Indiana University, Bloomington, and Center for the Study of Institutional Diversity, Arizona State University, Tempe.

Ostrom, E and Nagendra, H (2006) "Insights on linking forests, trees, and people from the air, on the ground, and in the laboratory," *PNAS* 103:51, 19224–19231.

Ostrom, E, Burger, J, Field, C B, Norgaard, R B and Policansky, D (1999) "Revisiting the commons: local lessons, global challenges," *Science* 284, 278–282.

Ostrom, E, Gardner, R and Walker, J (1994) *Rules, Games, and Common-Pool Resources*, The University of Michigan Press, Michigan.

Peluso, N L (1992) *Rich Forests, Poor People: Resource Control and Resistance in Java*, University of California Press, Berkeley.

Pirie, Fernanda (2006) "Legal complexity on the Tibetan plateau," *Journal of Legal Pluralism* nrs, 77–98.

Reid, A (2003) *The Shaman's Coat: A Native History of Siberia*, Phoenix, London.

Reid, R S, Galvin, K A and Kruska, R S (2008a) "Global significance of extensive grazing lands and pastoral societies: an introduction" in K A Galvin, R S Reid, Jr., R H Behnke and N Th Hobbs (eds.) *Fragmentation in Semi-Arid and Arid Landscapes: Consequences for Human and Natural Systems*, Springer, Dordrecht.

Reid, Robin S, Gichohi, Helen, Said, Mohammed Y, Nkedianye, David, Ogutu, Joseph O, Kshatriya, Mrigesh, Kristjanson, Patti, Kifugo, Shem C, Agatsiva, Jasphat L, Adanje, Samuel A and Bagine, Richard (2008b) "Fragmentation of a peri-urban savanna, Athi-Kaputiei Plains, Kenya" in Kathleen A Galvin, Robin S Reid, Jr., Roy H Behnke and N Thompson Hobbs (eds.) *Fragmentation in Semi-Arid and Arid Landscapes: Consequences for Human and Natural Systems*, Springer, Dordrecht, 195–224.

Ribot, J C (1998) "Theorizing access: forest profits along Senegal's charcoal commodity chain," *Development and Change* 29, 307–341.

Ribot, J C and Peluso, N L (2003) "A theory of access," *Rural Sociology* 68:2, 153–181.

Robbins, P (2004) *Political Ecology: A Critical Introduction*, Blackwell, Malden, MA.

Robinson, S, Milner-Gullandw, E J and Alimaevz, I (2003) "Rangeland degradation in Kazakhstan during the Soviet era: re-examining the evidence," *Journal of Arid Environments* 53, 419–439.

Rowe, W T (2009) *China's Last Empire: The Great Qing*, The Belknap Press of Harvard University Press, MA, London.

Saunders, F P (2014) "The promise of common pool resource theory and the reality of commons projects," *International Journal of the Commons* 8:2, 636–656.

Schlager, E (ed.) (2004) *Common-Pool Resource Theory*, MIT Press, Cambridge, MA.

Shayakhmetov, Mukhamet (2007) *The Silent Steppe: The Memoir of a Kazakh Nomad under Stalin*, The Rookery Press, New York.

Simukov, A D (1931) "Kulturno-bytovyye usloviya jizni Mongol (tesisy k dokladu)" in Yuki Konagaya, Sanjaasurengiin Bayaraa and Ichinkhorloogiin Lkhagvasuren (eds.) *Kratkaya geographiya Mongolskoi Narodnoi Respubliki: Hozyaistvo, cultura, i byt nasyelyeniya, Tom II*, Gosudarstvyennyi muzei etnologii Osaka, 593–599.

Simukov, A D (1934) "Краткая география Монгольской Народной Республики Часть II: Население, его хозяйство и государственное устройство страны" in Yuki Konagaya, Sanjaasurengiin Bayaraa and Ichinkhorloogiin Lkhagvasuren (eds.) *Труды о Монголии и для Монголии*, Государственный музей этнологии, Osaka, 709–773.

Sneath, D (1998) "State policy and pasture degradation in Inner Asia," *Science's Compass* 281:21, 1147–1148.

Sneath, D (2003) "Land use, the environment and development in post-socialist Mongolia," *Oxford Development Studies* 31:4, 441–457.

Sneath, D (2004) "Property regimes and sociotechnical systems: rights over land in Mongolia's 'Age of the Market'" in K Verdery and C Humphrey (eds.) *Property in Question: Value Transformation in the Global Economy*, Berg, Oxford, New York, 161–182.

Sneath, D (2007) *The Headless State*, Columbia University Press, New York.

Sneath, D (2010) "Political mobilization and the construction of collective identity in Mongolia," *Central Asian Survey* 29:3, 251–267.

Spooner, B (1973) *The Cultural Ecology of Pastoral Nomads*, Addison-Wesley Publishing, Reading, MA.

Stacey, Tom (2007) "Introduction" in Mukhamet Shayakhmetov, *The Silent Steppe: The Memoir of a Kazakh Nomad under Stalin*, The Rookery Press, New York, vii–xii.

Sternberg, T (2008) "Environmental challenges in Mongolia's dryland pastoral landscape," *Journal of Arid Environments* 72, 1294–1304.

Sturgeon, J C and Sikor, T (2004) "Post-socialist property in Asia and Europe: variations on 'fuzziness'," *Conservation & Society* 2:1, 2–17.

Swift, J (1988) "Major issues in pastoral development with special emphasis on selected African countries," FAO, Rome.

Swift, J and Mearns, R (1993) "Pastoralism in Mongolia," *Nomadic Peoples* 33, 3–239.

Tsevel, Ya (2013) "Mongol Helnii Tovch Tailbar Toli" in Ts Shagdarsuren (ed.) *Mongol Helnii Tovch Tailbar Toli*, Ulaanbaatar University, Ulaanbaatar, 1311.

Upton, C (2009) "'Custom' and contestation: land reform in post-socialist Mongolia', *World Development* 37:8, 1400–1410.

48 *Understanding CPR and rangeland management*

Verdery, K (1999) "Fuzzy property: rights, power, and identity in Transylvania's decollectivization" in M Burawoy and K Verdery (eds.) *Uncertain Transition: Ethnographies of Change in the Post-socialist World*, Rowman and Littlefield Publishers, Lanham, MD, 53–82.

Verdery, K (2004) "The property regime of socialism," *Conservation & Society* 2:1, 190–198.

Vetter, S (2005) "Rangelands at equilibrium and non-equilibrium: recent developments in the debate," *Journal of Arid Environments* 62, 321–341.

Vreeland, H H (1954) "Mongol community and kinship structure," Walter Hines Page School of International Relations, The Johns Hopkins University, New Haven.

William, D M (1996) "The barbed walls of China: a contemporary grassland drama," *The Journal of Asian Studies* 55:3, 665–691.

Wollenberg, E, Merino, L, Agrawal, A and Ostrom, E (2007) "Fourteen years of monitoring community-managed forests: learning from IFRI's experience," *International Forestry Review* 9:2, 670–684.

Xie, Yina and Li, Wenjun (2008) "Why do herders insist on *otor*? Maintaining mobility in Inner Mongolia," *Nomadic Peoples* 12:2, 35–52.

Zhizhong, Wu and Wen, Du (2008) "Pastoral nomad rights in Inner Mongolia," *Nomadic Peoples* 12:2, 13–33.

3 Mobile pastoralism and the pre-collective period (*c.*1206–*c.*1921)

Historically, property institutions in Mongolia were much more complex and the use of pastureland was more sophisticated than currently perceived. This sophistication was rooted in a common interest to herders, namely, the pursuit of pastoralism to obtain and maintain political and economic power. Such power seems important for the existence of pastoral societies, particularly when looking at their relationship with sedentary societies. Some scholars argue that it is misleading to interpret mobile pastoralism as independent of an agrarian lifestyle (Khazanov, 1994; Lattimore, 1962). Mobile people, culturally, ideologically as well as economically, are instead dependent on sedentary or agrarian lifestyles because of their technological capacity (Khazanov, 1994). However, this can be understood in a way that the power of expansion and the annexation of more pastoral territory was a marginal interest as they were also interested in securing political and economic alliances, by maintaining close proximity with other settled societies like the Roman and Chinese Empires (Heather, 2010). Early scholars and travellers observed, documented and recorded nomads' constant contact with sedentary societies through warfare and trade (Larson, 1930; Lattimore, 1941, 1962). Keeping close alliance or contact with settled societies was politically advantageous in order to spread their influence throughout the region and history (Grousset, 1970, p. 72).

This type of nomadic polity was ruled by powerful confederate chieftains (Sneath, 2007). As Gibson (2011) stated, "a chiefdom of a confederacy consists of a number of genealogically related and unrelated chiefdoms which were unified through coercion or common agreement" (p. 217). These powerful confederations managed their pastoral production and its institutions through a system of state territorial administrations. The origination of this system dated back to the Xiongnu, which was the first historically recorded state polity established in the late third century BCE and controlled the Inner Asian steppes including the current territory of Mongolia (Grousset, 1970, p. 26). This system was rooted in an aristocratic, military administrative system, which was based on "a series of decimal[1] units that could raise a nominal number of horsemen in times of war" (Di Cosmo, 2002 cited in Sneath, 2007, p. 23). Since then several different state polities employed these systems until the time

50 *Mobile pastoralism and the pre-collective period*

of the Mongol Empire in the thirteenth century (Grousset, 1970). The Mongol Empire established the foundation of the modern Mongol nation state. Its state organization was based on a pre-existing aristocratic order, in which hereditary rulers conveyed administrative power over their political subjects in a similar centralized state governance structure (Sneath, 2007). This was functional for pursuing pastoral production under existing geographical and climatic conditions (Sneath, 2007). Noble lords directed their thriving livestock production towards producing "large numbers of horsemen and mobile food supplies in the form of livestock" to solidify political[2] and economic[3] power (Sneath, 2007, p. 20). For this purpose, these steppe polities developed a sophisticated institutional framework for managing the movement of their mobile subjects and their pastoral production system.

Pastoral production management in the Mongol Empire

The formalization of the historical framework for the institution of pastoral production in current Mongolia perhaps dated back to the establishment of the Mongol Empire. The structure of this framework prevails in the jurisdictional administration; state territorial administrative units, instead of landed property ownership. In 1206, *Chinggis Khaan*[4] organized his subjects using the pre-existing decimal units system (Natsagdorj, 1972, p. 8). This was an organizational structure comprising "groups of ten, hundred, thousand and ten thousand, with a direct conveyance of orders through a chain of command from above to below" (Bold, 2001, p. 84). The main unit was based on the pre-existing one thousand (*myangat*) system, and the members were now a mixture from different chiefdoms (Natsagdorj, 1972, p. 12). The role of the thousand was to serve the empire through the military and civil services (postal service[5] and to herd livestock for the ruling elite and pay livestock tax) to the *Khaan.* He also changed the basis of the lords, from hereditary nobility, and bestowed titles on his military generals and colleagues who were without a noble background (Natsagdorj, 1972; Sneath, 2007). It was for both military/civil purposes[6] of administering/distributing nomadic population to nobles (Bold, 2001; Grousset, 1970; Natsagdorj, 1975; Sneath, 2007). Natsagdorj (1972) concluded that this jurisdictional administration was more for controlling the movement of the nomadic population by prioritizing the attachment of subjects to a specific ruler, instead of a specific territory. Thus, the khan first divided his subjects to his sons and then divided the territory (*nutag zaah*) (Natsagdorj, 1972, p. 8). "Secret History of Mongolia" is full of records about distribution of the population to specific jurisdictional authorities. Although jurisdictional social boundaries were clear, its resource-territorial boundaries were more fluid and dynamic before the Manchu period (Barfield, 2011, p. 117). This reflects the notion of labor control (Chapter 2), which shapes resource access for the purpose of controlling benefits from production even in land ploughing or crop cultivating contexts (Berry, 1993; Peluso, 1992).

Mobile pastoralism and the pre-collective period   51

Here, it is important to clarify the nature of property relations in land in the context of pastoralism. Natsagdorj (1972) noted that many commentators have argued that the Mongolian pastoral setting experienced no socio-economic development, and in particular, there was no private property (Natsagdorj, 1972). The author (1972, 1975) noted that, in the pastoral context, private ownership emerged beside state ownership over both subjects and territory/land when the sons of Chinggis *Khaan* independently controlled their respective territory under a feudal relationship. "Their power and rights were limited to their own immediate apanages"[7] (Natsagdorj, 1967, p. 267), even though the territory and subjects nominally belonged to the Great *Khaan* by virtue of paying tribute and forming military alliances (Lamb, 1927; Weatherford, 2004). Although Natsagdorj (1975) explained property relations in pastoralism in terms of European concepts of property ownership and Marxist feudal class relations, the author acknowledged that Mongolian feudal land ownership was much more unique and different than those in other countries (pp. 5–10). Also, many of his statements on feudal land relationships were not exclusive to land ownership as he simultaneously referred to owner-ship of subjects and livestock. His statement of land ownership was often based on general terms like assignment or allocation of certain territory/land (*gazar/nutag zaah*) identified by landmarks, rather than specific land measure-ment (pp. 13–15). Barfield (2011) noted the emergence of a feudal system under the Manchu period based on the position of another Mongolian scholar (p. 117). However, arguing the notion of nomadic feudalism in Mongolian society, Khazanov (1994) noted, "Superficial similarity to European feudalism in the organization of power should not overshadow the qualitative differ-ences with regard to the ownership of key resources" (p. 237). Lattimore (1962) considered Mongolian Pastoralism as quasi-feudalism, explaining that Marxist writers overlooked the difference between land-bound peasants and herders, whose survival was not bound to specific land, but dependent on their access to livestock through private ownership or working for their lords (p. 58). Other scholars are also critical about the position of using Marxist notions of feudalism to explain Mongolian history, social development and landed property relations[8] in the context of pastoralism due to the influence of socialist ideology, which prevailed at the time in Mongolia (Bold, 2001; Sneath, 2007).

In Mongolia, property relations in pastureland seem to present territorial authority or custodianship more than feudal land ownership. Grousset (1970) described that Chinggis' sons had received,

> *ulus* – that is, a certain number of tribes ... or territorial appanage of grazing land (*nutag*)[9] sufficient to support these tribes.... The only divisi-ble asset was Turko-Mongol prairie, the nomads' grazing grounds.... The cultivated country around Peking and Samarkand remained imperial territory.
>
> (pp. 221–222, 253)

52 *Mobile pastoralism and the pre-collective period*

The authority of the Great *Khaan* can also be seen when Guyuk[10] *Khaan* challenged Batu[11] *Khan* with a war campaign "to stamp out the growing autonomy which had begun to be enjoyed by the other Jenghiz-Khanate branches" or Mungkhu *Khaan* limited the arbitrary rule of the Khans of other Mongol appanages, who changed laws regarding taxes and revenues on behalf of him (Grousset, 1970, pp. 272, 275; Khazanov, 1994, p. 242). This indicates that property relations in pastoralism referred to subjects and objects such as livestock and pastoral territory, embedded together in the state territorial administration. Here, exclusive property ownership was fixed in subjects and livestock as taxable property.[12] Unlike feudal relations fixed in specific measurable land, the patchy pasture led to a territorial use of land with fuzzy dynamic boundary, and was not measurable/taxable or fixed asset for exclusive ownership. The use of territory was not fixed, but flexible pertaining to exclusive as well as inclusive of households between and within jurisdictions to manage their pastoral production. Instead of private property, Khazanov (1994) promoted the idea of possible corporate ownership, which varied in much more different forms than private ownership of livestock, due to a vague or no fixed boundary for owning the land (pp. 124–125). Lattimore (1962) considered it ownership by political unit (p. 39). Even then the notion of ownership of pastureland or the concept of property in the Mongolian context appears problematic. How do we recognize or identify who owns what land "in which persons and things are not seen as clearly bounded and separate but as participating in one another?" (Humphrey and Verdery, 2004, p. 8). This is particularly when territorial (social and resource) boundaries of different social subdivisions within a jurisdiction were often dynamic between different administrative levels and jurisdictions, and would often change under different socio-political orders following expansion or loss of territory from war and/or shifting climatic conditions.

Land tenure in the pastoral context embodies state territorial relations under custodianship. Entitlement to exclusive authority to control access to human and natural resources seems to be embedded in the jurisdictional structure, which is more territorial rather than through exclusive ownership via a modern property regime. Noble lords functioned as a jurisdictional authority as they now enjoyed a hereditary title, ruling over subjects of mixed groups in addition to re-assigning territory for political administrations. The *Khaan* granted a few elite members absolute authority (*darha*) to use or control their territory besides being exempt from some taxes. The nobles' subjects and territory were subordinate to the *Khaan*'s jurisdiction as the state was the supreme owner of the land (Natsagdorj, 1967). Thus, a concept of territorial-based land management existed. Each thousand and its micro-units had its own defined *nutag* territory (Rachewiltz, 1972 cited in Munkh-Erdene, 2011). This boundary delineation seems to represent a recognizable territory (*nutag zaah*) as it was identified by approximate geographical location of certain ethnic groups or geographical land marks (Munkh-Erdene, 2011, p. 217). Thus, it is worth noting that in pastoral contexts this form of territorial delineation is often fuzzy in nature (Lattimore,

Mobile pastoralism and the pre-collective period 53

1941). This is different from a rigid demarcation of boundary for parceling out land in a modern sense of exclusive property ownership. Nobles appointed officials (*nutagchid*) to assign grazing territory (*nutag zaah*) to their subjects (Natsagdorj, 1972, p. 55; Rachewiltz, 1972 cited in Munkh-Erdene, 2011, p. 217). Subjects had the right to use certain grazing lands in a flexible and territorial manner to accommodate their seasonal migration, which needs to be beyond a plot of land as a commodity in a sense of modern exclusive property rights. Nobles also issued or revoked pasture use rights to their subjects (Natsagdorj, 1967). In addition, pasture was expanded by the digging of wells in unused areas throughout Mongol territory (Damdinsuren, 1976, p. 237; Natsagdorj, 1972). This jurisdictional arrangement was centred on distribution of the population as "land was not conceptualized as an asset to be carefully divided up and parcelled out" (Endicott, 2012, p. 44). Others also noted that this territorial arrangement continued under the Manchu period; land remained under public ownership without any exclusive land ownership by noblemen or monks, and was governed by *hoshuu* territorial administration (Jagchid and Hyer, 1979; Maiskii 1921, pp. 223–269, cited in Khazanov, 1994, p. 124).

Therefore, it is questionable to perceive property relations in land from the perspective of property ownership in a modern economic sense. The reason to perceive it as private ownership may have been due to the fact that mainly those with a "monopoly of livestock holdings" controlled land use, even though it nominally belonged to a jurisdictional community (Tolstov, 1934 cited in Vainshtein, 1980, p. 233). Lattimore (1932) emphasized it well that neither individuals nor rulers prescribe individual ownership as land belongs to the whole tribal community, even the understanding of which is different from any modern state ownership (Lattimore, 1932, p. 48). This also reflects crop-cultivating societies elsewhere under aristocratic order, in which the monarch's claim over all the territory "could not be defined as state land ownership as it would be today; nor would it match European conceptions of property at that time" (Peluso, 1992, p. 33). In fact, Bold (2001) noted that "these ownership conditions did not relate to property in the economic sense, but rather to access to pastureland" (Bold, 2001, p. 41). This is more likely an authority or custodianship over territory, which is not the same as exclusive individual marketable private property ownership and it "does not equal ownership per se of land" (Endicott, 2012, p. 44).

If anything seemed private, it was for the use right for private personal purpose or abuse of authority under the given authority over the territory and subjects. Noble lords allowed themselves to categorize land for personal uses, for instance hunting and herding (Bold, 1996, p. 124; Bold, 2001; Khazanov, 1994). The purpose was mostly for the "reservation of the animals for large scale hunts," rather than the ownership in a modern sense (Endicott, 2012, p. 44). Although he acknowledged the absence of private ownership of land, Lattimore (1941) also discussed that noble lords employed their jurisdictional authority as a mechanism to gain benefits for their private needs. Lattimore observed Mongolian Pastoralism as follows:

54 *Mobile pastoralism and the pre-collective period*

There was no private property in land, though there was private property in livestock. There is no doubt that this Mongol system was decadent (corrupt); it had become so distorted that by the very fact that there was no property in land the great nobles and the great monastic "corporations" could use their authority to get all the profit that they could have had out of ownership of the land, without the responsibilities.

(1941, p. 249)

Although they control land use in practice, Natsagdorj (1975) noted that these lords were more often seen as the proprietor-manager of their assigned territory and subjects rather than the sole beneficiary, as they paid services and taxes to the *Khaan* (Natsagdorj, 1975, p. 7). Such arrangements were also the case under the rule of the Manchu Dynasty. Despite abuses,[13] their authorities were simply "the carrying out of socially expedient managerial functions and their rewards, rather than rights towards private property" (Khazanov, 1994, pp. 124, 125). Although abuse by authorities occurred, particularly at the end of the Manchu period, it is not a uniform characteristic throughout the history of the Mongolian pastoral system. Strict rules of law had prevailed at every level and sector of daily life, especially during the reigns of Chinggis to Munkh *Khan* (Grousset, 1970; Lamb, 1927; Weatherford, 2004). Regarding this framework of pastoral production Sneath (2004) argued

these systems of knowledge were not merely instruments of domination; they reflected a much wider range of human experience, including the technical constraints on production imposed by an "environmental" externality – be that conceived in spiritual or in materialistic terms. Based as they were on pastoral mobility and general access to land, these socio-technical systems tended to maintain and support those of land use, and this seems to have provided very real benefits for pastoralists.

(p. 171)

Thus, state territorial control is not the same in the western economic sense of entitling a "bundle of rights" to land as a pre-condition for a market-based economic system as it is not recorded whether this territorial ownership included alienation[14] rights. This may be because rights may not have rested directly in the land or water resources alone due to the dynamics of controlling both human and natural resources together as property (fluid territorial boundaries); issuing their subjects residency rights that transfer into right to use pasture within their jurisdictional territory. This form of right to land did not conform to land as marketable commodity. The lords' ownership over their subjects and territory was embedded in a framework regulating jurisdictional territory to retain political and economic power to exclude and include access to the pastoral resources. This was the fundamental structure of maintaining pastoral production management. This state territorial management

Mobile pastoralism and the pre-collective period 55

was characterized by communality in land use because of the characteristics of pastoral production, which defines the norms of shared use and pastoral institutions that I discuss in the next section.

Pastoralism under the Manchu Qing Dynasty

Over time, changes in the jurisdictional administration, particularly reduction in the jurisdictional territories, would affect future local pasture management. This began with the fact that the Manchu Qing Dynasty (1691–1911) reorganized Mongolia's once fluid territorial boundaries into permanent territorial units with fixed boundaries for its military defense purposes (Barfield, 2011, p. 117; Khazanov, 1994, p. 178; Vreeland, 1954, p. 10).

Territorial administration

In 1725, the Manchu changed Khalkha's three *aimags* (approximately current Mongolia) into four *aimags*,[15] by separating 22 *khoshuu* territories from Tusheet Khan *aimag* and created Sain Noyon Khan *aimag*[16] (Regsuren and Baljinnyam, 1973, p. 15; Sukhbaatar and Jamsran, 1968, p. 131). It divided each *aimag* (the highest territorial unit) into *hoshuu*[17] (banner), a military-territorial structure (Natsagdorj, 1972, p. 24). There were around 24 *hoshuuns*[18] in each *aimag* (Baabar, 1999). The *hoshuu* administration contained five types of settlement (herdsmen camps,[19] relay station, monastery, a headquarter camp and commercial center/town) within the *hoshuu* (Vreeland, 1954). Within the *hoshuu*, the Manchu also introduced the *soum*, an administrative unit containing 150 households[20] for the purpose of recruiting soldiers (Natsagdorj, 1972). The *soum* was divided into several *bags*, which contained 50 households and was led by the noble families (Bold, 2001; Fernandez-Gimenez, 1999; Humphrey, 1978; Natsagdorj, 1955; Sneath, 2007; Vreeland, 1954). Moreover, a group *aravt* or *arvan*, of ten households was used for administrative purposes (Regsuren and Baljinnyam, 1973, p. 21; Vreeland, 1954, p. 21). Except for the *hoshuu*, these smaller units were structured as group households living in close proximity to each other (Vainshtein, 1980, p. 19). The main function of these groups was to administer civil registration[21] of a group of households, their members, their taxable properties (only livestock,[22] occasionally silver), group members' civil offences and services, and occasionally organizing social events like sacred rituals (Natsagdorj, 1967; Vreeland, 1954). Although these territorial units equated formal control regarding their administrative duties, the extent of control in some units[23] would vary in the future following socio-political and economic transitions.

Hoshuu became a key territorial administrative unit within each *aimag* and the primary structure for controlling pastoral production. The Manchus formalized *hoshuu* territory, which reflected the customary boundaries with land marks and stone cairns (*ovoo*) to control the production and the movement of subjects. In this way, the Manchus changed the characteristics of Mongol

56 *Mobile pastoralism and the pre-collective period*

territorial administrative units with fixed territory. This was to avoid territorial disputes whilst continuing to allow the pre-existing pastoral production system for regulating pasture use (Vreeland, 1954, p. 10). In Manchu documents, borderlines were clearly drawn, but in reality the boundaries were rather fuzzy due to the complex features of herding strategies for pastoral production (Lattimore, 1941, p. 209). Maintaining the customary structure of jurisdictional boundaries was significant in accommodating flexibility of movement for herders pursuing pastoral production as this comprised a combination of forest, steppe and *gobi* zones (Natsagdorj, 1972, p. 59). This is due to the fact that herders needed to find free-range seasonal grazing for different species year-round. The management of pastoral production was rooted in the customary (*ulamjlalt*) system, which shaped movements for grazing while providing herder flexibility (Bazargur, 1998; Erdenetsogt, 1998). In other words, the Manchu administration adjusted its policy in Mongolia to take advantage of the political economy of pastoral production. During this period, the lord of each *hoshuu* was to be selected from *Chinggis Khaan*'s descendants rather than from among his military leaders and colleagues (Natsagdorj, 1975). Although Mongol nobles still controlled their *hoshuu* territory and subjects, the Manchu limited their exclusive ownership rights in order to facilitate Manchu control over benefits derived from taxes and services (Humphrey, 1978; Natsagdorj, 1972). At least in Outer Mongolia, until the collapse of the monarchy in 1921, the Manchu Emperor and the Mongol monarch Bogd *Khaan* (1869–1924) in general did not permit the sale of land to outsiders. For instance, local nobilities or commoners often reported their complaints to the highest level authority when foreign and local lords under the Manchu exercised their authority to pursue gold mining for personal benefit without acknowledging the interests of local herders (High and Schlesinger, 2010; Sukhbaatar and Jamsran, 1968, p. 167). Some small scale land sales were permitted for agrarian and mining purposes, but were not on a scale large enough to affect pastoral production[24] (Lattimore, 1941, 1962; Sukhbaatar and Jamsran, 1968). In other words, the nobles did not have the right to alienate (rent or sell) their land as both human and natural resources now belonged to the Manchu Emperor (Natsagdorj, 1972, 1975).

Parallel to the *hoshuu* jurisdiction, another politically and economically significant administrative institution emerged to control production. Most monasteries were owned by the banners, and lamas were subject to the jurisdiction they lived in and were subject to all civil matters except military service (Vreeland, 1954). Livestock owned by these monasteries could be herded by both monastery subjects and *hoshuu* commoners on *hoshuu* territory for performing religious merit (Natsagdorj, 1972). Besides, some higher ranking *Huvilgaan* (Reincarnated) or *Hutagt* (Saint) controlled their own monastery and its territory called *Shavi Gazar*. Once they were awarded a seal for leading more than 800 disciples, they established influence over a larger territory, usually contributed from different neighboring *hoshuus* (Sukhbaatar and Jamsran, 1968, p. 134) (Table 3.1). They acquired separate jurisdictional

Mobile pastoralism and the pre-collective period 57

Table 3.1 Pre-collective governance structure

	Monarchy	
	Centralized political & religious government	
	Local governance	
Central governance (approval & enforcement)		**Religious governance (Buddhist Monastery)**
Aimag (country)		*Aimag*
Hoshuu (province)	*Soum* (military unit)	*Shavi Gazar*
Bag (district)		Buddhist temple, *otog, bag* or *datsan*
Aravt		*Aravt*

status parallel to *hoshuu* within an *aimag* (province) (Natsagdorj, 1972; Regsuren and Baljinnyam, 1973; Vreeland, 1954). For instance, during the eighteenth and nineteenth centuries, *Sain Noyon Khan Aimag* changed from 24 *khoshuu* into 31 administrative units by adding more Shavi Gazar (Regsuren and Baljinnyam, 1973, p. 19). *Shavi Gazar* had an administrative system similar to banners and was divided into *otog, bag* or *datsan* (monastery) units (Regsuren and Baljinnyam, 1973). Buddhist monasteries gained rights to land through political means because Buddhism was such an influential political and economic institution (Baabar, 2005; Fernandez-Gimenez, 2006; Kaplonski, 2010; Lattimore, 1941; Natsagdorj, 1975; Vreeland, 1954). The *hoshuu* lords allocated the best part of their territories, and their willing subjects, to monastery control in return for spiritual as well as political favors. Some subjects, particularly nobles, rejected transfer to the monastery's jurisdiction often to avoid losing their hereditary noble status. In this case, their *nutag* territory would be excluded from the grant to the monastery (Vreeland, 1954, p. 20). Livestock was controlled under an institution called *jas*, meaning monks' "collective property" (Lattimore, 1962, p. 99; Natsagdorj, 1972, p. 75) and it was different from *hoshuu*.

These monasteries managed their own livestock production (Sneath, 2007, p. 19; Vreeland, 1954). Although different in terms of function, the monasteries were similar to *hoshuu* with regard to benefiting from their subjects' labor. The size of the territory and the number of subjects often increased due to religious and social influences (Vreeland 1954, pp. 16–17). In general, all monastery subjects were subject to all civil matters like *hoshuu* jurisdiction but with lighter taxes. Many households preferred to become the subjects of a monastery, because monastery subjects were exempt from state military service and other compulsory taxes (Natsagdorj, 1967, 1972, 1975; Regsuren and Baljinnyam, 1973; Vreeland, 1954). Also, the transfer of subjects was very strict, particularly from a *hoshuu* to a monastery community, because this meant that *hoshuu* princes were essentially losing subjects who would have paid them taxes and provided services (Vreeland, 1954).

Although both jurisdictions had mixed members, community social boundaries became relatively fixed as rulers were given the right to administer

58 *Mobile pastoralism and the pre-collective period*

their own subjects. Subjects were not allowed to migrate anywhere without the permission of the nobles or the monasteries (Khalkha Juram cited in Sukhbaatar and Jamsran, 1968, p. 131; Natsagdorj, 1972; Regsuren and Baljinnyam, 1973, p. 21). Fleeing subjects were common due to the heavy burden of taxes, services and conflicts with local nobles and rulers (Natsagdorj, 1955). People were encouraged to inform on and capture absconders (*bosuul*) for rewards (Khalkha Juram cited in Sukhbaatar and Jamsran, 1968, p. 131). Rulers often organized gathering up of their subjects (*Nutag huraihui*) who had migrated to another *soum* or *bag* in order to maintain their territory, and collect taxes and services from their subjects (Natsagdorj, 1967, p. 269). Thus, lords needed to manage livestock, labor and territory altogether to benefit from pastoralism. Both *hoshuu* and the monasteries independently managed their own production. The production management system roughly depended upon two historical fundamentals.

Production components

First, similar to the context of production of crop cultivation (Chapter 2), the management of pastoral production also involves balancing the availability of components of production: different types of livestock (hereafter called as "livestock"), labor and pastoral resources (Bazargur, 1998; Bjorklund, 2003; Erdenetsogt, 1998). Some debate whether the primary production resource is the livestock or the land in order to figure out the property relations in pastoral context (Natsagdorj, 1967; Sneath, 2007; Vainshtein, 1980). Exclusive individual property is referred to as livestock ownership. Therefore, some consider that without livestock there is no production, thus land can be considered as a secondary resource for pastoral production management (Tosltov, 1934, Tolybekov, 1959 and Markov, 1971 cited in Vainshtein, 1980, p. 233). Others argue that regarding the feudal relationship, land should be considered the primary production resource, in accordance with the historical perception, because "a large territory is the means of life ... to increase the herds it is necessary to expand the territory for ample migration and grazing" (Natsagdorj, 1967, p. 266; Natsagdorj, 1975). This is particularly when much of the livestock was in the hands of a few nobles and the monasteries[25] (Humphrey, 1978; Natsagdorj, 1972; Vainshtein, 1980). Consequently, both *hoshuu* and *Shavi Gazar* contained separate territories that were ecologically preferable land (EPL), a diversity of vegetation and ecology (Bazargur, 1998). This was an important resource to accommodate the needs of herders for flexibility of movement (Fernandez-Gimenez, 1999; Larson, 1930; Lattimore, 1962; Sneath, 2007; Vreeland, 1954). This is why the focus on jurisdictional territory is critical for the management of pastoral production.[26] Thus, I argue that land, if not the primary production resource, is one of the key production resources in addition to livestock and labor.

Another equally important resource is labor or the jurisdictional resident, as property relations in pastureland depend on the management of all production

Mobile pastoralism and the pre-collective period 59

components. There has been major debate over whether community structure was pre-state tribal, where membership was based strictly on lineal descent, or alternatively state-based aristocracy. The latter argues that jurisdictional authority was hereditary and rulers had common lineal descents. As noted earlier, the lords of *hoshuu* banner were hereditary from the line of Chinggis *Khaan* (Vreeland, 1954). Some subjects were called *dagaldah ard* or *khamjlaga/khamjaanii ail* (retainer of a noble family) (Sukhbaatar and Jamsran, 1968, p. 129). Although their subjects were hereditary serfs, they did not necessarily share the same lineage or have kin ties with their rulers and were mostly non-consanguineous (Khazanov, 1994, p. 158; Sneath, 2007, p. 97; Vreeland, 1954, p. 12). Although the lords maintained hereditary lineage, their subjects did not portray the characteristics of an homogenous group as membership was "subject to periodic reorganization, not by clan or lineage" (Sneath, 2007, p. 97). It was common among nomadic societies that lords and their subjects would separate or join one another depending on the recruitment of soldiers for war or intermarriage[27] (Lattimore, 1962). Their membership was often extended to subjects transferred from other rulers (Damdinsuren, 1976). *Shavi Gazar* was also composed of mixed community members, as it was established primarily in the border regions of several *hoshuu* territories (Natsagdorj, 1972; Regsuren and Baljinnyam, 1973; Vreeland, 1954). Thus, community collective identity was defined by locality or jurisdiction rather than by ethnicity (Sneath, 2007, 2010). In other words, each territorial administration embodied ones *nutag* and its fluid social boundary (not strictly from the same kin lineage).

Dual control

As the second historical fundamental, the system of controlling these three components tends to be dual (co-management). As explained further below, a system of formal institutions (state) combined with a system regulated by informal, customary institutions (Fernandez-Gimenez, 1999; Mearns, 2004). Consequently a form of property relation over pastureland functioned that involved both interdependent forms of formal and informal control over pastoral production. "Formal control" refers to the state and its use of regulations set forth in statutory law. The state formally employed jurisdictional mechanisms to control components of *ulamjlalt* pastoral production. In this regard, those who exercised jurisdictional authority over the residents also controlled their access to production and pastoral resources (land and water). Control of production under an administrative territorial unit increased the significance of a jurisdictional authority, whilst allowing them to obtain incessant benefits from pastoralism. Both the monasteries and the *hoshuu* lords had their own administrators who controlled their subjects' civil matters and production. Each regulated the balance between the three components of production in their jurisdiction using formal mechanisms – such as civil registration (jurisdictional residency-labor), taxes (taxable property was mostly production

60 *Mobile pastoralism and the pre-collective period*

from different types of livestock) and civil services (*urtuu* and *ulaa* [postal], military, household work, wage herding or rental livestock herding (*sureg tavih*) (Natsagdorj, 1967, 1972; Sneath, 2007; Sukhbaatar and Jamsran, 1968, p. 130; Vreeland, 1954). Taxing livestock production was the main mechanism for authorities to benefit from rangeland as livestock were countable in contrast to migratory pastoral resources. In this way, subjects were entitled to pasture use rights within their territory (Vreeland, 1954). Thus, formal control is limited to legal mechanisms like civil administration, civil services and taxation over livestock to manage the balance between labor, livestock and available pastoral resources within jurisdictional territory.

Jurisdiction also functioned as a mechanism for defining community social and resource boundaries and for exclusion and inclusion of outsiders under various climatic conditions, by offering EPL for herding different types of livestock. Within each jurisdiction, smaller administrative groups or individual herding camps had locally recognized winter areas, but shared summer pasture within their jurisdiction based on customary use (Natsagdorj, 1967; Vreeland, 1954). This type of public ownership needs to be distinguished from modern "state ownership" (Lattimore, 1932, p. 48). Under this arrangement, several processes helped ensure that the state and herders continued to benefit from pastoral production. Reciprocal arrangements under both formal (between jurisdictional rulers) and informal (between herders through connection, relations) control allowed for cross-boundary movements to take place in the process allowing for fees earned from pasture use (Larson, 1930; Natsagdorj, 1967). These arrangements depended on social relationships, not only between herders, but between jurisdictional authorities as well (Vreeland, 1954).

In this state/public ownership, herders also play their partial role of custodians justifying the legitimacy of the jurisdictional authority. Herders' informal control was often at play when lords abused their jurisdictional authority, allowing outsiders at local herders' expense.[28] Local herders severely resisted such abuses by lords, because they held that jurisdictional territory for the use of the jurisdictional community (Lattimore, 1932; Natsagdorj, 1967). Such abuse is detrimental not as it was "to encroach on its [community] land, but to challenge its [herders'] freedom of movement" (Lattimore, 1932, p. 49). Several sources recorded that jurisdictional herders often expressed their dissatisfaction or concern over unfair acts of their lords at formal jurisdictional meetings or to the monarch (Larson, 1930; Natsagdorj, 1972; Regsuren and Baljinnyam, 1973). Sometimes the state shifted the jurisdictional authority to the next lord in the hereditary line who was more widely accepted; alternatively herders could abandon a lord and join a better noble (Dilavhutagt, 1991, p. 13; Lattimore, 1941, p. 317). Again, according to Sneath (2004),

> these systems of knowledge were not merely instruments of domination; they reflected a much wider range of human experience, including the technical constraints on production imposed by an "environmental"

Mobile pastoralism and the pre-collective period 61

externality – be that conceived in spiritual or in materialistic terms. Based as they were on pastoral mobility and general access to land, these socio-technical systems tended to maintain and support those of land use, and this seems to have provided very real benefits for pastoralists.

(p. 171)

Thus, herders' production outcome was influential to the overall benefits the lords and the state obtained from pastoralism.

Balancing the availability of livestock, labor and pastoral resources requires herders' informal and solid control over micro management of pastoral production and pastureland. This in turn is shaped by extremely complex *ulamjlalt* rules and norms of managing the production of the combination of different species of livestock (as risk management), the herding strategies (different grazing distances, amount of attention and time spent herding) based on their types, size, age, gender and pregnancy basis due to changing weather conditions and the seasons under diverse and imbalanced ecological conditions (Erdenetsogt, 1998). Although the state controlled herders' movement through a formal mechanism of jurisdictional residency, it could not formalize all these *ulamjlalt* rules and norms in order to maintain the flexibility of movement that is required for production between and within jurisdictional boundaries. Authorities focused on overall population and production administration for labor control, but "did not assign pasturage rights and did nothing to regulate pasturing techniques" (Vreeland 1954, p. 26). Instead, the state recognized herders' practice of *ulamjlalt* rules and norms, granting herders a certain amount of informal control (Fernandez-Gimenez, 1999). In this regard, "informal control" refers to herders and their practice of *ulamjlalt* rules and norms for micro-managing both production and pasture use. Herders could more effectively enforce these complex production rules and norms than the authorities and maintained flexibility in movement. This is similar to the context of crop-cultivating societies, where pre-colonial aristocratic rulers often had loose control over peasant strategies for production in terms of "where when and how to cut the forest" (Peluso, 1992, p. 32). Thus, lords often consulted with experienced herders as they had expertise in this complex production of livestock (Humphrey, 1978; Natsagdorj, 1972). The need to micro-manage the components of production determined pasture use. In fulfilling complex production strategies, herders utilized different forms of movement which included daily herding, four-season mobility or *otor* temporary movement within and beyond jurisdictional boundaries (Bazargur, 1998; Erdenetsogt, 1998; Sampildendev, 1985; Vreeland, 1954). The herders decided when, where and how often to move depending on herd size, type of livestock, taking into account their ability to mobilize resources and how weather conditions affected EPL (Bazargur, 1998; Erdenetsogt, 1998; Fernandez-Gimenez, 1999; Vreeland, 1954).

Herders combined several formal and informal mechanisms that worked together to underpin the arrangements that allowed herders the right to

62 *Mobile pastoralism and the pre-collective period*

manage production and pastoral resources. In term of formal mechanisms, the state offered herders equal opportunity to exercise use rights to campsites and pasture through jurisdictional residency and registration of ownership of private herds (Natsagdorj, 1972; Vreeland, 1954). Commoners gained use rights according to their social status. Some herders tended livestock for princes (for tax service), or noblemen or monks, who leased out livestock for herding (*sureg tavih*) (Natsagdorj, 1967, 1972; Sneath, 2007). For instance, in 1919, Jun-Van Dorjpalam, a noble in Setsen Han *aimag*, owned 8506 livestock and 30 households herded his livestock on his behalf (Natsagdorj, 1972). Other herders were independent commoners, who herded their own private livestock and paid income taxes. Others were very wealthy commoners but still herded for princes, noblemen and monasteries. Nobles considered poor people without livestock too inexperienced to be reliable herders. Thus, they hired wealthy commoners because of their experience. In contrast, the monasteries permitted herders to tend livestock regardless of their status (Natsagdorj, 1972; Vreeland, 1954). These were essentially categorized as subsistence and yield-focused herding modes. Most households herded for their subsistence following essential seasonal movement patterns. Wealthy herders also focused on yield from their large number of livestock (Humphrey and Sneath, 1999, p. 225). They pursued a pattern of specialized herding (Fernandez-Gimenez, 1999; Sneath, 2004). This involved much more complex rotational movements and the labor support from average or poor herders in exchange for access to other resources for specialized herding of different types of livestock (based on private livestock ownership unlike centralized management of collective ownership) and access to larger pasture (Humphrey and Sneath, 1999, p. 226). Within this system, the arrangements that determined who uses how much of the pastoral resource were not egalitarian; rather the way in which herders inherit and own livestock determined this (Natsagdorj, 1967; Sneath, 2007). Informally, customary practices of reciprocity and social networking allowed herders to pool household labor (Natsagdorj, 1972; Sneath, 2007; Vreeland, 1954). This balanced inequality by allowing everyone access to pastoral resources to the extent of their wealth. The authorities in fact encouraged this by arranging households to support each other's needs regarding livestock production. This was to protect the production of taxable property of livestock (Vreeland, 1954, p. 26). This indicates that authorities were indirectly involved in land management via taxing production as pasture was not directly a taxable property. The system of residency and payment of taxes and services justifies herders exercising their right/claim to produce and use pasture by pursuing seasonal movement. This involves flexible arrangements and freedom of movement (Lattimore, 1932).

Freedom of movement was possible due to several informal and customary rules and norms of pasture use. The first *ulamjlalt* rule is, "first to camp claims the pasture use" (Fernandez-Gimenez, 1999, 2006; Natsagdorj, 1972; Vreeland, 1954). This principle was codified as customary law in the Manchu period (Fernandez-Gimenez, 2006). This rule allowed those who could afford

Mobile pastoralism and the pre-collective period   63

to be mobile, the time and resources to be the first to camp. Others followed and established themselves around the initial camp with certain distances that suited for the grazing of their herd size. For instance, small sized herds do not require as much pasture as large herds (Fernandez-Gimenez, 1999, 2006). This norm was usually used mainly for selecting permanent winter and spring campsites or temporary camping on summer and autumn pasture, which was available to commoners unless nobles selected specific areas for their own use (Natsagdorj, 1967). This context raises the question of the concept of property in land again, particularly, how to recognize who owns what when users and resources are not clearly identified for ownership? Referring to feudal land relations, some concluded that this customary use of winter/spring campsites and pasture use for long periods automatically led to private ownership (Natsagdorj, 1967, p. 269). As we discussed earlier, with the example of territorial use of pasture, herders could not informally or formally own campsite plots as exclusive property because of the flexibility needed in establishing and using these resources. Barfield (2011) noted the possible idea of proprietary rights over fixed assets like wells or winter campsites, particularly when herders invested in building barns or houses (p. 116). Ownership in this context may refer more to herders' investments in movable assets rather than actual plot of land or water. Otherwise, the author acknowledged that there was merely a concept of exclusive land ownership at the household level (Barfield, 2011, p. 116). Also, in the example of a well, the notion of individual or group ownership hardly implies private property as their use is limited to "preferential use and the right to immediate access, but not at all times and in all circumstances; it also allows other individuals and groups access to the well, usually without payment" (Khazanov, 1994, p. 126). A similar principle applies to the second *ulamjlalt* rule of using campsites and the surrounding pasture. Campsites are location points for shelters and other production resources (such as thick layers of livestock dung accumulated over time (*buuts*) and used for livestock shelters and as a fuel resource), and to access the wider pasture area around it (Fernandez-Gimenez, 2002; Sneath, 2003). Also, herders often move their livestock shelters/*buuts* and create other campsites on the same pasture due to herd size, or to avoid livestock diseases, and/or unhygienic conditions or burned *buuts* (Undargaa, 2013). Moreover, the use right to a campsite was flexible. Herders left informal markers (e.g., a large stone) at particular campsites, indicating that it was occupied for the year. During unstable weather conditions, the herd would graze elsewhere and the marker would be removed from the campsite, thus leaving the campsite available for others to use if it suited their herd size (Vreeland, 1954). In this way, herders became familiar with all possible campsites for accessing alternate pasture. Therefore, some herders maintained several campsites (Vreeland, 1954, p. 42). This is a locally recognized use right, which permitted flexible use depending on the balance between production components. In addition, Humphrey and Verdery (2004) were concerned with interpreting terms such as "my land" as private ownership. This regards the fact that

64 *Mobile pastoralism and the pre-collective period*

this term may easily refer to "land over which he or she has only use rights but for which those rights are sufficient for him or her to think of the land as 'his' or 'hers'" or refer to "mastery rather than ownership" and "dominion or lordship" rather than "property ... owning" (Humphrey and Verdery, 2004, p. 12). Similarly, in Mongolia, some campsites and wells/boreholes were often named after specific landmarks or someone who created or maintained the *buuts* or well, or who had been using the site for many years. This hardly refers to any exclusive ownership or possession. Herders did not use these specific terms and they could not refuse access to campsites and wells as long as there was room to share. Instead, it could refer to local acknowledgement and respect for landmarks[29] and custodianship. In this case, both herder (subject) and campsite (object) do not have clearly identified or fixed relationship to land as "owner" and "property," particularly campsite location is often fixed only with the establishment of movable assets. *Aimag* and *hoshuu* may also have been named after individual lords for their dominion or lordship due to similar reasons, but the socialist regime based on Marxist ideology later denounced it exclusively as a notion of private ownership and changed these to mountain names (see next chapter).

Pasture around campsites would have landmarks as territorial boundaries rather than exclusive boundaries. Individual territorial use may have occurred due to spaciousness of grazing land during stable weather conditions. Otherwise, during times of scarcity, herders would share pasture by implementing the third *ulamjlalt* rule by letting supervised herds pass each other without mixing (*zonuulj hariulah*) (Undargaa, 2013). Besides, when sharing local resources with outsiders, this has always been the jurisdictional authority, who often collected formal fees for pasture use from outsiders, and not individual herders, who had customary use claims to campsites[30] and pasture (Natsagdorj, 1967; Undargaa, 2013). This flexible camping arrangement often led to a concentration of households that gathered in the best pastoral area. In this case, households essentially employed the fourth *ulamjlalt* rule of sharing *haya bagtahaar buuj hamar bagtahaar id* (camp and grazing to the extent the pasture allows or as many as the pasture accommodates[31]) (Fernandez-Gimenez, 2000). Thereby, they share scarce pasture during unstable weather conditions or at border pastures between campsites, seasonal pastures or jurisdictional boundaries (Fernandez-Gimenez, 1999, 2000; Vreeland, 1954). Herders employed the first two rules to arrange camping. Then they grazed their livestock by letting herds pass by each other (Undargaa, 2013). Thus, use rights comprised informal and locally recognized *ulamjlalt* rules and norms to access campsites in all seasons. All these *ulamjlalt* rules and norms originated from and were suited for the context of Mongolian Pastoralism allowing both exclusion and inclusion. The decisive factor to access pasture is the overall management of the production components (formal control), instead of exclusive rights attached to land. Depending on balancing their production components (labor, pasture, livestock and their size, type, age, herding environment and

Mobile pastoralism and the pre-collective period   65

partnership with others), herders (informal control) would decide whether to exclude, include or join others to share pasture of any type or condition. These rules and norms are not easily interpreted by western concepts of property rights to land, which focus on exclusion.

Under flexible arrangements, herders moved between and within jurisdictional territories. Even with flexible dual control, there were certainly disputes over pasture and campsites. These disputes did not lead to a parceling out of land for exclusive use by individuals or groups. Disputes over pasture use were solved by herders or their group leaders or the next higher jurisdictional authority (Fernandez-Gimenez, 1999; Natsagdorj, 1967, 1972; Vreeland, 1954). Jurisdictional authorities continued to formally assign specific subjects (including wealthy ones) to grazing areas on a territorial basis for public services like *urtuu* (postal) or *haruul* (border guard) or for livestock owned by state or religious elites. They even issued decrees indicating specific purposes for the use of certain pastures (Dilavhutagt, 1991, p. 14; Natsagdorj, 1967). During times of scarcity, the jurisdictional authority attempted to allocate the right to use specific plots of land, using the "15 man" measurement, which may have been legally applicable mostly for plowing or haymaking. However, parceling out land with formal property rights remained impractical as herders would move to other jurisdictions during times of scarcity (Natsagdorj, 1967, p. 268). This indicates that state territorial management for pastoralism was the key logic for the state to formally regulate the flexible use of pastureland.

Primary production unit

Herders are able to pursue different movements by forming a specific camp of herding households. This camping structure shapes herders' use of pasture. Bold (1996) defined different levels of socio-economic segments as: *ail* (a single household), *hoton* or *hot* (*hot ail*)[32] (more than two households), *saahalt-ail* (a group of neighboring households, who herd livestock) and *neg nutag usniihan*[33] (livestock keeping families from the same region) (p. 76).

Hoton became a basic form of camping and the production unit regarding its structure, function and the role in the management of pastoral production and land. Herders used two different camping forms until the fourteenth century: a large group of households including hundreds of households (*huree*); and separate families or *ails* (relatives' or friends' households) of 2–3 *gers* (Simukov, 1933, p. 495).[34] These were considered a collective institution for managing pastureland (Natsagdorj, 1975, p. 4). Simukov (1933) clarified that *huree* was good for defense, but it was not necessarily ideal for grazing large numbers of livestock. That is why herders also camped as *ail*. As a result, Mongolians at the time either combined both the *huree* and *ail* regarding pasture use or to create *huree* in a situation of external danger (Simukov, 1933, p. 495). Simukov noted that the current *hoton* is similar to the form of *ail* (2–3 households). Vladimortsov

66 *Mobile pastoralism and the pre-collective period*

defined *hoton* as ten or more households camping together, and referred to *ail* as 2–3 households (Simukov, 1933). Yet, *ail* can also refer to a single household (Simukov, 1933). Simukov (1933) noted the full use of *hoton* in the eighteenth century, whereas Bold (2001) noted that it may have emerged earlier, but became an institutionalized production unit later in the nineteenth century (Bold, 2001, p. 68).

The definition of *hoton* seems to depend on its size, social structure and functionality. Regarding size, in northern and central Mongolia, *hoton* encompasses more than two households, whereas in the Gobi region, there is no such *hoton* as it has only a single household as *ail* (Bold 1996; Fernandez-Gimenez 1999). Erdenetsogt (1998) noted that *hoton* was composed of 1–2 households in the Gobi (p. 37). Simukov (1933) also noted that the Gobi single household is actually called *ail* or *hot ail* due to the fact that *hoton/hot* also refers to livestock shelter (p. 496). The author refers to a livestock shelter as a *hashaa* on a pile of dried dung as a livestock bed (*buuts*), which is the most important production asset for creating *hoton* and accessing pasture. Mostly, average or well-to-do herders create *hashaa/buuts* due to their large herd size and they attract those who lack access to such assets. In fact, the use of *hashaa/buuts* had regional differences. *Buuts* built with short walls out of dung or rocks were common everywhere. In northern *aimags* with forests, some herders used wood instead of rocks to build fences (*shurgaag horoo*) around *buuts* (Simukov, 1934, pp. 735–735; Regsuren and Baljinnyam, 1973, p. 24). Simukov (1933) also noted the changes in the meaning of *hoton*, which became more obscure and sometimes overlapped with the use of *ail*.

The structure of the *hoton* is based on relationships between neighbors, friends and kin who own similar types of livestock, but in different numbers (Bazargur, 1998, p. 183; Simukov, 1933). Anyone can join or leave a *hoton* as long as they are suitable in terms of herd type and size, various livelihood skills, and personality. Undesirable herders are often pressured to leave and seek another *hoton*. Prior arrangement is necessary, although sometimes it happens without prior arrangement. Essentially, a *hoton* has no constant organization/structure and has no significant administrative role (Simukov, 1933). Bold (1996) noted that a *hoton* has a designated leader who essentially manages the pastoral resources (Bold, 1996, pp. 73, 74). As Simukov (1933) explained, the leader took on an advisory role in household matters and *hoton* production management, rather than formal assignment of pasture management (p. 8). Each *hoton* contained a maximum of a thousand sheep (Vreeland, 1954, p. 36). This was a manageable size to maintain hygienic conditions of the shelter/*buuts*, provide sufficient grazing and labor for herding (very intensive work) (Undargaa, 2013). This is why, Simukov (1933) emphasized households with different herd sizes join each other to pool labor and contribute to herding and other activities. They complemented each other's socio-economic needs, and well-to-do herders used the labor of poor herders in return for food. Also, herders joined one

Mobile pastoralism and the pre-collective period   67

another based on the desire to camp with skilled persons in cattle breeding, hunting, crafts, etc. Simukov (1933) also emphasized that there was no specific arrangement for labor value regarding the nature of exploitation that existed within a *hoton* (wage labor, collaborative works equal contribution, reciprocity and use of relative/friend). Yet, it is important to note that in non-egalitarian pastoralism of the time, poor households' access to both food and other socio-economic resources such as livestock, campsites, seasonal pasture and networking, were important to maintain subsistence. Further chapters discuss ways in which socialist and post-socialist Mongolia sought to ensure equality and the impacts on pastoral institution and rangeland management.[35]

In a *hoton*, several households camp together for a period of time, even two days if necessary, to share pastoral resources and pool labor/collaborate for intensive economic activities such as herding and milking different types of livestock,[36] providing protection from weather, predators and to make felt, etc. These activities have a seasonal basis, and shape the number of herding households in each *hoton* (2–13) (Simukov, 1933). For instance, summer is the most intensive season and requires pooling of labor for milking, mating and herding based on age and gender of livestock as well as for felt making (Undargaa, 2013). Thus, during summer, a good pasture enables more households to camp together. In winter, the number may decrease to four or five households only to pool labor on herding in cold winter (Simukov, 1933). *Hoton's* collaboration on herding (separately by age, gender and milking/non-milking categories) and processing livestock products balances the production components as well as increases the productivity. As a result, *hoton* collaboration extends to an inter-*hoton* level. For instance, two *hoton* camps (as neighbor (*saakhalt*) within the vicinity (500 m) of each other can swap juvenile livestock to separate them from their mothers to prevent suckling. This saved and provided milk for human needs (Simukov, 1933). Conclusively, the *hot ail* is a production unit with "fluid residential groups of about one to eight *gers* ... that often come together temporarily for a season or more, before the constituent households combine with others" (Sneath, 2007, p. 97). This was to balance the production components: managing their seasonal pasture and mobility to ensure production (Sneath, 2007). Often, *hoton* structure (household relations and numbers), its function and its *hashaa/buuts* structure depends on the different conditions of geography (radius of a nomadic orbit), socio-economy (population density, household socio-economic needs), season and ecology modes of pastures and weather, rather than a static structure/function shaped by certain ecological zones.

In different historical periods in the past, the state territorial structure changed social and resource boundaries via the units of the state territorial administration and pastoral production. As such, both the *hoton* and the whole jurisdictional community had fluid social and resource boundaries. They often had the possibility to mingle with members beyond their *hot* or community, even if they were not all subject to pursue seasonal mobility. It was considered normal for households with sizable herds to leave for other seasonal pastures, leaving behind very poor or so called "lazy" households (with little or no livestock) or those who took care of cattle with forage during winter, etc. They were not obliged to move due to small herd size, which needed much less pasture with fewer adverse impacts on greater pasture area. They, in return, acted as informants for those who left about weather conditions back home, so herders could decide whether to return (Fernandez-Gimenez, 1999,

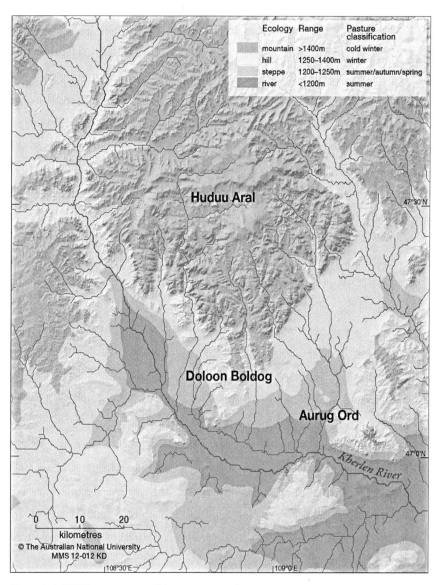

Figure 3.1 HBU case area until late seventeenth century.

2006; Vreeland, 1954). The state framework allowed these dynamic social structures and pasture use due to the flexible nature of pastoral production, except it assigned the lords to control its population movement due to a tax purpose. Therefore, a *hot ail* and *neg nutag usniihan* are analytical categories to understand these dynamics in social segments rather than a formal fixed administrative unit or fixed collective action institution.[37]

Therefore, unlike other mobile pastoral societies colonized or influenced by European powers, Mongolia (current) retained to a full extent the historical fundamentals of dual control over the integrated management of pastoral production components during the Manchu period, owing it to the uniqueness of Mongolian Pastoralism in its geo-political and geographical position. The next chapter reviews the development approach of the modern Mongolian state, which continued to change the units of the state territorial administration and the pastoral production and re-create new social and resource boundaries to obtain socio-political and economic benefits.

The HBU case study area, located in the territory of Delgerhaan *soum* in Hentii *aimag* is historically well-known (Figure 3.1). Regarding the names of historical places, some Mongolian sources noted that this was where "The Secret History of Mongols" was completed at "Ih Huraldai" (Great Gathering), while camping between "Doloon Boldog" and "Shilhentseg" at "Huduu Aral" (Damdinsuren, 1976). In addition, Chinggis *Khaan* seasonally camped in and around Huduu aral (Damdinsuren, 1957, p. 53; Ulziisuren et al., 2010). The HBU *bag* territory was renowned as the "Huduu Aral" (Country Island). DD *bag* was called "Doloon boldog," which took its name from seven small hills stretching from HBU Mountain to the "Herlen" River at "Huduu Aral" (Damdinsuren, 1976, pp. 14–16) (Figures 3.2 and 3.3). Historically, HBU Mountain was uninhabited but well-known among herders. It was "rich and fertile grazing land where nomadic herders did not experience drought or dzud when using its long developed thousand *buuts* and ten thousand springs" (Ulziisuren et al., 2010, p. 64). Well-off families used it as a reserve pasture for *otor* and moved to the HBU Mountain to escape harsh winter conditions. More historical events were to take place here in the future. For instance, Chinggis *Khaan*'s son Ugudei reigned as *Khaan* in 1228 and Galdanboshigt of Oirad stayed prior to his battle with the Manchus in the seventeenth century.

Figure 3.2 Huduu Aral from the southwest: Dolood hills (right) stretch to the south from HBU Mountain (left), May 2010.

70 *Mobile pastoralism and the pre-collective period*

Figure 3.3 Huduu Aral from the southeast: the Dolood hills (right), the end of the HBU Mountain, May 2010.

Notes

1 This was a numerical politico-administrative structure of "groups of ten, hundred, thousand and ten thousand, with a direct conveyance of orders from above to below" (Bold, 2001, p. 84).
2 Pastoral production supported war campaigns by mobilizing economic resources.
3 Booming livestock production was directed towards producing large amounts of food and transportation resources.
4 *Khaan* is translated as King or Supreme Khan in English (Grousset, 1970). The Secret History uses the word "*Khaan*/Hagan," whereas some historians, e.g., Pelliot question whether Chinggis ever bore the Hagan (Grousset, 1970, p. 585).
5 The postal service was newly created under the Chinggis period. Each thousandth territory had a postal service station for resting and exchanging their transportation. Each territorial unit provided horses and food for this service free of charge for matters of state.
6 These two categories were hardly distinguishable (Grousset, 1970, p. 221).
7 Inherited subjects and territory.
8 See, for instance, Puntsagnorov, 1955, p. 94.
9 See earlier discussion of the meaning of *nutag* in this chapter. It means broader than a plot of land.
10 A son of Ogudei and a grandson of Chinggis *Khaan*.
11 A son of Zuch or Jochi and a grandson of Chinggis *Khaan*.
12 In pastoralism, the question of private ownership of livestock is indisputable, whereas private or group land ownership with feudal relation in character is a matter of debate, particularly in Mongolian Pastoralism (Khazanov, 1994, p. 124).

Mobile pastoralism and the pre-collective period   71

13 These abuses were not often by individual jurisdictional authorities, but by heavy handed taxes, military and postal services imposed by the government without the regard to weakening pastoral production under severe weather conditions (see Puntsagnorov, 1955, pp. 124–128).

14 "Bundle of rights" is defined as the right to rent, sell or give away the rights (Meinzen-Dick et al., 2004).

15 Setsen *Han*, Tusheet *Han*, Zasagt *Han* and Sain Noyon *Han aimags*.

16 Sain Noyon *Han aimag* appeared to be founded earlier as a vassal to Tusheet *Han aimag*, but gained its independence in 1724 (see Grousset, 1970, p. 512).

17 Banner (*hoshuu*) unit in Mongolia may precede Manchu period (see Grousset, 1970, p. 530; Natsagdorj 1972).

18 Different sources come up with slightly different numbers of *khoshuus* in each *aimag*. For instance, Vreeland (1954) noted that there were 23 in Tsetsen Han, 20 in Tusheet Han, 19 in Zasagt Han, 24 in Sain Noyon Khan by 1912 (p. 10). There were 25 in Tsetsen Khan, 21 in Tusheet Khan, 23 in Zasagt Khan, 25 in Sain Noyon Khan between 1911 and 1924 (Munkh-ochir, 2012, pp. 6–16).

19 One or several more households.

20 Military service was frequently traded, with a poor man replacing a wealthy one.

21 Civil registration of a group of households, its members, their taxable properties (only livestock, occasionally silver), group members' civil offences and services and occasionally organized social events like sacred rituals. A comprehensive tax collection system from livestock production existed within each jurisdiction (Vreeland, 1954).

22 A comprehensive tax collection system from livestock production existed within each jurisdiction (Vreeland, 1954).

23 For instance, *aravt* would no longer be formalized in some constitutions. Although *bag* continued to carry out its formal administrative tasks over citizens and territory, it would have no formal status of territorial unit or budget control during the collective and post-collective periods. See chapters 4 and 5.

24 See also Endicott (2012).

25 For instance, in 1918 in Outer Mongolia, the population was about 647,500 (Humphrey, 1978) and the total livestock number was 9,645,563. Around 25–30 percent of the livestock belonged to the few noble families and monasteries (Natsagdorj, 1972). Each noble family and religious official owned much larger numbers of livestock than the majority of commoners. For instance, in 1858, feudal nobles owned on average 4.3 *bod mal*, big livestock per head, officials owned on average 1.1 and *hamjlaga* retainers of noble families owned on average 0.9 in Darhan Chin-van *hosuu*, Tusheet-Han *aimag* (Humphrey, 1978). In 1918, Dorjtseren, a prince in Setsen-Han *aimag* privately owned 15,000 head of livestock (Natsagdorj, 1972).

26 Some even compared land resources to the raw material and the livestock to the factory machine in a context of industrial production (Namjig, 2000).

27 The bride joins another group, and is followed by a group of households in her attendance as well.

28 As discussed earlier, lords abusing their authority for personal use continued under the Manchu period. Some lords would host herders from other jurisdictions on local pastures at the expense of local herders and would pocket the fees for pasture use; or they might allocate herders' customary pasture for postal households or other purposes (Natsagdorj, 1967).

29 Interview 49 (Undargaa, 2013).

30 Once allowed, an outsider may need to exchange some payment (in the form of livestock, labor or reciprocity) for sharing campsites with a local household, which matched their need (Undargaa, 2013).

31 An alternative translation is "occupy the land to the edges of your home and eat as much as the bridge allows" (Fernandez-Gimenez, 2000, p. 1323).

72 Mobile pastoralism and the pre-collective period

32 Modern version.
33 This is an analytical category. This is not a formal or official administrative unit.
34 Translation from Russian to Mongolian and English by L. Sandagsuren and S. Undargaa.
35 This is particularly relevant to how this pre-collective situation is similar to the post-socialist reality, regarding the production management in a condition for socio-economic need and the unstable ecology. The observation on the combination of unbalanced wealth is important for examining the process in current development projects, where they target same wealth herders to share their problems in order re-create collective action and equality among herders to ensure their access to land, instead of their access to production.
36 Herders unite their larger and/or non-milking livestock such as horse herd or male (except mating season) and/or younger age cattle, but let them graze on their own with loose supervision (Undargaa, 2013).
37 This was perhaps interpreted as shared pastoral resources by neighboring groups of households, thus becoming the basis for herder group formation. This was also defined as "social networking" to accommodate flexibility in *nutag* seasonal camping and mobility (Sneath, 2007).

References

Baabar, B (1999) *History of Mongolia*, Monsudar Pub, Ulaanbaatar.

Baabar, B (2005) *Twentieth Century Mongolia*, Global Oriental, Kent.

Barfield, Th (2011) "Nomadic pastoralism in Mongolia and beyond" in P L W Sabloff (ed.) *Mapping Mongolia: Situating Mongolia in the World from Geologic Time to the Present*, University of Pennsylvania Museum of Archeology and Anthropology, Philadelphia, 273.

Bazargur, D (ed.) (1998) *Geography of Pastoral Animal Husbandry*, TTC Company, Mongolian Academy of Science, Ulaanbaatar.

Berry, S (1993) *No Condition Is Permanent: The Social Dynamics of Agrarian Change in Sub-Saharan Africa*, University of Wisconsin Press, Madison.

Bjorklund, I (2003) "Sami pastoral society in Northern Norway: national integration of an indigenous management system" in David Anderson and Mark Nuttall (eds.) *Cultivating Arctic Landscapes*, Berghahn Press, New York, 124–135.

Bold, B (1996) "Socio-economic segmentation: khot-ail in nomadic livestock keeping of Mongolia," *Nomadic Peoples* 39, 69–86.

Bold, B (2001) *Mongolian Nomadic Society: A Reconstruction of the "Medieval" History of Mongolia*, The Nordic Institute of Asian Studies, Richmond, Surrey.

Damdinsuren, Ts (1957) *Mongoliin uran zohioliin toim*, State Publishing House, Ulaanbaatar.

Damdinsuren, Ts (1976) *Secret History of Mongolia*, State Printing Place, Ulaanbaatar.

Dilavhutagt, J (1991) *Ar Mongoliin uls turiin durtgal*, Soyombo Hevleliin Gazar, Ulaanbaatar.

Endicott, E (2012) *A History of Land Use in Mongolia*, Palgrave Macmillan, New York.

Erdenetsogt, N (ed.) (1998) *Mongolian Nomadic Livestock*, "MMM" Association, Ulaanbaatar.

Fernandez-Gimenez, M E (1999) "Sustaining the steppes: a geographical history of pastoral land use in Mongolia," *The Geographical Review* 89:3, 315–336.

Fernandez-Gimenez, M E (2002) "Spatial and social boundaries and the paradox of pastoral land tenure: a case study from post-socialist Mongolia," *Human Ecology* 30:1, 49–78.

Mobile pastoralism and the pre-collective period 73

Fernandez-Gimenez, M E (2006) "Land use and land tenure in Mongolia: a brief history and current issues," in Donald J Bedunah, E McArthur and M Fernandez-Gimenez, *Proceedings of the Conference on Transformations, Issues, and Future Challenges*, Salt Lake City, UT, Proceedings RMRS-P-39, Fort Collins, CO: US Department of Agriculture, Forest Service, Rocky Mountain Research Station.

Fernandez-Gimenez, Maria E (2000) "The role of Mongolian nomadic pastoralists' ecological knowledge in rangeland management," *Ecological Applications* 10:5, 1318–1326.

Gibson, B D (2011) "Chiefdom confederacies and state origins," *Social Evolution & History* 10:1, 215–233.

Grousset, Rene (1970) *The Empire of the Steppes: A History of Central Asia*, Rutgers, New Brunswick, New Jersey, London.

Heather, P (2010) *Empires and Barbarians: Fall of Rome and the Birth of Europe*, Oxford University Press, Oxford.

High, M M and Schlesinger, J (2010) "Rulers and rascals: the politics of gold in Mongolian Qing history," *Central Asian Survey* 29:3, 289–304.

Humphrey, C and Sneath, D (1999) *The End of Nomadism?*, Duke University Press, Durham, NC.

Humphrey, Caroline (1978) "Pastoral nomadism in Mongolia: the role of herdsmen's cooperatives in the national economy," *Development and Change* 9, 133–160.

Humphrey, Caroline and Verdery, Katherine (2004) "Introduction: raising questions about property" in Katherine Verdery and Caroline Humphrey (eds.) *Property in Question: Value Transformation in the Global Economy*, Berg, Oxford, New York, 1–25.

Jagchid, S and Hyer, P (1979) *Mongolia's Culture and Society*, Westview Press, Boulder, CO.

Kaplonski, Ch (2010) 'Introduction' in D Sneath and Ch Kaplonski (eds.) *The History of Mongolia, Volume III: The Qing Period Twentieth-century Mongolia*, Global Oriental, Kent.

Khazanov, A M (1994) *Nomads and the Outside World, second edition*, University of Wisconsin Press, Madison.

Lamb, H (1927) *Genghis Khan, the Emperor of All Men*, International Collectors Library American Headquarters, Garden City, New York.

Larson, F A (1930) *Duke of Mongolia*, Little, Brown, and Company, Boston.

Lattimore, O (1932) *Manchuria, Cradle of Conflict*, The Macmillan Company of Canada, Toronto.

Lattimore, O (1941) *Mongol Journey*, Doubleday, Doran and Co, New York.

Lattimore, O (1962) *Nomads and Commissars: Mongolia Revisited*, Oxford University Press, New York.

Mearns, R (2004) "Decentralisation, rural livelihoods and pasture-land management in post socialist Mongolia," *European Journal of Development Research* 16:1, 133–152.

Meinzen-Dick, R, Pradhan, R and Grigorio, M D (2004) *Collective Action and Property Rights for Sustainable Development*, CAPRI, Washington DC.

Munkh-Erdene, Lhamsuren (2011) "Where did the Mongol Empire come from? Medieval Mongol ideas of people, state and empire," *Inner Asia* 13:2, 211–237.

Munkh-ochir, D (2012) *Mongol Ulsiin aimag, hoshuu, sumiin lavlah*, Ulaanbaatar.

Namjig, N (2000) *Tuulsan Amidral mini*, "Shuvuun Saaral," Military Press, Ulaanbaatar.

Natsagdorj, Sh (1955) "The life of Sukebatur" in Owen Lattimore (ed.) *Nationalism and Revolution in Mongolia*, E J Brill, Leiden, 94–186.

Natsagdorj, Sh (1967) "The economic basis of feudalism in Mongolia," *Modern Asian Studies* 1:3, 265–281.

74 *Mobile pastoralism and the pre-collective period*

Natsagdorj, Sh (1972) *Soum, khamjlaga, shavi, ard*, Academy of Science Publishing, Ulaanbaatar.

Natsagdorj, Sh (1975) "Main characters of feudalism: the Mongolian society as an example" in *XIV International Congress of Historical* Sciences, Ulaanbaatar, San-Francisco, 1–18.

Peluso, N L (1992) *Rich Forests, Poor People: Resource Control and Resistance in Java*, University of California Press, Berkeley.

Puntsagnorov, Ts (1955) *Mongoliin avtonomit uyeiin tuukh*, BNMAU Shinjleh Uhaanii Hureelengiin Tuuhiin Sector, Ulaanbaatar.

Regsuren, D and Baljinnyam, A (1973) *BNMAU: Arkhangai Aimagiin Tuuh*, ADKh Executive Administration, The Party Committee of Arkhangai Aimag, Tsetserleg.

Sampildendev, H (1985) *Malchin ardiin zal uiliin ulamjlal*, State Printing Place, Ulaanbaatar.

Simukov, A D (1933) "Hotony" in Yuki Konagaya, Sanjaasurengiin Bayaraa and Ichinkhorloogiin Lkhagvasuren (eds.) *Kratkaya geographiya Mongolskoi Narodnoi Respubliki: Chast II Nasyelyeniye, ego hozaistva, i gosudarstvennoye ustroistvo strany, Tom II*, Gosudarstvyennyi muzei etnologii, Osaka, 493–508.

Simukov, A D (1934) "Kratkaya geographiya Mongolskoi Narodnoi Respubliki: Chast II Nasyelyeniye, ego hozaistva, i gosudarstvennoye ustroistvo strany" in Yuki Konagaya, Sanjaasurengiin Bayaraa and Ichinkhorloogiin Lkhagvasuren (eds.) *Trudy o Mongolii i dlya Mongolii Tom I*, Gosudarstvyennyi muzei etnologii, Osaka, 709–773.

Sneath, D (2003) "Land use, the environment and development in post-socialist Mongolia," *Oxford Development Studies* 31:4, 441–457.

Sneath, D (2004) "Property regimes and sociotechnical systems: rights over land in Mongolia's 'Age of the Market'" in K Verdery and C Humphrey (eds.) *Property in Question: Value Transformation in the Global Economy*, Berg, Oxford, New York, 161–182.

Sneath, D (2007) *The Headless State*, Columbia University Press, New York.

Sneath, D (2010) "Political mobilization and the construction of collective identity in Mongolia," *Central Asian Survey* 29:3, 251–267.

Sukhbaatar, G and Jamsran, L (1968) *BNMAU tuuhiin deej bichig I*, Sukhbaatar Printing Press, Ulaanbaatar.

Ulziisuren, B, Tsogtbaatar, B and Shagdar, Sh (2010) *Han Hentii Tovchoon*, Beat Press, Ulaanbaatar.

Undargaa, S (2013) "Property 'owners' without rights? Exploring property relations and access in the Herlen Bayan-Ulaan Reserve Pasture Area of Mongolia," Crawford School of Public Policy, Australian National University, Canberra.

Vainshtein, S (1980) *Nomads of South Siberia*, Cambridge University Press, Cambridge.

Vreeland, H H (1954) "Mongol community and kinship structure," Walter Hines Page School of International Relations, The Johns Hopkins University, New Haven.

Weatherford, J (2004) *Genghis Khan and the Making of the Modern World*, Crown Publishers, New York.

4 Mobile pastoralism and the collectivization period (1921–1991)

Revolution and production management

The 1921 revolution in Mongolia depicted the process of transitioning from aristocracy to collectivization of pastoral production under a modern state. After regaining its independence in 1921, the Mongolian People's Republic (MPR) followed the Soviet Russia model of developing a modern state, by abolishing the aristocracy and providing equal rights to its citizens. Simultaneously, the government of Mongolia retained several historical aspects of running a nomadic state (population and the pastoral production). First, in the constitution of 1924, it formalized the public's leadership in the governance of state matters,[1] particularly of natural resources by (a) declaring public ownership of land-based resources:

> All mineral, forest, water and natural resources within the territory of the current MPR have always been the property/asset (*hurungu*) of its public (*ard niit*) since the ancient past. As this custom still matches the principles of the current Republic (*ard uls*), this property/asset shall be under the power/authority/sovereignty (*medel*) of the public, and private property shall not be established regarding these resources.[2]

(b) by formalizing the public's power/authority via the state *Hurals* (High and lower level National Legislative Assemblies[3] along with the government make up the executive branch), which passed specific rules of law regarding the use of land, setting up *aimag* boundaries and the use of natural resources,[4] and (c) via publicly elected Assembly of People's Deputies at local level territorial units, has the authority of establishing and controlling local level government.[5] This was the earliest form of a formalized co-management of territorial administrations and production management. Second, the state territorial administration retained the units of *aimag, hoshuu, soum, bag, arvan* (see previous chapter[6]). The management of these units was not adequate for abolishing the aristocratic order, inequality and promoting public involvement in governance. Thus, the government replaced control over territories and pastoral production by the nobility and the monasteries with new boundaries of territorial units, changed

76 *Mobile pastoralism and the collectivization period*

jurisdictional names and locations for administrative centers to weaken religious dominance and publicly elected local deputies meeting and the government at each level (Kaser, 1982; Regsuren and Baljinnyam, 1973; Simukov, 1933a, p. 62). This policy, for instance, re-transferred monastery subjects to the authority of *hoshuu* administration and re-assigned the monastery livestock to other grazing grounds to open the best pastures for ordinary herders (Dilavhutagt, 1991, p. 48; Regsuren and Baljinnyam, 1973).

Third, pastoral production remained the primary agricultural industry. The majority of the population, both socially and culturally, still relied on mobile pastoralism for their livelihoods (Lattimore, 1962; Rosenberg, 1981). Mobile pastoralism was not merely "a 'traditional' sector of a national economy; it was the national economy" (Humphrey, 1978, p. 139). In other words, extensive pastoralism was the main food production system (to state officials) with regard to the existing ecology. As Lattimore noted: "Foreign journalists and travelers have made the mistake of assuming that the development of agriculture and industry in Mongolia means displacement and replacement of the pastoral economy. In other countries, perhaps; not in Mongolia" (1962, p. 164).

The socialist regime in Mongolia recognized the value of pastoral production in dry-land ecology when settling parts of the rural population (Humphrey and Sneath, 1999). The only challenge was that all livestock was still under private ownership. The production was heavily dependent on natural conditions. Since wealthy monasteries, nobles and commoners controlled most of the livestock for yield-focused production (see previous chapter), they exported mainly raw materials (89 percent of the export[7]) either by paying heavy debts[8] to traders for extremely cheap prices often set by traders or wholesale trade with Russia and other countries via Chinese traders (Amar, 1989, p. 16; Puntsagnorov, 1955, pp. 27, 28, 75, 94; Simukov, 1934, pp. 755, 756; Sukhbaatar and Jamsran, 1968, p. 156; J. Sambuu cited in Endicott, 2012, p. 61). Thus, it was difficult for the government to control economic development (Bradsher, 1972). The Mongolian People's Republic Party sought to collectivize extensive livestock husbandry under a new economic development plan with the aid of Soviet Russia[9] (Bradsher, 1972; Khazanov, 1998; Lattimore, 1962). The government aimed at modernizing and simplifying the extensive pastoral system and shifting it to a more sedentary, intensive pastoral system for industrial scale production based on Soviet Russia's design for its rural agricultural production (Scott, 1998). In other words, as Rosenberg noted, the new policy was a response to a "dramatically changing social and physical environment (due to such factors as drought, environmental depletion, tribal wars, incursion of government policies and authority, the introduction of new technology, reduction in available pasturage, and changing market accessibility)" (1981, p. 23).

In the 1930s, under the influence of the "Left Deviation" political movement, the state abolished the feudal production system and instituted collectivization (Rosenberg, 1981). The state and the Mongolian People's Republic Party (MPRP) political apparatus imposed social groups called *nuhurlul, hamtral,*

Mobile pastoralism and the collectivization period   77

horshoo, commun or *artel*[10] (forms of collectives) as an initial form of collectivization for livestock production, hunting, caravan, haymaking and crop cultivation (Regsuren and Baljinnyam, 1973, p. 138). These groups were unstable and unpopular regarding their collective action due to the poor quality of political works. Many advisers were not familiar with the new form of collective action. Many poor/average herders and the elders were forced to join these groups. Although increased in numbers, herder membership was valid only on paper as they lived remotely (Regsuren and Baljinnyam, 1973, p. 140; Simukov, 1931, pp. 131, 132, 140). Forced collectivization essentially failed following mass confiscation of private livestock properties from ordinary herders, nobles, monasteries, and others who owned more than a hundred large animals[11] (cattle, horses) to redistribute to the poor; the centralization of the tax system and the imposition of heavy taxes on all levels of herders and traders under new regressive taxes reforms (1924–1950), which were based on equalitarian ideology and in the context of mixed species herding (Dilavhutagt, 1991, pp. 49–53; Holzman, 1956, p. 508; Regsuren and Baljinnyam, 1973, p. 141).

As a result, livestock numbers decreased,[12] and many migrants lost their *nutag* which caused large deficits in the state revenue and damaged the national economy (Dilavhutagt, 1991, p. 54; Holzman, 1957; Rosenberg, 1981; Simukov, 1931, p. 128). This period also witnessed chaos in pasture use practices and unbalanced production components. The collapse of the historical aristocratic and ecclesiastical order, which provided for the customary pasture use, created an absence of solid socio-economic institutions (Upton, 2005, p. 581). It shifted customary *khot ail* or local wealthy/poor herders' collaboration based on supplementing their needs, to individual herding households struggling to manage different types of livestock independently. This may also have occurred due to the forced distribution of livestock to many poor households. Dilavhutagt noted:

> All the confiscated livestock was distributed to the local poor households, who were assigned to a certain area as a *homoon* (commune) to herd these livestock. These households began to seek a way out of the *homoon* as they soon became weary of *homoon* rules, which they were obligated to comply with.
>
> (1991, p. 51)

Many poor households were inexperienced in herding large number of herds without support (Natsagdorj, 1972, p. 502; Simukov, 1933b). That is why Sambuu (1945) suggested the need for experienced herders to share their expertise in increasing livestock numbers for those who lacked experience (Sambuu, 1945, p. 5). The state ended outmigration and revolts against reform by its decision to allow *ulamjlalt* livestock production, to return some of the confiscated livestock, and also to allow increases in livestock (Dilavhutagt, 1991, p. 54). In other words, the changes and instability in pastoral institutions affected the ways in which herders collaborated on balancing

78 *Mobile pastoralism and the collectivization period*

production components. Replacing the aristocratic order with smaller (social/territorial boundaries) socially engineered groups was perhaps a very challenging task regarding its capacity to control production components.

Complete collectivization

The government prioritized stabilizing the pastoral institutions and maximizing pastoral production, which involved major reforms in its approach to collectivization and the integrated management of the state territorial administration and production components. First, to complete collectivization and improve the national economy, the state employed a series of strategies; tax exemption (1949~), interest-free loans, other moral and material incentives designed to attract herders, who would improve livestock shelters and wells, and increase their livestock numbers, etc. (Holzman, 1957; Regsuren and Baljinnyam, 1973; Rosenberg, 1981). There were 19 livestock per person in 1924, this increased to 33 livestock per person in 1945 (Sambuu, 1945, p. 4). The state increased veterinary services as well as the number of old *buuts* and rock/dung walls by building more shelters with canopies (Regsuren and Baljinnyam, 1973, p. 121; Simukov, 1934, pp. 735, 741). By the mid-1950s, the state had control over completing collectivization and developed an intensive "ranch style" livestock husbandry (Bruun, 2006; McMillan, 1969, p. 23; Simukov, 1933a, p. 61). Collective membership eventually became attractive as the process did not alienate or exclude herders from gaining access to local pastoral resources. Moreover, it promoted collective membership by propaganda and material and financial incentives such as gifts of household items and salary payments in return for livestock owners giving up their private household production. Many eventually joined collectivization due to the heavy tax on private livestock owners (Fernandez-Gimenez, 1999; Rosenberg, 1981) and to gain access to better pastoral resources and the massive aid from Soviet Russia that was allocated to *negdels* (Bruun, 2006; Humphrey, 1978). By 1958–1960, the state had accomplished complete collectivization throughout the country (Fernandez-Gimenez, 1999; Rosenberg, 1981). The state, now the ultimate power, continued to pursue pastoral production to gain, maintain and control economic benefits from the existing ecology.

Second, the state was able to continue to pursue pastoral production by retaining the historical fundamentals of pastoral production (dual control over the production components). The 1940 and 1960 constitutions continued to emphasize the public's sovereignty in the governance[13] of natural resources by declaring (a) natural resources as the Republic's property (*ulsiin umch*) and public/republic[14] property/asset (*hurungu*), (b) governed by Assembly (*Hural*) of Working People's Deputies as the organs of state power at each level of territorial units[15] and (c) the pasture and agrarian plots would be placed at the disposal of individuals and collectives free of charge.[16] This matched with the ideology of socialist state property (Verdery, 2004). This period changed

Mobile pastoralism and the collectivization period   79

the nature of dual control a bit at least on paper. Although the *Hurals* formalized the herders' role and involvement in decision making as a formal control, de facto it was mainly used as an approval mechanism for top-down party decision making (Kaser, 1982). The state managed all productive resources as public property/assets, allocating administrative duties along different vertical hierarchical levels (Sturgeon and Sikor, 2004). Thus, the state adjusted the integrated management of the state territorial administration and production (components) by reforming the units of territorial administration and production management.

Reforms in the state territorial administration

Regarding modern economic development and the future progress of livestock production in Mongolia, particularly concerning future carrying capacity in relation to expected growth in the number of livestock, the state experimented with re-structuring territorial units. Simukov (1929) highlighted the importance of studying saturation of future livestock numbers and the maximum carrying capacity of the land in Mongolia. His concern was based on other's prediction of possible limitations of extensive pastoralism in the future regarding problems of overgrazing or the lack of carrying capacity for ever increasing numbers of livestock. Although the author acknowledged that the prediction was based on exaggerated and underestimated calculations of data from each category, he concluded that this prediction inspired an idea of the "dead-end" of extensive pastoralism. Then he suggested taking a wide range of actions such as improving fodder production, the quality and the rational use of pasture, and settling down some parts of the population for developing crop cultivation in desirable areas, and the mining industry. The author's position was that modern economic development was impossible by just relying on extensive pastoralism and without diversifying livelihoods of the population, and national agricultural, industrial development based on scientific measurements (Simukov, 1929, pp. 359–360). Later in 1930, the author noted that the size, boundary and centers of previous territorial administrative units needed further reforms to develop economic and agricultural zones, involve commercial and administrative institutions to integrate the national economy and simplify its economic units, administration costs and statistical registration. Additional development in the communication, veterinary services[17] and transportation sectors were also needed to expand livestock production and the trade industry (Simukov and Stulov, 1930, pp. 33–41).

Simultaneously, Amar (1989), a member of Mongolian intelligentsia and a politician, called for serious consideration of the knowledge base of Mongolian *ulamjlalt* pastoralism in developing a modern livestock production system in addition to scientific knowledge, because the former had always been critical in Mongolia's economic and political development as an independent food production system (p. 8). Reflecting Simukov's research and planning (Simukov and Stulov, 1930), which considered the historical role of the state territorial

80 *Mobile pastoralism and the collectivization period*

administration in pastoralism, on February 7, 1931, the government changed five *aimags* into 13, and abolished *hoshuu* and consolidated *soums*[18] according to population density (Regsuren and Baljinnyam, 1973; Simukov and Stulov, 1930, pp. 33–41). However, government implementation was not satisfactory as Simukov (1936) noted that the new *soums* were too small, with very vague territorial borders for developing effective economic units (pp. 67–68). It may be the case that the government was unable to exactly follow Simukov's 1930 blueprint on territorial administrative units and production management.

Nevertheless, the state divided rural territories into *aimag*, *soum* and *bag* units to be governed by the local *Hural* and the national government.[19] There were 12 *aimags*. An *aimag* is the largest territorial administrative unit with some degree of distinctive border, which is further divided into *soums*, consisting of some 15–40 *soums* per *aimag* (Simukov, 1934, pp. 751–752). Once the government abolished the *hoshuu*, it adopted the former military *soum* as the territorial administrative unit. Eighty-six former *hoshuuns* were divided into 300–304 *soums*, re-drawing their boundaries on a much smaller scale (Fernandez-Gimenez, 1999; Humphrey, 1978). *Soums* had nominal borders, which were more defined in areas where herders tended to move more regularly for shorter distances. The average *soum* area was about 500 sq. km and contained an average population of 2300. The *soum Hural*, which consisted of *bag* representatives, selected three members and two candidates as *soum* administrators, which in turn selected one as a chairman to be approved by the *aimag* administration (Simukov, 1934, p. 752). The *soum* was responsible for administering public services, receiving funds from the state and dealing with social and political matters such as the population census and military service. It also represented the state and provided these services to the *negdel* (collective) (Humphrey, 1978). Managing the production and its components was now integrated under the *soum* unit as it had replaced the *hoshuu* function. In other words, the state left the main responsibility for production management to nested enterprises – a much smaller rural district (*soum*) or urban micro-district (*horoo*). *Soums* were then divided into *bags*, the smallest administrative and territorial unit. Although there was no *bag* border, it can be distinguished if necessary. It contained an average area of 62.5 sq. km and 30–100 (in fact up to 150) households (300 people). There were around 2400 *bags* in Mongolia. A *bag* governor and his assistant were selected for a one-year term at the *bag Hural* (Simukov, 1934, pp. 751–752).

Therefore, following various socio-political changes that occurred, the state territorial structure often changed re-creating new social and resource boundaries of its territorial units. For instance, as shown in Table 4.1, the HBU case study area went through major changes in its territorial boundaries and administrative units. The restructuring of territorial administrative units affected the management of production and pasture use. According to research participants in the 1950s, "Bayanerhtii" *bag* residents (*bag* 2–4 in 1930 in Figure 4.2) were assembled into DD *bag*, Delgerhaan *soum*, whilst their territory remained in Nyalga *soum* (Figure 4.3). This re-settlement involved around 200 herding

Table 4.1 Changes in the state territorial administrative units in the HBU case study areas

Case study bags	Names of the areas	1911–1924 (Figure 4.1)	1923–1930 (Figure 4.2)	1931–1974 (Figure 4.3)	1992-current (see map in Chapter 5)
HBU & DD *bags*	HBU, DD and riverside of UU *bag*	Zorigt zasagiin *hoshuu* in Setsen Han *aimag*	Dashbalbar *hoshuu* in Han-Hentii *aimag* (maybe as HBU *soum*)	Belonged to Delgerhaan *soum*, Hentii *aimag*. In 1956, several *bags*[20] were re-structured. In 1974,[21] HBU *bag* separated from Delgerhaan as HBU *horoo* (urban micro-district) for HBU RPA, Hentii *aimag*.	HBU as a *bag* re-united[22] with Delgerhaan *soum* DD *bag*, Delgerhaan *soum*, Hentii *aimag*
UU *bag*	Western hillside of UU *bag*: Bayan-Erhtiin Mountain, Nyalga hills	Approximately[23] in between Darhan Zasagiin *hoshuu*, Tusheet Han *aimag* and the northern end of Ahai Zasagiin *hoshuu*, Setsen Han *aimag*	Bogd Han Mountain *hoshuu*, Bogd Han Mountain *aimag* and Darhan Mountain *hoshuu*, Han-Hentii *aimag*	A new border was drawn by the Herlen River between Tuv and Khentii *aimags*. Riverside of the rest of the UU *bag* belonged to Nyalga *soum*, Tuv *aimag*. In 1956,[24] Nyalga *soum* was separated. Its 1st, 3rd–6th *bags* joined Bayan *soum*, Tuv *aimag* and 2nd *bag* joined Govisumber *soum*, Dorno-govi *aimag*. In 1959, it was re-established as Bayan-jargalan *soum*, Tuv *aimag*.	UU *bag*, Bayan-jargalan *soum*, Tuv *aimag*

Sources: GIMAS, 2009; Munkh-ochir, 2012; Munkh-Ochir and Azzaya, 2014; Shirendev and Natsagdorj, 1966).

82 *Mobile pastoralism and the collectivization period*

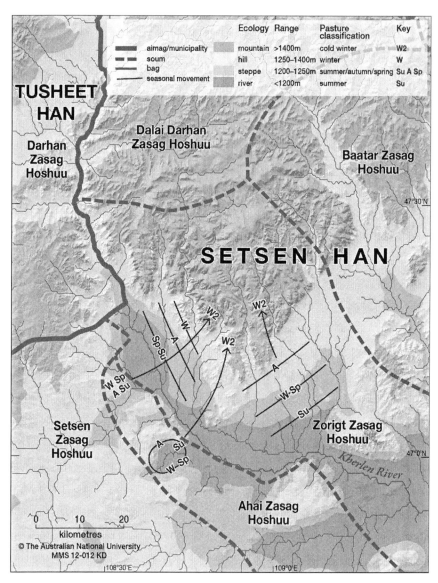

Figure 4.1 Territorial boundaries in HBU case area prior to 1923.[25]

households and about 200,000 head of livestock.[26] Because of this, the herders' seasonal mobility was restricted to a much smaller *soum* or former *bag* than the previously larger *hoshuu* territory (Figures 4.1–4.3). This reduced the ecologically preferable land for grazing. For instance, the seasonal mobility of resettled households changed from the right hand side of the river to the left hand side and their grazing was limited to only the DD territory (Figure 4.2). The grazing

Mobile pastoralism and the collectivization period 83

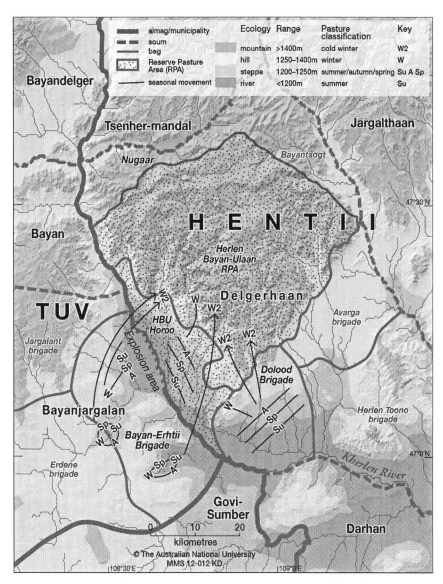

Figure 4.2 Territorial boundaries in HBU case area prior to 1962.[27]

area of the former DD herders was reduced due to the establishment of the RPA and some additional households moving from the other side of the river (Figure 4.3). Those remaining in the UU territory could no longer use the river valley as it had been handed over to the Soviet army for testing explosives and they thus used Bayan-Erkhtii Mountain and UU hills for seasonal mobilization (Figure 4.3).

84 *Mobile pastoralism and the collectivization period*

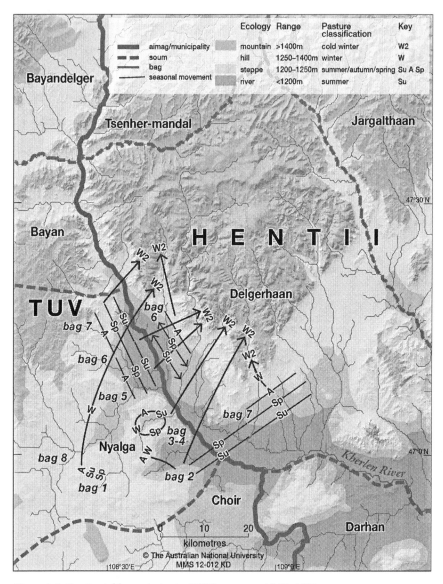

Figure 4.3 Territorial boundaries in HBU case area 1962–1991.

Reforms in the production management and the collective entity

The state developed a collective (*negdel*) enterprise within the *soum* territories as a formal pastoral institution to manage the production components. First, the *negdel* divided a *soum* territory into 4–7 *brigades*[28] at the *bag* level as the smallest production unit (Bruun, 2006; Fernandez-Gimenez, 1999; Sneath, 2003). A *brigade* was based on a former *bag*, which was no longer a formal territorial/ budget unit as the 1960 constitution changed rural territorial administrative units to *aimag* and *soum*.[29] The *brigade* functioned as a basic unit to integrate the components of production for developing intensive livestock husbandry. Second, kinship and neighborhood-based *hot ail* were replaced with non-kinship-based *suuri ail*, which consisted of one or two households for herding a single species of livestock instead of mixed herds (Fernandez-Gimenez, 1999; Humphrey, 1978). This structure aimed to "rationalize herding so that overall productivity would rise without bringing undue benefit or dis-advantage to any individual" (Humphrey, 1978, p. 142). The chairmen of the *soum* also governed the *negdel* and provided the *negdel* with state and public services (Humphrey, 1978). The *negdel* comprised about 1000 households or employees with a total population of 4000; half of these were herding house-holds (Humphrey, 1978; Sneath, 2003). *Negdel* restructuring was crucial to the country's economy (Lattimore, 1962). This was done under pressure from the Socialist development policy to shift Inner Asian nomadic pastoral production to a collectivized settled production system. The *negdel* production system comprised 85.2 percent of the rural economy in 1969 and 76.1 percent in 1975, indicating its continuing major contribution to the national economy (Humphrey, 1978). The socialist production system also had parallel produc-tion enterprises. Besides the *negdels*, the state also established farms (*aj ahui*), which operated within the *horoo* (urban equivalent to *soum*). In 1975, there were 259 *negdels* compared to 36 state farms (*sangiin aj ahui*). The main func-tion of these state farms was agriculture which involved raising crops, but some were involved in pastoral production and cross-breeding. These state farms owned much smaller numbers of livestock compared to *negdels* (Hum-phrey, 1978; Sneath, 2003). The state farms had their own jurisdictional ter-ritory, which was divided into *brigades*. *Negdel* and *aj ahui* became major pastoral parallel production institutions. Shrinking territorial boundaries of production management into *soums* meant that herders' seasonal movements were limited within the territorial boundaries of the *brigade*, which resulted in much less flexibility in mobility over an ecologically less diverse terrain, and offered fewer types of forage resources (Fernandez-Gimenez, 1999; Hum-phrey, 1978; Sneath, 2003). Compensating for the loss of EPL as well as the vulnerabilities of the risks of severe weather conditions like *dzud* and *gan*, the *negdel* and *aj ahui* opened up available pasture by using mechanized transport, engineered wells and provided extra forage (Heaton, 1979, p. 59).

The state also involved herders in production management under dual control. This allowed herders a certain amount of informal control (Fernandez-Gimenez, 1999; Mearns, 2004b, p. 140). There are hardly any collective period *ulamjlalt* rules and norms, because collectives mostly pro-vided mechanized support, which was an established practice, rather than pragmatic adaptation. Instead, the state formalized a few of the pre-collective *ulamjlalt* production and pasture use rules and norms regarding seasonal movement based on the type, age and gender of livestock. Although these

86 *Mobile pastoralism and the collectivization period*

enterprises strictly oversaw the components of production, planning and implementation, they continued to allow herders a certain degree of use of other informal *ulamjlalt* production and pasture use rules. This included allowing herders to maintain discretionary authority over selecting the location of campsites and continue to pursue basic seasonal movements according to their herding expertise (Humphrey, 1978; Mearns, 2004; Undargaa, 2013). This was significant in terms of accommodating herders' *ulamjlalt* flexible movements during unstable climatic conditions. In other words, this formal production structure had, in fact, many major characteristics of *ulamjlalt* pastoral production embedded within it. Thus, despite changes, what was most important was that historically up to the end of the collective period, the state retained the historical fundamentals of dual control over integrated management of the production components under *negdel* and *aj ahui*. This was because, as Lattimore (1962) noted, Mongolians, all of whom had direct relations to their pastoral background, led their own government and requested Russian technical advice. The collectivization activities "are traceable to Russian originals, but all have peculiarities which derived from Mongolian conditions" (Lattimore, 1962, p. 191). This was unlike the ways in which Soviet Russia had absolute control over the socio-economic and political reforms in Khazakhstan, damaging its pastoral production system and causing nationwide food insecurity (Shayakhmetov, 2007). The following subsections explain the *negdel*'s general pattern of controlling the three production components, as it slightly differs from the *aj ahui*.

Livestock

The negdel owned and controlled livestock production by means of a formalized herding strategy. It formalized production specialization to introduce an industrial-style working process and "the administrative routinization of work and hence the power and knowledge of central officials" (Scott, 1998, p. 212). Each *suuri* herded specific species, sex or age class of livestock, instead of mixed species, such as only sheep/goat herds, horses or castrated rams or two-year old lambs or cross-bred sheep. This strategy was based on a precollective pattern of specialized herding, which was much more flexible than the collective arrangement (Fernandez-Gimenez, 1999; Sneath, 2004). All livestock belonged to the *negdels*, except a few private livestock for household consumption (Fernandez-Gimenez, 1999; Humphrey, 1978). For instance, each individual herding household was allowed to own 30–75 head of private livestock in the HBU case area. Again, the *negdel* assigned one *suuri* to herd private livestock (Humphrey, 1978). The *negdels* had compulsory insurance through the state-owned insurance company,[30] which fully covered livestock loss due to natural disasters (Templer et al., 1993). Herders were responsible for paying for other types of loss,[31] in line with their responsibilities. State insurance rarely covered privately owned livestock (Fernandez-Gimenez, 1999; Templer et al., 1993).

Labor

The *negdel* also regulated labor resources. The *negdel* and the *soum*[32] shared the same leader (Fernandez-Gimenez, 1999), "known as the *soum darga* (boss), he enjoyed considerable discretionary power within his jurisdiction, while being upwardly accountable only to superiors at higher levels in the highly centralized state structure" (Mearns, 2004, p. 142). Scott (1998, p. 213) compared the power and authority of collective officials over collective members in Soviet Russia to feudal lords, who legally controlled the movement of its peasants. Although the constitution of 1940 allowed citizens freedom of locomotion,[33] the 1960 constitution did not mention any such right. The government controlled the labor movement for its centralized planning. In pastoral production, which was based on the need to balance the production components, the *negdel* structure in effect almost continued the pre-collective state territorial structure, assigning the use of pastoral resources to *suuri* households in *brigade* territory. Each *brigade* had a leader who led about 100–200 herding households (Fernandez-Gimenez, 1999). A *brigade leader* assigned at least two households in each *suuri*, depending on the task, to pool labor resources (Fernandez-Gimenez, 1999; Humphrey, 1978). Although, in the DD *bag* in the HBU case, a *suuri* also consisted of one household if they were herding non-milking livestock. Under *suuri* structure, inequalities between the wealthy and the poor were replaced by inequality in capacity and willingness to fulfill production plans (Humphrey, 1978, p. 153). For each suuri, the *negdel* assigned tasks to herders based on their capacity, which was dependent on gender, age or experience.[34] Each sheep *suuri* contained around 600 animals for two herders, whereas a milking *suuri* had 160 animals and ten milkmaids (Humphrey, 1978). The *negdel* also assigned a *suuri* leader to report to the *brigade* leader about livestock and machinery. *Negdels* continued utilizing propaganda or socialist competition which was supported by honors and awards to encourage herders to maximize collective production at the expense of private livestock. Due to limits of economic incentives, herders were often unable to utilize cash as there were few consumer goods available. Furthermore, having too many goods hampered mobility (Humphrey, 1978).

Pastureland and tenure

Although it may seem like there was no specific legislation or an institution for rural land management, historical records, including the collective period, discussed management of pastureland and its rehabilitation within the management of livestock production and its components. Protecting and improving pastureland was critical for production rather than specifically for conservation purposes (Namjig, 2000). Reflecting the constitutional (1940 and 1960) provisions, the 1971 law on land use granted *negdels* and *sangiin aj ahui* the right to "free and perpetual use" (Fernandez-Gimenez, 1999, p. 332). The management of pastureland was embedded in management of the whole

88 *Mobile pastoralism and the collectivization period*

production. The *negdels* took the following measures to compensate the loss of available pasture, natural water resources or handmade boreholes and minerals that existed under *hoshuu* territory. First, the *negdels* developed and drilled new wells, boreholes and transportation or delivered large tanks of water to remote areas to efficiently utilize pastures in small *brigade* and *soum* territories with state funding (Fernandez-Gimenez, 1999; Humphrey, 1978; Sneath, 2003). It assigned responsibility for the maintenance of these wells to special sections of each *brigade* (Humphrey, 1978). Second, the *negdels* replaced rock/dung walls with more sophisticated livestock shelters with canopies or byres to reduce the risk of livestock loss during severe winters (Fernandez-Gimenez, 1999; Humphrey, 1978). The byres were particularly necessary in newly expanded pastures. For instance, in UU *bag* territory, "Shine Amidral" *negdel* had to build new winter and spring shelters in the bare UU hills, because a Russian military division used the river valley (Figure 4.3). In contrast, in "Bayanbadral" *negdel* in DD territory, herders used rock/dung walls under the shelter of the HBU Mountain.[35] Third, the use of byres was supported by the production of hay and fodder in large amounts (more than in previous times) for an "emergency fodder fund" (Fernandez-Gimenez, 1999). The *negdels* established their own hay-making *brigades* annually and bought hay from *sangiin aj ahui* (Humphrey, 1978). In other words, herders became directly dependent on state support for their mobility and pastoral production, because the state replaced the production system that is dependent on customary technology with one based on advanced technology of machinery (Scott, 1998, p. 217).

However, the *negdel* structure resulted in some changes in the herders' customary patterns of access to pastoral resources. These changes affected the *ulamjlalt* patterns of social networking and herding strategies in pre-collective period (Mearns, 1996 cited in Fernandez-Gimenez, 2000). The changes in the grazing patterns of specific species led to overgrazing (Sokolewitz, 1982 cited in Fernandez-Gimenez, 1999). These changes diminished the practice of *ulamjlalt* pastoral production and pastureland management by placing limits on the herders' traditional patterns of cooperation (Mearns, 1996). Herders were losing their skills in keeping mixed herds, skills that were well known to most older herders familiar with *ulamjlalt* herding practices (Humphrey, 1978). The government's attempt to simplify and intensify pastoral production shifted once self-supporting pastoral production (Amar, 1989) to a production system economically dependent on mechanized modern technology, infrastructure, fuel and government subsidies (Barfield, 2011). To some extent, it had failed and was not supported by herders, because it contradicted the existing resource use management which was still based on strong *ulamjlalt* livestock production and pasture use rules and norms (Fernandez-Gimenez, 1999; Humphrey, 1978; Scott, 1998). A science-based experiment on improving grazing patterns had to cease due to financial constraints, though it resulted in a 15 percent increase in livestock production (MNE, 1996, p. 54). Also, many of the newly drilled wells were not properly constructed or suitably located

Mobile pastoralism and the collectivization period 89

and the knowledge of maintaining the wells was also lacking. Also, according to *ulamjlalt* herding strategies, permanent campsites can crowd too many live-stock into one byre and cause damage to animals or affect the quality of wool (Humphrey, 1978, pp. 148–149). Crowding animals together in permanent shelters can create unhygienic conditions which may lead to disease or injury and damage the quality of wool (Fernandez-Gimenez, 1999; Humphrey, 1978). Also, the locations and functions of newly fixed campsites with byres and wells were unfavorable to herders as *negdels'* mobility routes were mostly based on pre-collective routes, which already provided natural or traditionally built shelters suited to use during bad weather conditions without much forage or hay (Humphrey, 1978, p. 149). For these reasons, herders changed campsites quite often or used different campsites in pre-collective times under the flexibility of locally recognized use rights. Therefore, *negdels* had to rely on historical dual control over *ulamjlalt* management of pastoral production, which also embedded the pastureland management.

Seasonal mobility: Under formal control, the state-appointed *negdels* assigned management rights over production and pastoral resources to herders. The *soum/negdel* had its own four-season pasture (Humphrey, 1978). The *negdel* confirmed the location of each *brigade*'s *nutag* seasonal pastures (Sneath, 2003). Each *brigade* decided on the specific herd species and seasonal migration routes that each *suuri* would follow within their *brigade* territory (Fernandez-Gimenez, 1999; Humphrey, 1978). The *brigade* governor was also in charge of the final decisions on the choice of winter and spring campsites.[36] Following the policy of introducing sedentary production management, more inten-sive grazing occurred near population centers in *soum* territories, particularly of dairy farms, which had much less seasonal mobility than other *suuri* (Fernandez-Gimenez, 1999; Humphrey, 1978; Undargaa, 2013). The changes leading to overgrazing did not necessarily occur on a large scale, but at a small local level. When such concentration happens to sheep *suuri*, the *brigade* leader followed the *negdel*'s decision and organized *ulamjlalt* short/long-distance *otor*, regardless of the wishes of some herders to stay close to the center (Hum-phrey, 1978). The *brigades* mainly followed *ulamjlalt* patterns of seasonal mobility and pasture use with regard to the geographical location of water and mineral resources already available within its territory (Mearns, 2004).

With regard to herders' informal control, the herders made independent decisions about daily herding management. Since most of the new infrastruc-ture could not be relied on to avoid risk, the *negdel*'s modern pasture use rules and norms were based on *ulamjlalt* rules and norms to avoid overgrazing (Humphrey, 1978, p. 146). Herders employed much of the *ulamjlalt* know-ledge for their pastoral production and pasture use (Fernandez-Gimenez, 1999, 2000). Herders even coined the saying: *Mal mallahaa Marxismaar zaal-gahgui* (we herders would not be taught by Marxism how to herd our live-stock[37]). For instance, in the HBU case area in 2010, a former *negdel* herder in DD and UU explained how they selected where to establish campsites and camp seasonally:

90 *Mobile pastoralism and the collectivization period*

Our spring campsite used to be to the south. Then, the *negdel* head wanted to build a spring shelter for us. So, we chose this "XXX" as our [new] spring campsite.... And the *negdel* allowed another *suuri* herder to use our old one, because they used to stay to the south of DD and wanted to stay on our old site....[38] We chose to stay there. The pasture was really good and there was nothing like this was mine or yours etc. So, we were able to choose where to graze our livestock....[39] We would suggest to the *negdel* that we would like to stay in this and/or that winter or spring campsites....[40] The *negdel* used to organize everything, but we chose where to stay; the *negdel* would provide us with shelters and everything.[41]

Therefore, the *negdel*'s formal decisions about herders' movements were based on the herders' own suggestions taking into account local patterns of pasture use, whereas the *negdels* assigned herding tasks and supported herders' mobility with infrastructure. Herders were the main actors, balancing livestock herding with available pasture and labor. These regarded the type of species they herded as well as the selection of campsites, which was related to the social conditions of the herding households. Although a *suuri* was not necessarily composed of kin-based relatives, it was common that herders selected their campsites based on proximity to relatives. Another herder in DD explained that:

I chose it because it was closer to my relatives. You herded *negdel* livestock and you had your own little kids and there were only two of you. One of you had to leave for elsewhere for some business. In this case, I usually stayed at home with my kids. So, I could go and ask one of my relatives to come and stay with me and take care of the herding.[42]

Thus, herders' movement was influenced by their informal control over pooling and balancing their labor needs.

Herders had the use right to campsites rather than holding a right of private possession. Herders' annual use of the same campsites/shelters may resemble private property (Bawden, 1968 cited in Fernandez-Gimenez, 1999). In fact, the *negdels* recognized herders' rights to particular campsites (Sneath, 2003). For instance, in the HBU case area, former *negdel* herders in both DD and UU *bags* would stay on their same winter or spring campsites during favorable weather conditions. This practice had also occurred in pre-collective times as locally recognized use rights and the *negdels* continued to practice it. Locally recognized use rights meant herders annually used the same campsites and pastures during usual weather conditions. It would take time to adjust their livestock to the specific terrain/water in order to fatten them. As one of the *negdel* herders in UU *bag* explained, "It is not your livestock that got used to the area. It is the herder who made his livestock used to the area.... You rotate around different areas and choose where it was suitable to stay."[43] This adjustment helps the livestock avoid losing fat from changing their grazing in different[44] geographical conditions (Undargaa, 2013). Based on this, the

Mobile pastoralism and the collectivization period   91

negdels perhaps tried to establish sedentary production by creating fixed live-stock shelters and provided extra fodder for emergencies. This was to replace pre-collective flexible camping arrangements. Herders, back then, selected locally recognized campsites with or without shelters or camped elsewhere temporarily for extra forage under unstable weather conditions (see Chapter 3). As such, *negdel* herders also continued the *ulamjlalt* strategy of changing campsites during unstable weather conditions. For instance, a participant from HBU *bag* explained, "If it was snowy and the situation was very difficult [around the campsite], then the herder would move and stay somewhere else."[45] Also, as in the pre-collective period, herders could not own/possess specific campsites that they often moved their livestock shelters/*buuts* to another nearby spot on the same pasture to create a new one due to the herd size, livestock disease or unhygienic conditions. Individual territorial use may have been a common practice due to the spaciousness of the pastoral resources regulated by the controlled production management (see previous chapter).

However, the *negdel* pursued strict pastureland management, which was embedded within the overall production system. Setting strict controls over planning, monitoring, managing and appropriating production through the hierarchical administrative system was the main accomplishment of the col-lective system (Scott, 1998). Although continuing to employ *ulamjlalt* seasonal or cross-boundary mobility rules and norms, the *negdel* formalized the *ulamjlalt* rule of seasonal mobility compulsory for all herders in order to avoid over-grazing. The *negdel* enforced this by providing equal opportunity for herders to access transportation support and pastoral resources (livestock pasture and labor) and transportation support (Fernandez-Gimenez, 1999). Unlike some contemporary positions, in which strict enforcement of this rule was con-sidered as a collective time custom (Upton, 2009), seasonal mobility was/is still a fundamental pre-collective informal *ulamjlal*, which was only formalized and enforced in the collective period due to absolute collective control of the production components. Unlike the pre-collective period, where poor herders without support were allowed to overstay *nutag* seasonal pastures (Vreeland, 1954), no one stayed behind, because everyone worked for the collective and equally received the collective's support. The *negdels* imposed a penalty of a 30 percent pay cut for breaking collective rules on pasture use and norms (Fernandez-Gimenez, 1999). This indicates that the herders' basic pasture use rules and norms were based on *ulamjlalt* patterns, but the rota-tional movement and the time was compulsory for everyone.

Cross-boundary mobility: The *negdel* promoted *ulamjlalt* cross-territorial short-long distance mobility (*otor*) as compulsory to maximize production. This was for fattening livestock (looking for newer pastures or salty minerals) or to overcome severe weather conditions (Fernandez-Gimenez, 1999; Humphrey, 1978). For instance, in the HBU case area, after shearing the livestock by August or September, "Bayanbadral" *negdel* (DD *bag*) would remind herders to go on summer *otor* on the other side of the river in the territory of "Shine Amidral" *negdel* (UU *bag*), which was rich in minerals.

92 Mobile pastoralism and the collectivization period

They arranged this exchange. Also, within its territory, each *aimag* and *soum* reserved certain pastoral areas for emergency use and haymaking areas for the state fodder fund, and designed stock routes. In the HBU case, an absence of mixed species herding enabled *negdels* to assign all of their territory for specific purposes including reserve pasture[46] even with reduced territorial boundaries. Although the *negdels* made the ultimate decisions on *otor* movement, they consulted with herders on the timing and locations regarding the type and condition of the livestock under given seasonal climate conditions. Regardless of improved infrastructure and expanded pasture, herders still need *ulamjlalt* knowledge for coping with variations in terrain and climatic conditions to gain access to pastoral resources. Local leaders often negotiated directly with each other to gain reciprocal pasture-use privileges in case of emergency. These exchanges were then approved by the next-highest level of authority, a *soum* for a *brigade* or an *aimag* for a *soum* (Fernandez-Gimenez, 1999). In other words, the pre-collective dual control continued for herders gaining access to pastoral resources. Similar to the pre-collective period, any land disputes arisen from *ulamjlalt* use of pasture within or between jurisdictions were settled at the local *Hural* or next-highest level of *Hural*[47] (Butler, 1982 cited in Fernandez-Gimenez, 1999). Disputes between different *suuri* over the sharing of grazing land were rare during this time of controlled production. Regarding the lack of grass growth in winter and spring pasture, the *brigade* clearly defined territorial boundaries (herders would know each other's daily livestock grazing pattern) for each *suuri* (Humphrey, 1978). For instance, in UU *bag*, there was 5 km distance between each *suuri*, which contained permanent shelters. Such divisions between *suuri* were less formal and clear-cut because grass grew more quickly in summer, even after grazing (Humphrey, 1978). The boundary was based on the scientific calculation of carrying capacity (Humphrey, 1978). It was also based on *ulamjlalt* ways of approximate estimation.[48] Overall, the *negdel* succeeded in maximizing production. Despite pressure to use new intensive techniques of herding, combining it with *ulamjlalt* extensive herding techniques led to the success of some collectives or herders winning prizes in "socialist competitions" for their livestock products (Humphrey, 1978, p. 149). The state maintained integrated management that allowed formal *negdel* and herders' informal control over production and pasture use practices.

Enterprise of the Herlen Bayan Ulaan Reserve Pasture Area (HBU RPA)

This section discusses the *sangiin aj ahui*, a state funded and managed production entity established in the collective period to support *negdel* production. Some literature exists on agrarian *sangiin aj ahui*: agrarian production for supplying forage, hay and grain at the national level. As a parallel pastoral production institution to *negdels*, here we discuss *otriin aj ahui*, a rarely talked about business entity, the state-funded Inter-*Aimag* Cross-territorial Reserve Pasture Area

(RPA). This was involved in providing services of reserve pasture area (RPA), cross-breeding, and hay and forage supply to *negdels* which needed state intervention to arrange inter-*aimag* RPA; thus, all collectives could use it without any disputes, particularly under the state induced production plan. The state assigned management authority to the Ministry of Food and Agriculture (MFA). The MFA along with the Supreme Council of *Negdels* was in charge of all policies and planning with regard to agricultural land use (Mearns, 2004). The ministry also regulated management of the production and pastureland of the RPA.

The HBU RPA, the largest *otriin aj ahui*, presents a case regarding the ways in which the parallel institutions collaborated on production and organizing *otor*. Although the state controlled everything, territorial issues were sensitive as territorial units including their herders were concerned about losing their *nutag* (pastoral areas) as had occurred in the pre-collective period. Five years into collectivization, the *negdels'* intensive pastoral production lacked the full capacity to function on their own, particularly in terms of taking care of newborn livestock during the severe winters which occurred in the 1960s (Templer et al., 1993). In 1962, the government established the HBU Mountain as *Otor* Tejeeliin Station (HBU Station for Pasture Fodder Production[49]). Similar to the agrarian *aj ahui*,[50] the HBU RPA had jurisdiction over its own territory. The government strategically targeted the HBU Mountain because of the area's history and reputation as "a thousand *buuts/hond*"[51] for winter (see Chapter 3). The Delgerhaan *soum* governor changed the initial suggestion of the state to locate the RPA center in the Delgerhaan *soum* center to the HBU *bag* center in order to avoid losing their historical territory to the ministry controlled RPA.[52] The HBU RPA covered an area of 122 sq. km which included territories from Jargalthaan, Delgerhaan and Tsenhermandal (Figure 4.3). Nevertheless, Delgerhaan and other *soums* lost some of their territories: the HBU Mountain, which was used for winter, and other seasonal pasture around it, which were used by households from DD *bag*. Although this affected the grazing territory of DD *bag* even further, the establishment of the HBU RPA did not provoke much resistance. As in *negdels*, the state maintained the historical management of the components of production.

The administrative structure and production management

In response to the 1968 *dzud* and the massive loss of livestock,[53] the HBU Mountain expanded to *Otor tejeeliin aj ahui*[54] (Reserve Pasture and Fodder Enterprise) in 1972 to support *negdels* and farms in Tuv, Dorno-Govi and Hentii provinces and their herders on *otor*. The enterprise administration (RPAA) had approximately 300 employees excluding the enterprise herders, which numbered around nine at the beginning. *Aj ahui* had around 500 workers, much smaller than the *negdel's* 1000 workers (Humphrey, 1978). By 1975, 270–280 households were based at the HBU RPA enterprise center.[55] At some point the enterprise population reached 2800 growing larger than the *soum* population[56] and the HBU RPA center became a *horoo*,[57] an urban administrative unit.[58] Different

94   *Mobile pastoralism and the collectivization period*

state-based actors were involved in decision making regarding the use of PRA. Similar to a *negdel*, the HBU RPAA and the *Horoo* were governed by the same official, who was in charge of production, finances and property issues. The HBU *Horoo* secretary represented the local government and was in charge of overseeing population demography and statistics. "The *Horoo* had independent decision making power regarding who was in charge."[59] The ministry also established a committee called the Interprovincial RPA Committee (*Aimag dundiin otriin zuvlul*, hereafter called "the Committee") under its jurisdiction. The committee was run by the vice minister and the secretary of the HBU RPAA. Other members included the governors of any visiting *aimags* and *soums*. Unlike *negdels*, its production was state property. The state fully provided technical and financial support, funding and loans to the HBU RPA.

Although it was supposed to be a business entity financing itself from sales of forage to fund the *otor* service, its financial management failed. Initially, by the 1960s, the *aj ahui* cultivated 1300–1306 ha of land with wheat and oats as livestock fodder near the *horoo* center. This land proved unsuitable for cultivation as it lacked an effective irrigation system and the earth was rocky. The RPA abandoned cultivation for a while. Then, the state funded millions of *tugrugs*[60] for the irrigation system for the establishment of the dairy farm. The *aj ahui* planted small amounts of root vegetables along with silage (*uhriin darsh*) as winter food[61] for the cattle. The *aj ahui* also had six haymaking *brigades* with 120 tractors and 40 trucks. It harvested 20,000 tons of grass annually from the HBU Mountain[62] or remote parts of the eastern *aimags* such as the Suhbaatar and Hentii, where no one stayed in the winter for grazing.[63] It sold the hay to *negdels* from DornoGovi, Dundgovi and UmnuGovi *aimags*. Its history well-reflected what Templer et al. (1993) described for the state emergency fodder fund. The original purpose was to provide emergency fodder, but it eventually became the regular supplier of cheap fodder and resources to *negdels* (Templer et al., 1993). It also experienced "high cost, poor quality of the supplements it provided, high levels of wastage, disincentive effects to local feed supplement production, and the market distortions it produced" (Templer et al., 1993, p. 111). It lost more than it gained, as there was no payment imposed for hosting *otor*. A former official stated "many livestock [were] here for grazing and providing the *suuri* with all sorts of services including hospital, vets, schools, wells and hay bales reserved for them. It used to be a big burden and there was no benefit for us."[64] Thus, the RPA was dependent on the loans from the state to provide its services.

Labor

The ministry supplied the labor component of the RPA production. It mobilized migrants from all over Mongolia to work with the newly acquired farm machinery and at an administration center with a school, hospital and kindergarten built for the employees of the enterprise. The state tightly controlled the inter-provincial migration to avoid unemployment and population

Mobile pastoralism and the collectivization period   95

concentration. For instance, someone migrated only when the hosting jurisdictional government provided an official letter, indicating that the local government had the employment capacity to accept this individual as a resident.[65]

Livestock

The HBU *horoo* managed the following livestock production. Each employee household was allowed to own only 16 private livestock (almost half the amount allowed in the *negdel*), because most of the households comprised non-herding employees and a salary. The RPA also had 10,000–14,000 head of livestock belonging to the *aj ahui*. In 1985, the RPA also established a dairy farm with 400 specially bred cows to provide milk and dairy products to settled areas like "Baganuur" and "Bor-Undur." The enterprise employed around 100 herders and about 20 *suuri*.[66] By 1990, the *horoo* owned 26 sheep herding *suuri* and 10 small cow *suuri*.[67] Each *suuri* had around 500 sheep and goats. These herders would volunteer to work for the *horoo*, and would receive a 50 percent discount on livestock. This included one horse for riding, one pregnant cow and five two-year-old female sheep.[68]

Pastureland and its tenure

The *aj ahui* pursued the following land tenure. First, the *horoo* managed small residential areas as well as seasonal pasture of the HBU RPA around the HBU Mountain. Similar to *negdels*, it assigned administrative responsibilities, rather than imposing exclusive property rights to manage pastureland. It allocated its herders all the four-season pastures between HBU Mountain and the Herlen River. Then, it assigned *brigades* to define specific locations for establishing winter and spring campsites, as there were no local herders to suggest camp and shelter locations. The RPAA decreed that:

> When defining locations for winter and spring campsites, consider areas with abundant pasture to graze livestock in winter and spring, which are well protected from cold winters and storms, and which is adequate for livestock in winter and spring.[69]

Thus, the campsite selection was based on *ulamjlalt* herding strategies, but with the addition of more modern management practices. The *horoo* was responsible for the quality of construction of livestock shelters. Based on consultation with its herders, the *horoo* finalized decisions on assigning certain individuals to a *suuri* for herding tasks such as livestock delivery.[70] As in the *negdels*, the *horoo* also allocated the dairy farm a separate grazing territory with specific boundaries[71] and kept out[72] all other state and private livestock to protect the special breed dairy cows from livestock diseases. In emergency situations, where cows were suspected of having an infectious disease, the *horoo* would organize quarantine zones and restrict mobility of others grazing

96 *Mobile pastoralism and the collectivization period*

their livestock around the area, and quarantined the *suuri* within a certain pasture. It allocated only particular wells for use, so as to not mix with other *suuri*,[73] thus creating a very complex care system. Although *horoo* herders resided in the HBU RPA throughout all four seasons, they stayed outside of the HBU Mountain. The mountain pasture was specifically reserved for visiting *otor* herders.

Second, the *aj ahui* managed RPA, covering the HBU Mountain. The state's financial support for the development of the RPA contributed to the effectiveness of the institution in providing services to gain access to the RPA. Using many old *buuts* made of dung and rock walls in the mountain, the *aj ahui* then built 178 large solid wooden shelters with canopies with capacity for 500–1000 head of livestock and maintained its structure and hygiene (Figure 4.4). It created around 22 deep engineered wells and established mechanic brigades to maintain these wells. During the spring to autumn off-season, a guard was installed at the entrance to each mountain valley to protect these livestock shelters and wells. It also delivered tanks full of water and firewood on tractors to remote valleys, which lacked these resources. The *aj ahui* also provided *otor* services including veterinary services to maintain livestock hygiene in the HBU RPA.

Then, at an annual meeting the Committee made decisions with regard to organizing *otor* in the HBU RPA. Prior to the meeting, the Committee members would tour around the HBU RPA, defining pasture conditions and capacity for hosting *otor*. This definition was based on: (a) the number of livestock with regard to the number of *buuts;* and (b) the type of livestock to graze. Each *suuri* herded 500 head of livestock with regard to capacity of the *buuts* and its pasture in certain terrain. Then, each collective head presented their number of *suuri* herders that should come on *otor*. Calculating these two factors, the committee would decide the number of *suuri* and the livestock from each *negdel* that the HBU *aj ahui* would host on *otor*. Visiting *negdels* organized the mobility of their herders. They would leave their herders behind with camel caravans for them to herd the livestock in and out of the HBU RPA. They would also assign extra herders to assist them. Simultaneously, they would send trucks to move herders' *gers* and other household goods in and out of the HBU RPA. During heavy snow, the *aj ahui* would clear roads and make trails for the herders to follow. In this way, mobility could be carried out within one day without affecting the *horoo* seasonal pasture and campsites. *Otor* herders would enter the RPA following the instructions of the Committee. *Negdels* would vaccinate all their livestock prior to *otor* mobilization. The *aj ahui* vet would check the herders' livestock inspection records for infectious disease at the river bridges, en route to the RPA. The *aj ahui* hosted on average 100–200 *suuri* with 400,000–500,000 head of livestock annually. The *aj ahui* would be in charge of enforcing and monitoring the Committee rules of using pasture for all the *suuri*. The enterprise[74] secretary would be in charge of implementation.

(a)

(b)

Figure 4.4 A *buuts* with rock wall, outskirt of the HBU Mountain (a). A winter *buuts* with an old wooden shelter in the mountain (b), 2010.

The *aj ahui* organized a temporary tenure system for visiting *otor* herders. The HBU RPA mainly provided grazing for sheep and goats, not for horses. Horses were sent to the steppe area or elsewhere for winter *otor* which was well protected, particularly for horses from neighboring *bags*. The *aj ahui* organized *otor* between November and the *Tsagaan Sar* holiday in February, from the 10th to

98 *Mobile pastoralism and the collectivization period*

the 20th.[75] After this period, it would be too hot for adult livestock to stay on the mountain due to increased temperatures nearing spring. The mountain valleys also cannot avoid the spring storms and livestock was often driven off by these storms. Especially young animals were vulnerable to these storms, often acquiring diarrhea, and increasing mortality. After this period, herders usually returned to their spring area to assist with livestock delivery, which usually occurred in early spring. Thus, the timeline for *otor* was based on *ulamjlalt* strategies of pursuing *otor* in the HBU Mountain. Then, the *aj ahui* allocated a single valley for all *otor* herders from the same *negdel* and *aimag*, deep in the mountain away from the local HBU RPA seasonal pastures. For instance, to accommodate herders from neighboring *bags* and their *ulamjlalt* use patterns on the mountain, the Committee mainly sent Dundgovi *aimag* into the Delgerhundii valley in Zuun Bayanbulag and Govisumer *aimag* into the Burgaltai valley, and Bayandelger *soum* from Tuv *aimag* to the Huhtii valley. The HBU *Horoo* would allocate certain staff from each *aimag* to be in charge of their *otor* herders from their provincial *soums* (Table 4.2). The *aj ahui* also collaborated with a management unit called *otriin shtab*,[76] a temporary *otor* headquarters (TOH) sent by each *aimag* to organize herders and enforce the RPAA rules and norms. Each TOH established its own *ger* base in the valley allocated to them. It would be composed of a vet, a doctor and a livestock husbandry officer, who were from the same *aimag* and led by one of them. TOH corresponded with its herders regarding *otor* issues and communicated this to the *aimag* via radio-communication for further instructions to avoid disputes among herders staying in the same valley. TOH also allocated campsites based on herders' suggestions with regard to the number and type of livestock of each *suuri*. It would divide the valley into five parts to accommodate the herders from different *negdels*. Occasionally, *otor* households could stay close to local households since the boundaries between valleys were quite imprecise. Each *aimag* or *negdel* would camp in the same valley year after year creating customary use to preserve the valley for ready-use next time.

Overall, the collectivization in Mongolia was completed with an extremely top-down and domineering approach for developing a socialist system. It involved a massive amount of Soviet aid (Kaser, 1982, pp. 14–16; McMillan, 1969) which made it possible to pursue all the socio-economic and political engineering experiments and reforms through the following mechanisms: political and ideological propaganda, organized eradication of diverse political opinions and purges, social and geo-political research with an analysis framed by a simplistic version of Marxian ideology as it was in Russia (Payne, 1964; Scott, 1998) and technical support and human expertise. However, Mongolians adjusted these to their socio-economic needs given their geo-political status (Lattimore, 1962). Unlike other former mobile pastoral societies under the Soviet Republic and other socialist countries satellite to Russia, the Mongolian government retained the historical framework of pre-collective pastoralism: the fundamentals of dual control over the integrated management of pastoral production components until the end of the twentieth century due

Table 4.2 1983–1984 schedule assigned for officials from provinces on *otor* in HBU RPA approved by Party Committee, HBU *Horoo*

Aimag	Responsible individual	Soum	Responsible individual
Tuv	Seterhaan	Sergelen	Seterhaan
		Bayan	Mamerbek
		Bayandelger	Baranchuluun
		Bayanjargalan (case study area)	Purevjav
		Bayantsagaan	Suhbaatar
Dundgovi	Dorjgotov, T	Tsagaandelger	Narangerel
		Deren	Battulga
Dornogovi	Jamyanhorloo	Airag	Jamyanhorloo
The administration of the Ministry of Defence	Hasbazar	National Army	Hasbazar
Hentii	Tserenjav, L	Delgerhaan (case study area)	Saindemberel
		Bayanmunh	Baljir
		Darhan	Tserenjav
		Jargalthaan	Tsogtoo
		Tsenhermandal	Lhagvadash

Sources: XN81, DNo, XHNo48, HBU *Horoo*, MFA, Hentii *aimag* Archive, February 14, 1983.

100 *Mobile pastoralism and the collectivization period*

to the uniqueness of Mongolian Pastoralism in its geo-political and geographical position. The next chapter discusses Mongolia's transition to a market economy and its management of pastoral production under the environment of diverse socio-political and economic interests, whilst struggling to engineer its socio-economic institutions to adjust to a market economy and cope with changing climate conditions in the absence of massive and organized political and socio-economic aid and support.

Notes

1 Author's translation from Mongolian language, Article 1.3, Constitution of Mongolia, 1924.
2 Article 1.3.1, Constitution of Mongolia, 1924.
3 These *Hurals* were initially established in 1914 at the monarch's state/religious government for consulting state matter based on the example of DUM at the Tsarist Russian government. These were appointed from the hereditary noble line rather than public election (Puntsagnorov, 1955, p. 108).
4 Article 2.5.10, Constitution of Mongolia, 1924.
5 Article 3.30–32, Constitution of Mongolia, 1924.
6 Article 3.30, Constitution of Mongolia, 1924. See detailed change in the administrative structure in Munkh-ochir (2012).
7 Domestic marketing of these products were not popular as "it was hard for nomads to sell a surplus product (when they had one) within their own society with its undiversified economy" (Khazanov, 1994, p. 202).
8 See Puntsagnorov, 1955, pp. 114–122.
9 The Russian financial (loans) and technical support to Mongolia pre-dated back to Tsarist Russia when the Mongolian government sought to gain its independence from the Manchu Dynasty (Dilavhutagt, 1991, p. 14). Such supports came with many strings attached (complete rights to trade and exploit natural resources), which were more favorable for Russians than Mongolians (Puntsagnorov, 1955, p. 56).
10 A Russian word for a cooperative of workers or producers. In Arkhangai *aimag*, the number of households in these units varies between nine and 80 mainly poor/average households in 1929 (Regsuren and Baljinnyam, 1973).
11 7 sheep = 1 big livestock, 1 camel = 2 big livestock (Dilavhutagt, 1991, p. 49).
12 Many herders rejected the idea of collectivization as the economy was heavily based on private pastoral production at the household level. Commoners, both wealthy and poor, followed the nobles or the heads of monasteries. Many slaughtered their livestock or left the country with their livestock, moving to Inner Mongolia to avoid confiscation (Fernandez-Gimenez, 1999; Lattimore, 1941).
13 Chapter 2, Article 10, Constitution of Mongolia, 1940 (in Uigar Mongol script).
14 Chapter 1, Article 5, Constitution of Mongolia, 1940 (in Uigar Mongol script). Also, Chapter 2, Article 9–10, Constitution of Mongolia, 1960 (in Cyrillic Mongolian script) added the "Republic's property," which has two forms: the property/asset of the "Republic/public" and the rural production "collectives/cooperatives" including other forms of cooperatives.
15 Chapter 2, Article 12 and Chapter 6, Article 37, Constitution of Mongolia, 1940. Also, Chapter 1, Article 3, Constitution of Mongolia, 1960.
16 Chapter 1, Article 8, Constitution of Mongolia, 1940. Also, Chapter 2, Article 12, Constitution of Mongolia, 1960.
17 The Russian government sent its veterinary experts as early as 1914 as its traders were interested in exporting from Mongolia cheap livestock products (Puntsagnorov, 1955, p. 90).

Mobile pastoralism and the collectivization period   101

18 In 1920s, *hoshuus* witnessed difficulties in state territorial administration due to the increasing number of *soums*, *bags* and *aravts* resulted from the changes in the socio-political order in Arkhangai. The *aimag* government even took some measures including the abolishment of all the *bags* in 1926 (Regsuren and Baljinnyam, 1973 p. 118).
19 Chapter 2, Article 12, Constitution of Mongolia, 1940.
20 For instance, 3rd *bag* was separated to join into 2nd and 4th *bags*. 7th *bag* was united with 1st *bag* according to the BNMAU People's Assembly, Decree 9, August 1, 1956, No 104, Ulaanbaatar. By, 1930s, Delgerkhaan *soum* in Khentii *aimag* had total six *bags* (see Simukov, 1934).
21 BNMAU People's Assembly (AUH), Decree 13, July 27, 1974, No 204, Ulaanbaatar.
22 Great Assembly (*Ikh Hural*), Decree 20, August 21, 1992, No 24, Ulaanbaatar.
23 Due to an unclear border line on different maps, it is not exactly clear which *hoshuu* and *aimags* these border territories of Bayan-Erkhtii Mountain and Nyalga hills belonged. The author followed the data from the research participants, who camped around these areas and claimed that they belonged to Setsen Han *aimag*. These areas then belonged to the Tuv *aimag* in 1931 when the border was drawn by Herlen River between Tuv and Hentii *Aimag* (GIMAS, 2009). Another source indicated that Bayan-Erhtii Mountain and Nyalga *soums* were already in Bogd Han *hoshuu*, Bogd Han *aimag* between 1923 and 1930 (Munkh-ochir and Azzaya, 2014, p. 171).
24 By 1930s, Nyalga *soum* in Tuv *aimag* had a total of nine *bags* (Simukov, 1934).
25 Movement patterns are based on participants' approximate data.
26 Interview 29, (Undargaa 2013).
27 *Bag* numbers are roughly based on participants. Simukov (1934) listed as nine *bags* of HBU and six in DD.
28 A Russian word for *brigade*.
29 Chapter 5, Article 46, Constitution of Mongolia, 1960. "The *bag* is not formally a territorial and budget entity" (Mearns, 1996, p. 149).
30 The state considered animal losses from epizootic disease, natural calamities like *dzud* and hail storms beyond herders' responsibility (Templer et al., 1993).
31 Accidents like falling off cliffs, losses due to rivers or wolves (Templer et al., 1993).
32 *Soum* was responsible for administering public services, receiving funds from the state and dealing with social and political matters such as population census and military service and represented the state and provided these services to the *negdel*, which was responsible for pastoral production.
33 Chapter 10, Article 84, Constitution of Mongolia, 1940.
34 For instance, men usually herded more physically challenging animals like horses, whereas women took care of baby lambs or milking cows (Humphrey, 1978). Similarly, in the DD *bag* in the HBU case, young and middle aged men mostly herded horses as this involved intense physical effort. Eventually, they herded sheep when they got older (Interview 29, Undargaa, 2013).
35 Interviews 29 and 33 (Undargaa, 2013).
36 Interview 54 (Undargaa, 2013).
37 Later this phrase was used in a poem "Herder" by the poet Chimiddorj.
38 Interview 26 (Undargaa, 2013).
39 Interview 33 (Undargaa, 2013).
40 Interview 37 (Undargaa, 2013).
41 Interview 45 (Undargaa, 2013).
42 Interview 37 (Undargaa, 2013).
43 Interview 45 (Undargaa, 2013).
44 In summer and autumn *otor*, a herder rotates a lot for specific vegetations and mineral, but this case he selects good pasture for a certain period and herds his livestock in a stable manner, so the livestock graze well and fatten. Then he moves to another patch of grass.

102 *Mobile pastoralism and the collectivization period*

45 Interview 29 (Undargaa, 2013).

46 Interview 45 (Undargaa, 2013).

47 Disputes between herders of one *brigade* would be settled by the *brigade Hural*, between those of a *soum*, at the *aimag Hural*.

48 Interview 16 (Undargaa, 2013).

48 September 1, 1962 with Decree No. 470 of the Minister's Committee of People's Republic of Mongolia. In 1965, this was expanded from HBU Station to HBU Reserve Pasture Area.

50 Agrarian *aj ahui* had much larger jurisdictional territory for agricultural activities than the collectives (see Humphrey, 1978).

51 This was a metaphor. In fact, the *buuts* were around 700–800 and HBU RPA was easily able to host 300–400 households on *otor* at a time.

52 Interview 29 (Undargaa, 2013).

53 See McMillan, 1969.

54 This also functioned as the State Emergency Fodder Fund (Templer et al., 1993).

55 Interview 4 (Undargaa, 2013).

56 Interview 21 (Undargaa, 2013).

57 In accordance with Decree 13, No. 204, July 27, 1974, approved by "*Ardiin Ih Hurliin Terguulegchdiin Huraldaan,*" People's Great Gathering Representative Meeting of the People's Republic of Mongolia at the national level.

58 Equivalent to a *bag*.

59 Interview 24 (Undargaa, 2013).

60 Currency of Mongolia; it was strong in the collective period.

61 The plant is harvested when it is very green and then pickled for feeding cattle in winter.

62 The HBU Mountain was rich in grass as tall as 40–50 cm. According to the local people, "when you lie down to shoot a marmot, you cannot see the marmot" (Interview 4, Undargaa, 2013).

63 Specifically, HBU Mt, Huree Mt, Gutliin Mt and east Henui Mt, One Thousand Sheep Mt in Batshireet and Bayanadarga Hentii *aimag*.

64 Interview 11 (Undargaa, 2013).

65 Interview 11 (Undargaa, 2013).

66 Decree by Ardiin Deputatuudiin *Hural*, June 23, 1976XN81, DNo, XHNo114, HBU *Horoo*, Hentii *aimag* Archive.

67 XN81, DNo, XHNo113, HBU *Horoo* Emergency Meeting Minute, December 11, 1990, HBU *Horoo*, MFA, Hentii *aimag* Archive.

68 Decree of 1989, by HBU *Otor* and forage enterprise (HBU OTFE) secretary, XN104, DNo1, XHNo313, HBU OFE, MFA, Hentii *aimag* Archive. At this decree, the enterprise allocated one horse for riding, one pregnant cow and five two-year-old female sheep to each voluntary herder.

69 Decree by Ardiin Deputatuudiin *Hural*, April 3, 1976, XN81, DNo, XHNo6, HBU *Horoo*, MFA, Hentii *aimag* archive.

70 Meeting minutes on February 26, 1985, XN 104, DNo1, XHNo38, HBUOFE, Hentii *aimag* Archive, National Archive.

71 Decree by Ardiin Deputatuudiin *Hural*, August 6, 1985, CP N81, DNo, XHNo55, HBU *Horoo*, MFA, Hentii *aimag* Archive.

72 Decree by Ardiin Deputatuudiin *Hural*, September 9, 1974, XN81, DNo, XHNo1, HBU *Horoo*, MFA, Hentii *aimag* Archive.

73 Decree by Ardiin Deputatuudiin *Hural*, September, 17, 1976, XN81, DNo, XHNo, HBU *Horoo*, MFA, Hentii *aimag* Archive.

74 Party secretary would be on top of every executive (Kaser, 1982, p. 14).

75 According to locals, this was related to weather changes and because spring comes earlier in the collective period. Nowadays, spring usually comes in March or April.

76 A Russian word for headquarter.

Mobile pastoralism and the collectivization period 103

References

Amár, A (1989) *Mongoliin tovch tuuh*, Ulsiin Hevleliin Gazar, Ulaanbaatar.

Barfield, Th (2011) "Nomadic pastoralism in Mongolia and beyond" in P L W Sabloff (ed.) *Mapping Mongolia: Situating Mongolia in the World from Geologic Time to the Present*, University of Pennsylvania Museum of Archeology and Anthropology, Philadelphia, 273.

Bradsher, Henry S (1972) "The sovietization of Mongolia," *Foreign Affairs* 50:3, 545–553.

Bruun, Ole (2006) *Precious Steppe*, Lexington Books, Oxford.

Dilavhutagt, J (1991) *Ar Mongoliin uls turiin durtgal*, Soyombo Hevleliin Gazar, Ulaanbaatar.

Endicott, E (2012) *A History of Land Use in Mongolia*, Palgrave Macmillan, New York.

Fernandez-Gimenez, M E (1999) "Sustaining the steppes: a geographical history of pastoral land use in Mongolia," *The Geographical Review* 89:3, 315–336.

Fernandez-Gimenez, Maria E (2000) "The role of Mongolian nomadic pastoralists' ecological knowledge in rangeland management," *Ecological Applications* 10:5, 1318–1326.

GIMAS (2009) "Mongolian National Atlas," Geography Institute of Mongolian Academy of Science, II Press, Ulaanbaatar.

Heaton, W R (1979) "Mongolia 1978: continuing the transition," *Asian Survey* 19:1, 58–64.

Holzman, F D (1956) "Equity of the livestock tax of Outer Mongolia," *American Slavic and East European Review* 15:4, 506–510.

Holzman, F D (1957) "The tax system of Outer Mongolia, 1911–55: a brief history," *The Journal of Asian Studies* 16:2, 221–236.

Humphrey, C and Sneath, D (1999) *The End of Nomadism?*, Duke University Press, Durham, NC.

Humphrey, Caroline (1978) "Pastoral nomadism in Mongolia: the role of herdsmen's cooperatives in the national economy," *Development and Change* 9, 133–160.

Kaser, M (1982) "The industrial revolution in Mongolia," *World Today* 38:1, 12–17.

Khazanov, A M (1994) *Nomads and the Outside World, second edition*, University of Wisconsin Press, Madison.

Khazanov, A M (1998) "Pastoralists in the contemporary world: the problems of survival," in J Ginat and A M Khazanov (eds.) *Changing Nomads in a Changing World*, Sussex Academic Press, Brighton, 7–23.

Lattimore, O (1941) *Mongol Journey*, Doubleday, Doran and Co, New York.

Lattimore, O (1962) *Nomads and Commissars: Mongolia Revisited*, Oxford University Press, New York.

McMillan, J (1969) "Mongolia: the economy in 1968," *Asian Survey* 9:1, 23–28.

Mearns, R (1996) "Community, collective action and common grazing: the case of post-socialist Mongolia," *The Journal of Development Studies* 32, 297–339.

Mearns, R (2004) "Decentralisation, rural livelihoods and pasture-land management in post socialist Mongolia," *European Journal of Development Research* 16:1, 133–152.

MNE (1996) *Biodiversity Conservation Action Plan for Mongolia*, GEF/UNDP/MNE, Ulaanbaatar.

Munkh-ochir, D (2012) *Mongol Ulsiin aimag, hoshuu, sumiin lavlah*, Ulaanbaatar.

Munkh-ochir, D and Azzaya, D (2014) *Mongol ulsiin aimag, hoshuu, soumiin tovchoon*, Ulaanbaatar.

Namjig, N (2000) *Tuulsan Amidral mini*, "Shuvuun Saaral," Military Press, Ulaanbaatar.

104   *Mobile pastoralism and the collectivization period*

Natsagdorj, Sh (1972) *Soum, khamjlaga, shavi, ard*, Academy of Science Publishing, Ulaanbaatar.

Payne, R (1964) *Lenin*, Simon & Schuster, New York.

Puntsagnorov, Ts (1955) *Mongoliin avtonomit uyeiin tuukh*, BNMAU Shinjleh Uhaanii Hureelengiin Tuuhiin Sector, Ulaanbaatar.

Regsuren, D and Baljinnyam, A (1973) *BNMAU: Arkhangai Aimagiin Tuuh*, ADKh Executive Administration, The Party Committee of Arkhangai Aimag, Tsetserleg.

Rosenberg, Daniel (1981) "The collectivization of Mongolia's pastoral production," *Commission on Nomadic Peoples* 9, 23–39.

Sambuu, J (1945) *Mal aj ahui deer ba yaj ajillah tuhai ardad uguh sanuulga surgaal* (in Uigar Mongol script), Mal Aj Ahuin Yam, Ulaanbaatar.

Scott, J C (1998) *Seeing Like a State: How Certain Schemes to Improve the Human Condition Have Failed*, Yale University Press, New Haven, London.

Shayakhmetov, Mukhamet (2007) *The Silent Steppe: The Memoir of a Kazakh Nomad under Stalin*, The Rookery Press, New York.

Shirendev, B and Natsagdorj, Sh (1966) *BNMAUyn tuuh, terguun boti*, Ulsiin Hevleh Uildver, Ulaanbaatar.

Simukov, A D (1929) "O kochyevkakh i pastbishakh Mongolii" in Sanjaasurengiin Bayaraa, Ichinkhorloogiin Lkhagvasuren and Yuki Konagaya (eds.) *Kratkaya geographiya Mongolskoi Narodnoi Respubliki: Chast II Nasyelyeniye, ego hozaistva, i gosudarstvennoye ustroistvo strany*, Gosudarstvyennyi muzei etnologii, Osaka, 358–376.

Simukov, A D (1931) "Zamyetki o polojyenii na peripherii MNR za 1931 god" in Yuki Konagaya, Sanjaasurengiin Bayaraa and Ichinkhorloogiin Lkhagvasuren (eds.) *Trudy o Mongolii i dlya Mongolii Tom (3) Chast (2)*, Gosudarstvyennyi muzei etnologii, Osaka, 127–143.

Simukov, A D (1933a) "Bazy Sovmonbunera1) v svyazi s administrativnym deleniyem MNR i sushyestvuyushimi administrativno-economicheskimi tsentrami" in Yuki Konagaya, Sanjaasurengiin Bayaraa and Ichinkhorloogiin Lkhagvasuren (eds.) *Trudy o Mongolii i dlya Mongolii Tom (3) Chast (2)*, Gosudarstvyennyi muzei etnologii, Osaka, 61–64.

Simukov, A D (1933b) "Hotony" in Yuki Konagaya, Sanjaasurengiin Bayaraa and Ichinkhorloogiin Lkhagvasuren (eds.) *Kratkaya geographiya Mongolskoi Narodnoi Respubliki: Chast II Nasyelyeniye, ego hozaistva, i gosudarstvennoye ustroistvo strany, Tom II*, Gosudarstvyennyi muzei etnologii, Osaka, 493–508.

Simukov, A D (1934) "Kratkaya geographiya Mongolskoi Narodnoi Respubliki: Chast II Nasyelyeniye, ego hozaistva, i gosudarstvennoye ustroistvo strany" in Yuki Konagaya, Sanjaasurengiin Bayaraa and Ichinkhorloogiin Lkhagvasuren (eds.) *Trudy o Mongolii i dlya Mongolii Tom I*, Gosudarstvyennyi muzei etnologii, Osaka, 709–773.

Simukov, A D (1936) "Selskohozaistvennoye i economicheskoye raionirovaniye MNR (thesis)" in Yuki Konagaya, Sanjaasurengiin Bayaraa and Ichinkhorloogiin Lkhagvasuren (eds.) *Trudy o Mongolii i dlya Mongolii Tom (3) Chast (2)*, Gosudarstvyennyi muzei etnologii, Osaka, 65–72.

Simukov, A D and Stulov, E A (1930) " 'K voprosu o raionirovanii Mongolskoi Narodnoi Respubliki' published originally in journal *Hozaistvo Mongolii* 2, (20)" in Yuki Konagaya, Sanjaasurengiin Bayaraa and Ichinkhorloogiin Lkhagvasuren (eds.) *Trudy o Mongolii i dlya Mongolii Tom (3) Chast (2)*, Gosudarstvyennyi muzei etnologii, Osaka, 33–60.

Sneath, D (2003) "Land use, the environment and development in post-socialist Mongolia," *Oxford Development Studies* 31:4, 441–457.

Mobile pastoralism and the collectivization period 105

Sneath, D (2004) "Property regimes and sociotechnical systems: rights over land in Mongolia's 'Age of the Market'" in K Verdery and C Humphrey (eds.) *Property in Question: Value Transformation in the Global Economy*, Berg, Oxford, New York, 161–182.

Sturgeon, J C and Sikor, T (2004) "Post-socialist property in Asia and Europe: variations on 'fuzziness'," *Conservation & Society* 2:1, 2–17.

Sukhbaatar, G and Jamsran, L (1968) *BNMAU tuuhiin deej bichig I*, Sukhbaatar Printing Press, Ulaanbaatar.

Templer, G, Swift, J and Payne, P (1993) "The changing significance of risk in the Mongolian pastoral economy," *Nomadic Peoples* 33, 105–122.

Undargaa, S (2013) "Property 'owners' without rights? Exploring property relations and access in the Herlen Bayan-Ulaan Reserve Pasture Area of Mongolia," Crawford School of Public Policy, Australian National University, Canberra.

Upton, C (2005) "Institutions in a pastoral society: processes of formation and transformation in post-socialist Mongolia," *Comparative Studies of South Asia, Africa and the Middle East* 25:3, 584–599.

Upton, C (2009) "'Custom' and contestation: land reform in post-socialist Mongolia," *World Development* 37:8, 1400–1410.

Verdery, K (2004) "The property regime of socialism," *Conservation & Society* 2:1, 190–198.

Vreeland, H H (1954) "Mongol community and kinship structure," Walter Hines Page School of International Relations, The Johns Hopkins University, New Haven.

5 Pastoral production and pastureland management during transition to a market economy

In 1991, Mongolia witnessed a major shift in its socio-economic and political system that would result in an utterly different agricultural and environmental policy from previous systems. Following the collapse of the Soviet Union, and the loss of its political alliance and economic support, Mongolia joined other former satellite countries in reforming its political and economic system from an inefficient and moribund centrally planned socialist system to a free market democratic system (Mearns, 2004a; Sneath, 2006). A newly formed government led by the former Mongolian People's Revolutionary Party (MPRP) (Korsun and Murrel, 1995), introduced a structural adjustment program (SAP) following the advice of the IMF and the World Bank (Sneath, 2006). The aim of the program was to "emancipate" the economy from its political structure, and allow it to assume its latent "natural form," composed of private property and the market (Sneath, 2006, p. 149). One of the activities of the SAP along with other fiscal reforms was the privatization of public assets (Sneath, 2006). The objectives of privatization were mainly to promote private property ownership, a move that the World Bank saw as important for joining a free-market economy and to create an effective distribution system through "compensation, entitlement and equity in the transfer of property" (Korsun and Murrel, 1995, p. 474). According to this scenario, SAP would enable Mongolia to interact with the global market economy with hope for potential economic growth. This chapter critically discusses (a) the impacts of privatization on the management of production and pastureland, (b) popular policy discourse of open access (absence of property rights), which prevailed in the rangeland, and (c) a case study analysis, which reveals the underlying problems on the issue of rangeland management.

Privatization and its impact on pastoral production management

In 1991, the Mongolian government pursued privatization of the pastoral production sector, dismantling the management of the three components of pastoral production. The collective institutions (*negdel*) and state-owned enterprises (*sangiin aj ahui*) privatized their livestock assets along with livestock

Transition to a market economy 107

shelters, storage buildings and machinery by allocating free privatization shares to their employees, with the exception of pastureland and water (Fernandez-Gimenez, 2001; Fratkin, 1997; Sneath, 2003). They sold these assets to someone who possessed a certain value in shares of privatized assets through the stock exchange system[1] (Korsun and Murrel, 1995). In 1992, the government liberalized the labor market through a constitutional amendment,[2] which allowed all citizens of Mongolia to live and travel wherever they chose within the national territory. Mass unemployment resulted from privatization and triggered countrywide migration and movement without state control over the labor market. Regarding pastureland, the government attempted to adjust the status of existing republic/public governance of natural resources to the market economy. In the 1992 constitution, the state specified the terminology for the ownership of natural resources in the standard of western property regimes. The land and its underground (*hevlii*) resources, water, flora and fauna and other natural resources stays solely under the power/authority or sovereignty (*medel*) of the public (*ard tumen*) and under the state protection in a form of state property (*turiin umch*).[3]

This seems different from seeing Mongolia from the perspectives of popular property regimes such as open access or de jure state property and de facto communal management in the CPR literature.[4] Despite formalizing state property as in an analytically narrow framework of a property regimes approach, the constitutional provisions retained an historical notion of public sovereignty in governance. The decentralization policy encouraged developing states to transfer their power over resources to lower level political-administrative units and the territorial hierarchy, which became accountable for local populations (Ribot et al., 2006). Following this, the Mongolian government formalized co-management of a centralized state government and a local self-governing institution[5] (local assembly) at each level of territorial units. It allowed this local level government to inherit the state's significant legal power in managing communal use of pastureland (Mearns, 2004b). In other words, the historical dual control under the framework of state territorial units continued under the combined formal governance:[6] state territorial units of *bag*, *soum* and *aimag* represents central government and the assemblies (*Hural*) of *bag* residents, and *soum or aimag* residents' representatives[7] represented self-governance (Table 5.1). Yet, this co-management was to regulate only pastoral resources (pasture and water) instead of the whole production system and all its other components, even though the wealth of livestock constitutionally remained under the protection of the state.[8]

The state territorial administration retained the division of *aimag*, *soum* and *bag*.[9] Among these, the *soum* and *bag* governors and their *Hurals* were to regulate their level of pastoral resources. The *bag Hural* continued with the herders' formal role in decision making, though we will discuss its effectiveness as a formal control. *Soums* and their *Hural* were responsible for the resolution of disputes and allocation of campsites and pasture reserves. *Bag* governors, with the

108   *Transition to a market economy*

Table 5.1 Administrative and territorial governance structure after transition

		Constitution
		Ih Hural Parliament
		National government
		Local governance
Central governance		*Self-governance*
(approval & enforcement)		*(formulating proposal & decision making)*
Urban	Rural	Civil Representative *Hural* (Assembly) (CRH)
Niislel (capital city)	*Aimag* (province)	Civil Representative *Hural* (capital/ province)
Duureg (district)	*Soum* (district)	Civil Representative *Hural* (district)
Horoo (micro-district)	*Bag* (micro-district)	Public *Hural* (PM) (micro-district)

Source: Environmental Challenges of Urban Development, The World Bank document, 2004.

support of their *Hural*, are authorized to regulate *bag* herders' use of seasonal pasture, its rehabilitation and the possession of campsites (Fernandez-Gimenez, 2001; Fernandez-Gimenez and Batbuyan, 2004; Sneath, 2003). These were stipulated in the "Law of Mongolia on Administrative and Territorial Units and their Governance," 1993,[10] the "Law of Mongolia on Land," 1994[11] and the "Law of Mongolia on Environmental Protection," 1995[12] for pasture management and improvement. These laws stipulate that the local territorial administrations comply with the *ulamjlalt* or local resource use patterns.[13] To a certain extent, the state continued to enforce *ulamjlalt*[14] pasture use rules and norms for *bag* community access (Spoor, 2009). This formalized *ulamjlalt* rule mainly referred to seasonal movement as occurred in the collective period, because the state was unable to formalize all other informal *ulamjlalt* production and pasture use rules and norms. Also, these territorial units continued to administer the territorial population's socio-political matters such as elections, army recruiting and population census and taxes.[15] Therefore, dismantling the historical system resulted in the absence of any formal institution for integrated management of pastoral production. The components of production were to be managed in a compartmentalized manner by herders (labor), who independently dealt with livestock production in the market system, and the state, which shifted its control only to pastureland resources. Along with the privatization process, these changes in the management of the production components impacted herders' living conditions and their mobility, ultimately re-shaping local practices of pasture management.

Livestock

Open access prevailed in the privatization of state and *negdel* assets. Political power of various interest groups shaped privatization of *negdel* assets, including

Transition to a market economy 109

livestock, in order to secure benefits. Pastoral production was the main economic activity and an important safety net for many people (Griffin, 2003; Mearns, 2004a, 2004b; Sneath, 2006). Between 1989 and 1999, the total agricultural output (the largest sector) increased from 70.1 to 90 percent (Griffin, 2003, p. 61). Privatization of the pastoral sector became a mechanism for rapid economic benefits under the condition of an exhausted economy, in which it was difficult to provide general benefits (Nixson and Walters, 2006). Korsun and Murrel (1995) noted that "responding to political power of the agricultural section, the *Ih Hural*[16] gave the *negdels* control over their own privatization" (p. 477). It allowed each collective to make its own decisions on privatization procedures at their meetings (Korsun and Murrel, 1995). Consequently, the government was not totally responsible for controlling the process of privatization of state and collective assets, but maintained general records of the details of allocations (Nixson and Walters, 2006). Although the Union of Agricultural Cooperatives, representing all *negdels*, issued guidelines for privatization methods to help *negdels* control their own process of privatization, this guideline was ambiguous (Korsun and Murrel, 1995, p. 481). This resulted in the markedly different privatization process among each *negdel*, making it difficult to generalize about the direct impacts of each privatization on social inequity and its environmental outcomes (Fernandez-Gimenez, 2001; Nixson and Walters, 2006). In general, *negdels* distributed their assets based on the principle of total number of years any one put into the *negdel*, prioritizing "those whose property had been collectivized and who were still working on the cooperative" (Korsun and Murrel, 1995, p. 481). Remnants of cooperative assets were to be retained intact in order to sustain infrastructure, organization and trade services, and were bought with larger shares by those who established newly constituted limited companies and *horshoo*[17] (Nixson and Walters, 2006; Potanski, 1993; Sneath, 2006).

This trend allowed us to identify general social and environmental outcomes. Privatizing livestock resulted in a significant decline in herders' mobility (Fernandez-Gimenez and Batbuyan, 2004; Mearns, 2004a; Sneath, 2003). Dismantling the management of production and its components shifted the primary production unit from *suuri* to a re-emerging *hot ail* (Mearns, 2004b, p. 140). The re-emergence of *hot ail* mainly refers to the "individual ownership of livestock" (Bold, 1996, p. 75) by households who voluntarily camp together based on their connection through kinship and friendship (Sneath, 1993). This indicates individual production management. *Hot ail* mobility was reduced in relation to the widening gap between wealthy and poor households, a phenomena which was inherently absent in the former system (Griffin, 2003; Mearns, 2004a). Privatization assets were distributed based on the general criteria of the number of household members, the herders' experience and prior status in the *negdel* period, as well as claims to *negdel* assets by non-members from urban areas (Fernandez-Gimenez, 2001). These criteria were overridden by a process known as "underground" privatization and led to unequal distribution, as a few former officials (local elite) dominated the

110 *Transition to a market economy*

allocation and selection of the best assets (Nixson and Walters, 2006). Those who used to be *soum* or *negdel* officials, and others, who had connections or those with wealth and status who profited from purchases of livestock, acquired some of the remaining collective assets for establishing cooperatives or companies. In other words, they maintained their status in controlling access to some of the best seasonal pasture and livestock shelters (Mearns, 2004b). This pattern of opportunism affected those who were less opportunistic and who had no connections with officials. This affected those households with more than four children, the unemployed, small scale-herders in remote areas, female-headed households, the elderly without family support, handicapped people and orphans (Bruun et al., 1999). They received fewer head of livestock or missed out entirely on their shares under the privatization process.[18] They were less able to maintain viable numbers of livestock,[19] particularly when they sold off the few head of livestock in order to survive under the rapid inflation which characterized the early 1990s (Mearns, 2004a; Namkhainyambuu, 2000). As a result, these households lost their access to key resources, leading to less mobility (Fernandez-Gimenez, 2002). This gap in herders' wealth had implications for their mobility patterns.

Labor

Unemployment and the collapse of state control over the labor market led to massive urban to rural migration. Since livestock was the only capital available for making an independent living, many of the former collective herders and their staff as well as former state employees from settled areas relied on herding as their livelihood option (Sneath, 2006). The number of people relying on livestock herding increased from 135,420 (20 percent of the total working population) in 1989 to 414,433 in 1998, which is 50 percent of the total working population (Sneath, 2003, p. 442). Herders began to rely more on livestock than cash during times of higher inflation (Sneath, 2006, p. 152), following the *ulamjlalt* practice of keeping livestock as "money" (Lattimore, 1941, 1962). Without specific control over regulating the labor aspect of pastoral production, migration eventually resulted in increasing numbers of livestock and concentration in certain pasture areas. The total number of livestock increased from 26 million in 1989 to almost 34 million by 1999 (Mearns, 2004a, p. 112). Although the trend of herders and livestock was increasing, the decline of formal management of pastoral production prevailed, contributing to poverty (Nixson and Walters, 2006).

Pastureland and its tenure

Changes in the management of livestock and labor led to changes in the management of pastureland. The *negdels'* once integrated pastoral sector was atomized and de-mechanized, because of the unavailability of cheap fuel resources from Russia (Sneath, 2006). Provisioning of oil was mainly

Transition to a market economy 111

regulated by the government and was always dependent on national economic conditions. The lack of an oil supply ended the maintenance of the *negdel* infrastructure support for organized mobility, mechanized water to access more pastoral resources, and forage supplies, veterinary services and other public services (Fernandez-Gimenez, 2001; Mearns, 2004a). An open access prevailed particularly in the management of these assets. During the "underground" privatization process, a few former officials seized control over the allocation and selection of the best assets such as trucks and transportation, resulting in the total collapse of the *negdel* infrastructure. Since a *negdel* could not support itself, the *negdel*'s institution of management of pastoral production, its support mechanism and marketing all collapsed. Such a collapse also affected the management of water resources. Although the state retained responsibility over all water resources, no one was specifically assigned to maintain such resources including the engineered wells. This led to individuals looting the main parts of the engineered wells and selling them for cash.[20] Many wells, which had been capable of providing abundant amounts of water and access to expansive pasture, broke down (Fernandez-Gimenez, 2001; Sneath, 2003). Eighty percent of the usable engineered wells and approximately 15,000 usable hand wells became unusable between 1990 and 2000 (Tanaka et al., 2005 cited in Sternberg, 2008). The lack of mechanical support for pastoral production depleted once-available pastoral resources surrounding these wells within their jurisdictional boundary.

Besides these resources, the absence of an integrated formal institution as a legal mechanism for monitoring pastoral production units and their use of pastoral resources led to a decline in the management of pastoral production. The decentralization process failed to improve local pasture management. The process of transferring power was incomplete in terms of delivering legal and fiscal power[21] down to local government levels due to the emergence of contested power among state agencies and the corrupt process of electing local officials (Mearns, 2004b). At the national level, two different ministries were now involved in pastoral production issues, with two different purposes. The Ministry of Food Agriculture (MFA) was formerly responsible for issues relating to agricultural land and pastoral production management. Following the de-coupling of production components, now, the state assigned the responsibility for land-based CPR resources to the Ministry of Nature and Environment (MNE) in order to conform to a more "western notion of environmental management." The ministry acts in accordance with several different environmental protection laws (Mearns, 2004b, p. 142). No separate law was promulgated on pastureland. Since the MFA was responsible for protecting livestock via organizing and preparing for winter and *dzud* emergencies, supplying fodder, and disease control at the national level, the MFA attempted to resurrect its former influence over pastureland management through the unsuccessful drafting of a separate law on pastureland[22] (Mearns, 2004b). At the local level, the *soum* still played a significant role. Since the *soum* no longer exercised influence over production and a larger budget

112 *Transition to a market economy*

administration supported by the state, it manipulated a largely corrupt administrative process to gain benefits from controlling only pastureland, inheriting the authority previously exercised by the *negdel*. Different ministries assigned power to the *soum* to enforce their policies. Mainly former *soum* or *negdel* bureaucrats remained as *soum* or *bag* governors, exploiting their authority over regulating pastureland management (Mearns, 2004b).

The local administration's control over land created room to maneuver since it was ineffective or absent in addressing the use of pastoral resources. Although de jure local *bag* administration regulates *bag* members' use of *bag* pastureland following *ulamjlalt* pasture use rules and norms, they were unable to enforce it because herders independently controlled production (Fernandez-Gimenez, 2001, 2002). Consequently, local administrations allowed herders to make decisions themselves on the use of pastureland (Fernandez-Gimenez, 2002). Individual herding households informally controlled pasture use patterns, rather than utilizing formal control mechanisms of the *bag* and its *Hural*, because it was ineffective. In other words, the local adminsitration de facto returned to herders' micro-management as in the pre-collective period letting them select their own seasonal pasture and campsites as long as the herders were residents of that jurisdiction. Adding to the absence of an integrated control over the production components, ineffective control over herders' land use led to a concentration of herding households and disputed pasture use. Many so-called "new herders" derived from migration and claimed their ancestral or customary grazing areas. They stayed close to local relatives or friends in order to gain access to campsites and pasture. Increasing numbers of herders became concentrated in smaller areas, selecting their grazing areas near larger settlements with better access to market (Fernandez-Gimenez, 2001; Mearns, 2004a). This was to replace the absence of *negdel* support and reduce transaction costs for marketing livestock products and other goods (Griffin, 2003; Sneath, 2006). As access to such places became highly competitive, concentrating on rapidly depleting seasonal pastures near large settlements often led to disputes over pasture use and overgrazing (Griffin, 2003; Mearns, 2004a; Sneath, 2006). Local officials often turned a blind eye to disputes among herders with lower status, less wealth or background, whilst favoring those whose relationships they could benefit from, in terms of maintaining access to better pastoral resources. This was particularly when visiting herders from other jurisdictions needed a substantial connection to local actors to access pastoral resources in the host area (Mearns, 2004b). Sneath (2003) observed insecurity of access rights as herders changed their strategies to maintain access to pastoral resources. They pursued seasonal herding by staying near areas with public services during the summer and withdrew from herding during winter, leaving their livestock with full-time herder relatives in the country. Also, herders overstayed their time on seasonal pastures for fear of losing it to others (Sneath, 2003). Mostly new herders pursued these strategies abandoning the *ulamjlalt* norms that regulated the use of pasture, because they had less ecological awareness, little social

Transition to a market economy 113

support and unequal asset holdings (Fernandez-Gimenez and Batbuyan, 2004; Mearns, 2004a; Nixson and Walters, 2006). These strategies led to reduced mobility and a certain degree of sedentary pastoralism, leading to increasing pressure on the grazing area (Griffin, 2003; Ickowitz, 2003; Sneath, 2006). Herding households' concentration on grazing land often changed depending on climatic conditions, and the availability of water, transport and labor resources. Therefore, the pressure from overgrazing was not necessarily "uniform" on all pastureland (Griffin, 2003, p. 65).

Defining the problem of pastureland management

In contrast to privatized assets, disputed use of pasture and overgrazing was hardly a problem of open access. The increasing numbers of households and livestock depending on fewer pastoral resources reduced the herders' mobility and led to overgrazing (Griffin, 2003; Ickowitz, 2003; Mearns, 2004b). Overgrazing was also a matter of uneven distribution of herding households and livestock populations (Fratkin, 1997). Further, overgrazing has nothing to do with herd size exceeding the "carrying capacity of the land in general, it is a response to specific economic incentives and institutional weakness" (Griffin, 2003, p. 65). Thus, at the heart of the problem was the loss of the pastoral institutions that regulated pastureland use. However, it is questionable to interpret property relations in land in Mongolia from the perspective of a property rights and regimes concept. Some see local pasture use rules and norms as "traditional open-access property rights," which would lead to a "Tragedy of the Commons" under an incentive oriented market system (Ickowitz, 2003, p. 97). Others interpret the problem from the perspective of CPR management theory. As one analyst observed, "while pastureland [in Mongolia] remains under state ownership, it is de facto managed as common property" (Upton, 2005, p. 586). Common property theoretical framework suggests that increasing heterogeneity in wealth, social status and membership within a community "should lead to increasingly different interests among herders and a breakdown in the ability to self-regulate pasture use" (Ostrom, 1990, cited in Fernandez-Gimenez, 2001, p. 53). Those who define Mongolia as "open access" often argue that rising heterogeneity within a herding community has led to a "weakening in the observance of customary norms surrounding pasture use" (Mearns, 2004a, p. 116). As this body of thinking was applied to Mongolia, many scholars were concerned about the problem of open access, which prevailed to pastoral resources due to the failure of formal and informal institutions (Griffin, 2003; Ickowitz, 2003; Mearns, 2004b). As Griffin (2003) noted: "No one in Mongolia owns the vast grassland of the steppe: no one regulates the use of land. Anyone may graze their livestock on this common land and everyone is free to graze as many animals as they wish" (Griffin, 2003, p. 67). Thus, this perspective suggested that property rights should be specified as clearly as possible.

114 *Transition to a market economy*

However, others hold contrary positions to the problems in pastureland management. For instance, Upton maintained:

> An ideal of rights to pasture for all ... may convey the impression of an open-access regime as defined in CPR literature.... However, this is to overlook or misunderstand the complex system of rights, norms, and rules that inform practice on Mongolia's herding commons.
>
> (2005, p. 589)

In a similar vein, some analysts maintained that herders' pasture use patterns at this time remained homogenous, or changed less, given that they adhered to seasonal mobility practices (Addison et al., 2012; Fernandez-Gimenez, 2001; Upton, 2010). Rather than asserting that herders' mobility and flexibility were necessarily obstructed by an emerging heterogeneity, in this view the lack of mobility of resources such as labor, transportation, petrol and livestock obstructed such practices (Fernandez-Gimenez, 2001, p. 63; Sneath, 2003). Thus, absence of support for herders' mobility has led to not necessarily weakening of informal practices, but reduced mobility. Moreover, the problem may rest in the state's direct control of regulating herders' access to pastoral resources. In Mongolia, it is certain that problems emerged in the use of pastoral resources due to the absence of a formal institution that once regulated pastoral resources. This is because the imposed decentralization process failed to replace the local formal pastoral institution with local administration. The state is no longer able to arrange inter and intra-*bag soum* and *aimag* level mobility among the different levels of local territorial administration (Griffin, 2003; Mearns, 2004b). The power of *soums* and *bags* has also been restricted by the enforcement of laws[23] emphasizing *ulamjlalt* rules and norms of pasture use and intended to reduce the incidence of free-riding or trespassing (Fernandez-Gimenez, 2001; Griffin, 2003). Although local administrations replaced former collectives, it appeared ineffective in that by controlling land use only. These laws, particularly the land law, were primarily conservation-oriented, focusing rather on natural resource protection than being production-oriented as it used to be in the collective time (Mearns, 2004b, p. 142). Thus, the legislation did not necessarily equip the local administrations with an adequate mechanisms (nor capacity) for resolving the disputes regarding seasonal use patterns, allocating reserve pasture, or individual and communal pasture (Fernandez-Gimenez and Batbuyan, 2004; Griffin, 2003; Tumenbayar, 2000). Therefore, understanding problems in pastureland management would involve more than simply reallocating property rights to land. The next section discusses the absence of the state in regulating pastoral production in an integrated manner and its impact on some forms of sanctions deriving from herders' informal control in regulating access to pastoral resources in the HBU case.

Privatized management of pastoral production in the HBU case area

The HBU case illustrates the impacts of privatization of the *negdel* and *otriin aj ahui* assets and its implication for environmental outcomes in three *bags* by focusing on how and why: (a) the local administration struggles and failed to regulate herders' access to pastoral resources; and (b) herders in both former *negdel* areas and former HBU *aj ahui* adjusted their access to resources and their mobility. As elsewhere, the process of dismantling the integrated management of pastoral production occurred in a similar fashion among the *negdels* and *otriin aj ahui*.

Livestock

Although private livestock ownership had been a characteristic of non-egalitarian pastoralism, the state privatized former collective or state livestock without concern for distributional justice in all three *bags*. In a top-down privatization process, herders had less control over selection, but accepted what was allocated to them based on the size of their household, *negdel* membership status and type of animal each member herded during the collective period. In terms of *negdels*, "Bayanbadral" (current Delgerhaan *soum*) and "Shine Amidral" (current Bayanjargal *soum*) *negdels* controlled their own privatization process, because they distributed their communalized assets back to their members. Herders had held conflicting ideas about the distribution process based on current *negdel* membership as it was less than fair. First, *negdels* excluded those who communalized their private livestock and then left the *negdel* (Nixson and Walters, 2006). For instance, a former *negdel* member, who became a city dweller later due to the state assignment, stated that "I thought I was supposed to get assets from a collective privatization.... But at the time, the law was privatizing collective assets for current members...."[24] Those who became members of a collective later in the 1960s after completing professional school in Ulaanbaatar received an allocation of shares regardless of their contribution to the starting-up of the *negdel*.[25]

Second, *negdels*' distributed shares, which were hardly worth the livestock herders initially had communalized to their *negdels* even if they remained members until privatization. The distributional justice at the HBU *aj ahii* was even worse due to its institutional difference from *negdels*. First, all *aj ahui* assets belonged to the state, because the state established and managed it with its credit funding. The ministry allocated shares for small privatization, which was worth 3000 MNT, to its employees, because it privatized only three-fourths of its 14,000 livestock.[26] The number of livestock each employee was able to buy with their small share amount was much smaller than for collective members, who received all ten sets of shares. Second, the distribution was based on per household rather than the number of family members. Many employees received unequitable allocation of shares. For instance, a

116 *Transition to a market economy*

family with 7–8 members was allocated ten sheep and one cow or per household was given 10–16 small livestock.[27] Third, the ambiguity in the privatization arrangement was disadvantageous to some *aj ahui* employees. Some were told to claim their shares not from the *aj ahui*, but from their former collectives, where they used to be members. Some sought out an alternative strategy[28] to benefit from privatization. For instance, by personal arrangement, one participant's parents, who were members of other collectives at the same time, included their children, who were *aj ahui* employees, as their family members to claim a few livestock, regardless of the children's work and locality.[29]

Besides the criteria discussed above for distribution of livestock, the distribution of livestock shelters by these two entities followed patterns that were based on different localized contexts of livestock production in the three *bags*. First, the difference in the terrain of the *bags* defined herders' access to shelters. UU herders were able to obtain both winter and spring shelters as these were located on UU hill away from HBU RPA[30] (see Chapter 4). In contrast, herders in HBU and DD *bags* only obtained spring shelters. Their winter campsites were located in the HBU Mountain, in which all the wooden shelters belonged to the state, whereas few DD campsites were made of dung or rock walls.[31] Second, herders received shelters based on their experience and background, particularly the type of livestock they once herded for *negdel* or *aj ahui*. As the difference in terrain shaped the production management of the different *bags*, those who herded horses in the steppe, mostly in UU and DD *bags*, were less able to claim livestock shelters compared to those who herded small livestock which required shelters in the hills. Third, was the difference in the entities themselves. Unlike *negdels*, HBU *aj ahui* employees did not obtain state owned winter shelters. The ministry privatized a few spring shelters for those who used to herd for the *aj ahui*. It reduced the price from 21,000 MNT to 3000 MNT, so, herders were able to buy one with their small amount of shares.[32] These patterns of unequal distribution of livestock and shelters, particularly among *aj ahui* employees, had further implications for pasture management of all three *bags:* herders' selection of their grazing areas, increasing disputed use and overgrazing of the HBU Mountain.

Labor

Since private livestock ownership is fundamental in developing pastoral production in a market economy, dismantling the integrated management of the production components, particularly the labor components, created challenges to land management. Three *bags* also witnessed large inter-migration. The differences in the privatization of *negdel* and *aj ahui*, however, led to a different nature of migration and the growth of the local population. Since the *negdel* had distributed its livestock among all its members, regardless of their herding background, they had more than 100 livestock which were

Transition to a market economy 117

viable[33] to begin herding. Increasing numbers of migrants, who were born there or who had relatives in the area, came from the settled areas to herd in DD and UU *bags*. During the *dzud* of 2000, the number of herders in these *bags* reduced dramatically as many new migrant herders left the area. According to former *negdel* herders in DD and UU *bags*:

> Since the 2000 *dzud*, many households left and moved away. Before the *dzud* there were many people around here ... Perhaps many of them lost their livestock and moved away to the city.[34]
>
> Well, in the 1990s, the numbers of households were many more than at this time. Then, people moved elsewhere for school and other purposes ... When the pasture is not good anymore, people are likely to leave this place.[35]

With no major migration movements since 2000,[36] these *bags* witnessed natural growth in population, which was composed of former *negdel* herders and their offspring. Table 5.2 shows that almost all of the participants from DD and UU *bags* had lived in these *bags* before 1990 or were born in these *bags*.

In contrast, HBU witnessed artificial growth in its population of households and livestock as the majority of participants from HBU *bag* came from elsewhere. First, the collapse of *aj ahui* led to de-urbanization of the HBU *horoo*. Most *aj ahui* employees were unable to pursue herding with the less viable numbers of livestock they received from privatization.[37] As was common elsewhere in Mongolia, they mainly consumed the few head of livestock they had received from the privatization exercise or had sold them to buy food. They also unpacked and sold livestock shelters and storage buildings and other machinery for cash. They returned to where they had come from during the enterprise or joined their relatives elsewhere or in urban areas.[38] The number of households in HBU *bag* fell from 270 to fewer than 100 following privatization.[39] Very few[40] in HBU *bag* built a viable herd size by purchasing stock from others and stayed in herding. These were mainly people who had lived nearby the HBU Mountain at the time of the establishment of the *aj ahui*. Table 5.2 shows that fewer than half of the HBU *bag* participants and their offspring had been living in HBU RPA before the 1990s. Second, following the constitutional freedom, herders employed

Table 5.2 Migration status of herders from each *bag* since 1958

Three bags	Migration trend by %			
	1958–1990	*1991–1994*	*1995–1999*	*2000~*
HBU *bag* (n = 40)	40	18	18	25
DD *bag* (n = 23)	95	0	0	4
UU *bag* (n = 34)	100	0	0	0

118   *Transition to a market economy*

migration as a mechanism to access better pastoral resources and markets, particularly during unstable climatic conditions. Since 1994, this de-urbanization attracted more incoming migration to HBU *bag* due to its proximity to markets and pastoral resources. At the beginning, only a few individual households arrived in HBU *bag* as they had obtained viable numbers of stock for their herds. Later, more migrated from western and southern *aimags* following a national trend, particularly after the 2000 *dzud*.[41] According to a HBU *bag* participant, "There were only a few HBU [*bag*] households; not like these many households from all western *aimags* such as Govi-Altai and Zavhan etc."[42] A former *negdel* herder in DD, who lived nearby the HBU *bag* boundary, shared a similar observation "In HBU [*bag*], not so many of them are local people; perhaps around 15 of them could be from this area. Others are all from outside."[43] As Table 5.2 showed, more than half of the HBU *bag* participants had migrated from elsewhere since 1990. This trend of increasing numbers of herding households and livestock also reduced the availability of ecologically preferable land, in addition to failed infrastructure.

Pastureland and its tenure

The collapse of the *negdel* and *aj ahui* infrastructure contributed to the depletion of resources and the reduction of ecologically preferable land as much as the historical pattern of change in the boundaries of territorial units did. In all three *bags*, the "underground" privatization process triggered open access to state owned assets such as the transportation infrastructure, livestock shelters and particularly the engineered wells, which had helped to maintain access to pastureland. Since the local administrations lost the capacity to take care of the wells, many were seized and looted, leaving them broken down in DD and UU *bag*. This free right to seize assets also occurred widely in HBU *bag*. The state retained its ownership over the RPA winter livestock shelters and wells in the mountain for future use of the RPA, because it considered *otor* as necessary for herders' production even in the transition period. The ministry transferred the management responsibility of these assets to *soum* administrations, which used to visit HBU RPA on *otor* in the *negdel* period. The idea was that they should maintain the *otor* service with the collaboration of the HBU *bag* administration[44] following the arrangement utilized in the collective period.[45] However, the ministry failed to make the necessary transfer due to the lack of an arrangement that suited the existing situation. In the absence of *negdel* transportation, many officials and herders from other *soums* were no longer able to travel to HBU *bag* to take care of or to use these assets. Although the surrounding *soums* privatized these *otor* assets eventually to the herders, many assets, along with the storage buildings, were essentially ruined (Figure 5.1). A HBU *bag* herder noted that within a few months of privatization, those who could afford to come from other *soums*, dismantled the shelters and looted the important parts of the engineered wells.[46]

Figure 5.1 Storage buildings from HBU RPA, half looted and used by other households.

In the presence of increasing numbers of households, the deterioration in both quantity and quality of pasture resources became a major factor for herders' access to pasture, and *bag* and *soum* pasture management. As discussed earlier, Dergerlhaan and Bayanjargal *soum* government and their *Hural* were to manage the pastoral resources by adopting *ulamjlalt* pasture use rules and norms[47] as in the *negdel* period. In HBU *bag*, the former HBU *horoo* territory became HBU *bag*, 1st *bag* of Delgerhaan *soum*,[48] Hentii *aimag* as shown in Table 5.3. Simultaneously, this *bag* also contained the status of a village, which replaced the former *horoo*[49] based on its former settlement status with more than 500 residents.[50] Unlike the other two *bag* governments, it is administered by a village/*bag* government, which has its own land office and state budget. Also, the ministry transferred responsibility for managing incoming *otor* households to the HBU *bag*/village government, allowing it control over the HBU *bag* seasonal pastures and the HBU Mountain. These assets enhanced the authority of the HBU *bag*/village governor and its *Hural* over that of *soum* government in terms of controlling access to RPA pasture on its *bag* territory. Although *bag* governors along with their *Hurals* enforced their *soum* government and the *Hural*'s decisions on herders' pursuit of seasonal and long/short distance cross-boundary movements, the local *soum* and *bag* governments were unable to control herders' access to pastoral resources due to the absence of authority they once had over migration (labor) and production (livestock)[51] management. Migrants registered at the inter-*aimag*

120 *Transition to a market economy*

Table 5.3 Changes in the territorial administrative and production management units in three *bags*

Three bags	Collective period		Transition period	
	Territorial administrative unit	Production unit	Territorial administrative unit	Town/village centre
HBU	HBU *horoo*	HBU *aj ahui*	HBU *bag*, Delgerhaan *soum*	HBU village-*bag* centre
DD	Delgerhaan *soum*	DD *brigade*, 'Bayanbadral' *negdel*	DD *bag*, Delgerhaan *soum*	*Bag* center
UU	Bayanjargalan *soum*	Bayanerhtii *brigade*, Shine Amidral' *negdel*	UU *bag*, Bayanjargalan *soum*	*Bag* center

level for residency, but not for employment. The *soum* and *bag* administrations had to accept them as residents. They claimed that their action to control migration was illegal and that they may be infringing on someone's constitutional rights to live in a place of their choosing. Migration then became a legal mechanism that was mutually beneficial, particularly the HBU *bag*/village administration and visiting herders, in controlling and maintaining their access to the RPA pasture. The HBU *bag* officials favored incoming migrants in order to re-build resident numbers up to the minimum population of 500 and maintain the status of village and for that matter the state budget and the responsibility for *otor* management. Simultaneously, they allowed herders to select their *nutag* (seasonal pastures), decide when and where to move seasonally, and gain access to reserve pasture, because local governments were unable to control their land use. It resulted in the concentration of herding households in smaller pasture areas around the village center.

Control over selection of nutag: Bag officials' inability to control herders' land use hardly led to conditions of open access in pastureland. As was the case in pre-collective patterns, herders resumed to have much more control over access to pastoral resources than the administration due to their micro-management of private livestock production. Although the land law (1994) allowed individual households to possess residential plots,[52] this chapter discusses how herders initially selected the location of their privatized shelters to create campsites and grazing *nutag* prior to the enforcement of the legal campsite possession in 1998. Herders in all three *bags* have equal opportunity to access pastoral resources in their jurisdictional boundaries through their residency and private livestock ownership. However, the ways in which they legitimized their access was different in the former *negdel* and *aj ahui* area due to differences in migration trends. In former *negdel* areas like DD and UU *bags*, as in the pre-collective period, migrants legitimized their access through dual control: connection to local herders and the administration. Former *negdel* or local herders, particularly wealthy ones, initially, selected *nutag* and set up a campsite with their shelters in the Herlen river valley in DD and UU *bags* (Figure 5.2) on primary spring pasture (surrounded by summer and autumn pastures) as a priority for livestock birthing and delivery. Before registering with the local administration, the migrants selected *nutag* following their connection to local kinsmen and families, who had found the best pastoral areas. New migrant herders without a local connection also stayed close to these

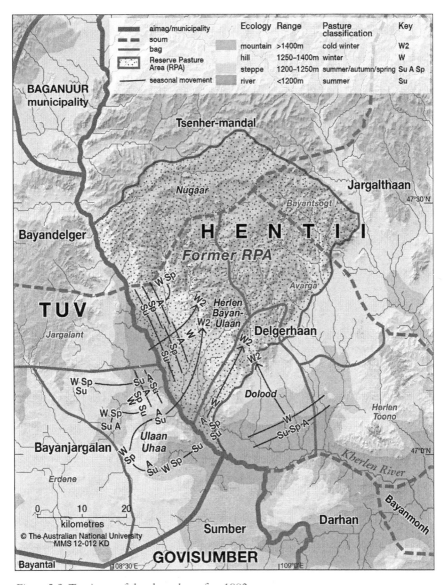

Figure 5.2 Territory of the three *bags* after 1992.

122 Transition to a market economy

herders following the good pasture and water resources. In contrast, in the former *aj ahui* area, the absence of local herders resulted in the fact that many migrant herders legitimized their access only through the connection with local *bag*/village administrations. The de-urbanization allowed a few local HBU *bag* herders to build their shelters on available primary spring pastures. Later, migrant herders were unable to claim these areas, because they had no connection to local herders. Regardless of their livestock and other wealth to afford such a distant migration, they had to select other available pasture that was suited to their style of livestock herding. For instance, those who came from the western *aimags* built their spring shelters in the winter pasture area at the northern mountainous part of the HBU *bag*, because they were used to herding in the mountains. Those who came from the Gobi region settled in the border of summer and autumn pasture areas at the southern steppe part of the HBU *bag*, as they were used to herding in a desert-steppe environment. The *bag*/village administration legitimized the migrants as local residents by accepting their off-seasonal use of these pastures despite the fact that HBU *bag* lacked enough seasonal pastures for their increasing number of migrants and despite the disagreement from local herders. This indicates that initially migrants in all three *bags* employed under dual control to access pastoral resources. Later, particularly in the HBU *bag*, negotiation with local officials to obtain residency (legal mechanism) to access pastureland became paramount. The difference in mechanisms for gaining access to pastoral resources between former *negdel* and *aj ahui* areas indicates that the shift in state policies to control pastureland changed how the components of production were controlled and how herders and the state as dual control legitimized access to pasture in the past. This difference had crucial implications for the future with regard to the heterogeneity of *bag* membership and the role of informal and formal control over access to pastureland in all three *bags*.

Second, instead of open access, herders selected seasonal pasture based on pre-collective *ulamjlalt* rules and norms: their herd type and size, besides the specific terrain they use to herd. In both DD and UU *bags*, herders who predominantly owned sheep defined the river valley as their grazing area for three seasons. Some UU herders, who had horse herds, selected drier open steppe areas on the southwest of UU *bag* as it offered more potential grazing area for horses and sheep. Describing the reason for this, one UU participant explained,

> This area is great in winter to leave your horses and other livestock on *otor*. That's why we chose to come here. The old area [in *negdel* period] was not really appropriate especially in winter, when livestock was likely to get lost following winter storms. But here, the pasture was much more expansive.[53]

Third, herders in DD and UU *bags* used their ancestral claims over specific pastoral production and pastoral resources. Herders stated that they were following their ancestors' pre-collective pastoral areas. For instance, one DD herder acknowledged that changes in mobility and campsite locations had occurred, but were not necessarily in the general pasture area or jurisdiction. "Ah, this was my husband's ancestral place. His ancestors stayed around here in the old time."[54] Ancestral claims over specific grazing land were mainly shaped by ancestors' involvement in herding specific types of livestock. Particularly in UU, regardless of what they herded in the *negdel*, many herders returned to herd sheep in the river valleys following their ancestors. Thus, instead of open access, a variety of production related factors including herd size, type, ancestral claims and herding experience in a specific terrain limited everyone, even wealthier herders, in the three *bags* in gaining and maintaining access to pasture everywhere, besides the different patterns of legitimizing access.

Control over seasonal mobility: In fact, these factors played as much a role as heterogeneity in *bag* members (wealth of livestock and vehicles, social status and collective and new herding background) in pursuing seasonal movements. Although the privatization and migration contributed in heterogeneity in *bag* members and resulted in a concentration of herding households and livestock in the river valley, it did not necessarily lead to open access. This is related to a small but important distinction that helps us understand the ways in which this heterogeneity in *bag* members affected their compliance with pasture use rule and norms. First, collectives uniformly enforced *ulamjlalt* seasonal movement as a formalized rule (instead of collective period *ulamjlal*[55]) thanks to their integrated management of balancing the production components with the support of transportation and labor assistance equally provided to all herders. In contrast, current local administrations are unable to enforce this formalized rule in the absence of an integrated management of the production components and logistical support. As a result, herders returned to pursue seasonal mobility in an informal and flexible manner according to the pre-collective *ulamjlal* insomuch as they could afford the labor and transportation. Hence, heterogeneity in herders' seasonal movement becomes inevitable regarding non-egalitarian pastoralism due to heterogeneity in members' wealth, social status, herding background as well as production related factors such as herd type, size, specific herding terrain and need for pooling labor (including poor). Those, who could afford to balance the production components and logistical support (by owning, renting camel caravan or privatized vehicles or wage herding), continued to move to other seasonal pastures in order to increase and strengthen their private production. For example, one newly migrated city dweller in HBU *bag* was successful in increasing the size of his small, but viable herds by being seasonally mobile.[56] This was also the case for the remaining *aj ahui* employees who were able to increase their livestock numbers in HBU *bag*. Those who cannot afford to balance the production components (e.g., by wage herding) and logistical support stay behind, which is what occurred in the pre-collective period. This hardly portrays ignorance of customary rules and norms.

Second, changes in members' wealth, social status and herding background affects community compliance with *ulamjlalt* rules and norms and becomes a real problem only when some members ignore the rules and norms, only even

124 *Transition to a market economy*

when they can afford logistical support to access pastoral resources. Even so, the problem was/is related to the concentration of households in areas of depleted resources,[57] which indicates the lack of legal mechanisms to support herders in balancing the production components. Nevertheless, in this period, local herders continued to impose informal sanctions over households regardless of their migration status. For instance, in Dolood *bag*, a former *negdel* herder was forced to comply with pasture use rules, because "everybody complained that we were grazing over their winter pasture in the off-season."[58] Thus, to a certain extent, herders remained homogenous in their pursuit of seasonal movement, but within a much shorter distance due to the reduction of EPL and the lack of logistical support to access other pastoral areas within their jurisdiction. Informal sanctions and seasonal rotations for short distances were possible due to the small herd size that each household owned.[59] A participant from UU commented on the numbers of households in relation to the numbers of livestock right after privatization: "There were many more households, but there were not that many livestock."[60] According to a participant from DD *bag*, "If there are 500 livestock [in each camp], then it is possible to rotate and graze without any problem."[61] As a result, according to former *negdel* and *aj ahui* herders, their pattern of using seasonal pastures had changed less, except the seasonal mobility within a much smaller radius. In all three *bags*, herders spent three seasons in the river valley,[62] except for winter. This was how they moved in both the pre-collective or collective periods except for some UU *bag* herders, whose pre-collective spring camps shifted from the river valley to the UU hills[63] in the collective period. Therefore, all three *bags* witnessed little change in livestock numbers and herder mobility.

Production factors based on weather conditions also shaped the ways in which herders set up winter shelters and pursued winter rotations. Winter camping patterns were quite different from those of other seasons in all three *bags*. Herders travelled much shorter distances in winter than they had in the *negdel* period as they no longer selected winter campsites deep in the HBU Mountain in anticipation of *dzud* conditions.[64] In HBU *bag*, the few local households with established locally recognized winter shelters and campsites were located on winter pastures close to the village center, nearby other seasonal pastures. New migrants, who did not have winter shelters, used temporary wooden fences for the livestock, and changed the location of their winter campsites for several years in an abundant mountain *buuts* in order to work out which mountain valleys had potential for establishing locally recognized winter campsites.[65] As in the pre-collective period, local herders from all three *bags* had flexible winter camping patterns depending on the weather conditions. They stayed within their jurisdictions without any need for long distance migration[66] due to stable weather and rich grazing conditions that continued until 1999/2000. Occasionally, when the winter was severe and there were not any visiting *otor* herders from other jurisdictions,[67] they stayed in specific valleys in the HBU Mountain as they had customarily during the pre-collective and collective periods.[68]

Absence of a property institution?

After privatization, in the absence of formal control, the concentration of households on reduced pastoral areas did not necessarily lead to overgrazing or disputes of pasture use due to compliance with *ulamjlalt* seasonal rotations. Reduced mobility occurred due to the shift in dual control over pastoral production, which conflicted with the historically proven principles of pastoral production management. The state created a contradictory legal environment by controlling only land-based resources under exclusive state ownership. As a formal control, it allowed the local co-management government to enforce the formalized version of *ulamjlalt* pasture use rules and norms. However, rather than the local government, herders had much more informal control over land use, because they managed all the production components. As a result, they were able to enforce *ulamjlalt* pasture use rules and norms and impose sanctions exerted within their *bag*. Instead of the absence of a property institution, the institutional arrangement currently portrays institutional bricolage as Upton (2009) referred to in post-socialist Mongolian land tenure, where custom was contested in terms of enforcing pasture use rules and norms. In fact, this period portrays institutional bricolage in the overall production management.

Formal control: Historically, local co-management authority was able to regulate herders' access to pastoral resources via controlling the production under expansive pre-collective administrative territory or collective mechanized production support even within reduced administrative territories. Now, in the presence of depleted pastoral resources without mechanized support within small *bag* boundaries, they were no longer able to regulate access to these resources during periods of complex seasonal mobility and cross-territorial mobility. Without the historical formal control mechanisms over the labor and livestock, they are ill-equipped to enforce formalized *ulamjlalt* pasture use rules and norms and solve disputes such as free-riding or trespassing. The number of labor and livestock was controlled more by weather conditions and the market than the local administration. Its role was limited to registration of migrants and ownership of the livestock for the sake of the census rather than a mechanism to regulate labor markets and access to pastoral resources as occurred in the past. There is no correlation between the registration of residency at the *aimag* level and the flow of livestock following migrants. In other words, the legislation on registering population movements did not reflect its impacts on local pastoral production and resource management. In this case, Mearns' (2004b) argument is valid, that local administration as a law enforcement body was mainly focused on protecting land with *ulamjlalt* rules, instead of regulating production components. The historical practice of pre-collective *ulamjlalt* rules and norms extends to both the land use and the whole production management.

However, the local administration as a state-based actor made the most of its opportunities under the new land regime and this affected pasture use

126 *Transition to a market economy*

patterns. The local administration's inability to control access to pastoral resources and migration created a fuzziness in the roles and responsibilities of different actors (Ribot and Peluso, 2003; Sturgeon and Sikor, 2004). In other words, the state overestimated its ability to regulate access to natural resources without effective jurisdictional mechanisms (Berry, 1993). Mearns (2004b) argued that local officials exploited their state administrative positions to secure control over access to pastoral resources for personal gain by inheriting official positions from the previous system. Although this argument explains one of the reasons for ineffective formal control, it is limited when the problem is examined only within the issue of land, rather than the whole production management. The local administrations, particularly HBU *bag* government, in fact, exercised their formal territorial authority and took advantage of a gap in the legislation by allowing more migrants at the expense of local herders' access to the HBU Mountain and diminishing the legitimacy of local herders' informal control. This was to compensate for its loss of control over production (livestock and labor) and maintain control over access to pastoral resources. This was a case of taking advantage of their authority as a crucial mechanism to control access to resources (Sikor and Lund, 2009). This condition created patron-client relationships in which herders utilized their wealth and social status as a strategy to maintain their access to the best pasture resources with the approval of state-based local actors over their actions (Sikor and Lund, 2009; Verdery, 1999).

Regarding informal control, these are the main reasons why, in the HBU case area, state control over land, in fact, shifted to the herders as herders managed the labor and livestock components in accordance with the historical principle of "those who control the production regulate the land." Based on my findings I support the argument that informal control remained in place (Fernandez-Gimenez, 2001). Herders' reduced mobility did not necessarily lead to overgrazing due to the continued compliance with the *ulamjlalt* rules and norms. First, herders, particularly migrants, legitimized their access either with formal or informal control in each *bag* instead of dual control. In DD and UU *bags*, the affirmation from local herders (informal) was more important than from the local administration (formal), because there were enough local herders to control the production process. Migrant herders gained residency status, which was legitimized more strongly by relational mechanisms such as ancestral or birth place as found elsewhere (Fernandez-Gimenez, 2001; Mearns, 2004a). This strategy secured their membership in the *bag* community and followed the *ulamjlalt* rule of "camp and graze as many as fit." This informal control was only practiced by individual herding households unlike the integrated formal control by lords or collectives in the pre-collective and collective period. In contrast, in HBU *bag*, legitimate registration by the local administration was more important than affirmation from the local herders in HBU *bag* due to the gap in the law, under which the local administration had an obligation to accept migration. Second, herders' *ulamjlalt* way of selecting seasonal pastures does conform less to the concept of open access even in the absence of formal control. Instead, they followed the *ulamjlalt* concept of use rights, "first to land claims the right to pasture." Local herders claimed the best pastoral resources in their *bags* and shaped the migrant herders' access to pastoral resources, regardless of their wealth and social status, in the three *bags*. Herders selected their seasonal pastures solely based on *ulamjlalt* production management and pasture use rules and norms. This depended on the type of livestock being herded and on herding experience, which was shaped by their ancestral style of herding livestock in particular terrain as found elsewhere (Fernandez-Gimenez, 2001; Mearns, 2004a). These patterns were apparent in previous systems as lords or *negdels*, regarding their production strategy, consulted with individual herding households on where and when to camp under the arrangement of territorial administration and use rights rather than exclusive land ownership.

Third, the issue of the heterogeneity in members' wealth, social status and background did not necessarily lead to uniform non-compliance with *ulamjlalt* seasonal mobility rules as argued elsewhere (Fernandez-Gimenez, 2001). Heterogeneity in herders' seasonal movements occurs due to their production related factors besides the heterogeneity of the herders' background, wealth and social status. The heterogeneity in the members' compliance of rules and norms becomes a problem depending on the ways in which the state managed production components in different historical periods. Heterogeneity among members with privately owned livestock is inevitable due to non-egalitarian pastoralism as was practiced in the pre-collective period. It only becomes a problem when even well-to-do able members ignore the rules and norms. As in the HBU case, this is related to the problems with the current legal environment, which lacked integrated management to balance the production components. Nevertheless, in the HBU case even under reduced EPL and the concentration of households, herders remained homogenous in their pursuit of seasonal movements as compliance with seasonal mobility is inherent in pursuing pastoral production under mainly non-equilibrium climatic conditions in Mongolia (Fernandez-Gimenez and Allen-Diaz, 1999; Ickowitz, 2003; Sneath, 2003). They moved seasonally, but in a much reduced distance as found elsewhere (Bazargur, 1998; Fernandez-Gimenez, 2001; Mearns, 2004b; Sneath, 2003). Herders' mobility and flexibility were not necessarily obstructed by the emerging heterogeneity among members, but mainly by the lack of logistical support such as labor, transportation and petrol (Fernandez-Gimenez, 2001; Sneath, 2003). Thus, in the absence of the former *negdel* mechanized mobility support, herders were able to move short distances with camel caravans or tractors as found elsewhere (Fernandez-Gimenez, 2001, p. 57). Also, this was enabled by the small numbers of livestock herders owned during moderate weather conditions until 1999. This reflected a nationwide trend that right after privatization, a majority of the households owned small-size herds (fewer than 200 head) (Griffin, 2001 cited in Nixson and Walters, 2006). A similar trend was observed in Bayanhongor right after privatization, of no dramatic livestock increase and this did not

128 *Transition to a market economy*

necessarily contribute to herders' changing mobility (Fernandez-Gimenez, 2002). Livestock numbers did not increase but in fact reduced in some areas due to the inexperience of new herders (Fernandez-Gimenez, 2002; Humphrey, 1999). Thus, all three *bags* witnessed little change in livestock numbers and herders' mobility as found elsewhere (Addison et al., 2012; Fernandez-Gimenez, 2002; Upton, 2010).

Overall, exploring the nature of property relations in pastureland beyond the property regimes and rights concept is crucial for understanding the problems with pastureland management in Mongolia. The property regime concept defines the problem of CPR management by identifying whether actors have property rights to any CPR. Instead, the HBU case shows us the need to understand the ways in which different actors exercise various rights to access pastoral resources is shaped by changes in overall management of the production system (dual control over the integrated management of pastoral production and its components) under different historical periods. The next chapter discusses the ways in which further policy on land reform affected *ulamjlalt* production management, particularly on community compliance with *ulamjlalt* rules and norms.

Notes

1 Privatization proceeded in two stages. Stage one was large scale privatization, in which collective and state farms and enterprise assets were privatized. The second was small scale privatization, in which livestock was privatized. Every citizen was to be allocated a set of ten privatization shares worth 10,000 MNT (three red shares, each worth 1000 MNT [in 1994, 400 MNT = US$1]) for small privatization and one blue share worth 7000 MNT for big privatization), which were sold for a nominal fee (Fernandez-Gimenez, 2001; Korsun and Murrell, 1995; Nixson and Walters, 2006).
2 Article 6.3 Constitution, 1992.
3 Article 6.1 and 6.2, Constitution, 1992.
4 See for instance Fernandez-Gimenez and Batbuyan (2004), Ickowitz (2003), Mearns (2004b) and Upton (2005).
5 Article 4.59.1, Constitution 1992.
6 Article 59.1, Constitution, 1992.
7 *Bagiin Irgediin Hural* or *Soum, Aimagiin Irgediin Tuluulugchdiin Hural*, which replaced *Ardiin Depytatyydiin Hural* in the socialist government. *Hural* would be led by governors for each level of territorial administration, who are nominated by this *Hural* and approved by a senior at the next higher level. An exception is *bag Hurals*, which are not a formal territorial and budget entity. *Bag Hurals* are composed of its residents and led by its representatives and nominates its own head. *Soum Hurals* are represented by heads of *bag Hurals* and *aimag Hurals* are represented by *soum* governors and *Hural* heads (Mearns, 2004b).
8 Article 1.5.5, Constitution, 1992.
9 *Aimags* have a population of around 75,000, *soum* around 5000 and *bags* fewer than 1000.
10 Law of Mongolia on Administrative and Territorial Units and their Governance 1993: Article, 18.1.2 k, *Soum Hural* "to develop and approve integrated program for use, rehabilitation and protection of *soum* territorial land." Article, 29.1.3 b, *Soum* governor, to present a proposal of program on to *soum Hural* and organize implementing the program on sustainable use ... protection of natural environment.

Article, 17.1.8, *Bag Hural* "to discuss and present the proposal to *soum Hural* on local cooperative, organization and group on a use, protection and possession of specific natural resources in their territory." Article 28.1.2, *Bag* governor organizes preparation for winter by haymaking, forage making and *otor* movement etc.... Article, 28.1.13, *Bag* governor's role on monitoring resource use management in their territory. Article, 28.1.16, *Bag* governor receives locals' complaints and comments and solve it in terms of his duties and responsibilities and present these to relevant legal authorities and organizations. Article, 28.1.18, *Bag* governor monitors its permanent and temporary residents complying their citizen's duties.

11 Law of Mongolia on land 1994: Article 51.2, *Soum* governor in collaboration with relevant state institute enforce land use and management of pastureland for protection and its capacity. Article 51.3, when using and managing pastureland, refer to traditional land use division such as winter, spring, summer and autumn pasture. Summer and autumn pasture and *otor* reserve pasture will be communally used within *bag hot ails.*

12 Law of Mongolia on Environmental Protection 1995: Article 18.1.1, *Bag Hural* "to develop and administer schedules for protection and use of hayfields, pasture and water sources no designated for possession or use by others," Article 18.1.1, *Bag Hural,* "to supervise the protection and use of natural resources in common use."

13 Article 28.1.2 of Law on administrative and territorial units and their governance 1993/2006 and Article 51.3, Land law 1994.

14 Pre-collective and collective (some pre-collective rules and norms were formalized).

15 Amendment 2006, Law on administrative and territorial units and their governance 1993/2006.

16 Great Assembly, the New parliament.

17 Small scale voluntary cooperatives mainly focused on trade rather than land management. Literally, *horshoo* means "to collaborate or combine an effort."

18 This was quite popular among several poor and wealthier households I met during this fieldwork and other fieldwork as well (2005). Mainly female-headed households emphasized that they were not able to receive their shares due to lack of an adult male member, who could collect their shares from the collectives.

19 The viable number fluctuates. After privatization, the viable number was 100–125 according to authorities in the rural areas (Namkhainyambuu, 2000). This rose to 200 head of livestock by the late 1990s (Mearns, 2004a).

20 This was a period of so-called "iron rush," in which the Chinese were paying a higher market price for iron following their industrial development.

21 Power in this thesis refers to "the capacity of some actors to affect the practices and ideas of others" (Weber, 1978 and Luke, 1986 cited in Ribot and Peluso, 2003, p. 156).

22 The ministry and other donor agencies are currently attempting to pass revised drafts.

23 The enforcement of legislation on campsite possession has been effective since 1998, thus, its impact is not clear at this stage.

24 Interview 18 (Undargaa, 2013).

25 Interview 11 (Undargaa, 2013).

26 Interview 4 (Undargaa, 2013). The state was not privatizing HBU *aj ahui* assets to its employees. However, the former *aj ahui* employees argued that they would be unemployed and disadvantaged due to the collapse of *otriin aj ahui* without receiving any privatized assets (Interview 11 and 12, Undargaa, 2013). The state decided to pursue privatization of *otriin aj ahui,* but only to a limited extent. The government assigned the MFA to directly control both the design and process of HBU *aj ahui* privatization. The vice minister led the privatization push. It aimed to retain most of the assets in order to maintain its function as state enterprise under joint companies or *horshoo.*

130 Transition to a market economy

27 Interview 11 and 12 (Undargaa, 2013).
28 Strategy here refers to "a plan, method, or series of maneuvers or stratagems for obtaining a specific goal or result" http://dictionary.reference.com/browse/strategy.
29 Interview 13 (Undargaa, 2013).
30 Interview 45 (Undargaa, 2013).
31 The only shelters available were eight milk farm winter shelters or those built by HBU RPA in DD territory. The latter were supposed to be given to Delgerhaan, which is to say, DD. However, it appeared that the local people did not receive any of these. "HBU [*bag*] got all of those shelters and ruined them" (Interview 29, Undargaa, 2013). The former, the milk farming shelters, were divided and allocated among several individual households, who were mostly relatives. "There used to be eight big winter shelters. So, we divided these shelters among us four, between me and my sister" (Interview 34, Undargaa, 2013). In this way, only a few were able to get what they had had in the collective time.
32 Interview 13 (Undargaa, 2013).
33 Viable numbers fluctuate. After privatization, viable numbers were around 100–125 according to authorities in rural areas (Namkhainyambuu, 2000). Namkhainyambuu (2000, p. 19) also wrote that herders in Zavkhan *aimag* in the western part of Mongolia had to slaughter these for food if they had fewer than 75 head of livestock, thus they were unable to increase numbers of livestock for viable herding. The viable number rose to 200 head of livestock by the late 1990s (Mearns, 2004a).
34 Interview 49 (Undargaa, 2013).
35 Interview 29, (Undargaa, 2013).
36 1990–2000 migration data in these *bags* and *soums* were unavailable at the local *soum* administration.
37 Most of the herders in HBU *bag* received fewer than 100 livestock, which they considered insufficient to make a living out of herding. As one remaining herder in HBU *bag* explained,

> If you had 15 small livestock, 7–8 of them would give birth to babies each year for 10 years and it would make up to 70 livestock. This was not really enough, especially if you consume some of these for food every year. What you keep as an asset was not so much.
>
> (Interview 11)

In other words, the number of livestock HBU *aj ahui* employees received was much lower than the nationally recognized average minimum viable herd number. In addition, the unequal distribution among the HBU *aj ahui* employees contributed to their inability to create viable herd sizes.
38 There is a large suburb full of former HBU *bag* migrants in Baganuur city, 80 km away from HBU *bag*. They began migrating to bigger cities like Ulaanbaatar and Baganuur in the mid-1990s.
39 Interview 3 and 23 (Undargaa, 2013).
40 These people essentially remained herders for the new companies' livestock. Herding for the company was beneficial for increasing their own small numbers of livestock. As they were herding 252 head of sheep or cattle and breeding them, 70 percent of these herders were able to keep the remaining 30 percent of the livestock as a bonus. After the company collapsed, they began herding privately (Interview 13, Undargaa, 2013).
41 The period 1999–2003 saw much migration from the western to the central area due to the loss of livestock in *dzuds* (Batbayar, 2007; Sneath, 2003). Livestock insurance has no longer been compulsory since 1991, but voluntarily includes loss of livestock to wolves (Templer et al. 1993). After the *dzud*, rural migrant herders

from other parts of Mongolia, particularly from western *aimag*s, looked for abundant pastoral resources, which were closer to urban markets during 1995–2000 (Mearns, 2004a; Solongo, 2007).

42 Interview 12 (Undargaa, 2013).

43 Interview 26 (Undargaa, 2013).

44 Interview 11 (Undargaa, 2013).

45 For instance, Dundgovi *aimag* would be responsible for maintaining shelters and wells in a valley which they used to use in the *negdel* period. The same idea was also applied to *soums* surrounding HBU *bag*. These *soum* administrations were supposed to be responsible for all winter shelters, storage houses and wells established in their territory by the ministry during the *aj ahui* period. For instance, Delgerhaan *soum* would be responsible for all the assets established by the ministry in their territory (Interview 39, Undargaa, 2013).

46 Interview 11 (Undargaa, 2013).

47 Article 28.1.2 of Law on administrative and territorial units and their governance 1993/2006 and Article 51.3, Land law 1994.

48 There are four *bags*: HBU, DD, Avarga and *soum* center *bag*.

49 *Horoo* is an urban settlement equivalent of *soum*. In the collective period, HBU *bag*'s administrative status was that of a *horoo* as it contained more than 500 residents.

50 The law on territorial and administrative units articulated that the rural territory of Mongolia will be divided into the hierarchical administrative units of *bag*, *soum* and *aimag* and allowed village or town center on these rural territories. Provision 1, Article 3 in the law on Administrative and Territorial units and their governance, 2006. Provision 1, Article 5 in the law on town and village administration, 1993.

51 In 1990s, Delgerhaan *soum* administration made an effort to control migration as it did in the *negdel* period. For instance, the *soum* administration monitored migrants' permission of movement and employment and fined those who came without any official transfer of residency (XN46, DNo, XHNo125, Ardiin *Hural* Executive Administration, HBU *Horoo*, MFA, Hentii *Aimag* Archive).

52 Article 30.1, the Law on land, 1994.

53 Interview 45 (Undargaa, 2013).

54 Interview 26 (Undargaa, 2013).

55 See Upton (2009).

56 Interview 18 (Undargaa, 2013).

57 Interview 29 (Undargaa, 2013).

58 Interview 29 (Undargaa, 2013).

59 Interview 20 (Undargaa, 2013).

60 Interview 48 (Undargaa, 2013).

61 Questionnaire 52 (Undargaa, 2013).

62 Spring campsites are on *denj* (dry slope area along the *ders*, broom grass between the mountain and the river grass). Summer camping usually fluctuates between the river grass and *denj* areas, depending on the weather because of several rotations occurring there during the summer. Autumn camping is often between the *denj* and the bottom of the mountain, away from the summer and spring pasture.

63 See Chapters 3 and 4.

64 This trend is more apparent among herders in HBU, DD and the hillside of UU *bags*, because of their close proximity and easy access to the mountains and hills. In particular, the DD and HBU *bag* herders assumed they could go deep into the mountains as there were plenty of unoccupied campsites with warm *buuts*.

65 Interview 8 (Undargaa, 2013).

66 As in the pre-collective period, in UU and DD, households in the river valley were more likely to remain around their spring shelters, along the river among the broom grasses.

132 *Transition to a market economy*

67 Local administrations also did not have much presence in regulating cross-territorial mobility. Until 1999, the number of visiting *otor* households from distant provinces was particularly low. This was due to the fact that only a few herders were able to afford transportation to pursue long distance *otor* mobility as a result of the collapse of mechanized support of *negdel* institutions. Also, moderate weather conditions were a factor and herders from other provinces had no significant reason to pursue long distance *otor* mobility. Thus, all three areas experienced minimal need for arranging *otor*. The exception was a few herders from the area around the HBU *bag* who stayed at HBU Mountain following the *ulamjlalt* pattern of winter camping for a few cold winters. They essentially went in and out without any formal control, following their seasonal pattern of winter camping from November until January (see Chapter 4). The local HBU *bag* administration was largely absent in regulating their use, also a reflection of the pre-*negdel* pattern of reserve pasture use.

68 Herders from these three *bags* freely selected winter *buuts* in the mountain close to their spring sites, but without wooden shelters as the mountain offers abundant *buuts* sheltered by mountains and hills. Herders claiming *ulamjlalt* grazing land occurred more in DD and UU area than HBU *bag* where the majority of the households were migrants, and had no such claims. When claiming *ulamjlalt* winter pastoral areas, it was not necessarily specific campsites, but rather general geographically distinct areas such as dry hills or river valleys. Allocation of valleys for UU herders in the mountain in the collective time was generally based on their pre-collective ancestral camping areas in the mountains. In other words, the choice of valleys in the mountain was similar.

References

Addison, J, Friedel, M, Brown, C, Davies, J and Waldron, S (2012) "A critical review of degradation assumptions applied to Mongolia's Gobi Desert," *The Rangeland Journal* 34, 125–137.

Batbayar, Ts (2007) *Modern Mongolia*, Pentagon Press, Delhi.

Bazargur, D (ed.) (1998) *Geography of Pastoral Animal Husbandry*, TTC Company, Mongolian Academy of Science, Ulaanbaatar.

Berry, S (1993) *No Condition is Permanent: The Social Dynamics of Agrarian Change in Sub-Saharan Africa*, University of Wisconsin Press, Madison.

Bold, B (1996) "Socio-economic segmentation: khot-ail in nomadic livestock keeping of Mongolia," *Nomadic Peoples* 39, 69–86.

Bruun, O, Ronnas, P and Narangoa, L (1999) "Country analysis Mongolia," Nordic Institute of Asian Studies, SIDA.

Fernandez-Gimenez, M E (2001) "The effects of livestock privatization on pastoral land use and land tenure in post-socialist Mongolia," *Nomadic Peoples* 5:2, 49–66.

Fernandez-Gimenez, M E (2002) "Spatial and social boundaries and the paradox of pastoral land tenure: a case study from post-socialist Mongolia," *Human Ecology* 30:1, 49–78.

Fernandez-Gimenez, M E and Allen-Diaz, B (1999) "Testing a non-equilibrium model of rangeland vegetation dynamics in Mongolia," *Journal of Applied Ecology* 36, 871–885.

Fernandez-Gimenez, M E and Batbuyan, B (2004) "Law and disorder: local implementation of Mongolia's land law," *Development and Change* 35:1, 141–165.

Fratkin, E (1997) "Pastoralism: governance and development issues," *Annual Review of Anthropology* 26, 235–261.

Griffin, K (2003) "Urban-rural migration and involution in the livestock sector" in K Griffin (ed.) *Poverty Reduction in Mongolia*, Asia Pacific Press, Canberra, 56–71.

Humphrey, C (1999) "Rural institutions" in David Sneath and Caroline Humphrey (eds.) *The End of Nomadism: Society, State and the Environment in Inner Asia*, Duke University Press, Durham, NC, 68–136.

Ickowitz, A (2003) "Poverty and the environment," in K Griffin (ed.) *Poverty Reduction in Mongolia*, Asia Pacific Press, Canberra, 95–112.

Korsun, G and Murrel, P (1995) "Politics and economics of Mongolia's privatization program," *Asian Survey* XXXV:5, 472–486.

Lattimore, O (1941) *Mongol Journey*, Doubleday, Doran and Co, New York.

Lattimore, O (1962) *Nomads and Commissars: Mongolia Revisited*, Oxford University Press, New York.

"Law of Mongolia on Administrative and Territorial Units and their Governance" (1993).

"Law of Mongolia on Environmental Protection" (1995).

"Law of Mongolia on Land" (1994).

Mearns, R (2004a) "Sustaining livelihoods on Mongolia's pastoral commons: insights from a participatory poverty assessment," *Development and Change* 35:1, 107–139.

Mearns, R (2004b) "Decentralisation, rural livelihoods and pasture-land management in post socialist Mongolia," *European Journal of Development Research* 16:1, 133–152.

Namkhainyambuu, Ts (2000) *Bounty from the Sheep*, The White Horse Press, Cambridge.

Nixson, F and Walters, B (2006) "Privatization, income distribution, and poverty: the Mongolian experience," *World Development* 34:9, 1557–1579.

Potanski, T (1993) "Decollectivization of the Mongolian pastoral economy (1991–92): some economic and social consequences," *Nomadic Peoples* 33, 123–135.

Ribot, J C and Peluso, N L (2003) "A theory of access," *Rural Sociology* 68:2, 153–181.

Ribot, J C, Agrawal, A and Larson, A M (2006) "Recentralizing while decentralizing: how national governments reappropriate forest resources," *World Development* 34:11, 1864–1886.

Sikor, T and Lund, C (2009) "Access and property: a question of power and authority," *Development and Change* 40:1, 1–22.

Sneath, D (1993) "Social relations, networks and social organisation in post-socialist rural Mongolia," *Nomadic Peoples* 33, 193–207.

Sneath, D (2003) "Land use, the environment and development in post-socialist Mongolia," *Oxford Development Studies* 31:4, 441–457.

Sneath, D (2006) "The rural and the urban in pastoral Mongolia" in O Bruun and Li Narangoa (eds.) *Mongols from Country to City: Floating Boundaries, Pastoralism and City Life in the Mongol Lands*, Nordic Institute of Asian Studies, 140–161.

Solongo, A (2007) "Growth of internal and international migration in Mongolia" in *Migration, Development and Poverty Reduction, 8th International Conference of Asia Pacific Migration Research Network, May 25–29, 2007, Fuzhou, Fujain province, China*, Funian Normal University, Fujian, China.

Spoor, M (2009) *The Political Economy of Rural Livelihoods in Transition Economies: Land, Peasants and Rural Poverty in Transition*, Routledge, London and New York.

Sternberg, T (2008) "Environmental challenges in Mongolia's dryland pastoral landscape," *Journal of Arid Environments* 72, 1294–1304.

Sturgeon, J C and Sikor, T (2004) "Post-socialist property in Asia and Europe: variations on 'fuzziness'," *Conservation & Society* 2:1, 2–17.

134 *Transition to a market economy*

Templer, G, Swift, J and Payne, P (1993) "The changing significance of risk in the Mongolian pastoral economy," *Nomadic Peoples* 33, 105–122.

Tumenbayar, N (2000) "Land privatization option for Mongolia" in *Constituting the Commons: Crafting Sustainable Commons in the New Millennium, the Eighth Conference of the International Association for the Study of the Common Property*, Bloomington, Indiana, May 31–June 4.

Undargaa, S (2013) "Property 'owners' without rights? Exploring property relations and access in the Herlen Bayan-Ulaan Reserve Pasture Area of Mongolia," Crawford School of Public Policy, Australian National University, Canberra.

Upton, C (2005) "Institutions in a pastoral society: processes of formation and transformation in post-socialist Mongolia," *Comparative Studies of South Asia, Africa and the Middle East* 25:3, 584 599.

Upton, C (2009) "'Custom' and contestation: land reform in post-socialist Mongolia," *World Development* 37:8, 1400–1410.

Upton, C (2010) "Living off the land: nature and nomadism in Mongolia," *Geoforum* 41, 865–874.

Verdery, K (1999) "Fuzzy property: rights, power, and identity in Transylvania's decollectivization" in M Burawoy and K Verdery (eds.) *Uncertain Transition: Ethnographies of Change in the Post-socialist World*, Rowman and Littlefield Publishers, Lanham, MD, 53–82.

6 Land reform in pastureland management

Land reform in Mongolia

The government of Mongolia introduced land reform by passing new laws on land in 1994, which made provision for exclusive individual private property rights. The Asian Development Bank (ADB) argued that the existing property regime over land in Mongolia lacked exclusive private ownership, which it assumed would boost the efficiency of market-based land management (Fernandez-Gimenez and Batbuyan, 2004; Sneath, 2003; Tumenbayar, 2000). The law provided for three types of rights to land: ownership, possession/lease (*ezemshil*) and use (Fernandez-Gimenez and Batbuyan, 2004). In other words, the implication of the land law was to introduce de jure secure tenure to land. In the law, the state also incorporated legislations for pastureland "to provide positive incentives to herders, farmers and others to maximize production and to protect land from damage or degradation" (Sneath, 2003, p. 443), and solve overgrazing and disputed use of resources among herders (Fernandez-Gimenez and Batbuyan, 2004). There are two drastically different regulations referring to pastureland, which are the focus of this chapter.

The first regulation refers to exclusive individual/group land possession. It articulated that citizens possess their residential plot for their household use.[1] This did not specify herders' rights to possess residential land, except that citizens are allowed to pursue gardening within their campsites.[2] Then, the amendment to the land law ("Law of Mongolia on Land," 2002) clearly stated that "a citizen as a *hot ail* together [commonly] may possess land under winter and spring campsites (*uvuljuu havarjaanii buuts gazar*)."[3] The transition policy initiatives often reflected ways in which policy advocates understand Mongolian Pastoralism. Mongolian intellectuals were divided in opinion with regard to introducing such exclusive property rights to pastoral resources. Some criticized the influence of the ADB loan in passing the law to formalize such property rights to pastoral resources, which may deteriorate some herders' customary ways of accessing to pastoral resources (Sneath, 2003, pp. 445, 454). Others supported the idea of exclusive property rights to land or pastoral resources as a step forward to join the global (market) economy (Bazargur, 1998; Mashbat, 2004). For instance, Bazargur suggested a reformed

136 *Land reform in pastureland management*

structure of a *hot ail* in the market economy: "Ecologically preferable land (EPL) should be allocated among a *hot ail* [of households] to correct its seasonal movement. Winter and spring pastures as main EPL should be given under solid/strict possession with a passport/certificate" (1998, p. 186).

The author interpreted the pre-collective state territorial use of land as herders belonged to fixed socio-economic units such as "*hot ail*" (base unit) and "*neg nutag usniihan*" (community) with specific boundaries and strict possession of their EPL (referring to territorial units) (p. 180). Then, the author suggested, current individually operating herding households would re-unite as *hot ail* and *neg nutag usniihan* and formalize their property rights to land. This is to overcome the backwardness of the herders' current subsistence-based socio-economic production and step into a village-based sedentarization/sedentary production system by combining customary pastoral strategies with modern technologies and alternative livelihood sectors (pp. 171–190). Mobile pastoralism is considered an inadequate socio-economic production system in a period of modern development or market economy (Bazargur, 1998; Mashbat, 2004). These views almost echo the Marxist ideology once influential in the socialist period, depicting feudal ownership of campsites and pasture in the pre-collective period (e.g., Natsagdorj, 1972), and promotion of modernization based on scientific and advanced technology and the settled livestock production system (e.g. Simukov, 1931) in the collective period.

The second regulation refers to the pastureland surrounding campsites. The state assigned responsibility for pastureland management to local *bag* and *soum* jurisdictions.[4] Under this provision, summer and autumn pastures would be shared among the *bag* jurisdictional community.[5] However, there was no specific provision for winter and spring pasture, nor any guidance on whether these were for community use or possession of a group or individuals (Tumenbayar, 2000). In other words, the law allowed individuals and enterprises to possess land,[6] but without a clear distinction regarding whether pastureland as a CPR can be possessed (Fernandez-Gimenez and Batbuyan, 2004). Only in 2002 did amendments specifically exempt all pastureland from possession (Fernandez-Gimenez et al., 2008). Nonetheless, in reality, implementation of pastureland possession at the local level was not popular except for a few attempts by experimental development projects on herder groups' exclusive use right to pastureland[7] (Fernandez-Gimenez and Batbuyan, 2004; Sneath, 2003; Tumenbayar, 2000). Therefore, this chapter discusses only the implementation of legal rights to possess campsites and to use/share jurisdictional pastureland.

First, the implementation of legal campsite possession is merely to ensure herders' rights to exclusive individual/private property of land. By 1998, the government issued a possession certificate to individual or group herding households' winter and spring campsites (*hot ail uvuljuu havarjaanii buuts gazar*), as these were considered herders' residential plots in the 1994 provision (Fernandez-Gimenez and Batbuyan, 2004). This means a citizen, who leads a household or several households as a *hot ail*, may possess winter and spring campsites. Here, article 54.7 or 52.7 on different English versions of the land laws are confusing as a speculative translation was made as "citizens of Mongolia may jointly possess land under winter and spring settlements through their *hot ail* communities." This translation made the emphasis on *hot ail* communities without specifying what it is. It creates confusion that it did not refer to an individual household. In reality, the structures of *hot ail* range from individual to several households in different parts of Mongolia (see Chapter 3). Thus, depending on a structure of *hot ail*, local authorities could issue a certificate to an individual household and a certificate to several households' cluster of campsites *buuts* and livestock shelters (Fernandez-Gimenez and Batbuyan, 2004; Undargaa, 2006).[8] As shown in Figure 6.1, they each possess a campsite area of 0.07 ha under a certificate (*ezemshliin gerchilgee*) for 15–60 years (with another 40-year extension) (Fernandez-Gimenez, 2002; Tumenbayar, 2000). Now, herders can exercise exclusive rights to manage this small plot of land, which includes a camping spot and a nearby area that contains livestock shelter, *ger* and horse posts (Fernandez-Gimenez and Batbuyan 2004). This exclusive right refers to a bundle of rights (Meinzen-Dick et al., 2004). This includes decision making and use rights; right to mortgage the certificate,[9] the right to transfer use through inheritance and to another except through sale[10] (Fernandez-Gimenez and Batbuyan, 2004). Similar to privatized property rights (not the land) in China, this possession right de facto triggered land sale not necessarily through real state, but through trading the certificates (Mashbat, 2004, p. 327).

Figure 6.1 Winter campsite, 1 ha in HBU *bag*.

138 *Land reform in pastureland management*

However, in reality, winter and spring campsites are strategically important assets for pastoral production. These are "point locations rather than swathes of land, … they entail an implicit right to pasture of several kilometres radius around the site" (Sneath, 2003, p. 445). Also, these are location points for shelters and other production resources such as thick layers of livestock dung accumulated over time and used for livestock shelter and as a fuel resource (Fernandez-Gimenez, 2002, p. 61). Now, herders legally possess these campsites within their *bag* territory of residence. De jure, the *bag* governor registers a herder's application for legal possession of campsites. The *bag* governor submits profiles of applications to the *soum* land officer. The *soum* land officer designs and carries out the annual *soum* land management planning, including the land for legal possession of campsites. The *soum* land officer processes the applications[11] and verifies that the applicant's request for these campsites does not overlap with someone else's request for the same land.[12] Then, the land officer submits it to the *soum* self-governing *Hural*, which approves individual household[13] applications for legal campsite possession from the area designed in the annual *soum* land management plan.[14] Then the *soum* governor formalizes the decision of the *soum Hural*.[15] Although *soum* and *bag* central and self-governing *Hurals*[16] have legal authority to control over access to pastureland, de facto, these officials are unable to decide over the location and allocation of campsites, thus allow herders to select the location of the campsites. Therefore, herders often apply for possession certificates after having already established their campsites without the approval of the local administration (Upton, 2005). In some cases, local *soum* administration encouraged this pattern of legal campsite possession (Undargaa, 2006).

Second, the implementation of the land law was unsuccessful in terms of regulating herders' use rights to pastureland. Following the prevailing property regimes approach, Mongolian land tenure was defined as (failed) formal and informal institutions (Fernandez-Gimenez and Batbuyan, 2004; Mearns, 2004b), or de jure state or de facto common property (Upton, 2005, p. 586), or even customary or traditional open access commons (Griffin, 2003, p. 67; Ickowitz, 2003, pp. 96–97). Here, what constitutes formal and informal institutions, common property, customary, traditional or even open access regime is very vague, as Mongolian land tenure is currently based on, de jure, a combined formal control: the land law entitled *soum* and *bag* central and self-governing bodies to regulate local pastureland management[17] along with the allocation of *uvuljuu havarjaa* under the authority vested in them as territorial administrations of Mongolia. Nevertheless, these authorities also found it difficult to enforce pasture use rules of seasonal mobility and rotation (Fernandez-Gimenez and Batbuyan, 2004; Upton, 2009). On the one hand, some herders acknowledged the need for more involvement from local administration (Upton, 2009). On the other hand, some herders perceived that the management of seasonal pasture is more a matter for individual herding households than formal institutions (Undargaa, 2006; Upton, 2005). This dilemma occurs due to the fact that, since transition, formal authorities

Land reform in pastureland management 139

including *bag Hural* struggle to regulate only land use, as the overall management of pastoral production is left solely in the hands of individual herding households with their informal management.

Land reform outcome

As a result, the land reform led to a range of social and environmental impacts. The social outcome found that the prediction of diminishing herders' access to pasture came true (Sneath, 2003, pp. 445, 454). Land reform secured only individual/private access to campsites at the expense of *bag* community. Legal campsite possession changed the *ulamjlalt* way of gaining access to pastoral resources and contributed to growing inequalities among herders. Those who owned a viable number of livestock and shelters, and who legally possessed campsites de facto claimed right to use the surrounding pastures. Others, who lacked these assets, were only able to make a few claims to pasture[18] (Fernandez-Gimenez and Batbuyan, 2004; Sneath, 2003; Tumenbayar, 2000). This unequal opportunity to gain access to pasture may have been a result of a common confusion throughout Mongolia over whether legal campsite possession refers to a camping spot or to the surrounding pastureland (Fernandez-Gimenez and Batbuyan, 2004; Undargaa, 2006; Upton, 2005). For instance, in Bayandalai *soum*, Umnugovi, local officials interpreted the law to mean that those who did not own livestock shelters could not legally possess campsites (Undargaa, 2006, p. 57). Then, those who lost informal use right to a campsite would also lose their access to pastoral resources. Essentially, legal possession of campsites legitimized herders' use rights to pastureland (Sneath, 2003). Also, herders employed it as a mechanism to gain and maintain access to more pastoral resources. By a family-splitting strategy, wealthy herders were able to control more pasture by setting up several campsites near poor households with less livestock (Mearns, 2004a; Undargaa, 2006). This process diminished the poor herders' informal rights to campsites, leading to their exclusion from gaining access to pasture. Consequently, many poor herders have diversified their strategies for accessing pastureland. Previously, *hot ail* institution customarily supported poor herders in gaining access to pastoral resources as they stayed with wealthier kin or neighbors (Cooper, 1993; Fernandez-Gimenez, 2002; Mearns, 2004a). Since the implementation of legal possession of campsites, this strategy became less available to poor herders as "kin-based and other social-networks have begun to shift towards semi-commercial forms" (Mearns, 2004a, p. 128). In response, herders have turned either to wage herding, or become more mobile in their attempt to gain access to available pasture because they have no secure rights through legal possession of campsites (Fernandez-Gimenez and Batbuyan, 2004). Some choose to carry out fewer movements, staying longer on their campsites and leading an almost sedentary lifestyle in order to protect the pasture around the campsite (Mearns, 2004a). These actions, however, guarantee only temporary access to pasture without providing security to quality pasture that is essential for their production.

140 *Land reform in pastureland management*

Legal campsite possession conflicts with *ulamjlalt* pasture use rules and norms as it does not secure exclusive management rights to pasture and becomes only one of the many ways to gain access to pastureland. In general, in a context of spacious pasture, herders with legal possession of campsites may pursue exclusion, because "the sphere of influence over pasture is greatest close to the campsite and diminishes with distance" (Fernandez-Gimenez, 2002, p. 62). However, even with legal campsite possession, some poor herders were unable to exclude and are vulnerable to others' trespassing (Fernandez-Gimenez, 2002). This is because, customarily, herders' control of pasture depends on their wealth (herd size) and their ability to mobilize other resources (networking, transportation and labor). Large herd size uses more pasture than small herd size (see Chapter 3). These factors impact on herders' decision whether to claim legal possession of a campsite and then one could claim more pasture around a campsite. This is why the campsite is more a part of pastoral resources rather than a "common substance that can be owned or possessed" (Sneath, 2004, p. 170). Moreover, herders' wealth or ability to mobilize resources matters in using a certain amount of pasture around the campsite. With only a legal title, herders in general cannot exclude others from trespassing or sharing pasture around their campsites, particularly in a context of small pasture area. In fact, the sphere of influence over pasture around the campsite is "a matter of contention" (Upton, 2009, p. 5), because "inclusive and exclusive paradigms co-exist concerning pasture rights" based on the common strategy of "reciprocity" within the principle of pasture use (Upton, 2005, p. 589). This reciprocity is inherent in the *ulamjlal* and herders often by-pass each other's livestock to share the same pasture (see Chapter 3). The evidence suggests that reciprocity mainly occurs in relation to off-seasonal use of pasture or "trespassing" during the shortage of pasture. Trespassing is often judged as not ideal, but it is a regular process "justified by necessity, or so infrequent as to be of little real concern with respect to both local culprits and *otor* families" (Upton, 2005, p. 595). Trespassing incidents are usually temporary and solved by negotiation and mutual compromise and reciprocity, rather than seen as a source of conflict (Upton, 2005). Although herders could employ legal possession of campsites to gain access to pasture under stable weather condition, it is a contestable idea to exclude others from pasture through this formal mechanism, which does not reflect other flexible *ulamjlalt* arrangements of sharing pasture in different pastoral conditions. Also, legal possession of campsites may guarantee access to the land around it, but not often the use of the land due to the changing quality of the surrounding pasture under different weather conditions. In severe weather, pastures around these campsites are inaccessible, so, herders leave to go elsewhere. Thus herders do not employ legal possession of campsites as a mechanism to protect their seasonal pasture. For instance, prior to the winter *dzud* of 2000, Upton (2005, p. 599) reported that "herders grazed their winter pastures in early autumn with the expectation that they will go on *otor*, hence rendering the reservation of winter pasture unnecessary." Therefore, herders' security of tenure is still embedded in the *ulamjlalt* mobility strategies (short and long distance *otor*) rather than exclusive rights attached to a fixed plot of campsites.

In terms of environmental outcomes, the land law intensified the process of overgrazing. In the pastoral context, legal possession of campsites is against herders' constitutional right to camp and reside wherever they can (Fernandez-Gimenez and Batbuyan, 2004). This provision resulted in blocking herders' freedom of movement. It disrupts the *ulamjlalt* pasture use rules and norms, which allow herders to leave their locally recognized campsite for flexible camping arrangement in different locations to rotate, rehabilitate and pursue their production strategies (see Chapter 3). There is a trend of using seasonal pastures repeatedly or in the off-season or over time by establishing fixed campsites. For instance, research in Bayanhongor revealed that legal possession of campsites works as an incentive for wealthier herders to become sedentary. They use their campsites "repeatedly to protect improvements and pastures by staying in the area" (Fernandez-Gimenez and Batbuyan, 2004, p. 162). The same practice was revealed in the case of Bulgan *soum*, Umnugovi (Upton, 2005, p. 596). As seasonal pastures become scarce from an increasing number of livestock and campsites, herders face considerable challenges to find locations to establish camps and expand to other seasonal pasture. For instance, in Umnugovi *aimag*, wealthy herders expanded their legal possession of campsites to summer and autumn pastures (Undargaa, 2006). Legal possession of campsites reportedly hinders herders' flexibility and mobility by limiting their option to the same campsites every year (Undargaa, 2006, p. 68). Thus, the repeated use of seasonal pasture or expansion of legal possession of campsites into other seasonal pasture leads to overgrazing.

Defining the problem

Previously, many scholars already agreed on the ineffectiveness of local administration enforcing *ulamjlalt* pasture use rules and norms. Simultaneously, some argued that individual herding households still informally practice *ulamjlalt* rules and norms in their use of pasture even in the presence of increasing heterogeneity among *bag* members (see Chapter 5). Since the land reform, these scholars have agreed that the informal institution no longer works as herders did not comply with the *ulamjlalt* rules and norms of pursuing seasonal mobility or, at least, the *ulamjlalt* rules and norms are contested (various authors cited in Fernandez-Gimenez et al., 2008, pp. 12, 13; Upton, 2009). Some scholars predicted this failure in relation to the land law. For example, Sneath (2003) argued that exclusive property rights may hinder the existing "skills, techniques, institutions and co-ordination" that herders continue to pursue in their pastoral production (Sneath, 2003, p. 454). In other words, the land reform diminished herders' *ulamjlalt* way of accessing pastoral resources. Some scholars explained the problem from the perspective of the property rights approach. Tumenbayar (2000) argued that the law distinguished pastoral resources as state property, whilst limiting herders' rights to

142 *Land reform in pastureland management*

campsites only without protecting their rights to broader pastoral resources (Tumenbayar, 2000). Fernandez-Gimenez and Batbuyan (2004) argued that even though the law protects herders' rights to pastoral resources under shared use among the *bag* members, the problem is,

> "by mandating that these remain open to all," the Law potentially undermines initiatives to grant exclusive tenure over large areas to herding associations or groups to manage for their collective use ... make[s] it difficult to implement rangeland co-management schemes that aim to provide secure tenure over large areas of land to groups of herders constituted as grazing associations so that they can manage use among their membership.
>
> (pp. 146, 163)

These arguments focus on how herders, particularly poor herders, are losing their use rights to pastoral resources (Fernandez-Gimenez and Batbuyan, 2004; Mearns, 2004b), particularly when local administration neglects to address changes in the herders' access to pastoral resources with regard to wealth and local status (Mearns, 2004b). Therefore, the last two positions perceive the Mongolian CPR problem as an open access condition that emerged from the failure of both formal and informal institutions. The next section examines the problem within access as an ability, going beyond the property rights approach.

Land reform in the HBU case area

In this case study, the land reform resulted in similar social and environmental outcomes. However, the problem was the shifting access mechanism to pastoral resources from an informal use right to access both campsites and pasture to a hybrid statutory exclusive individual right to possess a campsite, and *bag* community use right to pasture. This section examines the ways in which the law overlooked acknowledging the importance of the flexible informal arrangement of locally recognized use rights to both campsite and pasture. Here, to adjust to existing conditions, formal control of local government and *Hurals* and informal control of individual herding households each implemented these provisions respectively altogether differently from the way stipulated on paper.

Implementation of legal possession of campsites

Formal control

The local *bag* and *soum* administration has no control over the allocation of legal possession of campsites just as they were unable to control where herders built their shelters after the privatization. First, the benign policies on migration and personal income tax for herders' livestock[19] resulted in local

Land reform in pastureland management 143

authorities' inability to regulate labor and livestock components in all three *bags*. Now, following the re-emergence of pre-collective subsistence and yield-focused production,[20] herders made decisions regarding the increase in[21] their stock levels after taking into account their value in the market and their ability to access markets. As discussed in Chapter 5, DD and UU *bags* witnessed a more natural growth in the number of livestock following the number of local herders' children forming their own independent herding households under stable weather conditions after the 2000 *dzud*. For instance, a UU herder explained the situation as: "A's children [four] have been all married and all B's children [six] got married and separated as independent households. They all have their own livestock. In the 1900s, they all belonged to one single household."[22]

Table 6.1 and Table 6.2 illustrate that almost all participants in DD and UU are local people and their children from the collective period, indicating that all migrant herders after 1991–1999 had left these *bags*. In contrast, the government's inability to control migration led to an artificial growth, increasing number of migrant households with their large herd sizes coming to HBU *bag* following the 2000 *dzud*. According to the observation of a local herder in HBU *bag*:

> HBU [*bag*] used to be the enterprise with the least number of livestock, but now it is the *bag* with the largest number of livestock and the largest number of households with "one thousand head of livestock." The reason is that those households with a thousand head of livestock came from other areas and managed to become residents here.[23]

Table 6.1 and 6.2 illustrate that 60 percent of HBU *bag* respondents had migrated to HBU *bag* since 1991 with more of them showing up by 2000. The majority of them had been herding elsewhere since 1991,[24] indicating their herding background and therefore their need to pursue *otor* in HBU *bag*.

The increase in livestock and population led to increasing demand for legal possession of campsites to access more pasture as occurred elsewhere (Tumen-bayar, 2000; Undargaa, 2006). Upon their arrival, the migrant herders employ combinations of *ulamjlalt* and statutory mechanisms to gain and maintain

Table 6.1 Inward migration status by each *bag* participant since 1991

Inward migration by 2010	Participating households by bag (by %)		
	HBU	DD	UU
Before 1990	40	96	100
1991–1994	18	0	0
1995–1999	18	0	0
Since 2000	25	4	0
Total (n = 97)	40	23	34

144 *Land reform in pastureland management*

Table 6.2 Herding experience by *bag*

Herding experience	Participating households by bag (by %)		
	HBU	DD	UU
Collective herders since 1958	10	52	18
Transition herders since 1991	75	43	68
New herders since 2005	15	4	15
Total (n = 97)	40	23	34

access to campsites and pasture. A HBU *bag* official described the migrant herders' strategy as follows: "They would go on *otor* for two or three years, and perhaps after staying one year here, they would apply for a certificate [legal campsite possession]."[25] In other words, they gain access through *ulamjlalt otor*. Then they legitimize their local residency and access through legal migration (see Chapter 5) and then maintain their access through legal possession of campsites.

Lack of effective residential registration system is a second reason for the local administration's incapacity to control the allocation of legal possession of campsites. In all three *bags*, the authorities provided certificates of possession to individual households as a *khot ail*, which were now a single household in the winter and spring seasons. For the application of legal possession of campsites, a *bag* governor first ensures that the application is from a resident of the *bag* (including migrant herders, who became residents) and that they are in the "A list," which is a *soum* list made up from the livestock census. The *soum* administration registers a family member who is at least 18 years old and married or separated from their parents. This list confirms that the member is from an independent, livestock-owning household.[26] Although a valid criterion for claiming residency registration, membership of the "A list" is problematic for local authorities in controlling access to legal possession of campsites. In HBU *bag* there are many young households that are in the "A list," because they are considered independent herding households and whose livestock is counted separately from that of their parents. Then, in all three *bags*, it was also not unusual for these young families stay with their parents or stay on the same campsites despite legally owning their separate campsites. Moreover, the "A list" apparently includes those who own the livestock, and also includes those who reside in the village or *soum* center and are not full-time herders. According to a UU official, "Campsite possession is allowed for 'citizens who own livestock.' This is, even I possess my own winter and spring campsites.... They can be there or they can allow their herders to stay there."[27] Thus, in all three *bags*, it was a very common strategy for anyone on the "A list" to claim legal possession of campsites, thereby increasing the demand for these. In other words, local administration is legally powerless to control migration, except registering those with livestock in the "A list." Although incapable of controlling the number of campsites, *bag* officials

Land reform in pastureland management 145

exercise particular control over access to it by providing clearance/reference letters, which increases their power and authority. The extent to which they exercised their power differs in the three *bags* due to the differences in their structure of state territorial administration. In DD and UU, the implementation remained ambiguous and chaotic at the beginning. For instance, one of the UU officials recalled that

> When legal possession of campsites was allowed at the beginning, the process was perhaps quite messy, there was no specific land planning…, it was approved either by land officer or *bag* governor. So anybody who thought he had the legal authority approved it; that is why there are many disputes [over campsites] like "this is mine or this is yours."[28]

Currently, their *soum* governments straightened this process out by decreeing that UU and DD *bag* governors now compile the application documents directly for the *soum* land office, which processes the application form for the *soum* governor's approval.

In contrast, HBU *bag*/village officials benefit from this procedural bureaucratic process, because the governor headed their own land office separate from the *soum*. A HBU *bag*/village official described their involvement in legal possession of campsites as "we [HBU *bag* administration] have a role in passing all documents [between local *soum* governor and herders], because we are a *bag*."[29] In reality, instead of the *soum* land officer, the HBU *bag* land officer processes application requests, checking, for example, whether the requested campsite has been claimed by others. Then, the HBU *bag*/village governor essentially approves it by issuing a clearance document for the *soum* governor's signature. This is why, to legitimize their access, migrant herders deal with HBU *bag* officials rather than HBU *bag* herders or Delgerhaan *soum* officials. For instance, by early 2000, this resulted in the HBU *bag* governor issuing more campsites to HBU migrants, which caused disputed claims over the same campsites (particularly some in DD territory, which will be discussed in Chapter 8). By approving migrants' residency via legal possession of campsites, these officials maintained the village population and the status for governing the state allocated budget (see Chapter 5). A local HBU *bag* herder reported the *bag* official's position on migration: "If we allow this many households, then we would qualify as a village, with our own independence."[30] A HBU *bag* official also affirms this: "Yes, they [migrant herders] would be included, that's how we reached a population of 500 or more and became a village."[31] The village status and state budget increase the officials' importance and benefits when dealing with the ministry and with migrant or *otor* herders to access winter campsites in valuable HBU RPA. Local HBU *bag* herders complained that HBU *bag* officials did not do anything to stop the migration, because migration was useful for them in governing the scarce reserve pasture. One of the participants articulated his perception of the conduct of HBU *bag* officials as follows: "This is very different in the HBU

146 Land reform in pastureland management

bag territory, because this is RPA. This is sort of an unofficial statement by locals; people are allowed to become residents there with some sort of bribe."[32] This concern resonated from several other participants from all three *bags*. For instance, migrant herders claimed winter pasture in some valleys of HBU RPA, which UU households customarily used for *otor* movement in pre-collective and collective periods.

Moreover, local officials employ legal possession of campsites only to obtain benefits rather than considering the local capacity of pasture. The HBU *bag* officials' conduct is contradictory to the capacity of the following seasonal pastures in the *bag*. Some migrant herders cannot claim possession of a spring campsite as well as summer and autumn pasture in the river valley. Although aware of the shortage of seasonal pasture for migrant households, HBU *bag* officials have left the matter to the herders to resolve. According to one of the officials,

> Once they come, then I will decide [to register them as resident] and allow them to legally possess winter campsites, which are abundant here.... About spring campsites, we tell them to arrange spring camping by themselves. We have nowhere else to send them for camping.[33]

Similar to a process of residency registration, local administration is limited to only registering/approving the application for campsites. Then, it is questionable whether legal possession of campsites is an adequate mechanism for controlling access to campsites and pasture. As occurred elsewhere and different from the legislation (Upton, 2009), the officials in all three *bags* de facto allow herders to select the location of their campsites before applying for a certificate. According to one HBU *bag* official: "Herders decide, that's actually easier for us, because we can say that "this was your decision [to establish your campsites here]."[34] The state could not bring the movements and livestock of herders into alignment with pasture conditions, since herders informally control their production. *Bag* officials were aware that herders select their campsites where they select their *nutag* pasture area as an important production factor. Local officials had to turn a blind eye to the different strategies herders exercise to access legal possession of campsites. Thus, control over access to pasture de facto shifted from the local administration to individual herding households. However, herders' ability to employ these strategies depends on their migrant status and the *bag*'s institutional background.[35]

Informal control

Formalizing herders' exclusive property rights to campsites led them to change their pattern of resource access. Herders select locations for their legal campsites carefully to access pasture, water and markets regarding their production, particularly, in the situation of the depleted pastoral resources (see

Chapter 5). A local HBU *bag* herder briefly described the de facto process of legal possession of campsite similar in all three *bags*: "We select a place and then inform the local administration where we wanted our winter place to be established."[36] Legal possession of campsite is a fixed pastoral asset[37] and becomes a legal mechanism for herders to gain and maintain access to their new *nutag* seasonal pasture. Increasing numbers of herding households select their campsites based on their production,[38] leading to competition for best pastoral areas in the HBU case. Then, as occurred elsewhere, herders split their families to utilize legal possession of campsites, replacing once legitimate locally recognized use rights to alternate their campsites. This works under stable weather conditions, because their seasonal movements have been restricted within their *bag* jurisdictional boundary due to their residency status. This strategy differs among herders depending on their migration status. There are overlapping forms of this strategy. First, local herders in three *bags* use a connection with local officials. An earlier migrant herder shared this observation:

> If you were working in or had a history of working for the local admin-istration at an earlier time, then they were very good at this kind of strategy. They registered several winter and spring campsites that they wanted under their children's names, when they were powerful. Now they are all retired and managing those campsites.... Those who worked at the local administration often employ this kind of strategy. Otherwise, not all households would be able to do such things.[39]

Second, herders involve extended family members to claim several campsites in close proximity and access larger pasture. A local HBU *bag* herder observed how migrant herders involve their relatives from other jurisdictions in this:

> [H]is wife is related to those households, who came from [western *aimags*]. Through her, over 10 households arrived in the HBU [*bag*]. Then another household [X] also brought many households from a [western *aimag*] and elsewhere. They are all his relatives.[40]

This manner of expansion affected spring pasture of neighboring local herders. A third form, in all three *bags*, involves non-herding relatives in the "A list" to claim more campsites. A local HBU *bag* herder shared this observation:

> They get more winter and spring campsites through their relatives who live in the village, e.g., a son who lives in the village center. They would have/possess all the *buuts* around their campsites in their relat-ives' names and prevent others/outsiders from camping around them. For instance, most households own around 500 livestock. Then if one household has five members who are all adults, then they would all possess campsites.[41]

148   *Land reform in pastureland management*

Migrant herders also use the residency identities of their family members, who left for elsewhere, regardless of their status as herders. A local HBU *bag* herder explained this strategy as follows:

> They would belong to the HBU *bag* at the beginning and get their camp-sites and then later those family members would transfer their residency to *Baganuur* or to the city [Ulaanbaatar]. Meanwhile, household members who stayed behind [here] would keep those campsite certificates that had been given to other members of the household and had already left for other areas. It actually is a rule that the local administration is supposed to take your name off the residency list of the HBU *bag* if you move or transfer your residency elsewhere. But it does not happen.[42]

These forms indicate that family splitting strategies often involve legitimacy of local authorities.[43] Besides the problematic "A list," the family splitting strategy exposes the contested or ambiguous notions of herding household or family. One of the officials raised his concern:

> This situation requires state policy [of clarification]; a household is some-thing like a married couple separated from their parents with their own private assets and property. These days, one senior lady would separate from her adult son and then she would be considered as a single house-hold. Then the meaning of a household is sort of lost. It is more likely that there are two or three households in one *ger*.[44]

Herders reinvented and reworked ambiguous legal notions of residency registration, household and the "A lists" from the past to gain access to legal possession of campsites or project aid,[45] as these are granted to an individual rather than household with several family members. Even if herders lacked property rights to land, they could still use their rights to residency and ownership of livestock to benefit from pastoral resources. The lack of state complementary mechanisms to control the number of herding households and the livestock generated changes to patterns of resource access, decreasing the availability of pastoral resources and making it more difficult for herders to balance the components of production. Thus, formalizing property rights to campsites may not function as an ade-quate mechanism without clear definition of users/subjects or with fluid notions and flexible structures of family or households in pastoral context.

Although these forms of strategies may depict that open access condition prevailed in selecting locations for campsites, herders use informal or formal control to a certain extent to legitimize their access to campsites. Individual herding households informally control others' access to campsites by employ-ing legal possession of campsites. A migrant herder in the HBU *bag* shared his experience of claiming legal possession of campsites as follows:

Well, it was difficult at the beginning [to settle]. Local herders were from here, that's why their attitude towards legal possession was quite different; they would claim "this is mine or that is mine" etc they would come and show their temper or tell us off.[46]

However, legal possession of campsites enables herders to only gain and maintain access to pasture rather than to exclusively manage specific pastoral resources. As elsewhere, legal possession of a campsite does not refer to excluding others from sharing the pasture between campsites. A DD herder explained the reason:

> ...since there is no exact definition, it does not matter whose livestock it is. Even [if] my livestock is out near that household, they would not chase ours away. They would pass their livestock by ours avoiding mixture.... It is better not to define the boundary of pasture, in general. We always manage to pass our herds by others depending on the possibility.... If we define the boundary, it will make things worse, causing local conflict.[47]

The distance between flocks observed by herders in grazing and sharing pasture around their campsites depends on specific terrain,[48] which shapes herders' decisions on where to build a campsite and thus, the distance between campsites. As another participant in DD explained, "there is not an exact definite radius, which indicates 'you can or cannot go further than this'."[49] Thus, acknowledging the diversity in terrain,[50] herders still conform to passing by each other (*zuruulj ideh*)[51] following the *ulamjlalt* way of sharing pasture.

Despite the fact that local herders are aware of who uses which campsites in an informal manner, formal control (if they cannot control where and how many campsites are built) also plays a role legitimizing herders' possession through *bag* (clearance) and *soum* (officials) approval for a certificate. As a local HBU *bag* herder explained:

> When we go and try to claim a campsite, knowing who camps on which campsites all the time, some would claim that this was their campsite that they already possessed. Then I would say "what do you mean, your campsite is that one (meaning another different campsite)," then he would say "this belongs to our son." But then the son would be staying in the city or elsewhere.... We can claim more campsites this way ... but, we know that everybody is aware of who uses which one.[52]

Herders including migrants employ formal legitimization process for both securing their access and controlling others' access to campsites. Legitimacy gained only through the new statutory entitlements system increases influence of formal authorities, who take advantage of it only to extract benefits, and

150 *Land reform in pastureland management*

Table 6.3 Seasonal campsites by *bag*

Legal possession of campsites	Bag households (by %)						Total number of legal possession of campsites
	HBU[53]		DD[54]		UU[55]		
	Yes	No	Yes	No	Yes	No	
Winter	97	3	96	4	81	19	
Spring	65	35	83	17	78	22	
Total (*n* = 97)	37		23		32		92

causes a loss of local endowments (informal control) such as legitimacy by local people, their knowledge of who uses which campsites, and the significance of locally recognized informal use rights.

Using both informal and formal control, herders established many campsites with legal possession and created the concentration[56] of campsites. Over 95 percent (*n* = 97) of all participants legally possess either winter or spring campsites or both in all three areas. However, the concentration of winter or spring campsites differs due to the different terrains in each *bag*. As shown in Table 6.3, the majority of DD and UU households were able to secure access to both spring and winter campsites, mostly by using the family-splitting strategy. In contrast, in HBU *bag*, the majority of those who legally possess campsites are more likely to claim winter campsites than spring ones, due to the abundance of winter pasture in the unoccupied former HBU RPA. Mainly local households already claimed all available spring campsites in the scarce other seasons' pastures, whereas the migrant herders do not due to their larger herd size (Figure 6.2). Thus, herd size shapes one's ability to access pastoral resources. Particularly in crowded areas, it enabled local herders to access campsites on scarce other season's pasture and complicates the process for

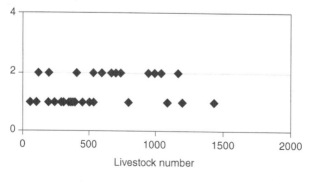

Figure 6.2 HBU *bag* participants' migration status by herd size.

migrant herders.[57] The scarcity of other season's pasture and lack of access to spring campsites led to the increasing number of campsites in the *bag*. Aware of the shortage of seasonal pasture, most migrant households from western *aimags* increasingly established legal winter campsites in the HBU Mountain to graze both the winter and spring seasons and over-stay winter pasture. In contrast, migrants from the Gobi increasingly established legal spring campsites on the southeastern steppe of the HBU *bag*, expanding to the summer and autumn pasture in the river valley. These patterns indicate a changing trend in seasonal pasture use, particularly off-season use of winter or summer/autumn pastures in the HBU *bag*. Therefore, instead of an open access, for the most part herders cannot simply access whatever campsites or pasture they desire. As in the pre-collective and collective period, coordination of the components of production regulated herders' access. In particular, the combinations of factors such as herd size, type and gender, herding strategy for each type of livestock, the availability of labor and pastoral resources within a particular jurisdiction, herders' herding practices that take into account particular ecological conditions, as well as herders' current ability to employ statutory or *ulamjlalt* mechanisms all affect access outcomes for any herders as much as heterogeneity in wealth, social status and herding experience.

Implementation of pastureland management

The local administration's lack of involvement in controlling the important production components diminishes its ability to exercise formal control over access to both legal possession of campsites and pastureland use. The lack of a strict tax[58] system on livestock and migration control affects pasture management in all three *bags*. The increasing number of (migrant) households with large numbers of livestock has led to establishing more campsites, because the capacity for each campsite is limited to 500–1000 livestock. One of the participants who were concerned about the lack of a mechanism to control the number of livestock in a condition of depleted pastoral resources commented that: "There should be a tax on those who have 1000 livestock. This way, there will be a limit on the increasing numbers of livestock. The pasture is getting worse, due to the increasing numbers of livestock and mining."[59] This indicates that an extremely benign tax policy enables herders to increase the number of their livestock.

Besides, currently, the land law is full of contradictory provisions for local administrations to regulate access to legal possession of campsites and pastureland. Although *bag* governors process applications for legal possession of campsites, the *bag Hural* is also authorized to regulate the use and protection of *bag* community[60] use of pastoral resources. Regarding the latter provisions, *bag* officials sought to address the impact of migration in the HBU *bag* on pasture management in all three *bags*. They agree that they have no power to say "no" to migration because of the migrant's constitutional rights.[61] Yet, they have interpreted their legal power under the constitution and the land

152 *Land reform in pastureland management*

law differently to defend their own interests in regulating access to pastureland. DD *bag* officials perceive herders' migration as purely a policy matter, which can be resolved at the *bag Hural*.

> We used to allow them [migrants] to apply for legal possession of campsites. These days, we have no place to give them.[62]
>
> Regarding the conditions that there are too many livestock and not enough capacity of pastureland, we [the *bag Hural*] passed a decree saying that we cannot allow migration of citizens with livestock within our *bag* territory.[63]

Disagreeing with this position of DD *bag*, the HBU *bag* officials argued that this decree impedes human (constitutional) rights.[64] They perceive that the *bag Hural* has a limited power in making such decisions:

> We are not supposed to intervene so much in the issue of legal possession of campsites. The *bag Hural* should only discuss and decide whether we support an entity that wants to possess land.... We [the *bag Hural*] can issue a decree, but not in serious matters that would break laws or abuse power.[65]

Although these are hardly an apparent evidence of misconduct by local officials, they maintain contradictory positions about their legal authority. In particular, their interpretation of their power over legal campsites possession is contested due to the ambiguities in the land law in articulating the authority of *soum* and *bag* governors and *Hurals*. First, *bag and soum Hural* land management planning is supposed to shape allocation of legal possessions of campsites. Both Bayanjargalan and Delgerhaan *soums* have similar interpretation of this process. As stated by one *soum* official:

> The *soum* administration is supposed to approve the *soum* annual land management plan, which is based on each *bag Hural* defining its territorial pastoral capacity, and indicating "in our *bag* there is capacity for how many campsites we can allow for legal possession."[66]

In reality, as discussed earlier, *bag* and *soum* governors and *Hurals* either cannot control herders' de facto selection of campsites based on their production or cannot object an individual's right to legal campsite possession.

Local officials interpret these provisions differently regarding the availability of the pastoral resources in each *bag*. DD officials perceive that their territory has insufficient seasonal pasture to host more migrant households with their large numbers of livestock, and attempt to issue legal possession of campsites to local herders only. Assuming all DD and UU households are local herders, fewer DD households with 700 livestock use the HBU Mountain than those of HBU *bag* (Figure 6.3). In other words, fewer DD households need more

Land reform in pastureland management 153

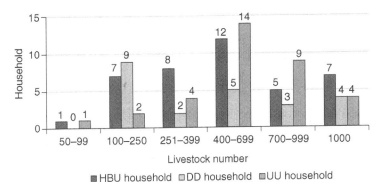

Figure 6.3 Participants' herd size by *bag*.

campsites through family-splitting strategies. Most households have already claimed all available spots for legal possession of campsites by splitting their herds into smaller sizes for better production outcomes. UU *bag* has more households with more than 700 livestock, but it has a much larger seasonal territory than HBU and DD *bags*. In contrast, the HBU *bag* officials perceive they cannot control migration attracted by abundant old RPA *buuts*[67] in the HBU Mountain. This perception encourages migrant herders secure access to pastoral resources by legal possession of campsites.

Moreover, the *bag Hural* exercises more de facto authority than the *soum*'s de jure authority in regulating pastureland use. The *bag* governor has the legal authority to ensure the implementation of decrees issued by *bag* and *soum Hurals* on pastoral issues.[68] Simultaneously, the *bag Hural* has legal discretion over decrees and proposals on pastoral issues[69] and disputes,[70] which are based on *bag* residents' comments and requests, to be approved by the *soum Hural*.[71] This is why DD *bag* officials argue for a *bag Hural*'s legal authority to limit the arrival of migrants, whereas it is illegal for (HBU) *bag Hural* to forbid migrants according to the HBU *bag* officials. Meanwhile, the *soum Hural* also experiences ambiguity in its authority. The *soum* government and *Hural* are authorized to approve legal possession of campsites regarding individuals' constitutional rights. Simultaneously, based on *soum Hural* decisions, it is also authorized to approve *bag Hural* decrees regarding pastoral issues. Ironically, the *soum*'s approval of these two resources (campsites and pasture issue) is supposed to be based on the *bag Hural*'s land management planning[72] and its decrees on pasture management. The *soum* governor and *Hural* faces a dilemma in making decisions over pastureland management versus migration, because *soum Hural* members include *bag Hural* heads who often defend their own interests.

These gaps in the law provides an opportunity for local officials to solidify their authority and influence over controlling herders' access to pastoral resources and reimburse the benefits they used to get from taxes (see Chapter 5).

154 *Land reform in pastureland management*

On one hand, HBU *bag* officials use this gap to maintain their village status,[73] and gain personal benefit from migrants herders. Participants[74] from all three *bags* challenged HBU *bag* officials' position on migration, regarding the fact that the HBU *bag Hural* reflects more the opinion of the officials than that of its herders. On the other hand, DD *bag* officials use their authority to reduce the impact of migration on *bag* herders' pastoral resources. HBU *bag* officials also criticized DD officials' concerns as coming only from a few wealthy herders, who are in the *bag Hural*, and are trying to control the pastoral resources in the RPA. Oppositely, the evidence suggests that regardless of wealth, DD participants, whose winter pasture was located in the RPA, were concerned that *otor* and migrant households affect their seasonal pasture.[75]

Institutional, social and environmental outcomes of the implementation of the legal possession of campsites

Institutionally, in the HBU case area, certain changes occurred in the informal practices of pasture use rules. The inability of the local administration led to individual herding households controlling access to pastoral resources as they control the livestock. As shown in Table 6.4, more than half of the respondents are content with individual herders' making decisions on daily pasture management given the current circumstances (climatic, socio-economic and legal) of regulating pasture use.[76] This reflects the historical pattern of "those who control the production manage the pasture use."[77] What concerns them is the lack of a historically complementary role of local administration controlling jurisdictional matters: in this case, the impact of migration and disputed use over their pasture. The dilemma is that the state created a legal environment in which neither the state nor herders (individually or by group) are able to control migration or the labor component of production,[78] except each using this situation to their own advantages.

Moreover, this situation led herders to change their mobility patterns, which in fact differed among herders regarding their migration status. Following the increasing demand for pasture and concerns over possible legislation of pasture possession/privatization,[80] local herders in all three *bags*

Table 6.4 Most practically involved actors in regulating daily pasture use and satisfaction[79]

Actors (n = 97)	By percentage		
	Herders		Local administration
	Herders		Local administration
Daily pasture management (multiple choices allowed)	99		12
Scale	Satisfied	Neutral	Dissatisfied
Satisfaction	52	31	18

expanded their spring campsites to jurisdictional autumn and summer pastures (Figure 6.4), for off-seasonal use to access more pasture, though it is not allowed (Table 6.5 and Table 6.6). Such expansion would compensate herders' fixed campsites with more flexibility for alternative camping in unstable weather conditions.[81] A local UU herder observed "more spring campsites are built along the river.... [These are actually summer pasture], yes [now it is given for spring campsites]."[82] Local herders see it as their need to utilize legal possession of campsites to legitimize their user rights of other seasonal pastures and stay on their campsites off-season. Lack of other seasonal pasture led HBU *bag* migrant herders to overstay in the mountain winter pasture for half the year in winter and spring. A migrant HBU *bag* explained his strategy for the rest of the year:

> We stay there in the open [mountain] in order to deliver our baby livestock [in spring]. We do not have spring campsite. Those early arrivals to the HBU [*bag*] already got these places, making it quite hard to find a spring place.... We often move [for other season] for greater distances. From X to here, it takes 4–5 days and around 200 km.[83]

This signifies changes in the informal control over access to pastoral resources. The informal cross-territorial *otor* mobility for severe winter conditions has become a strategy to pursue regular seasonal mobility outside of one's jurisdiction elsewhere[84] to cope with a shortage of pasture in their jurisdiction

Figure 6.4 Spring campsite next to the river.

Table 6.5 Impact of legal possession of campsites on changing pasture use rules and norms

Actors	Institutional background	Change	Reason		Mechanism
			Purpose	*Factors*	
HBU (Local herders) DD &UU	*Bag*/village & RPA *Bag*	Off-season use of summer & autumn pasture	Control other's ability to gain access to more seasonal pasture	Weather Need for recompensing flexibility in seasonal movement	Legal campsite possession
HBU (Migrant herders)		Overstaying on winter & spring pastures	Seasonal mobility	Lack of seasonal pasture	Legal campsite possession
		Summer & autumn seasonal mobility outside of the jurisdictional territory			Informal long-distance cross-territorial *otor* movement

Land reform in pastureland management 157

(Table 6.7). This is possible because summer and autumn pasture is more loosely coordinated as locally recognized use rights (Fernandez-Gimenez, 2002; Sneath, 2003). However, these patterns of seasonal mobility are to maintain their production. This is hardly a case of "open access," or "predatory pastoralism," which indicates that some herders take over others' pasture area (SDC, 2010; Upton, 2009). Instead of going everywhere they wanted under the pressure of increasing population, herders in the HBU case area relied either on local herders or the local administration to legitimize their access to pastoral resources via campsite possession or *ulamjlalt otor* movement and locally recognized use rights.

Environmentally, in all three *bags*, changes occurred in the herders' *ulamjlalt* seasonal mobility which resulted in a reduction of the distances between campsites and the use of different seasonal pastures. First, the concentration of legal possession of campsites increases the grazing pressure on pasture between campsites. A local UU herder shared her concern: "In the

Table 6.6 Seasonal mobility patterns of the local households with legal possession of campsites

Seasons	Seasonal mobility	Duration (flexible)	Camping locations	Territory
Winter	Winter	November–April	In the mountain or the lower mountain slopes between the mountain/hill and river	HBU, DD, UU
Spring	Spring	April–June	In the lower mountain slopes between the mountain/hill and river	HBU, DD, UU
Summer	Summer	June–September	Along the river grass	HBU, DD, UU
Autumn	Autumn	September–November	In the lower mountain slopes between the mountain/hill and river	HBU, DD, UU

Table 6.7 Seasonal mobility patterns of the migrant households without campsite possession

Seasons	Seasonal camping	Duration (flexible)	Camping locations	Territory
Winter	Winter	November–April	In the mountain	HBU
Spring	Spring	April–June	In the mountain	HBU
Summer	Summer	June–September	X	Elsewhere outside of HBU
Autumn	Autumn	September–November	X	Elsewhere outside of HBU

158 Land reform in pastureland management

river valley, some households built their shelters close to existing spring shelters, affecting the others nearby; in terms of pasture, these are too close, less than 500 m sometimes."[85] Second, the expansion of spring campsites to other seasonal pastures leads to crowding and depleted pastoral resources. In DD, a local herder noted that "The number of spring campsites increased and there are no more reserve pastures [in the *bag*] anymore. This has resulted in the shortage of pastureland."[86] Therefore, a reduced mobility distance within and between seasonal pastures led to constant grazing pressure. A local UU herder said that: "Local households are too crowded, the pasture is becoming worse. The grass does not really grow well these days, so local households are getting crowded wherever there is a little pasture."[87] As Table 6.8 illustrates, participants identified overgrazing as one of the key challenges along with climate change (as "other" in the table) in pursuing pastoralism in 2010[88] (Figure 6.5). This is particularly among the HBU *bag* participants, and especially regarding the HBU *bag*'s relationship to migration.[89] The legal possession of campsites for the spring becomes a primary factor shaping the availability of other pastoral resources such as water and services in the HBU case area. Reduced mobility diminished herders' freedom of movement (rotation or seasonal mobility) in alternative locations to rehabilitate pasture, an important strategy for maintaining pastoral production[90] and in managing the rangeland ecosystem (Miller and Sheehy, 2008).

Socially, legal possession of campsites affects herders' use rights to pastureland and private assets for pastoral production. This is apparent from the herders employing any available mechanisms to gain access to pastureland.[91] First, legal possession of campsites does not secure herders' gaining and maintaining access to alternative or quality pasture[92] as it is a migratory resource (Feeny et al., 1990). When there is lack of pasture or water around their campsites under unstable weather, with less faith on the regulatory power of these legislations, they seek out alternative camping areas following the *ulamjlal*,[93] an informal rule of capture[94] or locally recognized use rights

Table 6.8 The participants' perception of challenges to pursuing mobile pastoralism

Challenging issues	Bag households (multiple choices allowed) (by %)		
	HBU	DD	UU
Public services	3	0	3
Water	10	13	6
Overgrazing	60	43	38
Livestock thievery	50	57	32
Mining	0	3	18
Other	53	22	68
Total ($n = 97$)	40	23	34

(a)

(b)

Figure 6.5 HBU (a) and elsewhere (b) in the same Herlen River terrain in July, 2010.

160   *Land reform in pastureland management*

(Chapter 3). When asked about whether herders ever used other's campsites in their local area,[95] a UU herder explained the local herders' strategy:

> If this [campsite] is possessed by someone, ask "if you do not stay, can we stay?" The owners anyway, must be staying on another's campsites, too. This is how people find campsites following the available pasture. If they possess a campsite and the grass around this campsite does not grow, they will chase after a better pasture.... We [locally] know this household will not come, so we do not have to ask for permission as well. They will not mind about it.[96]

This indicates that herders have returned to the pre-collective way of sharing campsites to deal with uncertainty, and the need for flexibility in mobility. They still cannot say "no" to whoever asked to stay on their campsites as long as it is available. De jure formalization of property rights to campsites by individual household only resulted in a de facto practice that campsites are now likely to be called after the name of their legal possessors rather than a landmark, and herders usually expect one another to come and ask for the availability of a campsite first, if possible.[97] This is perhaps mainly for the protection of private, but movable assets such as livestock shelter and the reserve dung or *buuts*. In other words, similar to ambiguous notions of family or household, it is hardly the case for legal possession of campsites that the subject/user has clearly identified as the exclusive owner and their relation is strictly fixed to a plot of land as a private property.

Second, legal possession of campsites is an inadequate means of securing herders' private and movable pastoral assets (livestock shelters and fire fuel) in their absence.[98] Nobody including the local administration legally claims responsibility for protecting herders' campsites, resulting in the free-for-all capture of these assets. Thus, instead of building fixed shelters, the herders shifted toward an *ulamjlalt* structure of campsites using mobile fences or natural mountain shelters (Chapter 3). According to a UU respondent, "The grandpa gave us his shelter materials to establish a campsite. Although we are thinking about it, there is not enough grass growing around the campsite. Also, there is robbery or thievery of the spring shelters."[99] Avoidance of using a fixed livestock shelter enables herders to access campsites through both legal possession of campsites without a livestock shelter or informal use rights to alternative *buuts* and increase their ability to gain access to pastoral resources[100] under depleted pastoral resources. Research participants stated that local people hardly stay on their campsites, but camp and graze their livestock nearby. In particular, wealthy herders[101] move more often at increasing distances and seek out any available pasture, which is near herders with an average or small herd size. As one of the UU participants described: "those who are wealthy and powerful would grab the best pasture and those who are not wealthy and are powerless end up having nothing."[102] Wealthier herders (that is, those with 800–1000 head of livestock) claimed that their grazing

Land reform in pastureland management   161

does not affect poor herders with small numbers of livestock, by referring to *ulamjlalt* practices that the latter do not require as much pasture as large herds need (Fernandez-Gimenez, 1999, 2006). They justify their move by an *ulamjlalt* norm of sharing pasture, "camp and graze as many as the pasture allows" (Chapter 3). Simultaneously, some[103] herders including poor ones, who do not move often, attempt to exclude others from sharing pasture via legal possession of campsites, as perceived earlier by Fernandez-Gimenez and Batbuyan (2004). This may diminish herders' right to exercise the *ulamjlalt* rule of sharing pasture between campsites. Although de facto legal possession of campsites shapes herders' access to pasture, herders find it hard to exclude others regarding the *ulamjlalt*. As Upton (2009) argued about the exclusive and inclusive paradigm of sharing pasture, herders in the HBU case do use *ulamjlalt* reciprocal use rights to access pasture under unstable weather condition. Although access is based on one's wealth, this is not strictly a case of class distinction. As in the pre-collective period, regarding the difference in herd size, wealthy ones employ poor herders for labor in return for access to pastoral assets or resources, or wealthier herders could be hit by dramatic loss of livestock. Thus, regardless of wealth, herders employ both mechanisms whenever it suits their purpose of gaining access to pasture.

The collision and combinations of these two mechanisms challenge the legitimacy of both *ulamjlalt* use rights and the statutory possession right. No shelter to mark one's legal possession of campsite led asset-rich herders to employ the family-splitting strategy and legal possession of campsites to claim more winter campsites. This affects both locals and *otor* herders' former ability to gain access to pastoral resources as noted elsewhere[104] (Sneath, 2003). Particularly in the context of *otor* movement, herders face challenges in gaining access to *buuts* for short periods to cope with the extreme weather conditions. According to herders, who experienced the problem during 2009 *dzud*:

> It is ok; we are doing fine, free in our *soum* roaming anywhere we want without being controlled by our possessed campsites. In other *soum*, it is hard...[105]
>
> The worst thing is that when we go to HBU Mountain for *otor*, the available *buutses* are all possessed by someone, who says this is mine or yours, etc.[106]

The dispute over these winter *buuts* was a major problem among visiting *otor* herders from UU and hosting herders from HBU and DD *bags*. On one hand, local herders de facto claimed they legally possessed these *buuts* since there are no shelters to distinguish among them. According to a UU respondent: "HBU Mountain is filled with herders from western *aimags* calling them "local household." They perhaps bribe the local officials and claimed a place called Jaran. There is no place left for *otor* households in that area."[107]

On the other hand, UU herders argued that they have right to stay there using *ulamjlalt* mechanism of *otor*, because HBU Mountain was historically

162 *Land reform in pastureland management*

used as an *otor* area. Their attempt to re-establish their customary use right often fails. Another UU respondent explained, "If we stay here and build an extra *ger* on a closer *buuts*, then HBU *bag* households will come and pack it away. Those who are staying closer would be able to do so."[108] This changing nature of access to pastoral resources also diminished the herders' *ulamjlalt* pattern in accessing cross-territorial mobility. Disputed use of campsites in this context could portray a possible open access condition.

Questioning "the problem of the open access condition"

Some scholars related the "open access problem" to the fact that the land law did not protect herders' statutory property rights or allowed open access in pasture (Fernandez-Gimenez and Batbuyan, 2004; Tumenbayar, 2000). Another position explained that the land law introduced exclusive (possession[109]) property rights to pastoral resources, which may hinder the herders' ability to gain access to pastoral resources using *ulamjlalt* pasture use rules and norms (Sneath, 2003). The findings from the HBU case supported the last argument. Formalizing the herders' statutory property rights to pastureland does not by itself secure their ability to gain access to pastureland, whilst affecting dual control over the pasture management: changing local officials' complementary role in production management and herders' ability to pursue *ulamjlalt* pasture use rules and norms. This raises a question whether the state has capacity to directly regulate pastureland management, particularly via property mechanism (exclusive property rights), or the state needs to restore its historically complementary role in co-management of production (components) with its non-land-based legal mechanisms (livestock tax, labor movement and state territorial administration).

The land reform policy overlooked the importance of historical dual control (their complementary roles) over the production and the pastureland. First I argue that the land law overlooked the fact that a notion of a campsite with its *buuts* is inseparable from the surrounding pastureland, both of which were historically controlled under the same use rights. Whilst maintaining the use right to the surrounding pasture, formalizing exclusive rights to campsites and its *buuts* as residential plot devalued its significance beyond a location point to access pastoral resources. In the historical pastoral context, the herders' use rights go beyond these campsites as they were the ones who micro-manage the production (Chapter 3). Second, the land law overlooked acknowledging the importance of herders' historical role in enforcing *ulamjlalt* pasture use rules and norms better than local authorities for the purpose of micro-managing both pastureland and production in a flexible manner. By formalizing two different rights to campsites and pasture, the land law diminished herders this ability. Now, de jure, herders were supposed to manage only their campsites, whilst the local authority became the "legitimate body to control pastoral resources" employing *ulamjlalt* pasture use rule and norms

(Fernandez-Gimenez and Batbuyan, 2004). Authorities' complementary role was in macro-management of production via controlling labor and livestock based on territorial administration. The HBU case illustrated that the formal control of central-government and self-governing *Hurals* failed to enforce its authority over pastureland (territorial-based use rights to pasture and exclusive private rights to campsites) due to losing their complementary roles. This resulted in individual herding households informally controlling access to pasture based on their production. Therefore, the law swapped the role and places of the authorities and individual herders in overall production management, changing the dual control and hindering their roles and capacity in *bag* community pasture management. Third, land law formalized few of the *ulamjlalt* rules and norms that pertained only to pastureland. It overlooked recognizing the important role of overall management of *ulamjlalt* pastoral production in pastureland management. Therefore, more than anything, misinterpreting pastureland management with property rights approach and the lack of attention to the principles of dual control over the management of pastoral production resulted in breaking down the fundamentals of the pastoral production and pastureland management in Mongolia.

This discussion raises the question whether conditions in Mongolia are really open-access regime from the failed overlapping or nested formal and informal institutions. Instead of a separate exclusive state ownership and/or a group/communal management of pastoral resources, in Mongolia, these were historically integrated into a single system of dual control over the integrated management of production/components. Therefore, instead of focusing on whether the state recognized community rights to CPR (Feeny et al. 1990), the issue is to examine to what extent the system is broken down or persists during the socio-political and economic transitions. In other words, the problem is not necessarily an absence of property rights, but more a question of historical pluralism in pastoral institutions, a system that embeds both state and herders with their complimentary roles for pastoral production management. As the HBU case illustrates, land reform in Mongolia has led to a CPR dilemma by exacerbating conflict between formal and informal control over access to pastureland, instead of achieving sustainable land management. The problem is that national and international policy advisors examine the CPR dilemma only within the western oriented exclusive property rights concept.[110] As argued in Sneath (2003), the property rights approach often carries the risk of shaping a policy narrative that supports a push for imposing exclusive property rights. National and international policy advisors see the inability of the local administrations to regulate pastoral resources as an absence of formal pastoral institution, which leads to open access. Instead of understanding the historical property relationship in the pastoral context in Mongolia, such a view has led to a further push to define property rights for pastureland management. The next chapter discusses engineering herder groups as a formal property institution to strengthen community-led or CBNRM.

Notes

1 Article 29.1 the Law on land, 1994.
2 Article 53.4 the Law on land, 1994.
3 Article 52.7 (in Mongolian) of the Land law, 2002 "*Uvuljuu havarjaanii doorhi gazriig Mongol Ulsiin irgen hot ailaar dundaa hamtran ezemshij bolno.*"
4 Article 51 the Law on land, 1994.
5 Article 51.3 the Law on land, 1994.
6 Article 30.1 the Law on land, 1994.
7 Article 6.2 the Law on land, 2002. Experimental group use has been conducted by donor projects. This will be discussed in Chapter 7.
8 In some places mostly in northern parts of Mongolia, several households share a cluster of campsites, on which each individual household has separate *buuts* to shelter their own livestock. Thus, local administrations allocate one possession certificate among several households, listing the names of the heads of these households on the back of the certificate. In other words, each can claim their small plot of campsites through one certificate. In some places, one household stays on one small camp, then, the local administration allocates one certificate in the name of that household (Undargaa, 2006).
9 Article 35.1.7 of the Land law, 2002 (added July 9, 2009).
10 Article 35.1 of the Land law, 2002.
11 Article 23.2.13 of the Land law, 2002.
12 Article 31.3 of the Land law, 2002.
13 Article 29.4, 31.2 and 33.1 of the Land law, 2002.
14 Article 33.4 of the Land law, 2002.
15 Article 52.1 of the Land law, 2002 (see Chapter 5).
16 Since transitions, the *bag Hural* became an ineffective body as fewer people in fact attend the meeting.
17 Article 52.10 of the Land law, 2002, says that the local *soum* administration and its *Hural* should manage the pastureland by, first, employing traditional pasture use rules and norms; second, classifying *soum* seasonal pasture into winter, spring, summer, autumn; and third, classifying reserve pasture for sustainable use and conservation. A *bag Hural* would be in charge of enforcing a *soum* governor's decision on *bag* pastureland management and would also resolve any disputed use of pastoral resources.
18 For instance, in Jinst and Bayan-Ovoo *soums*, in Bayanhongor *aimag*, most poor households did not possess *uvuljuu havarjaa* because they did not have viable numbers of livestock (Fernandez-Gimenez and Batbuyan, 2004).
19 Herders do not pay a grazing fee, but only *maliin huliin tatvar* (a tax on livestock). After privatization the government adopted a more benign tax policy in order to avoid imposing an excessive tax burden on herders, and levied a special reduced income tax on herders. Thus, herders paid only 50 MNT (4 cents by 2000) per sheep unit with 100 percent exemption of tax from a 20 sheep unit per family member for the purpose of risk management during severe weather conditions (The law on personal income tax, 1993). However, under the 2006 law, the amount of tax was increased and fluctuated between 50 and 100 MNT per sheep unit depending on the province, with fewer and fewer exemptions being allowed. Under this law, they also obtain a discount on their tax for creating wells and for paying tuition fees for their children attending university (The law on personal income tax, 2006). However, in 2009, the government exempted herders from tax on livestock, due to the heavy losses of livestock herders faced during the 2009 *dzud* (Article 16, law on personal income tax 2009 amendments; SDC, 2010). Livestock tax does not earn a significant amount of revenue for the central government as it only covers 2 percent of the national budget, but it is important for the revenue of *soum* governments (SDC, 2010).

20 See Humphrey (1999).
21 According to Bruce and Mearns (2002), herders increased the numbers of their live-stock rather than selling due to the unfavorable market price after the privatization.
22 Interview 47 (Undargaa, 2013).
23 Interview 25 (Undargaa, 2013).
24 This includes children of collective herders.
25 Interview 14 (Undargaa, 2013).
26 Interview 14 (Undargaa, 2013).
27 Interview 54 (Undargaa, 2013).
28 Interview 56 (Undargaa, 2013).
29 Interview 21 (Undargaa, 2013).
30 Interview 20 (Undargaa, 2013).
31 Interview 21 (Undargaa, 2013).
32 Interview 25 (Undargaa, 2013).
33 Interview 23 (Undargaa, 2013).
34 Interview 25 (Undargaa, 2013).
35 Local herders in all three areas used the family-splitting strategy to gain control over more seasonal pasture, expanding to summer and autumn pasture with campsite possession, even though these are not allowed to be individually pos-sessed. The HBU *bag*'s lack of seasonal pasture led migrant herders to use camp-site possession through the family-splitting strategy in order to pursue their regular seasonal mobility. They maintained their usual access to winter pasture and gained access to spring pasture in the HBU Mountain.
36 Interview 8 (Undargaa, 2013).
37 As discussed in Chapter 5, in all three *bags*, spring pasture was a strategically important seasonal pasture for production. Most herders in all three *bags* legally possessed their spring campsites along the river since they had livestock shelters there (see previous Chapter 5). In terms of winter campsites, it has to be a spot where thick *buuts* has already accumulated, in a location which receives less snowfall and provides more protection from the wind for accessing winter grass. In the HBU and DD *bag* cases, local herders and early migrants mainly claimed old *buuts* or *hond* on HBU Mountain, but these were usually close to their spring campsites and village. Simultaneously, herders also continued to use other un-owned *buuts* as they were necessary for their production strategy. This is because of the abundant availability of other *buuts* in the area. This indicates that winter campsite possession had not become the main legal mechanism to gain access to pastoral resources in HBU *bag*.
38 As discussed in Chapter 5, the herding patterns of migrant households differ from those of local herders and shape their selection of the location for building their spring and winter livestock shelters. Similar to the patterns adopted by earlier migrants, new migrants sought mountainous or steppe terrain which they were used to for herding livestock.
39 Interview 7 (Undargaa, 2013).
40 Interview 18 (Undargaa, 2013).
41 Interview 7 (Undargaa, 2013).
42 Interview 7 (Undargaa, 2013).
43 Herders are able to employ the family-splitting strategy because of the use of the "A list," which acts as an ineffective formal control over the migration mech-anism, for their own advantage and split their family to claim more pasture.
44 Interview 24 (Undargaa, 2013).
45 This problematic notion of household also artificially inflates the number of poor households and both herders and local officials take advantage of it to distribute or receive aid (Interview 24, Undargaa, 2013).
46 Interview 23 (Undargaa, 2013).

166   *Land reform in pastureland management*

47 Interview 26 (Undargaa, 2013).
48 Who uses how much depends on herd size.
49 Interview 29 (Undargaa, 2013).
50 *Ulamjlalt* management pattern includes rehabilitation through seasonal movements and rotations.
51 Interview 8, 26 and 40 (Undargaa, 2013).
52 Interview 7 (Undargaa, 2013).
53 In 2004, there were 30 households who legally possessed campsite possession (Interview 14). Now, since 2009, several new households reside in the HBU *bag*. Since 2009 17 new winter and 13 new spring campsite certificates have been issued in 2011.2.15, decree 16 of *soum* governor. These applications for campsites were all from HBU *bag*. In 2011–2012 no outsiders came to the HBU *bag* as residents (Interview 25). By 2010, there were 209 winter campsites registered and herders (overlapping) registered to possess (not clear whether de jure or de facto) 101 of these campsites (HBU *bag* document 2010.03.12). There are 32 herders registered as HBU *bag* herders and 31 registered as households with livestock (HBU bag document 2010.01.18).
54 In DD, according to a *bag* document, 78 herding households possess winter and spring campsites. However, 7–8 households in the *bag* do not possess campsites.
55 In UU, according to a *soum* document, 93 winter campsites and 83 spring campsites are possessed by residents (Interview 42, Undargaa, 2013).
56 It is impossible to calculate the range of the distances traveled between seasonal mobility in all three areas. This is because the three areas differ immensely between and within each other due to differences in terrain, thus the availability of seasonal pasture.
57 Migrant herders in the HBU *bag* shared his experience of finding a spring campsite:

> The households who lived here before [us] got their [spring] campsite earlier at the beginning [of the privatization] in the river area for spring, summer and autumn [Interview 21].... We do not have spring campsites ... So it looks like it is quite hard to find spring pasture [Interview 23].

They were not even able to employ spring campsite possession as a mechanism to gain access to seasonal pasture due to the lack of spring pastoral resources in HBU *bag* territory. Otherwise, once they found a *nutag* and campsite, then a large herd uses more pasture around the campsite, depending on the available pasture around the campsite.

58 SDC (2010) argued that controlling herd size with tax alone does not necessarily change herders' behavior towards the sustainable use of pasture and may contribute to exacerbating poverty. They assume "neither tax nor subsidies alone cannot solve [the] open access problem" (SDC, 2010, p. 3).
59 Questionnaire 49 (Undargaa, 2013).
60 Article 22.2.2, Land law, 2002.
61 Interview 14, 24 (Undargaa, 2013).
62 Interview 24 (Undargaa, 2013).
63 Interview 36 (Undargaa, 2013).
64 Interview 21 and 36 (Undargaa, 2013).
65 Interview 22 (Undargaa, 2013).
66 Interview 25 (Undargaa, 2013).
67 About 60 percent of the DD winter pasture area is included in the RPA (Interview 24, Undargaa, 2013). That is why many DD households possess winter campsites in the RPA. The DD spring area is not included in the RPA, but it is heavily used by *otor* households from the Gobi, because it is the corridor to the HBU RPA.

Land reform in pastureland management 167

68 It appears that during the peak migration period there was no clarification by earlier *soum* and *bag* officials regarding speedy migration.

69 Article 22.1.1, Land law 2002.

70 Article 52.10, Land law, 2002.

71 Article 52.2, Land law, 2002.

72 Article 7.1.3–7.1.5, Methodology for *soum* annual land management plan, Agency for Land affairs, Geodesy and Cartography, Ulaanbaatar (2006).

73 The *soum* has no legal authority to say "no" to legal possession of campsites, once it is de facto allowed at the *bag* level. As a result, since 2009 the Delgerhaan *soum* administration has allowed 17 new winter and 13 new spring campsites under the decree of 2011.2.15, following the migration trend. Yet, these applications were all from HBU *bag* (Interview 25, Undargaa, 2013).

74 There are many such quotes from herders from all three areas regarding the increasing number of migrant households taking over RPA sites for *otor*. This is also a serious matter for DD herders, whose winter campsites are in the RPA, thus *otor* and migrant herders are expanding to DD winter pasture areas and competing with local herders.

75 Interview 22, 24, 28, 29, 31, 32, 33, 36 and 37 (Undargaa, 2013). Fewer people in fact attend the meeting. Those who do attend are usually bound to officials for guidance in making policy.

76 This is because local officials cannot decide even in the case of disputes between different applicants over the same campsites. For instance in UU *bag*, the local officials' role is limited to mediating the matter for negotiation among the claimants (Interview 40 and 50, Undargaa, 2013). Also, herders are reluctant to acknowledge the legitimacy of the current law, or its capacity to regulate pastoral resources as herders own their private livestock.

77 In this time of independent herding management, herders are aware that their access strategy to pastoral resources is after all shaped by their production. A UU herder explained:

> Well, it depends on how many livestock they have and how long they would stay around here etc.... Usually, households with many livestock do not come and stay around here, because they also need to look at the availability of the pasture...
>
> (Interview 48, Undargaa, 2013)

78 Local jurisdiction used to control migration movements, but now it only registers them. Informally, herders balanced labor through production under jurisdictional control, but since this type of jurisdiction has no control over migration, this informal practice has weakened.

79 This survey was conducted in May 2010 when herders were in their spring camps. Some of the respondents were in their winter pasture in the mountains as they either had no spring place or their spring place was not good for pasture.

80 Interview 48 (Undargaa, 2013).

81 In 2010, HBU, UU and DD *bags* were seriously affected by drought as summer began with rain in June and the green grass had completely dried up due to heat over 40°C with no more rain. This continued until late September, and then cold rain fell and damaged the last remaining river grass for fattening the livestock before the cold winter. Grazing conditions were quite bad, particularly because the drought was followed by a serious *dzud* in 2009, when *otor* herders filled HBU Mountain and grazed over all the pasture in the winter and spring of 2009 and 2010.

82 Interview 48 (Undargaa, 2013).

83 Interview 23 (Undargaa, 2013). Twice, I drove 200 km one way to another *aimag* and *soum* territory to pursue one of the migrant households for an

168   *Land reform in pastureland management*

interview during the summer and autumn. I missed him both times, only to meet his wife in the HBU RPA the following winter.

84 These households seek out access to pasture not just anywhere they prefer, but available spacious pastoral areas elsewhere and gain access through local connections. The area where they spend summer and autumn was available as it was less crowded due to the absence of some local households, many of whom had lost their livestock and migrated to urban areas. Thus, these herders went there to rely on relatives, who were married to locals. I limited my inquiry here, but they must have negotiations with local officials as well, because there were several migrant households with more than a thousand livestock each.

85 Interview 49 (Undargaa, 2013).

86 Interview 36 (Undargaa, 2013).

87 Questionnaire 50 (Undargaa, 2013).

88 After a severe winter in 2009, HBU case area (all three *bags*) was also affected by a bad drought and a stormy spring and summer. A small amount of rain fell in early June and then no rain at all until late September, 2010.

89 This is because of higher concerns with livestock thievery resulting from outsiders in and out of the HBU RPA area. Also, they identified climate change as a challenge in all three *bags*. They used to experience *dzud* once every decade. It was also recorded that *dzud* occurred once in 14 years in eastern *aimags* during *negdel* period (Templer et al. 1993). Now, they experience more *dzud* in periods shorter than ten years.

90 In other words, in the HBU case, the flexibility embedded in the *ulamjlalt* locally recognized use rights, is now restricted under the current regulatory environment, leading herders to rely on legal campsite possession to gain, maintain and control access to pastoral resources.

91 Right after the transition, herders returned to the informal mechanism of locally recognized use rights to campsite. Then under the land reform, they turned to legal campsite possession to secure their rights to pastureland. Currently, herders face the dilemma of employing both (legal campsite possession and *ulamjlalt* rules and norms) as a mechanism, which I discuss in this section.

92 Water does not alone shape access to pasture. Access to pasture depends also on weather. Herders had to leave the Herlen river area and move elsewhere in autumn because of the drought and lack of grass.

93 The concentration of campsites under unstable climate conditions or overgrazing has led to pasture degradation, particularly over the last five years. Thus, the research participants "move wherever there is grass and water," using this principle widely to cope with drought in 2010. However, this principle does not lead to open access as herders confront the many limitations to gaining access to pastoral resources elsewhere.

94 The informal rules of capture includes "any place not occupied is mine," "small herds use smaller pasture" or "camp and graze as many as the pasture accommodates," etc.

95 Questionnaire 43 (Undargaa, 2013).

96 Questionnaire 71 (Undargaa, 2013).

97 Interview 53 and others (Undargaa, 2013).

98 Herders from three *bags* often lose their livestock shelters and their *argal hurzun* fuel resources due to looting while they are on the move.

99 Interview 55 (Undargaa, 2013).

100 This is particularly where herders compete for any available *buuts* and its surrounding pasture.

101 Bayanjargalan *soum*, where UU *bag* is located, has the largest number of herders with one thousand livestock in the Tuv province.

102 Questionnaire 82 (Undargaa, 2013).
103 Interview 47 and 55 (Undargaa, 2013).
104 This suggests that campsite possession as a statutory law has become a mechanism to subtract the availability of pasture for others' use, instead of sharing pasture through *ulamjlalt* locally recognized use right to campsite. Thus, exclusive property rights to specific pastoral resource do not necessarily solve the problem of subtractability, but may exacerbate it.
105 Questionnaire 96 (Undargaa, 2013).
106 Questionnaire 68 (Undargaa, 2013).
107 Questionnaire 49 (Undargaa, 2013).
108 Interview 55 (Undargaa, 2013).
109 Possession/lease as exclusive management rights, otherwise, pastoral resources are all property of the state.
110 This is mainly for the purpose of integrating the land tenure to the current market system. However, the problem is that current economic policies designed to boost the market economy are not free of fault in their predictions. Enormous problems have been encountered in introducing exclusive individual property rights even in agrarian contexts, where the land tenure system does not require as much flexibility and mobility as in the pastoral context.

References

Bazargur, D (ed.) (1998) *Geography of Pastoral Animal Husbandry*, TTC Company, Mongolian Academy of Science, Ulaanbaatar.

Bruce, J W and Mearns, R (2002) "Natural resource management and land policy in developing countries: lessons learned and new challenges for the World Bank," IIED, London.

Cooper, L (1993) "Patterns of mutual assistance in the Mongolian pastoral economy," *Nomadic Peoples* 33, 153–162.

Feeny, D, Berkes, F, McCay, B J and Acheson, J M (1990) "The tragedy of the commons: twenty-two years later," *Human Ecology* 18:1.

Fernandez-Gimenez, M E (1999) "Sustaining the steppes: a geographical history of pastoral land use in Mongolia," *The Geographical Review* 89:3, 315–336.

Fernandez-Gimenez, M E (2002) "Spatial and social boundaries and the paradox of pastoral land tenure: a case study from post-socialist Mongolia," *Human Ecology* 30:1, 49–78.

Fernandez-Gimenez, M E (2006) "Land use and land tenure in Mongolia: a brief history and current issues" in Donald J Bedunah, E McArthur and M Fernandez-Gimenez *Proceedings of the Conference on Transformations, Issues, and Future Challenges*, Salt Lake City, UT, Proceedings RMRS-P-39, Fort Collins, CO: US Department of Agriculture, Forest Service, Rocky Mountain Research Station.

Fernandez-Gimenez, M E and Batbuyan, B (2004) "Law and disorder: local implementation of Mongolia's land law," *Development and Change* 35:1, 141–165.

Fernandez-Gimenez, M E, Kamimura, A and Batbuyan, B (2008) "Implementing Mongolia's land law: progress and issues," The Center for Asian Legal Exchange (CALE), Nagoya University, Japan.

Griffin, K (2003) "Urban-rural migration and involution in the livestock sector" in K Griffin (ed.) *Poverty Reduction in Mongolia*, Asia Pacific Press, Canberra, 56–71.

Humphrey, C (1999) "Rural institutions" in David Sneath and Caroline Humphrey (eds.) *The End of Nomadism: Society, State and the Environment in Inner Asia*, Duke University Press, Durham, NC, 68–136.

170 Land reform in pastureland management

Ickowitz, A (2003) "Poverty and the environment" in K Griffin (ed.) *Poverty Reduction in Mongolia*, Asia Pacific Press, Canberra, 95–112.

"Law of Mongolia on Land" (2002).

Mashbat, O S (2004) "Mongolia: managing the transition from nomadic to settled culture" in Jim Rolfe (ed.) *The Asia-Pacific: A Region in Transition*, The Asia-Pacific Center for Security Studies, Honolulu, 323–334.

Mearns, R (2004a) "Sustaining livelihoods on Mongolia's pastoral commons: insights from a participatory poverty assessment," *Development and Change* 35:1, 107–139.

Mearns, R (2004b) "Decentralisation, rural livelihoods and pasture-land management in post socialist Mongolia," *European Journal of Development Research* 16:1, 133–152.

Meinzen-Dick, R, Pradhan, R and Grigorio, M D (2004) *Collective Action and Property Rights for Sustainable Development*, CAPRI, Washington DC.

Miller, D and Sheehy, D (2008) "The relevance of Owen Lattimore's writings for nomadic pastoralism research and development in Inner Asia," *Nomadic Peoples* 12:2, 103–115.

Natsagdorj, Sh (1972) *Soum, khamjlaga, shavi, ard*, Academy of Science Publishing, Ulaanbaatar.

SDC (2010) "Livelihood study of herders in Mongolia," Swiss Agency for Development and Cooperation (SDC), Ulaanbaatar.

Simukov, A D (1931) "Kulturno-bytovyye usloviya jizni Mongol (tesisy k dokladu)" in Yuki Konagaya, Sanjaasurengiin Bayaraa and Ichinkhorloogiin Lkhagvasuren (eds.) *Kratkaya geographiya Mongolskoi Narodnoi Respubliki: Hozyaistvo, cultura, i byt nasyelyeniya, Tom II*, Gosudarstvyennyi muzei etnologii Osaka, 593–599.

Sneath, D (2003) "Land use, the environment and development in post-socialist Mongolia," *Oxford Development Studies* 31:4, 441–457.

Sneath, D (2004) "Property regimes and sociotechnical systems: rights over land in Mongolia's 'Age of the Market'," in K Verdery and C Humphrey (eds.) *Property in Question: Value Transformation in the Global Economy*, Berg, Oxford, New York, 161–182.

Templer, G, Swift, J and Payne, P (1993) "The changing significance of risk in the Mongolian pastoral economy," *Nomadic Peoples* 33, 105–122.

Tumenbayar, N (2000) "Land privatization option for Mongolia," in *Constituting the Commons: Crafting Sustainable Commons in the New Millennium, the Eighth Conference of the International Association for the Study of the Common Property*, Bloomington, Indiana, May 31–June 4.

Undargaa, S (2006) *Gender and Pastoral Land Use in Mongolia: Dilemmas of Pastoral Land Tenure*, Centre for Development Studies, The University of Auckland, Auckland.

Undargaa, S (2013) "Property 'owners' without rights? Exploring property relations and access in the Herlen Bayan-Ulaan Reserve Pasture Area of Mongolia," Crawford School of Public Policy, Australian National University, Canberra.

Upton, C (2005) "Institutions in a pastoral society: processes of formation and transformation in post-socialist Mongolia," *Comparative Studies of South Asia, Africa and the Middle East* 25:3, 584–599.

Upton, C (2009) "'Custom' and contestation: land reform in post-socialist Mongolia," *World Development* 37:8, 1400–1410.

7 Community-based natural resource management

Formation of herder groups in Mongolia

In addition to the state-led land reform to improve pasture management, international and national development organizations promoted CBNRM by restoring and improving the historical, or crafting new self-governing community institutions based on the CPR approach. In Mongolia, restoring the historical formal pastoral institutions involved the following options with regards to territorial structure (i) recreating the *hoshuu* (banner) level expansive jurisdictional boundary; (ii) using the current *bag* or *soum* level jurisdictional boundaries; or (iii) crafting or re-designing former smaller units as a self-governing community based on the notion of *neg nutag usnii-han*, a group of households that share the same pastoral resources (Fernandez-Gimenez, 1999a, 2002). Engineering individual herding households into smaller units than a *bag* or a *soum* as *neg nutag usniihan* as fixed socio-economic unit (referring to pre-collective territorial unit), was considered essential to shift an ineffective subsistence production to one that was modern and/or intensified livestock production, and a village sedentary lifestyle for alternative livelihood options that adjusted to a market economy (Bazargur, 1998, pp. 171–190; Khazanov, 1994). Also, referring to the CPR approach, many international agencies supported the herder group approach towards developing CBNRM and protecting herders' custodian/indigenous rights to pastureland and lifestyle. Regarding the contradictory legal environment, some suggested formalizing herder groups' statutory property rights to pastoral resources, nested within state territorial administration to enable them to pursue exclusion (Fernandez-Gimenez and Batbuyan, 2004; Griffin, 2003; Ickowitz, 2003; Mearns, 2004; Tumenbayar, 2000). The process of engineering this smaller socio-economic unit almost echoes earlier attempts to form voluntary collectives or communes (*nuhurlul, hamtral, horshoo, negdel*) in the 1930s, which struggled heavily due to the dependence on third party finances, and technical/ideological support, which mainly ended up on paper until the eventual forced collectivization (see Chapter 4).

172   *Community-based natural resource management*

Differing approaches by donor organizations

Understanding the process and implications of forming herder groups and their capacity for exclusion is critical for the future of local pasture management. Donor supported projects focused on developing the herder group as an autonomous property institution to exercise exclusive use or possession rights to pasture, mainly referring to Ostrom's concepts of institutional design principles (SDC, 2010, p. 33). GTZ[1] pioneered to engineer herder groups to strengthen a self-governing community institution (*nutagiin uuruu udirdah udirdlaga*). Here, the group formation was not explicitly designed to establish externally conceived "institution building" and it was rather simpler to "enforce this manifestation of traditional pasture management" and traditional collective action (Schmidt, 2004, p. 21). The emphasis on traditional collective action on pastureland management was also intended to correct the misleading perception that there was an absence of community among herders (Schmidt, 2004). Whilst attempting to restore or even redefine what traditional or customary institutions are, they adopted an approach more or less to mend the traditional institutions. They re-organized individual herding households into community organizations (*nuhurlul*) and required them to clearly define their social and resource boundaries to be credited as a community based on a notion of people, who shared the same resources (*neg nutag usniihan*).[2] In other words, this refers to a neighborhood of herding households that share pastureland around campsites to address the principle of flexible mobility and to collaborate on pastoral production (Schmidt, 2004; SDC, 2010; Upton, 2008), and form a group by selecting their own leaders and committees in a democratic participatory manner, developing their own pasture rules, if given legal property rights to pastoral resources (Fernandez-Gimenez, 2002; Griffin, 1995; Schmidt, 2004). Then, these actors would enforce and monitor group practices of more fixed routines under *ulamjlalt* pasture rules and norms. These principles essentially served to exclude non-members or trespassers from the local *bag* or outside (Undargaa et al., 2007; Upton, 2008). Regarding this re-imagined capacity of exclusion, many national and international programs shifted their experimental approach to scaling up the number of herder groups and proposing to allow group possession of pastureland under the newly drafted law on pastureland.[3]

However, defining *neg nutag usniihan* seems to present particular difficulties as donor programs redefined it differently for setting up herder groups' social and resource boundaries. First, GTZ supported the formation of a volunteer unit of 10–20 households based on kin, as well as neighborhood relationships (Schmidt 2006, p. 21; SDC 2010; Upton 2007). Their social and resource boundaries were mainly confined to the four-season pastureland within their *bag* or to the water sources shared between different jurisdictional territories, indicating that their social and resource boundaries went beyond jurisdictional boundaries. Second, UNDP supported households of relatives and their shared use of winter and spring seasonal pastures or wells. This approach

Community-based natural resource management   173

presented difficulties in matching a group's social and spatial boundaries for better institutional outcomes, because member households are often spatially mixed with non-member households (Fernandez-Gimenez et al., 2008). Third, the World Bank funded Sustainable Livelihood Program (SLP) shifted its approach of defining the herder group to one based on jurisdictional boundaries, aiming to reflect historical pasture management practices embedded in local territorial administrative structures. Local *soum* and *bag* administrations divided an entire *bag* into explicitly mapped and delineated group territories (SDC, 2010; Upton, 2009). The project staff acknowledged that delineating group territory in this way was not specifically for allocating exclusive rights to a particular group; thus, if needed, members can use another group's territory (Upton, 2009, p. 8). Fourth, the Green Gold program supported by the Swiss Development Cooperation (SDC-GG) changed its approach to the compulsory formation of a pasture-user group (PUG) in larger areas within an entire *soum* territory with larger numbers of households (40–100) (Fernandez-Gimenez et al., 2008; SDC, 2010). The social and resource boundaries would be confined to the *soum* boundary, so that "group membership is defined by locality and resource use, facilitating a match between spatial and social boundaries of pasture user groups and unit" (Fernandez-Gimenez et al., 2008, p. 42). Thus, similar to the GTZ and UNDP groups, the social and resource boundary of each group may lie outside their *bag* boundary, combining members and territories from two different *bag*s.[4] Setting social and resource boundaries of herder groups smaller or larger than their current *bag* will be discussed regarding the complexity in legally recognizing a group's exclusive management rights[5] to its territories.

Scaling up the number of herder groups leads to the question of translating these processes into actual positive outcomes of collective action. Defining a group's social boundaries often lead to classifying *bag* households into specific groups based on their living conditions. This was to achieve a balance in power relations, which is important for strengthening local community institutions (Agrawal, 2003; Dietz et al., 2003). Initially, in most cases, those who were more opportunistic and in a better socio-economic position took advantage of donor support for group formation (Fernandez-Gimenez et al., 2008; Undargaa, 2006; Upton, 2008). Regardless of whether they were a member or non-member, the older, poor or female-headed households were at some point excluded or marginalized from participating in group activities due to their geographical isolation, less capacity of mobility and/or fewer kin or social networking support. In some groups, some members were considered reluctant to collaborate or referred to as "lazy," a notion once used for some poor herders in the pre-collective period (Fernandez-Gimenez et al., 2008; Undargaa, 2006; Upton, 2008). Eventually by 2006, donor programs advocated for herder group formation, which was more inclusive of the poor. Emerging trends of group formation were mainly composed of average to poor households. This is because fixed group boundaries were less likely to correlate with members with differing herd sizes. In some parts of

174 *Community-based natural resource management*

the SDC-GG program, wealthy herders either avoided joining a PUG or were not accepted in a PUG because of their large herds (SDC, 2010). Similarly, in the UNDP project, poor herders with fewer livestock were less mobile and were able to remain within a group territory, whereas wealthier herders needed to move due to the group's small territory and depleting pastoral resources.[6] Therefore, not everyone is able to recognize and comply with the group's exclusive rights, particularly when herders legally claim pastoral resources within their *bag* territory via residency, livestock ownership and legal possession of campsites. In other words, it is challenging to delineate group social and resource boundaries between member and non-member households regarding their dynamic movement patterns during unstable weather conditions. As a result, many groups supported by GTZ and SLP were on paper only (Mau and Chantsallkham, 2006). Some members were unaware of their membership or non-members were reluctant to acknowledge groups' pasture use rules and norms (Undargaa et al., 2007). This situation generally reflects the 1930s when most collective groups were formed among the poor and average households and their production needs were segregated from those who were wealthy to engineer new socio-economic units that fit the egalitarian ideology of socialism (Simukov, 1931, p. 134). Therefore, drawing clearly defined social and resource boundaries, particularly based on living conditions in non-egalitarian pastoralism, had future implications on accomplishing collective action pastureland management coordination.

Moreover, concluding that group formation led to better pasture management is a complex issue, and is too simplistic. Research carried out among these experimental herder groups found that 11 percent more bio-mass was generated in group areas than in non-group areas due to group pasture management (Leisher et al., 2012). Simultaneously, the same research reported that there was no statistically significant difference between group members and non-members regarding their herd size, the level of collaboration with local administrations, and in the occurrence of disputes (over pastoral resources) (Leisher et al., 2012, p. 6). These findings seem to be contradictory regarding whether group collective action specifically explains the improved ecological conditions, because these three criteria for herder group are also supposed to indicate the level of group collective action on pasture management and be different from non-members. Another research conducted on similar experimental groups also concluded that the herder group as an institution and its project activities may not fully explain the difference in ecological conditions between group and non-group areas (Addison et al., 2013). In fact, another research in the same area revealed the opposite of collective action, regarding small size group territory, which raises questions of how to balance the production components among group members. Fernandez-Gimenez et al. (2008) highlighted that "some [herder group members] clearly expressed the idea that the total number of livestock within the group's territory would ultimately be limited" (Fernandez-Gimenez et al., 2008, p. 35). Then the question is open-ended as to whether group members prefer voluntary reduction in livestock numbers, when yield-focused production is popular and herders are interested in increasing their herd size due to the fact that the livestock product is undervalued at local market. Group members were expected to increase their household income from various project activities such as alternative income generating activities, and collectively and voluntarily reduce their livestock numbers to lessen the pressure on their pasture (Mau and Chantsallkham, 2006). However, there was almost no voluntary livestock reduction among members even with increased incomes. In fact, 44 percent of the participants in another research claimed they used concession credit from the project for purchasing more livestock. Thus, with regard to alternative livelihood options, the "underlying philosophy is unrealistic, and may even be counterproductive" (Mau and Chantsallkham, 2006, pp. 15, 23). In other words, the idea of group pasture management overlooks the complexity of pastoral production within larger social and economic conditions. Overall, group possession of pasture, a formalized grazing management, is not necessarily the key to collective action on improving pasture management (Fernandez-Gimenez et al., 2008). Herders' grazing strategies and pasture rehabilitation depend on the weather, which shapes their herding strategy and conditions of access to other production resources to pursue mobility (Fernandez-Gimenez et al., 2008, p. 45). Thus, the ways in which group social and resource boundaries are defined shape group effectiveness in collective action and improvements in pastureland management.

Challenges to group collective action and pasture management

These outcomes on collective action reveal three main challenges for herder group pasture management. First, herder groups' ability to pursue collective action heavily depends on group leadership and support from state-based actors (Batkhishig et al., 2012; Mau and Chantsallkham, 2006; Schmidt, 2004; SDC, 2010; Undargaa et al., 2007). Schmidt (2004) argued that leadership skill contributes to good governance of a group by making sure that all activities are transparent, involving joint decision making of all members, and that accountability is assured for the use of communal funds. Although the issue of imbalanced power relations among group members was of concern, whether or not group leadership balances power relations and provides equal opportunities for all members and collective action remains questionable. This is related to the ways in which the involvement of a third party defines groups' social and resource boundaries, as it is a popular notion that third party involvement leads to success (Batkhishig et al., 2012). As Upton (2008) explained, a successful group is particularly dependent on the involvement of the project team facilitating the members in fostering the "growth of interpersonal trust and cooperation," because herders' possibility of joining a group or its collective action is mainly shaped by whether they have the time to take part in and the labor required for organized collective action, the financial constraints, group size and/or their geographical distance from the

176 *Community-based natural resource management*

majority of members (Upton, 2008, p. 175). However, Sneath (1993) argued that grouping based on *neg nutag usniihan* is a form of an externally constructed social group and that it cannot be a pastoral institution. Even the involvement of a third party seldom leads to successful collaboration. An empirical research on group evaluation (Undargaa et al., 2007) revealed that respondents from only three groups out of 12, which were facilitated with PRA exercises and considered successful by the project team, stressed the existence of collaboration among the members. Among these three, some respondents were concerned that group leaders' preferred primarily capable members to be trained and involved in the activities for the success of the group (Undargaa et al., 2007).

Second, when group formation is based on a rigid definition of *neg nutag usniihan*, the challenge comes in accommodating the principle of "freedom of movement" of its members. The project design emphasized that "the approach to institution was not strategic and not based on a thorough prior analysis," whilst recognizing the existence of local power relations and heterogeneity within the herding community (Schmidt, 2004, p. 20). Upton (2008) argued that this approach to institution building was not necessarily based on the notion of a herding community as it once existed in its historical, socio-political and ecological context. Adopting a notion of *neg nutag usniihan* resulted in groups' social and resource boundaries, which are much smaller than *bag* and *soum* jurisdictional boundaries, in which herders' movement was confined in the past (Fernandez-Gimenez, 1999a; Lattimore, 1941; Mau and Chantsallkham, 2006; Sneath, 2003). Under this arrangement, some projects, which are experimenting with herder group pasture management, have already acknowledged the difficulties of pursuing exclusion and reciprocity, and the possession of pasture by herder groups.[7] In fact, *neg nutag usniihan* does not necessarily perform a crucial function as a production unit (Bold, 1996, p. 76). It is more a social networking mechanism, which enables herders to collaborate on their complex and flexible seasonal mobility and camping, rather than a territorially fixed group (Sneath, 1993). Thus, the group's effort to pursue exclusion based on this notion raises particular concerns over maintaining the fluid nature of social and resource boundaries of groups and their relationship to non-group areas (Fernandez-Gimenez et al., 2008a; Upton, 2008).

Third, although nested within a broader state territorial administration, herder groups assuming the role of formal control appears problematic in sharing power with other state-based or formal actors over governing pastureland. Successful cases of local pasture management involve both herder groups making and enforcing rules, which is legitimized by the re-enforcement of the local administration (Fernandez-Gimenez et al., 2008). With regard to different state-based actors sharing authority over pasture management, Schmidt (2004) raised the important question of "whether a parallel structure to the territorial administrative (government) structure has been developed through donor support; and if the local government sees community organizations as a threat" (Schmidt, 2004, p. 27). The author reported that a local administration accepts group formation as a positive contribution to strengthening local pastoral institutions. They were envisioned to reduce the workload and alleviate the financial constraints of local administrations in governing the herders (Mau and Chantsallkham, 2006; Schmidt, 2004). However, this portrayal overestimates the ability of herder groups in managing pasture independently, while underestimating the many difficulties they face. Some relate the groups' failure only to the lack of skill in organizing themselves and the lack of support from the local administration in understanding the significance of the herder group and supporting the groups' collaboration at the completion of project funding (Batkhishig et al., 2012; Chantsallkham, 2009; SDC, 2010). In reality, another project case reveals conflicting interests among herder groups and local administrations over who should claim benefits from visiting herders' use of local pastures.[8] Since group politics with local administrations are mainly shaped by group leadership (Mau and Chantsallkham, 2006; Schmidt, 2004; SDC, 2010), group pasture management is therefore dependent on both group collective action and its collaboration with local administrations, which have a bigger management role than just formalizing the group's legitimacy. In fact, Fernandez-Gimenez et al. (2008) found that the majority of respondents "supported joint regulation or co-management by herders and the local administration," though herders were the main actors (70 percent) in regulating seasonal pasture use (Fernandez-Gimenez et al., 2008, p. 34). Further difficulties occur due to the lack of collaboration between the donor projects, local administration and the herder groups, and neither of these actors "can alone effectively manage pasture or respond to disasters such as *dzud*" (Fernandez-Gimenez et al., 2012, p. 848). Therefore, forming herder groups and its collective action appears much more complicated, not to mention exercising exclusive possession rights for pasture management, because of the factors related to balancing pastoral production components within larger socio-economic conditions, beyond just defining social and resource boundaries for small groups. The next section examines these issues in the context of the HBU case area, discussing the challenges the SLP project faces in forming herder groups and their collective action.

Group formation in the HBU case area

In the HBU case study areas, the SLP project employed a top-down, but ambiguous approach to forming groups and defining their social and resource boundaries. *Bag* governors and *soum* SLP project extension officers were assigned to facilitate group formation for delivering aid-based activities to local communities,[9] instead of working with single households. Initially, they encouraged volunteer herders in all three *bags* to form small size groups. In the HBU *bag*, "volunteering" meant joining a group they liked, but all herders would belong to a group.[10] In DD *bag*, officials registered whoever decided to form a group. In UU, group formation was in the early stages. In

178 *Community-based natural resource management*

all three *bags*, local officials were reluctant to define a specific group resource boundary. Instead, they defined social boundaries by dividing all herders into the *aravt*, a group of ten households, which was used for administrative purpose in the past (see Chapter 3). Here, they considered *aravt* as *neg nutag usniihan* based on the geographical proximity of herders' key spring camp-sites and pasture as these shape herders' access to other seasonal pastures and keep them together most of the year. This division was for the purpose of improving management of pasture (protecting wells and springs) and pro-duction (pasture fencing for juvenile livestock, protection against livestock thievery).[11] They excluded herders' winter camping patterns for defining social boundaries, because herders separate by spreading across HBU Moun-tain. This indicates that group pastureland management does not necessarily include winter pasture, which is important for pastoral production. However, as elsewhere, this top-down approach only had reality on paper as very few herder groups were actually formed in the area. Table 7.1 shows that the majority of total participants stated "no" that they were not a member and that they had never heard of herder groups in their *bags*. The remaining participants mentioned that *soum* officials once attempted and failed to establish herder groups. Although a HBU *bag* official claimed that there was an active herder group in the area,[12] this group existed only on paper as its nominal members confirmed that there was no such group.[13] A voluntary group based on relatives also exists nominally in DD.[14] Also, according to one participant in UU *bag*, "the *soum* divided households into groups in top down manner; but none are active."[15] Thus, group formation was merely limited to an externally constructed process, since no group was actually reported to exist in the area.

Forming groups based on social boundaries failed for several reasons. First, this was an attempt to impose an assignment on herders, without taking into account their residency in different jurisdictions. One UU respondent, who claimed that their group was to be an NGO, explained:

> The group used to be the neighboring four households from UU and X *bag*. The local administration suggested we form a group to possess a well.... We grew vegetables, then we all did not have time; we dispersed and moved away from each other to follow pasture.[16]

Table 7.1 Herder group formation by *bag*

Herder group formation	Bag households (by %)			Total
	HBU	*DD*	*UU*	
Yes	3	22	12	10
No	98	78	88	90
Total (*n* = 97)	40	23	34	

Community-based natural resource management 179

This indicates that herders' collaboration is shaped by their pasture use patterns, which is often confined within their jurisdictional boundary. Second, herders, mostly opportunistic members, joined a group nominally or temporarily mostly for its incentives such as micro-credit and project support to obtain benefits,[17] rather than collaborating on their pasture and production management or preventing livestock theft. Third, groups formed in this manner, even among relatives, are unable to gather for collaboration. According to a member of a nominally existing group in DD *bag*:

> Although 10 relative households joined from our *soum* center, we were no longer involved in any [shared] activities. We were supposed to mend this hand-well, but we haven't done it yet. We were given a tractor to make hay and for moving between seasonal pastures. My son-in-law drives the tractor in the *soum* center now, cultivating agricultural land for others.... We actually mended one well before. We wanted to improve it but nobody is coming to do it anymore. Right now, there is no one, who supports it.[18]

Thus, project incentives remain in the hands of those who turn it into a personal gain, rather than for maintaining group collective action as envisioned by the project.

In fact, the group pastureland management idea conflicts with local norms and practices in several respects. First, in spite of failed attempts to strengthen herders' externally constructed social capital by setting social boundaries, herders maintain their social capital by collaborating informally on their production activities within their informal networks. None of the participants mentioned formal group collaboration and pasture management.[19] Of the total participants, 63 percent ($n = 97$) manage herding independently, hiring households with small or no herds to supplement the extra demand for labor. The remaining 37 percent collaborate informally with their neighbors or relatives for long distance *otor*, preparation of winter food, cleaning and fixing campsites, or milking mares. Second, local herders' idea of pasture management differs from those set down by the project. Development projects often fund establishment of reserve pasture or haymaking areas for strengthening group pasture management (Schmidt, 2006; SDA, 2010). In the HBU case, at the UU *bag* meeting in 2010,[20] herders did not vote for the project proposal for fencing small patches of pasture in their winter and spring or haymaking areas (Figure 7.1). They considered that these initiatives would mainly serve individual interests since there was no clear indication of who would be responsible for what, and how it would be done. Instead, herders voted for the support to protect saltlicks, springs and muddy areas, which are shared among local and neighboring *bag* and *soums*, and opted for improving their quality of livestock with a breeding program. Since SLP funds group activities in order to deliver its aid to responsible local actors, it required the herders to form a group and contribute 10 percent of the cost of these activities. According to a project officer:

180 *Community-based natural resource management*

If these initiatives really need to be done, then herders need to establish a group to be responsible for the possession [having exclusive title] of the land. It cannot be [held in] among a *bag* community (*dundiin*). Otherwise, nobody can take responsibility over it. If herders want to do it, then I will make those who wanted to be responsible for it to establish a herder group and include this proposal in the 2011 plan.[21]

Figure 7.1 At the UU *bag* meeting, herders were concerned about pollution on the salt lake.[22]

Interestingly, the project officials were incapable of supporting herders' initiatives in any other way, except the very rigid agenda for involving them in group pasture management.

Third, conflicting interests among stakeholders portray contradictory ideas on local pasture management. Addressing herders' needs through project funding is controversial. In one of the *bags*, tensions arose over control of the SLP project funding between the *soum Hural* and the *soum* SLP committee.[23] The *soum Hural* criticized the project committee for prioritizing fencing of pasture areas for the sake of the project, when it does not benefit any herders. The project officer also blamed the *Hural* for installing a livestock bath in the *soum* center, which is too far from the herders and overlooked their needs. Ironically, herders did not vote for either of these proposals.[24] These conflicting stakeholder interests essentially diminish the idea of group pasture management, because they rarely address the ways in which herders collaborate on production and pastureland management.

Understanding community social boundaries

This CBNRM project was limited in its ability to form an exclusive group management, because it overlooked the following factors that shape community social boundaries and its pasture management. First, *neg nutag usniihan* is an analytical term to identify those who are from the same jurisdiction, but distinguished by different levels of jurisdiction depending on the context.[25] Instead of the designation of geographical proximity to define social boundaries for a fixed group or social unit, herders employ it as a social networking[26] mechanism among all sorts of stakeholders, who are from the same jurisdiction. These include relatives, neighbors, local and national level officials and political representatives. In the HBU case area, the social boundary of *neg nutag usniihan* is fluid horizontally and vertically, and goes well beyond small size herder group members, particularly when herders collaborate on production and pasture management. For instance, without formal group formation, DD *bag* herders[27] collaborated with the *bag Hural* (which includes *bag* herder representatives), *soum* administration and an acting parliament member to halt the operation of a mining exploration company and protect their pasture and water.[28] In contrast, UU *bag* herders lacked support from their local administration and political representatives, and were unable to collaborate as *neg nutag usniihan* to stop mining exploration on their side of the territory.[29] One UU herder, whose pasture was affected by mining exploration, stated that "Our *soum* [officials] does not oppose these mining people, whereas Delgerhaan always does, particularly two years ago."[30] Thus, stakeholders from different localities have varying degrees of ability to collaborate as *neg nutag usniihan* depending on their interests. Even among herders, migration shapes their ability to collaborate as *neg nutag usniihan* on pasture management. In HBU *bag*, herders' networking pattern as *neg nutag usniihan* is based on their migration status, creating different levels of collaboration between local and migrant herders. Depending on their birth place,

182 *Community-based natural resource management*

migrants from certain *aimags* emerged as *neg nutag usniihan* and network less with local herders, unless connected through marriage. For instance, some never visit other local herders even though they share a valley in the same *bag*, or they dispute over pasture with neighboring local households.[31]

In contrast, herders in DD and UU *bag* widely network as *neg nutag usniihan* because they have belonged to the same jurisdictions for several generations (Figure 7.2). Regardless of their kin relations, herding households camp

(a)

(b)

Figure 7.2 Local herders milking mares for their friends, who were absent (a). Siblings herd and milk only their horses jointly due to scarce pasture and livestock thievery (b).

as neighbors in three successive seasonal pastures and consider themselves as *neg nutag usniihan* without necessarily referring to any group membership. They support each other's herding or production when necessary.[32] For instance, a UU herder explained that they use this "informal networking mechanism" for *otor* purposes: "We can go with our local friends and neighbors (*nutagiinhan*), and stay closer to each other in order to take care of all our horses in the HBU Mountain, where you are likely to lose your horses to livestock theft."[33] Thus, some herders linked by some common geographical residence also work as *neg nutag usniihan* depending on the context.

Second, herders' collaboration as *neg nutag usniihan* is a dynamic relationship shaped by their production strategies. Herders decide on their production based on their herd size and on the amount of pasture available. The relationship between these resources and collective action needs to be explored within the changing *hot ail* structure, which limits the possibilities of herders collaborating on their production and pasture management. In the past, each *hot ail*, regardless of the number of households, contained a maximum one thousand head of livestock regarding the capacity of a campsite[34] and surrounding pasture.[35] In the HBU case area, currently, a *hot ail* is mostly composed of single *ail* (a household) with more than two *gers* (extra kitchen or storage *gers*), due to the increasing numbers of livestock depending on depleting pastoral resources between campsites. For instance, one UU respondent's decision about camping as a single household on *otor* based on their herd size is as follows: "Last year, we kept my brothers' livestock. But this year, we may herd only our own, because we both have many livestock and there is not enough pasture capacity for staying in one place all together."[36]

In HBU and UU[37] *bags*, most *hot ail* is composed of a single household all year around, because the majority of participating households in these *bags* have larger than average herd sizes (Figure 7.3). Particularly, those who own more than 700 head of livestock are unable to camp, even with poor households pooling labor due to depleted pasture. Individual households manage their labor-intensive jobs on their own, unless they have time to help each

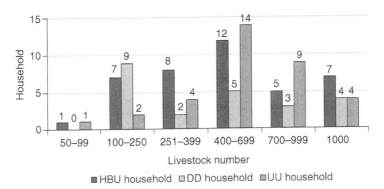

Figure 7.3 Range of livestock ownership by household per *bag*.

184 *Community-based natural resource management*

other, regardless of kin relations (Figure 7.4). In contrast in DD *bag*, more than two households at a time are able to camp together, because the majority of respondents have small size herds (Figure 7.3). This occurs particularly through autumn and winter to pool labor for milking, slaughtering, herding or pursuing seasonal or *otor* movements, as noted elsewhere (Bold,

Figure 7.4 Everyone in the family contributes to household production.

1996, p. 69). Thus, a household with an average herd size is able to camp with a household with a smaller herd size as a *hot ail*, keeping their combined herd size below one thousand head. Yet, herders with different herd sizes encountered in this research said they preferred camping alone to secure their production due to the reduced distance and depleted pasture between campsites. On the one hand, herders wish to camp with poor herders with good herding experience. On other hand, some local poor households, who own their own campsites, prefer camping alone, particularly in spring to increase their herd size.

Third, changing *hot ail* structure resulted in increasingly dynamic social boundaries, particularly for a *bag* community. Although the state maintains the *bag* herders' dynamic social boundary through a residency mechanism, many single households obtain extra labor resources outside of their *bag*. In the HBU case area, wealthy herders hire from outside a wage herder, who owns almost no livestock, in order to control the number of livestock in a *hot ail*. The wage herder stays with the host family or on his own to earn a living. Compensating labor demands by drawing on external sources existed in pre-collective period as it was easy to hire some migrants without livestock to integrate into the community rather than one with livestock regarding local pasture capacity.[38] After a one-year contract trial period, wage herders with non-resident status become legally registered as residents to gain access to campsites and other productive resources. Thus, compensating labor demands by drawing on external sources has increased the dynamics of community social boundaries. Also, as discussed elsewhere (Fernandez-Gimenez, 1999b, 2002), seasonal or absentee herding in the HBU case area also contributes to the dynamics due to fluctuations in household labor and herd size in different seasons. In some seasons, regardless of the living conditions, herders temporarily move to settled areas for trading, school children, teaching or for their elders. They often leave their livestock behind with relatives or wage herders, thus becoming absentee herders as noted elsewhere (Fernandez-Gimenez, 1999b; Sneath, 2003). For instance, a UU respondent described their strategy as an absentee/seasonal herder:

> Wage herders stay at my *ger* [alone] and use everything, like our family member. They do not have to have their own livestock, but herd for us for three seasons. We constantly come back and forth. Sometimes, we hire an assistant for him.[39]

Although seasonal herders are mostly local residents, their occasional presence in herding also affect community social boundaries and its pasture management. For instance, one HBU *bag* herder shared her observations on her seasonal neighbors:

> We usually camp in summer between X and Y. But now, there is someone staying on that area.... That household is from the outside,

from a city or province center. They are a relative of "A," who works in the village. "A" allowed them stay there. "A" camped near our spring camping spot.... That's why we moved to Z area.[40]

Under these changing resource access conditions, absentee or seasonal herding can be challenging for *bag* pasture management (Figure 7.5). These are among many examples, in which different actors benefit from natural resources by controlling livestock or other productive resources without claiming exclusive property rights to land. In fact, it raises the question of "who is a herder," the response to which has implications for defining the social boundaries of any small or big size groups and their pasture management.

Fourth, legal possession of campsites also affects community social boundaries and its pasture management as ascribing economic value to pastureland increases the exploitation of pasture more for gaining economic benefits than managing it properly. In the HBU *bag*, households with an average herd size and legal campsite possession rent out their campsites to visiting *otor* herders in exchange for 2–3 sheep if this is compatible with their herd size and production strategy.[41] This shows the changing nature of reciprocity, from mutual assistance to looking for economic incentives by controlling access to pastoral production resources. Also, it often leads to disputable use and overgrazing. Neighbors of those who are renting are forced to share the small pasture between the campsites with larger numbers of visiting livestock.[42]

Figure 7.5 Occasionally some herders claim pasture around their locally recognized summer camping spot by leaving a landmark. However, they need to camp elsewhere when other seasonal herders are camping nearby.

Similarly, in another project area, a member of a herder group rented their campsite to outsiders. In other incidents, more campsites were built in a group's territorial area or *otor* households moved into their area.[43] In these cases, local authorities are incapable of solving such disputes due to the incompatible legal environment, even though they have legitimized the influx in community membership (see Chapter 6). In other words, defining group social boundaries is difficult when herders legitimize their access to pastoral resources with legal possession of campsites. Following the increasing demand for campsites, herders employ legal possession of campsites to exploit any available pasture, regarding that it does not often secure their access to better pasture and production.

Understanding community resource boundaries

The CBNRM project overlooked several factors that affect community resource boundaries and its ability to exclude others in all seasons. First, under stable weather conditions, herders pursue four season mobility as a basic production strategy regarding their herd size and available pastoral resources. This mobility shapes the *bag* community resource boundaries, which embed fluidity to facilitate freedom of movement. In the HBU case area, participants in each *bag* carry out different numbers of seasonal movements annually, though the social boundaries for herder groups on paper were drawn through their three seasonal pastures. In DD and UU *bags*, households on average move four or more times,[44] whereas HBU *bag* households move between three and four times (Figure 7.6). Seasonal movements appear more dynamic as these are based more on the quantity of available pasture within the jurisdiction than on herd size. The majority of HBU *bag* respondents, regardless of herd size, move 3–4 times, which only indicates a basic seasonal mobility (Figure 7.7). In other words, a lack of seasonal pasture due to the RPA within the *bag* reduced most herders' possibility of pursuing summer *otor* to improve the

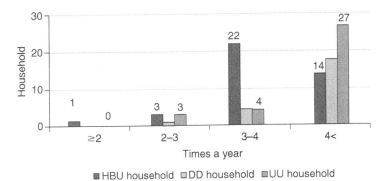

Figure 7.6 Movement frequencies by different *bag* households.

188 *Community-based natural resource management*

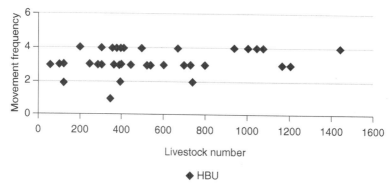

Figure 7.7 HBU participants' movement frequency by livestock number.

quality of their livestock. Only fewer households, of those who owned more than a thousand head of livestock, move more than four times a year within, or crossing the *bag* boundary for other seasons, and extend the resource boundary beyond the HBU *bag*. In contrast, UU and DD participants, regardless of herd size, are able to pursue more summer and autumn *otor* within their own territory, because of the ratio between household herd size and respective *bag* territory, outside of the RPA (Figures 7.8 and 7.9).

Second, resource boundaries become much more dynamic when herders change the characteristics of their usual seasonal pasture during unstable weather conditions, which destroys or blocks available pasture. Then, freedom of movement in search of pasture refers to summer and winter long or short distance *otor* movements in seasonally and geographically specific terrain, or crossing jurisdictional boundaries of different levels (Figure 7.10). The respondents in HBU and DD *bags* have a limited tendency to pursue cross-territorial *otor* movements, since they can winter in the HBU Mountain, which is an historical RPA located in the territory of their *bags*. In contrast,

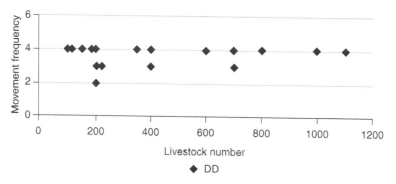

Figure 7.8 DD participants' movement frequency by livestock number.

Community-based natural resource management 189

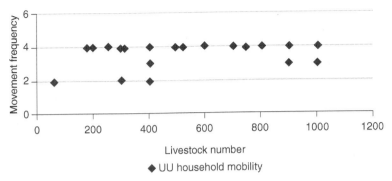

Figure 7.9 Ulaan Uhaa participants' movement frequency by livestock number.

UU herders pursue more cross-territorial *otor*, because their winter campsites are located away from the RPA. Simultaneously, in severe winter conditions,[45] herders move elsewhere regardless of their legal possession of campsites, following the pre-collective *ulamjlal*. Then, herders who usually share the same seasonal pastures pursue different camping patterns, depending on the type of herd, its size and labor demand for this type of herding. In particular, the movement of poor herders becomes quite unpredictable when they herd for different households annually, depending on their herd size, in order to gain access to a campsite. For instance, a DD wage herder described that his winter pattern depends on his employer's pattern:

> This household would usually go and stay close to the *soum* center. They came from the *soum* center and came here on *otor*. The year before last, we got their livestock and stayed at their winter campsite. Then we spent spring near the *soum* center at their spring campsite. Then we came here [to our own place].[46]

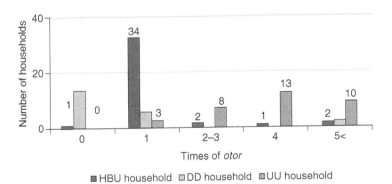

Figure 7.10 Otor frequencies by households in different *bags*.

Those who rent their campsites also follow an unstable camping pattern as they either stay with an *otor* household or stay elsewhere beyond their *bag* jurisdictional boundary if herding for someone else from a neighboring *bag*. Households with large and average numbers of livestock also separate their families or join other *bag* members to take care of specific types of livestock in specific areas, because each type of livestock has different strengths to cope with severe winters in certain areas. For instance, it is a common strategy in all three *bags* that parents stay behind at their campsites, even if the pasture were covered with snow, to take care of the cattle with fodder, whilst their children go on *otor* to the HBU Mountain with the sheep, goats and horses. Moreover, the herders' ability to use the same seasonal pasture is dependent on their seasonal herding strategy and their ability to pursue mobility. In severe spring conditions,[47] it is common that participants in all three *bags* are unable to use their spring campsites, as they are stuck in the snow or their campsite did not have sufficient pasture. Then, those with large herd size stay in the mountain pasture for its abundant *buuts*, along with the HBU *bag* migrant herders, who did not possess spring campsites. Spring camping for poor households also changes as they follow their employer. In contrast, households with average herds mainly aim to reach their campsites or anywhere in the local broom grass area (Figure 7.11) for greater stability in a familiar area, even though it means staying in different and/or empty campsites, whose owners were unable to return.[48] Unlike households with large herds, they avoid the risk of losing their small size herds whilst exploring alternative camping elsewhere.[49]

Figure 7.11 Broom grass area, where local herders spend spring in UU.

Third, depleting seasonal pastures also contributes to the dynamics of the resource boundary. In summer,[50] herders pursue increasingly dynamic movements in terms of distance and frequency, due to the lack of seasonal pasture in each *bag*. In HBU and DD *bags*, participants with large or average size herds pursue summer *otor* in other localities (Figure 7.8, 7.9 and 7.10). A migrant herder in the HBU *bag* shared his experience,

> We usually go and stay in [X area away from HBU *bag*] for most of the summer.... It is better there, because we do not have a place for spring and summer here. Our livestock does not fit in this area. The local households would complain and claim the river area [in the HBU *bag*]. Instead of causing trouble, we go elsewhere.[51]

In this case, the *ulamjlalt* pasture use principle of "camp and graze as many as the area will allow" sets the limit for gaining access to pastoral resources, instead of implying an "open access." Herders can pursue summer rotation in other *bags* in their same *soum*, using their residency. A DD herder described his summer rotation: "I do go around the *soum* a bit. Well, within the *soum* territory, there is less trouble from local people saying 'you have to move now' as long as you do not stay near someone's spring campsite."[52] In other words, *soum* herders employ *neg nutag usniihan* to reciprocate for sharing pasture with households with fewer livestock. Thus, herders' camping patterns are often composed of those households that have different herd sizes within each jurisdiction. This indicates that the *soum* boundary denotes a more legitimate exclusionary mechanism. Then, exclusion is dependent on production factors such as a combination of herd size and availability of the pastoral resources, rather than a matter of social sanctions for complying rules regardless of production and pasture conditions. For instance, in UU and DD *bags*, those with large herds were unable to camp in their own jurisdiction nearby river grass for summer rotation, because all other households were concentrated there due to a drought. They, instead, were able to pursue cross-territorial *otor*, as they had a wider network of connections with officials and herders elsewhere.

Fourth, specific herding strategies required for a season also increase the dynamics of herders' resource boundaries. In all three *bags* in autumn,[53] regarding their ability to create a *hot* with fewer than a thousand livestock each year, herders with small and average size herds negotiate with each other in pooling labor and selecting areas with sufficient pasture and water to condition their herds for winter. Migrant households with large herds also return to HBU *bag* to condition their livestock for winter. Some HBU *bag* herders with large herds also visit UU territory to access its abundant salty lake during summer and autumn to strengthen the herd.[54] A shortage of these saltlicks in other jurisdictional territories can affect the resource boundary due to the arrival of outsiders.

192 *Community-based natural resource management*

The limitations of group pasture management

Breaking the fundamentals of *ulamjlalt* integrated pastoral production management, which was suited for non-equilibrium conditions, during the transition period actually complicated the process of defining both social and resource boundaries for engineering a new nested social unit within a *bag* or between two different jurisdictional boundaries. As in different project areas elsewhere in Mongolia, the HBU case demonstrates the complexity involved in setting up herder groups. Here, community pasture management goes beyond herder groups due to the existing structure of the *bag* community and the dynamics of its social and resource boundaries for triggering collective action. Successful groups were reported to owe their collective action directly to the support given by a third party and to the group leadership (Mau and Chantsallkham, 2006; Schmidt, 2004; Upton, 2008). The HBU case revealed that neither of these was able to define group social and resource boundaries to trigger collective action on pasture management due to an ambiguous understanding of *neg nutag usniihan* to form a fixed social unit. Instead, different actors with unbalanced power relations ended up capturing the project benefits as reported elsewhere (Mau and Chantsallkham, 2006; Undargaa et al., 2007; Upton, 2009). Defining pastoral institutions based on *hot ail* and *neg nutag usniihan* is only one of the conditions for shaping community collective action, if it regards their production management. These may have appeared as fixed and stable socio-economic units due to the stability of the pastoral institution in the past. However, as in the HBU case, *neg nutag usniihan* is rather seen as a social networking mechanism and is an analytical term that underpins production-based collective action as argued elsewhere for accommodating flexibility in mobility and camping (Sneath, 1993, 2007). This way, herders still collaborate informally, regardless of third party involvement in attempting to strengthen group social capital.

However, particularly under the unstable institutional arrangements, herders possess different abilities to work as *neg nutag usniihan*. This is due to the changes in their migration status, political and economic interests among different actors, values attached to campsites, *hot ail* structure, and flexible movements or freedom of movements within and between jurisdictions based on seasonal production strategies under stable and unstable weather conditions as well as their ability to pursue mobility under depleting pastoral resources. These factors affect the group's ability to include everyone to enforce community rules and norms. Similar to what Sneath (1993) reported, the HBU case also revealed that a herder group smaller than *bag* level was more an externally constructed social group following the design principle of a well-defined group with small size, than a real institution. Defining resource boundaries based on four season mobility in fixed pastures in stable weather conditions is a simplification process to adjust herders' complex mobility patterns into a standardized model for small territory-based group pasture management. Due to the lack of pastoral resources and unstable weather conditions, herders' seasonal rotation is no longer restricted to a fixed number of movements, nor are they tied to a locally recognized pastoral resources or de jure legal possession of campsites within the *bag* territory. Instead, regarding the balance between production components, herders select a specific terrain with recognized characteristics of seasonal pasture under different weather related conditions to accommodate their needs for seasonal camping and grazing. As a result, herders from the same geographical area often do not pursue similar mobility patterns and are unable to pursue group pasture management.

The difficulty we see in group formation is related specifically to *hot ail*, which functions more for production than social grouping. Scholars and advocates set up a theoretical basis for group formation based on the collaboration of *hot ails*, because they assumed the *hot ail* to be more a fixed collaborative social unit for managing pastoral resources (Bazargur, 1998; Fernandez-Gimenez, 2006; Fernandez-Gimenez and Batbuyan, 2004; Ickowitz, 2003; Mearns, 2004; Tumenbayar, 2000). *Hot ail* is a production unit composed of more than two households camping together to manage production and the pastoral resources surrounding their campsites (Bold, 1996; Fernandez-Gimenez, 2001). A single household *ail* with a large herd size often has a poor household camping with them to provide labor support (Bold, 1996). Nevertheless, *hot ail* structure witnessed a shift to a single *ail* due to the privatization of livestock (Bold, 1996, p. 75). This single *ail* independently managing its production is seen as problematic because it is neither a formal nor an informal institution, and may thus point to the existence of an "open access" situation in Mongolia (Fernandez-Gimenez and Batbuyan, 2004; Ickowitz, 2003; Mearns, 2004; Tumenbayar, 2000). The problem attached to the single *ail* structure is quite misleading. First, instead of defining *hot ail* as a group of households, it can be composed of a single household. In fact, *hot* refers to a "livestock enclosure," so one household with a sizable herd creates such an enclosure[55] (Sneath, 2006, 2007). In other words, *hot ail* is defined more by a herd size large enough to create a *hot*, than by the number of households. Second, due to an increasing trend of household herd size, *hot ail* is less likely to consist of two independent households which collaborate in their production. Upton (2008) argued that herder group formation tends to institutionalize social capital building to try to achieve effective collective action. In other words, the lack of collaboration in *hot ails* becomes an indication of a lack of social capital. In the HBU case area, the *hot ail*'s non-collaboration with others was due to their mode of collaboration based on production strategy and the production components, rather than a single *ail* being reluctant or having weak social capital. For instance, in the HBU case, herders' ability to pursue collaboration on production was shaped by differences in herd size, time available to them and depleted pastoral resources. This often changes herders' mode of collaboration, which cannot be easily organized within clearly delineated social boundaries.

194 *Community-based natural resource management*

Third, if composed of more than two households, *hot ail* is not fixed as a social unit. The informal collaboration among herders is not limited to a geographically distinct area, because of the *ulamjlalt* inclusionary approach that necessitates pooling labor, regardless of wealth status. The "common basis for co-residence is unequal wealth ... wealthy households prefer to have two or three poor households" in their *hot ail* (Sneath, 2007, p. 97). In the HBU case, due to the *hot ail* being composed of a single *ail*, herders supplied their labor demand through visiting *otor* or migrant herders and their relatives or friends elsewhere, and asking who was available or who has compatible numbers of livestock to stay with them. As a result, herders with different social and wealth status often camp together in patterns of mixed social and spatial locations. This shows that the herders' informal collaboration involves those from outside of their *bag*. Thus, small geographical territory and weak social ties among group members cannot result in building an institution to pursue exclusion in the HBU case. The CPR theory attempts to address the issues of difficulty in exclusion and subtractability through applying the design principle of small group size with clearly defined social and resource boundaries and a fixed distributional outcome. By reflecting these design principles, many donor projects resulted in homogenous membership based on similar living conditions and, thus, similar production patterns. However, such group formation does not incorporate the fluid nature of the 'herders' mobility (Fernandez-Gimenez et al., 2008; Upton, 2008). As occurred elsewhere, the HBU case also confronted the problem with small group territory, revealing that the territorial approach to group formation does not take into account the fluid nature of *hot ail* structure and mobility.

Herder groups also face difficulties in pursuing exclusion due to conflicting informal and formal access mechanisms. A group's boundary is defined by the location of herders' legal possession of campsites as those who experience different living conditions now share pastoral resources via legal possession of campsites. Under stable weather conditions, herder groups can claim the pasture surrounding their legally possessed campsites. During unstable weather conditions, following the *ulamjlal*, those with large herd size along with poor herders, often come and go beyond their group territory in search of pasture. Also, those with average or small size herds pursue *ulamjlalt* reciprocation with both local and visiting herders from outside of their group, using their legally possessed campsites as well. The combined use of both of these conflicting mechanisms could easily cause disputed use of pasture among members when a group attempts to exclude outsiders. Setting up social boundaries based on a group territorial approach as proposed under a draft pastureland law will face challenges in accommodating the dynamics of inclusionary *ulamjlalt* strategies. Although the draft of the new pastureland law addresses the issues of flexibility in mobility, reciprocity and exclusion, these are still under much debate (Upton et al., 2013).

Also, dynamic herding movement does not mean that there are no well-defined boundaries beyond that of the herder group. The CPR design

Community-based natural resource management   195

principles promote a "small size" group with well-defined social and resource boundaries. Bazargur (1998) also considered that *bag* and *soum* level groups are too large to solve herders' socio-economic issues and suggested creating smaller socio-economic units for specific species herding nested within *soum* and *aimag* territorial administrations (pp. 187, 190) in order to move towards sedentary village-based livestock production along with alternative sedentary food production (p. 228). However, an absence of broader development or alternative, but costly livelihood options hardly triggered a reduction in dependency on herding and/or reducing herders' livestock numbers. In fact, reducing the number of livestock is hardly a main solution to pasture management as there are other underlying problems rooted in dismantling the integrated production management. This is why, as food security, herders still rely on independent multi-species *ulamjlalt* pastoral production to gain benefit from an undervalued local market price, particularly during increasingly unstable weather conditions. Thus, their mobility is still flexible and is confined to a larger *bag* or *soum* boundary as shown in the HBU case. For instance, in one case a social group boundary drawn through a cross-jurisdictional territory failed as members' seasonal movement was limited to their own jurisdictional boundary. Historical, dual control over exclusion and inclusion continued to be practiced at the *bag* level, which is beyond group pastureland management (Figure 7.12). This is why the majority (60 percent of choices overlapped) of total research participants expressed concerns over production and pasture use through their local *bag* administration, whereas 6 percent did individually, 6 percent by the Ministry of Food and Agriculture (MFA) and 0 percent by herder group. Simultaneously, many (47 percent) indicated they never expressed concerns, or if expressed, no one paid attention to their concerns. This is perhaps related to the inability of the *bag* and *soum* formal authority as they lack the complementary and historical regulatory mechanisms to control labor and livestock to support herders' micromanagement of production components. Moreover, projects also faced challenges in forming herder groups to pursue exclusive pasture management, because it contrasts previous institutional arrangements, when different administrative groups, including the smallest *aravt* group, were once only responsible for administering population and overall production (taxation) (Chapters 3–4), or current *bag* enforces its herders' use rights (Chapters 5–6). For instance, the earlier GTZ project experimented on forming herder groups to re-enforce traditional pasture management and re-emphasize traditional community and its collective action (Schmidt, 2004) perhaps referred to historical *aravt* unit. Similar to *aravt*, the project formation of the herder group was ideal and promising to improve the efficiency of local governments' territorial administration of population and overall production and re-enforce group collective action on heavier production duties, but its other goal of formalizing group-based exclusive pasture management did not have historical ground (see Chapter 3). Nevertheless, other projects continued to aim at forming PUG as an ideal collective pasture management institution, which is

Figure 7.12 Bag is also where herders gather for social and cultural events as a community.

based on: "territorial boundaries, which are defined in a deliberative process involving concerned herders and are validated by the *soum* government.... PUGs ... are autonomous organizations aimed at jointly developing, enforcing and monitoring PMP [Pasture Management Plans]" (SDC, 2010, p. 11).

However, SDC (2010) also acknowledged difficulties in running PUG based on this category due to the diverse factors related to differences in ecological zones (SDC, 2010). In the HBU case, defining group territory based on herders' spring camping as *neg nutag usniihan* conflicts with herders' actual seasonal movements, particularly in winter due to the need to balance the production components based on the herding strategy. The local community social and resource boundary is more confined to the *bag* or *soum*, where herders' grazing is limited due to their legitimate rights and access to pastoral resources via the residency mechanism.

An additional difficulty in forming a group is that herders' decisions on mobility are not subject to a fixed schedule of group formation, but require flexibility in the use of the pasture based on the production strategy during unstable weather. Although herders' weather dependent production and seasonal mobility are perceived as a subsistence production (Bazargur, 1998; Erdenetsogt, 1998; Mearns 2000), difficulties in forming groups is also related to their seasonal or cross-territorial movements, which can be seen as herders' strategy to maximize yield oriented production as argued elsewhere (Fernandez-Gimenez et al., 2008; Humphrey and Sneath, 1999). In this situation, scholars have argued, poor households have less mobility than wealthier households (Fernandez-Gimenez et al., 2008, SDA, 2010). Households with larger herd size can afford to pursue higher mobility over longer distances, which in some cases is referred to as "predatory pastoralism," which is "irrespective of the rules and norms of pasture use" (Blench personal communication cited in Upton, 2009, p. 9; SDC, 2010). Referring to *ulamjlalt* rules and norms, Upton (2009, p. 9) argued that this "reinvention and reworking of norms may be strategically employed by the wealthiest and most powerful to their own advantage." In the HBU case, they re-invented and reworked ambiguous legal notions such as household or residency registration, rather than pasture use rules and norms. Also, herders do not go anywhere blindly or practice predatory pastoralism by taking chances. Here, the re-invention is only that instead of using a formal organization, individual herders negotiate with a local administration and/or the local herders in the host area (Chapter 6). They seek approval to make sure that access beyond their jurisdiction is legitimate as it is a necessary step to pursue *ulamjlalt otor* due to depletion of seasonal pasture. This is the matter of a conflicting legal environment, in which herders employ any available legitimate mechanisms, both legal (residency or legal possession of campsites) and informal (e.g., *otor*). Besides, carrying out *otor* goes beyond wealthy herders, as those with different size herds, including poor herders, are dependent on each other for pooling resources. The HBU case illustrates that, under the transition economy, the actors pursued pastoralism more for economic than political benefit. Controlling

198 *Community-based natural resource management*

production, herders pursue economic benefits, leading to an increasing wealth gap as existed in the pre-collective period. This difference in wealth in fact facilitates reciprocity in times of scarce pastoral resources, particularly when there is no strong ruling institution to facilitate production and risk management. In this case, the perception that the poor are often disadvantaged in pastoralism is quite misleading because any herders may also easily fall into poverty by losing livestock. Wealthy herders do not agree with the idea of aid supporting only poor households, because aid creates dependency but not preparedness (Fernandez-Gimenez et al., 2012). Thus, in the HBU case area, local officials support helping herders, who have lost numbers of animals, to sustain production for the future. In this case, in non-egalitarian pastoralism, access to pastoral resources needs to be protected through state's social welfare policy (e.g., protect local herders' residency/production rights vs. mining, support herders' access to production and marketing, and increase minimum wage, etc.) rather than exclusive property rights to land that nobody can exercise.

Another difficulty in forming groups is conflicting interests among different actors in local pasture management. The aspect of stakeholder power in strengthening self-governing institutions has always been overlooked as donor support often perceives community institutions as independent of the state and the market (Agrawal and Gibson, 1999). Defining herders' legal role in pasture management through exclusive group possession rights to pasture overestimates the herder group's ability no differently than overestimating the state's ability to manage pastoral resources. This overlooks the historically complementary role of both the local authority (macro-level) and the herders (micro-level) managing the production components to regulate access to pastoral resources. The SLP acknowledges the weakness of the role of local administrations as regulatory pastoral institutions and perceives herder groups could potentially replace this role (Batkhishig et al., 2012; Chantsallkham, 2009; SDC, 2010). Herder group pasture management parallel to the local authority is seen both ways: a positive relationship created between the herder group and the local administration (Schmidt, 2004), or local authorities reluctant to support herder groups and their collective action even though there are adequate regulatory frameworks to accomplish this (Batkhishig et al., 2012; Schmidt, 2004; SDC, 2010). The latter position overlooks the fact that the content of the laws is incompatible for local authorities not only to regulate herders' changing access to pastoral resources, but also to support group formation. The state territorial unit in pastoralism is not a form of modern abstract territoriality set up to govern pastoral resources, but a historically political and administrative system to manage pastoral production. Parallel pastoral institutions (state territorial administration and monastery administration) historically succeeded, because each institution controlled all three components of production. Projects are unable to create a condition for herder groups to independently control the three components of production, because of the de-coupling of management of land from livestock and

Community-based natural resource management 199

labor. Thus, the HBU case revealed conflicting interests in who would control aid to represent broader local pasture management, or who would collect benefits gained from governing pastoral resources among different local actors. The self-governing authority of the group would become a matter of local politics in governing pastoral resources, because the local administration legitimizes the groups' social and resource boundaries (in- and out-movement of local, visiting and migrant herders) via residency, livestock ownership status and legal possession of campsites, and recognizes their legitimacy as it does for the *bag* community. Then, a group's legal status nested within a *bag* or *soum* jurisdiction may challenge the interests of the local authority in territorial administration and resource governance. By virtue of its power over regulating natural and human capital within its jurisdiction, they seek to maintain their economic interest to compensate for their loss from losing control over production. Herder groups are hardly able to replace the role of the aristocratic order in the pre-collective period and collectives in the socialist period, due to its inability to balance the production components within its smaller social and resource boundaries. Moreover, it is a challenging notion that a group independently reserves pasture within its territory for risk management (SDA, 2010). In the HBU case, it depends on the availability of pastureland in each *bag* and the ability of local authorities to maintain their territory to secure community access. These are real challenges, because there are other state-based actors, who are interested in controlling jurisdictional resource access. The next chapter discusses the role of the state RPA in HBU Mountain.

Notes

1 GTZ's programs are: "Nature Conservation and Buffer Zone Development," 1995–2002, and "Conservation and Sustainable Management of Natural Resources – Gobi Component" 2002–2006), currently implemented by the "Initiative for People Centred Conservation" (IPECON) of the "New Zealand Nature Institute" (NZNI).

2 The varying versions are people who share same territory, valley, river, well (*neg nutgiinhan, hudgiinhan, usniihan, amniihan* or *jalgiinhan*).

3 Herder groups were formed to manage pastureland on an experimental scale (Fernandez-Gimenez, 2002; Fernandez-Gimenez et al., 2008; Mearns 2004). Earlier accomplishments of GTZ projects in group formation and increasing incomes from alternative income generation activities led to other donor programs establishing more herder groups all over Mongolia (Schmidt, 2004; Undargaa, 2006). Twelve different donor and NGO supported programs including GTZ, IPECON-Mongolia, UNDP, IFAD, Swiss Development Agency and USAID have been operating in Mongolia since 2000. Scaling up the number of herder groups was the main agenda of donor support to the rural poor. For instance, during 1995–2004, 70 community organizations were formed and were active under the GTZ supported Conservation and Sustainable Management of Natural Resources – Gobi Component (Schmidt, 2004). According to project documents, from 2003 to 2006, 1957 herder groups were formed with the support of donor programs (Undargaa, 2006). These were mainly on paper as few were considered

200 *Community-based natural resource management*

active (see Mau and Chantsallkham, 2006; Undargaa et al., 2007). The increasing number of herder groups eventually led the state to legislate "natural resource group user rights" within the land and environmental laws. Also, national and international advocates presented new designs for a law on pastureland. 1. "Concepts of the law on pastureland," Unofficial version of Draft Law on Pasture Land developed and revised by a team of lawyers from the Mongolian Society for Rangeland Management and Green Gold (SDC), *Zuunii Medee* newspaper, 2009.11.4 No. 258 (3330), 2. Law on pastureland, law of Mongolia, Draft, 2008.03.27, UNDP MON/08/301,3. These versions are updated in two drafts: one by the Government of Mongolia in 2010.08.09 and one by MSRM in 2010.10.05, "Comparison of the drafts on law on pastureland" MSRM document. 4. Law on pastureland, law of Mongolia, No. 187 (3577), *Daily News* 2010.08.09. These drafts articulated *ezemshil erh* (possession right) of pasture to herder groups.

4 Interview 57 (Undargaa, 2013).

5 GTZ experimented with legal recognition of a few groups, setting up a binding tripartite contract between herder groups, the local administration and the buffer zone committee under the provision of group right to use pastoral resources under the laws (Schmidt 2004; Upton, 2009). The content of this contract is overtly exclusionary with clear size and boundary of the community managed area (CMA) with the intent of excluding any non-member households from other areas. However, this type of group territory is uncommon among other groups due to the locals', including officials', inability to define particular group territory (Undargaa, 2006). SLP advanced their legal standing by registering the groups as an NGO to comply with the land use provisions in the Land Law (Upton, 2009, p. 9). This was for the purpose of future institutional development and its authority, which will rest on the Association of herder groups' network or PUG (APUG) for higher level pasture management coordination with the support of local administrations (Fernandez-Gimenez et al., 2008; Schmidt, 2004; SDC, 2010). Essentially, this is a major shift, in which the formation of a group, with its clear social and resource boundaries, is legally recognized for exercising exclusive property rights in land tenure (Upton, 2009).

6 Interview 58 (Undargaa, 2013).

7 Interview 57 and 58 (Undargaa, 2013).

8 Interview 57 (Undargaa, 2013).

9 Interview 12 and 41 (Undargaa, 2013).

10 Interview 12 (Undargaa, 2013).

11 Interview 39 (Undargaa, 2013).

12 Interview 15 (Undargaa, 2013).

13 Questionnaire 3–6 (Undargaa, 2013).

14 Questionnaire 62 (Undargaa, 2013).

15 Questionnaire 83 (Undargaa 2013).

16 Questionnaire 95 (Undargaa, 2013).

17 Interview 24 (Undargaa, 2013).

18 Questionnaire 52 (Undargaa, 2013).

19 Other donor projects mainly refer to maintaining wells, fixing roads and agreeing to use pastures seasonally on fixed dates, which is essentially *ulamjlal*, but de jure formalized pasture use rules are limited to group members being involved in herder group pasture management.

20 Field note, Ulaan Uhaa *bag* meeting, Shiveet MT, August 15, 2010 (Undargaa, 2013).

21 Interview 41 (Undargaa, 2013).

22 This pollution is nearby their spring campsites and is caused by outsiders with their trucks loaded with heavy rocks, bricks and rubbish to weigh their light-weight

Korean trucks down, so they are able to drive in the snow. These outsiders then dump the rubbish at the lake and fill their trucks with salt for the return journey.

23 The SLP committee is composed of various *soum* officials along with a project officer. It has the power to select a project proposal to get funding. It can approve what it considers is the best proposal based on prioritization. It then sends it to the *aimag* SLP committee for approval, which allows funding to be obtained from the city SLP project.

24 Interview 41 (Undargaa, 2013).

25 For instance, those who come from the same *bag* would refer to each other as *neg nutag usniihan* in front of those who are from other *bags* at the bigger *soum* level. However, those who come from same *soum* define themselves as *neg nutag usniihan* at the bigger *aimag* level. Those who are from the same *aimag* define themselves as *neg nutag usniihan* at the national level. At the ministerial and national level, this concept has more social and political influence in terms of offering favors to each other. This concept of *neg nutag usniihan* is very powerful and provides a strong networking strategy that can benefit all levels in Mongolia.

26 Strong and wider social networking is popular among herders from same *nutag* or jurisdiction, because of their pastoral production strategy. It is even mentioned in a well-known 1980s poem "*Huduugiin aranshin*" by Choinom. It literally goes

> ... in the city, people do not know each other, even if they have been neighbors for ten, twenty years. In contrast, country herders get to know each other by following pasture and water, even though they live far from each other, and get to distinguish each other's every single foal or calf and get to know each other by inviting in those travelling away or passing by ...

27 In the decree approved by the representative herders of the *Dolood bag Hural* and Delgerhaan *soum Hural* in Hentii *Aimag*, 2009.04.19, *bag* herders demanded the mining company stop its operations and noted that *bag* members have a common understanding of the issue and signed the attachment to the decree. It continues: "If our proposal is not considered, we will take measures in the next level to fight for our *gazar* (territorial land) and *nutag* (home pastureland)."

28 Interview 24, 25 and Questionnaire 50 (Undargaa, 2013).

29 Questionnaire 84 (Undargaa, 2013).

30 Questionnaire 85 (Undargaa, 2013).

31 Interview 4 and 7 (Undargaa, 2013).

32 Interviews 26, 33, 43 and 48 (Undargaa, 2013).

33 Interview 43 (Undargaa, 2013).

34 It is hard to keep more than a thousand head of livestock in each campsite, because of the need for cleaning the livestock bedding area, and keeping it free of wet dung, particularly in winter.

35 Interview 4, Questionnaire 33 (Undargaa, 2013).

36 Interview 48 (Undargaa, 2013).

37 Bayanjargal *soum* contains the highest number of households with a thousand head of livestock in Tuv *aimag* (Interview 51 and 55, Undargaa, 2013).

38 See for instance, a Mongolian novel "Tungalag Tamir" by Lodoidamba, Ch.

39 Questionnaire 72 (Undargaa, 2013).

40 Interview 13 (Undargaa, 2013).

41 Interview 37 (Undargaa, 2013).

42 Interview 3 (Undargaa, 2013).

43 Interview 57 (Undargaa, 2013).

44 4< refers to number of movements, which can be 4–10 times a year including short summer *otor* movements or any other season when herders do not have secure access to a convenient camping spot.

202 *Community-based natural resource management*

45 The aim of winter mobility is to gain access to sufficient water and pasture resources in sheltered terrain to cope with the harsh winter conditions. Reflecting on conditions from previous seasons, herders prepare well ahead for winter.
46 Interview 30 (Undargaa, 2013).
47 Spring mobility is all about saving new livestock or helping weak ones that have survived the winter at their established spring livestock shelters.
48 Interview 6 and 48, Questionnaire 92 (Undargaa, 2013).
49 Interview 30 (Undargaa, 2013).
50 Summer movement is for fattening weak livestock left over from winter and spring. Thus, herders pursue summer *otor*, which are small rotations on available grassy areas in their jurisdictional territory.
51 Interview 23 (Undargaa, 2013).
52 Interview 35 (Undargaa, 2013).
53 The function of autumn mobility are maintaining and solidifying summer fattening and conditioning of both herders' camping and livestock for winter.
54 Interview 18 (Undargaa, 2013).
55 It seems that the *hot ail* is not strictly referring to only the number of households, but to a general residential camping structure inclusive of households as well as a sizable livestock herd that can create a *hot* (*buuts* area with or without a stable). This is because *hot* also refers to *maliin hot* (the area where livestock lie and sleep overnight at the camp) or to *malaa hotluulah* (to bring the herd back from grazing to the camp overnight). For instance, an HBU *bag* participant described her camping with one household in the following way. "Well, for instance, this *hot* contains [takes care of] the livestock, which belong to our six children…" (Interview 3, Undargaa, 2013). Herders in the southern and northern parts of Mongolia also explained this in a similar way during my previous fieldworks.

References

Addison, J, Davies, J, Friedel, M and Brown, C (2013) "Do pasture user groups lead to improved rangeland condition in the Mongolian Gobi Desert?," *Journal of Arid Environments* 94, 37–46.

Agrawal, A (2003) "Sustainable governance of common-pool resources: context, methods and politics," *Annual Revenue of Anthropology* 32, 243–262.

Agrawal, A and Gibson, C (1999) "Enchantment and disenchantment: the role of community in natural resource conservation," *World Development* 27:4, 629–649.

Batkhishig, B, Oyuntulkhuur, B, Altanzul, Ts and Fernandez-Gimenez, M E (2012) "A case study of community-based rangeland management in Jinst soum, Mongolia" in M E Fernandez-Gimenez, Xiaoyi Wang, B Batkhishig, Julia A Klein and Robin S Reid (eds.) *Restoring Community Connections to the Land: Building Resilience Through Community-based Rangeland Management in China and Mongolia*, CAB International, Wallingford, Cambridge.

Bazargur, D (ed.) (1998) *Geography of Pastoral Animal Husbandry*, TTC Company, Mongolian Academy of Science, Ulaanbaatar.

Bold, B (1996) "Socio-economic segmentation: khot-ail in nomadic livestock keeping of Mongolia," *Nomadic Peoples* 39, 69–86.

Chantsallkham, G (2009) "Sustainable rangeland management in Mongolia: the role of herder community institutions," Land Restoration Training Programme, Island, Ulaanbaatar.

Dietz, T, Ostrom, E and Stern, P C (2003) "The struggle to govern the commons," *Science* 302, 1907–1912.

Erdenetsogt, N (ed.) (1998) *Mongolian Nomadic Livestock*, "MMM" Association, Ulaanbaatar.

Fernandez-Gimenez, M E (1999a) "Sustaining the steppes: a geographical history of pastoral land use in Mongolia," *The Geographical Review* 89:3, 315–336.

Fernandez-Gimenez, M E (1999b) "Reconsidering the role of absentee herd owners: a view from Mongolia," *Human Ecology* 27:1, 1–27.

Fernandez-Gimenez, M E (2001) "The effects of livestock privatization on pastoral land use and land tenure in post-socialist Mongolia," *Nomadic Peoples* 5:2, 49–66.

Fernandez-Gimenez, M E (2002) "Spatial and social boundaries and the paradox of pastoral land tenure: a case study from post-socialist Mongolia," *Human Ecology* 30:1, 49–78.

Fernandez-Gimenez, M E (2006) "Land use and land tenure in Mongolia: a brief history and current issues," in Donald J Bedunah, E McArthur and M Fernandez-Gimenez *Proceedings of the Conference on Transformations, Issues, and Future Challenges*, Salt Lake City, UT, Proceedings RMRS-P-39, Fort Collins, CO: US Department of Agriculture, Forest Service, Rocky Mountain Research Station.

Fernandez-Gimenez, M E and Batbuyan, B (2004) "Law and disorder: local implementation of Mongolia's land law," *Development and Change* 35:1, 141–165.

Fernandez-Gimenez, M E, Batkhishig, B and Batbuyan, B (2012) "Cross-boundary and cross-level dynamics increase vulnerability to severe winter disaster (*dzud*) in Mongolia," *Global Environmental Change* 22, 836–851.

Fernandez-Gimenez, M E, Kamimura, A and Batbuyan, B (2008) "Implementing Mongolia's land law: progress and issues," The Center for Asian Legal Exchange (CALE), Nagoya University, Japan.

Griffin, K (1995) *Poverty and the Transition to a Market Economy in Mongolia*, St. Martin's Press, New York.

Griffin, K (2003) "Urban-rural migration and involution in the livestock sector" in K Griffin (ed.) *Poverty Reduction in Mongolia*, Asia Pacific Press, Canberra, 56–71.

Humphrey, C and Sneath, D (1999) *The End of Nomadism?*, Duke University Press, Durham, NC.

Ickowitz, A (2003) "Poverty and the environment" in K Griffin (ed.) *Poverty Reduction in Mongolia*, Asia Pacific Press, Canberra, 95–112.

Khazanov, A M (1994) *Nomads and the Outside World, second edition*, University of Wisconsin Press, Madison.

Lattimore, O (1941) *Mongol Journey*, Doubleday, Doran and Co, New York.

Leisher, C, Less, S, Boucher, T M, Beukering, P V and Sanjayan, M (2012) "Measuring the impacts of community-based grasslands management in Mongolia's Gobi," *PLoS ONE*, 7:2.

Mau, G and Chantsallkham, G (2006) "Herder group evaluation: a study of herder groups, their present status and future potential," UNDP, Ulaanbaatar.

Mearns, Robin (2004) "Decentralisation, rural livelihoods and pasture-land management in post socialist Mongolia," *European Journal of Development Research* 16:1, 133–152.

Schmidt, S M (2004) "Pastoral community organization, livelihoods and biodiversity conservation in Mongolia's Southern Gobi region," in *Annual Meeting of Society for Range Management*, Salt Lake City, USA.

SDC (2010) "Livelihood study of herders in Mongolia," Swiss Agency for Development and Cooperation (SDC), Ulaanbaatar.

Simukov, A D (1931) "Zamyetki o polojyenii na peripherii MNR za 1931 god" in Yuki Konagaya, Sanjaasurengiin Bayaraa and Ichinkhorloogiin Lkhagvasuren

204   *Community-based natural resource management*

(eds.) *Trudy o Mongolii i dlya Mongolii Tom (3) Chast (2)*, Gosudarstvyennyi muzei etnologii, Osaka, 127–143.

Sneath, D (1993) "Social relations, networks and social organisation in post-socialist rural Mongolia," *Nomadic Peoples* 33, 193–207.

Sneath, D (2003) "Land use, the environment and development in post-socialist Mongolia," *Oxford Development Studies* 31:4, 441–457.

Sneath, D (2006) "The rural and the urban in pastoral Mongolia" in O Bruun and Li Narangoa (eds.) *Mongols from Country to City: Floating Boundaries, Pastoralism and City Life in the Mongol Lands*, Nordic Institute of Asian Studies, 140–161.

Sneath, D (2007) *The Headless State*, Columbia University Press, New York.

Tumenbayar, N (2000) "Land privatization option for Mongolia," in *Constituting the Commons: Crafting Sustainable Commons in the New Millennium, the Eighth Conference of the International Association for the Study of the Common Property*, Bloomington, Indiana, May 31–June 4.

Undargaa, S (2006) *Gender and Pastoral Land Use in Mongolia: Dilemmas of Pastoral Land Tenure*, Centre for Development Studies, The University of Auckland, Auckland.

Undargaa, S (2013) "Property 'owners' without rights? Exploring property relations and access in the Herlen Bayan-Ulaan Reserve Pasture Area of Mongolia," Crawford School of Public Policy, Australian National University, Canberra.

Undargaa, S, Tungalagtuya, Kh and Narangerel, Ya (2007) "Community organization, mobility and common property management of pastureland resources in the Gobi," NZNI/IPECON, Ulaanbaatar.

Upton, C (2008) "Social capital, collective action and group formation: developmental trajectories in post-socialist Mongolia," *Human Ecology* 36, 175–188.

Upton, C (2009) "'Custom' and contestation: land reform in post-socialist Mongolia," *World Development* 37:8, 1400–1410.

Upton, C, Moore, Kate, Nyamaa, N and Erdenebaatar, B (2013) "Community, place and pastoralism: nature and society in Post-Soviet Central Asia: Mongolia Country Report," University of Leicester.

8 State territorial strategy for natural resource governance and pastoral production

State territorial strategy for natural resource management in Mongolia

In response to insignificant or no improvement in herders' livelihoods and their production after the state or so called community-led land reform approaches, the government re-established the historical state reserve pasture areas (RPA) to accommodate herders' long distance movement during unstable weather conditions. The state political and economic structures have often shaped herders' use of physical territory, which has not always been static in the past. Here, it is hardly a novel concept that the Mongolian state exercises its coercive power and employs a territorial strategy for territorial administration and natural resource management. This was on the grounds of its historical role in shaping the socio-political structure of pastoral community (Bold, 2001; Humphrey, 1978; Natsagdorj, 1972; Sneath, 2007; Vreeland, 1954). It is crucial then to understand what constitutes state territorial strategy for regulating herders' access to pastoral resources.

Pre-collective period

Historically, the state pursued a territorial strategy for controlling natural resources under a form of public ownership in order to benefit from pastoral production (see Chapter 3). Regarding their complementary formal role, central and local governments passed decrees setting up territorial controls for reserving/protecting wildlife, fauna and flora, and pasture areas for seasonal hunting and grazing as a risk management strategy for food security in the context of pastoralism[1] (Wingard and Odgerel, 2001, p. 52). As noted in a UNESCO document,[2] historical documents recorded:

> By the time of Marco Polo, there were already rules specifying closed hunting seasons for rabbits, deer, *saigas* and gazelles. Later, the laws of Khalkha Juram, promulgated between 1709 and 1799, designated 16 mountains to be protected from hunting, cultivation and logging. Bogd

206 *State territorial strategy*

> Khan Mountain has been continuously protected since the 13th century as a holy mountain. It became Mongolia's first officially protected area in 1778.[3]
>
> (Badarch et al., 2003, p. 23)

Although the intentions of these preservations for environmental conservation were contested elsewhere (Endicott, 2012, p. 45), these decrees indicate the state's legal mechanisms to control the use/hunting of natural resources by providing preservation rules and norms (Wingard and Odgerel, 2001, p. 54), regardless of its political or economic intentions. Territorial administrations at each level succeeded in enforcing the state's territorial strategy for several reasons. First, the state set it up within the authority of different levels of jurisdiction[4] which acted as a formal pastoral institution with its complementary mechanisms for controlling all components of production. The lords and monasteries reserved the best pasture for their yield-focused production within their jurisdiction (Bold, 1996; Sneath, 2007). Simultaneously, they regulated their subjects' access to strategic pastoral resources in times of *dzud* (Bold, 1996; Sneath, 2007, p. 127). Second, they used natural landmarks for territorial boundaries, which worked with local community socio-cultural rules and norms of using natural resources, in order to be able to control herders' access, and adjudicate any conflicting claims to these resources.

Collective period

The twentieth century marks the beginning of modern states applying zoning for their territorial strategies for controlling natural resources (Vandergeest and Peluso, 1995). Under socialism in the twentieth century, the Mongolian government formalized public ownership by constitutionally declaring all land-based natural resources as property/assets (*hurungu*) under the power/authority/sovereignty (*medel*) of the public,[5] or state property (*umch*), i.e., public property/asset (*hurungu*)[6] (see Chapter 4). Unlike in the pre-collective period, it pursued a territorial strategy in two different forms: conservation/hunting and production. First, from the 1920s after the revolution, the central government issued several decrees for restoring old or creating new reserves for regulating hunting and protecting rare wildlife, including the protection of Bogd Khan Mountain (Bedunah and Schmidt, 2004; MNE, 1996; Sokolov et al., 1991). From 1957 to 1976, the state established more protected areas, which provided a clarification on all aspects of resource use, the type of resources, and use rights within a well-defined territorial boundary. As a complementary formal mechanism, the *Great Hural*[7] introduced regulations for use, including for hunting and protecting natural resources in one-year or five-year production plans and created special offices for environmental management including the Society of Protection of the Environment and Nature in 1975 (Sokolov et al., 1991, pp. 252–253). Second, the state pursued a territorial strategy for establishing RPAs under the jurisdiction of the MFA

(Ministry of Food and Agriculture) (Undargaa, 2013). This was to support herders' production by securing herders' access to the RPAs as the government re-formalized the *ulamjlalt* short or long distance cross-boundary *otor* movements during times of emergency weather conditions. Unlike during the pre-collective period, the state imposed zoning over parts of the territories of different territorial administrative units.

The state managed to avoid any land related conflicts among these different state-based actors when territorializing their pastoral resources with zoning. The problem often arises from zoning as it is quite different from the local use of the physical territory and it often contradicts "people's social relationships and histories of their interactions with the land" (Vandergeest and Peluso, 1995, p. 389). The negative effects of the territorial strategy on the herders' historical use of land also became apparent in Mongolia. For instance, during the establishment of the Huh Serh National Park in the socialist era, "within five years of its 1977 establishment, all pastoralists and their livestock had been removed" (Bedunah and Schmidt, 2004, p. 168) in the effort to protect the wildlife habitat. Although changing herders' historical interactions with the physical territory, the government succeeded in its territorial strategy for conservation and production without much opposition from herders regarding resettlement due to the following reasons. First, the central government regulated land management and the interaction between different state-based actors such as MNE, MFA or local territorial administrations through assigning administrative tasks. Second, under centralized economic planning, the state allowed each *negdel* or RPA *aj ahui* to control its own production management (land, livestock and labor) within its jurisdictional boundary through its complementary mechanisms (Chapter 4). In other words, although exclusively emphasized on its property management role in the constitution, the central state retained the historical pattern of land management as embedded within the integrated pastoral production management.

Transition period

Although the state retained the historical notion of public sovereignty over natural resources, the state's role shifted from a complementary formal mechanism to direct exclusive management authority over the natural resources under its newly amended constitutional status of "the state protection or state property." The state now functions without its historical ability to govern natural resources, particularly in an absence of financial and technical supports provided in the collective period and of the historical mechanisms of pastureland management as embedded in the pastoral production management (see Chapters 5 and 6). As a result, the state's territorial strategy for both protected areas and RPAs began to contradict with herders' physical use of the grazing land to a certain extent, as its sole focus was on conservation rather than on incorporating the herders' production management. After establishing the first independent ministry in charge of environmental

208 *State territorial strategy*

protection in 1987–1988 (MNE, 1996, p. 60; Wingard and Odgerel, 2001, p. 28), the transition government continued to employ a territorial strategy to expand protected areas and manage land-based CPRs mostly for conservation purposes (Mearns, 2004, p. 142). Government expanded its protected areas under the advice of international development organizations in a response to a perceived loss of biodiversity and apparent land degradation from the pressure of a growing number of households and livestock after the transition (Bedunah and Schmidt, 2004). The government divided protected areas into four types: Strictly Protected Areas (SPA), National Parks (NP), Nature Reserves (NR) and Natural and Historical Monuments (NHM) in terms of function. In each group, it applied an extensive zoning approach in order to pursue exclusion as a protection mechanism (Bedunah and Schmidt, 2004). Three of these (except SPA) allow livestock grazing to a certain extent under: (a) a special use zone, with permits being issued in severe winters in the NPs; (b) a travel and tourism zone along with a limited use zone; and (c) in Nature Reserves (Wingard and Odgerel, 2001). Government protected areas increased to 20.5 million hectares by 2000, which comprises 13 percent of the total area of Mongolia. The state aimed to cover 30 percent of the national territory by 2030 (Bedunah and Schmidt, 2004; MNE, 1996). As occurred in the collective period, the zoning strategy resulted in changes in the herders' physical use of territory for their mobility and production. The government ignored herders' pasture use patterns when it expanded the protected areas by taking over parts of their territories from local territorial administrations. This restricted the access of local herders, who had long used these areas (Bedunah and Schmidt, 2004). For instance, whilst establishing Hustai Nature Reserve in order to re-introduce the Przewalskii horse (wild horse), Altanbulag *soum* administration lost some of its territory and herders were barred from using their seasonal grazing areas (Bedunah and Schmidt, 2004, p. 168). Moreover, the zoning led to herders' losing their seasonal grazing areas (Bedunah and Schmidt, 2004, p. 170). Furthermore, "the establishment of the Gobi B Ecological Reserve reduced winter grazing areas for local herders" (Bedunah and Schmidt, 2004, p. 168). The reduction in seasonal pastures in jurisdictional territories would result in a shortage of reserve pasture and constrain the flexibility of herder movements, particularly when these jurisdictions experienced an increasing number of campsites utilizing possession regulations (see Chapter 6).

In contrast to the collective period, the state's territorial strategy was constrained by an apparent fuzziness in the authority of the different state-based actors regulating pastoral resources. The government created a conflicting legal environment by regulating only the natural resources through its land-based policy approach, rather than acknowledging herders' jurisdiction-based production management. Although the state no longer controlled the herders' pastoral production management or supported it through PRA, each local administration was legally responsible for regulating the herders' access to seasonal pasture or organizing their cross-boundary movement to access pasture elsewhere. Since

State territorial strategy 209

local administrations lost authority over parts of their grazing land to the park administration for managing protected areas, during emergency weather conditions the local administration must now obtain a permit from the protected area administration for its herders to access reserve pasture in the protected areas. This process often results in contested claims among these actors for authority over pastoral resources. For instance, local official X claimed that his herders had the right to gain access to the special use zone in the nearby protected area due to severe winter weather, whereas park director Y argued that he could not issue such a permit because of the restrictions[8] to access the park zone. Moreover, the protected area has become more like a legal mechanism by which powerful or resourceful outsiders can derive benefits, instead of improving wildlife protection. Conflicting claims to authority over pastoral resources arise when protected area management weakly enforces exclusion of outsiders due to the lack of a budget and human resources and its inability to enforce protected area rules and regulations (Endicott, 2012; Rossabi, 2005, pp. 175–183). For instance, one local government was in dispute with the protected area administration in park X over the increasing trend of outsiders illegally logging with the help of protected area administration staff,[9] which was witnessed by herders. This is mainly related to the state's incapacity to enforce monitoring over abstract space (Vandergeest and Peluso, 1995). The fuzziness in authority is not due to the ambiguity of the herders' property rights over pastureland. On the contrary, the formal authority of the local administrations and the herders' informal control in resource management appear to be diminished in the conflicting legal environment (see Chapter 6). In other words, the state has overestimated its ability to govern natural resource independently without incorporating the relevance of pastoral production management in regulating the use of natural resources.

Only the MFA took over the pastoral production aspect as *negdel* and *aj ahui* no longer controlled herders' production (see Chapter 5). Currently, maintaining or re-establishing the reserve pasture area is becoming increasingly critical in supporting herders' production. The territorial administrative units have lost their former reserve pasture areas due to the depletion of the pastoral resources, which resulted from the destruction of the water resources and overgrazing as most former areas have already been occupied by herders and their campsites (SDC, 2010). Without access to reserve pasture, individual herding households struggle to cope with severe droughts or winter *dzud* during unstable climatic conditions, regardless of donor projects' efforts to form herder groups to pursue risk management and ensure preparedness (Fernandez-Gimenez et al., 2012). Advocates prioritize the national level policy initiative to re-introduce RPAs in all territorial level units (Fernandez-Gimenez et al., 2012; SDC, 2010). The significance lies in the "perils of unregulated *otor* movements during *dzud* and the way that this can increase the vulnerability of receiving communities if they are not prepared with designated *otor* reserves and cross-boundary agreements cannot be effectively monitored and enforced" (Fernandez-Gimenez et al., 2012, p. 847).

210 *State territorial strategy*

The state responded by re-establishing some of the former RPAs which existed in the collective period. The next section discusses the complexities which arose in re-introducing the territorial strategy with zoning in the form of the state RPA and the interaction between different state-based actors in governing pastureland.

Territoriality in natural resource management in the HBU case study area

RPA is a rarely examined form, in which (a) the state tries to resume its historical role of regulating herders' pastoral production partially by introducing RPAs, and (b) the PRA deals with various actors (the ministry, visiting and hosting local administration and herders) in supporting herders' production. Therefore, the examination of the state RPA, rather than protected areas, provides more insight in exploring challenges arising in the state territorial strategy through zoning. In 2007, the state re-introduced the RPA policy. Its aim was:

> to protect and maintain sustainable use and management of Interprovincial *otor* RPAs, and create or repair RPA resources including wells and water resources and ensure its proper use and maintenance, and overall establish a comfortable and convenient environment for herding households, who pursue extensive mobile pastoralism,[10] to overcome winter and spring [weather conditions] and reduce livestock loss.
>
> (MFA, 2010)

To reach these aims, the state set the following objectives: (a) to create a legal environment to support RPA management; (b) to establish new RPAs; (c) to improve herders' access to water resources in RPAs; (d) to improve livestock capacity to overcome severe weather conditions; and (e) to provide herders on *otor* movement with necessary services. The central government perceived these steps as necessary for several reasons. First, the state has a constitutional responsibility indicating that "Livestock is a national treasure and will be protected by the state"[11] (Constitution, 1992) due to state ownership of pastureland and its historical role in production management, if not currently responsible for the whole production management. Second, local administrations were ineffective in arranging herders' access to reserve pasture. Third, some state officials perceived that herder group formation had been ineffective in terms of strengthening local pastoral institutions and tackling herders' vulnerability to climate related production risks. Fourth, among the many agendas contained in the RPA policy,[12] the state took over former inter-provincial RPAs in different localities, leaving any local reserve pastures. This is because herders' individual production management was vulnerable when mobility was restricted to their particular jurisdictional territory, particularly during unstable climatic conditions. For instance, during a series of *dzud* and droughts since 2000, herders pursued long distance inter-provincial *otor* movements, with 4–5 million head of livestock annually.[13] The negotiations among local administrations were often ineffective, leading to increasing disputes over the use of pasture among hosting and visiting local administrations and herders. Also, visiting herders often lack a social welfare system that would provide them with services such as schools and hospitals whilst they are in a hosting area. Thus, the government has taken various state policy measures[14] including RPA management in response to herders' vulnerability to massive livestock loss and to support *ulamjlalt* livestock production.

Implementation of the HBU RPA

The HBU RPA case is critical as it was the first and largest RPA re-established after the transition. It also presents diverse patterns of herder mobility with regard to visiting herders gaining access to state RPAs. The state was to achieve its objectives through a territorial strategy of zoning RPAs under the status of the "state special needs territory" in the land law.[15] At the Ministry of Food, Agriculture and Light Industry (MFA), the *Ikh Hural* (Parliament) established the "Department of Interprovincial Reserve Pasture Area Management" (*Aimag dundiin Otriin Belcheer Ashiglaltiin Zahirgaa*) (hereafter called "The ministry")[16] on September 1st, 2007. The ministry designed a whole project and aimed at covering 10 percent of Mongolian territory (1,565,000 sq. km.) for establishing and managing inter-provincial RPAs. It drew[17] the boundaries of seven areas, covering 649,300 hectares or 0.6 percent of the total pastureland in all ecological zones (Figure 8.1). The largest (192.800 he) is the Herlen Bayan-Ulaan Reserve Pasture Area (HBU RPA), which hosts herders from eastern, central and south Gobi provinces.

Figure 8.1 Map of inter-provincial RPAs in Mongolia.[18]

212   *State territorial strategy*

The ministry re-introduced the RPA model, which had been used in managing production in the collective period. The ministry specially chose HBU RPA as a model given its historical role of being a reserve pasture. It also re-established a Temporary Committee which regulated access to the RPAs at the inter-provincial level and decided many management issues such as setting livestock entry quotas.[19] The committee is composed of ministry officials in charge of the RPA department and the *soum* governors and their livestock husbandry officials from hosting and visiting jurisdictions. As in the collective period, the ministry assigned the governor of the HBU *bag*/village to lead the committee until 2009, regarding the role of former and independent HBU *horoo* in hosting the RPA. Then in 2010, the ministry assigned the governor of the Delgerkhaan *soum* regarding its legitimacy[20] over the HBU *bag*/village. The ministry also assigned its representative officer to manage the RPA during *otor* and off-seasons. He regulates access to the RPA by issuing each herding household an entrance permit on their arrival based on their livestock health certificates, and collecting pasture use fees, the amount of which is dependent on the number of livestock (Table 8.1). The state invested approximately 400,000,000 MNT for constructing and fixing 20 wells, and setting up irrigation systems with fences for planting fodder, and expanding pasture use in the RPA. This also created employment.[21] To improve the condition of the HBU RPA pasture, the ministry enforced two exclusionary policies: reservation by zoning of the HBU RPA and rehabilitation for two years.

Reservation of the HBU RPA

The ministry established the RPA by zoning in order to reserve pasture for the use of winter only *otor* movement. In the pre-collective period, herders used the HBU Mountain for this purpose. Now, the ministry adopted the collective era boundary, which included parts of territories from the surrounding *bags* and *soums* in Hentii *Aimag*. In other words, the RPA includes four seasonal pastures in the HBU *bag* and partial winter and spring pasture from DD *bag* in the north (Figure 8.2). According to the ministry, the zoning over these seasonal pastures creates a useful buffer zone to protect the

Table 8.1 Pasture use fees in the HBU RPA

Livestock number	Fee amount (MNT)
300	10,000
300–500	20,000
500–1000	40,000
1001–1500	80,000
1501–2000	160,000
2000<	320,000

State territorial strategy 213

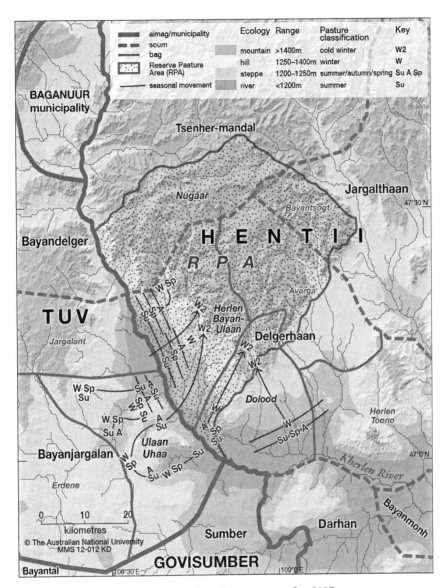

Figure 8.2 Territorial boundaries of the HBU case area after 2007.

HBU Mountain from any livestock use.[22] Previously according to the *ulamjlal*, the RPA was used during the coldest winter months, from December to February. Now, the department extended the period from November 1 to April 1.

Although successful during the collective period, state re-zoning faces challenges in pursuing exclusion for several reasons. First, in the presence of

214   *State territorial strategy*

inadequate legislation on land, the zoning system increases the significance of the legitimacy of local officials in protecting jurisdictional boundaries. The zoning of seasonal pastures exposed the sensitivity of disputed jurisdictional borders since herders' physical use of territory is limited to the *bag* jurisdictional boundary. Assigning the governor of the HBU *bag*/village for the management of the RPA has led to disputed claims over the border between HBU and DD *bags*, where herders from these two *bags* have overlapping claims of legal possession of the same campsites. With ministry authorization, the HBU *bag*/village government de facto assumed the former *otor* territory to be HBU *bag* territory and took advantage of the fuzziness of the buffer zone territory between the two *bags*. After the 2003 amendment of the land law, it provided clearance for legal possession of campsites for its migrant residents in this buffer territory, whilst disregarding DD households' existing legal possession of the same campsites issued earlier under the 1994 law. As a result, each *bag* disputed whose authority was legitimate, since this area is an important spring seasonal pasture which both *bags* lack. A herder in the HBU *bag* referred to the dispute as: "DD *bag* would tell us to leave.... The border area is in X, where our campsite is located. This is the old border. The new one is not clear. It happened before the *otor* administration in 2007 or 2008." DD officials pointed out that officials of HBU *bag* had taken advantage of being located within the former RPA territory and expanded its much needed seasonal pasture through legal possession of campsites. Thus, the contradictory legal environment for land management created the ambiguity among different state-based actors regarding which *bag* controls the disputed territory.

Second, disputes over the jurisdictional boundary reflect the different interests of state-based actors in controlling access to pastoral resources. The zoning of the RPA alarmed both the HBU and DD *bags*, because of the growing impact of allowing *otor* herders into the RPA territory. DD *bag* officials were concerned about losing their historical (pre-collective and current) claim to the HBU mountain area. Simultaneously, HBU *bag* had an historical claim over the collective era RPA territory, which included its spring and summer pastures. Currently, both *bag* officials employ legal possession of campsites to define their border. A HBU herder who was affected in this dispute claimed that:

> DD *bag* official would state that we either have to transfer our residency to DD [in order to keep our spring campsite possession] or give up the possession and leave [to maintain HBU residency]...[23]
>
> *Bag* governors had a dispute at a meeting I heard. There were 5–6 households on DD *bag* territory. Then our *bag* governor [HBU] told them that the governor will not give them up for DD...[24]

This indicates that the loss of legally possessed campsites would lead to a reduction of jurisdictional territory, which affects the ability of officials to

State territorial strategy 215

benefit from control of the *bag*. The HBU *bag* officials struggle to provide its new residents with spring pastoral resources in order to maintain its population, to retain the *bag*'s status as a village and to keep up its financial independence. In comparison, DD *bag* has been facing a shortage of seasonal pasture[25] from losing its historical authority over HBU Mountain. Thus, their interest in retaining authority over HBU Mountain and the border territory translates into controlling access to benefits.

Third, official interest in controlling access to benefits occurs in cross-level authorities, beyond the *bag* level. Since the transition, DD *bag* legally resumed some of its old territory after the collapse of the HBU RPA (see Chapter 5). Thus, the new governor[26] in Delgerkhaan *soum* resolved the dispute over legal possession of campsites in the border area by maintaining the claims of DD *bag* herders and invalidating the approval issued by the HBU *bag* governor. HBU *bag* officials disagreed with the *soum*'s decision, noting that the *soum Hural* could have maintained the claims of the HBU *bag* herders since both *bags* belong to the same *soum*.[27] To claim their territory back, HBU *bag* officials employed a new amendment to the law on territorial administration, which authorized the *bag Hural* to regulate access to resources and decide on its boundaries. They also solidified their position by gaining the support of the ministry to keep HBU village as the RPA center. These interests challenged the authority of Delgerhaan *soum* officials over the HBU *bag* territory. According to a *soum* level official:

> Since this law passed, the *bag Hural* head was authorized and emerged with more power and is authorized in exercising this power over this area and over other *bag* territories ... by telling *otor* households "you can or cannot enter and if you enter you have to deal with us."[28]

This is why Delgerhaan *soum* officials supported DD *bag* claims in order to maintain the *soum*'s historical authority over the HBU *bag* territory. They are in the process of changing the de facto power exercised by the HBU *bag* officials with regard to RPA matters, and their collaboration with the RPA administration and the temporary committee. They are developing a policy that allows the HBU RPA to conclude a contract with each *bag* administration with the approval of the *soum* governor in order to consider the HBU *bag* capacity for hosting *otor* households.[29] This border dispute represents the ultimate struggle between different state-based actors over important territorial control in order to maintain their benefits accruing from the exploitation of pastoral resources.

Two-year rehabilitation policy

Within its territorial strategy of controlling pastoral resources, the ministry also put in place an exclusionary policy by prohibiting all livestock grazing[30] in the HBU RPA for two years. This was a significant step to rehabilitate the

216 *State territorial strategy*

pasture which had been degraded by over-use prior to the establishment of the HBU RPA.[31] Initially, the DD *bag Hural* planned to use the RPA as a mechanism to reduce the number of unorganized *otor* or migrant households entering their territory,[32] and proposed the government to preserve the HBU Mountain pasture. The ministry translated this proposal into a policy of expulsion of all herders, including those from HBU and DD *bags*, from their seasonal pastures. The ministry enforced this edict by coercion in collaboration with the *soum* and *bag* governor's decree, demanding that the herders leave, otherwise large fines of 500,000 MNT would be levied.[33] It organized to relocate herders and their herds to sparsely populated border areas in the eastern *aimags* some 500 km away (MFA, 2009a). However, the herders refused to go to these areas due to the travel costs, and unsuitable pasture and water conditions in the area. Instead, they preferred to move to the neighboring UU *bag*, Bayanjargalan or Bayandelger *soums* in Tuv *aimag* due to the short distance (20–80 km), and local connections and familiarity with the landscape.[34] The department later accepted these choices. At the Interprovincial RPA temporary committee meeting, the department negotiated with visiting and hosting *soum* governments to formalize access rights for a specified number of visiting herders and livestock from HBU and DD *bags*, and allocate them grazing areas in hosting *soums*. The department allocated three million MNT of funding to the visiting *soum* government for enabling the movement for those with fewer than a hundred head of livestock or for those who could not afford transportation.[35]

However, the state failed to enforce this exclusion due to the lack of thorough consultation with local herders in accordance with the law.[36] The consultation regarding herders' production was necessary for the following reasons. First, the policy of exclusion again conflicted with the land law. Although the ministry zoned the whole seasonal pasture of the HBU *bag* as the RPA, it is responsible for protecting only the mountain campsites for *otor* herders, and not the local herders' legally possessed campsites on the seasonal pastures as the state does not protect herders' private assets under the law (MFA, 2009a). Consequently, some herders in DD *bag* refused to leave behind their campsites and livestock shelters unprotected (Figure 8.3). In response, the ministry criticized the Delgerhaan *soum* officials for not enforcing state policy, whereas the *soum* officials argued that the ministry needed to determine a mechanism for protecting the herders' private property when enforcing exclusion. Later, the ministry ruled to accept the *soum* proposal to protect the herders' private assets. Second, the state ignored the herders' production management in the situation of deteriorating pastoral conditions. The HBU *bag* administration struggled to enforce the exclusion for households who owned fewer than a hundred livestock and could not afford transportation[37] and labor costs, or households with large herds who were concerned about the lack of secure access to spare pastoral resources in hosting jurisdictions.[38] According to one of the respondents in HBU *bag*:

Figure 8.3 Spring shelter is an invaluable asset in pastoral production.

> Last year, local officials and the ministry said that no matter what, we should leave. There should be no such approach.... In fact, I think it is wrong to go and stay near someone else's pasture. That's why I stayed here.[39]

This indicates that herders were mostly concerned about their limited ability to gain access to depleting pastoral resources in a different jurisdiction.

Third, the state employed *otor* mechanism to exclude herders from particular pastures. It overlooked the fact that the herders' decision to pursue *otor* movement is shaped by their production strategy based on the prevailing ecological conditions. In the HBU case area, herders had different levels of experience in pursuing *otor* outside of their jurisdictional boundary. Herders in HBU and DD *bags* pursue *otor* less, because the HBU RPA is located within their jurisdiction (Figure 8.4). The two-year policy provided the first opportunity for a majority of the HBU *bag* participants to carry out a major *otor*, regardless of their herd size (Figure 8.5). Only a small number of migrant households have experienced moving a long distance outside of their own locality more than three times, because of the lack of opportunities to access seasonal pasture for their large herds (Figure 8.5). Similarly, a small number of DD participants pursued *otor* regardless of their herd size, because both their winter and spring campsites were located in the HBU RPA (Figure 8.6). Otherwise, the remaining DD participants had either

218 *State territorial strategy*

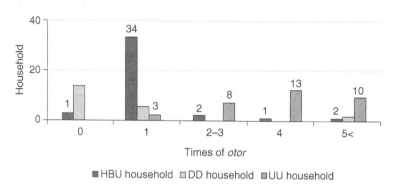

Figure 8.4 Otor frequency by household in different *bags* 2000–2010.

never experienced *otor* because their campsites were outside the HBU RPA, or had experienced *otor* only once, because their winter campsites were inside and spring ones were outside of the RPA. Interestingly, most UU participants have experienced long distance *otor*, regardless of their herd size (Figure 8.7), because they lived outside of the jurisdiction where HBU Mountain is located. In other words, the pursuit of distance *otor* refers to a cross-boundary movement. Therefore, unless otherwise decreed/forced by the state, herders mainly decide to pursue distance *otor* based on the availability of the pasture in their or hosting jurisdictions, rather than the size of their herd as *otor* is only a temporary stay.

Fourth, the state overlooked the conflicting interests among different levels of state-based actors regarding control over pastoral resources. Although having gained de jure access rights negotiated among the ministry and the officials from different jurisdictions, many herders in HBU and DD *bags* were unable to access pastoral resources in the hosting area. In fact, the experience

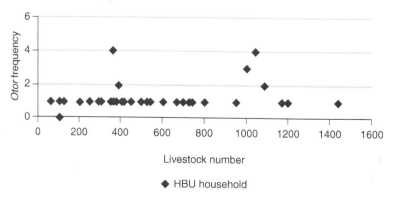

Figure 8.5 HBU participants' *otor* frequency by livestock number 2000–2010.

State territorial strategy 219

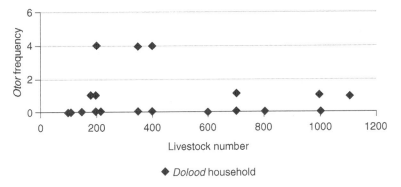

Figure 8.6 DD participants' *otor* frequency by livestock number 2000–2010.

they shared reveals the extent of the pressure[40] (MFA, 2009b) from local residents and local administrations. For instance, a herder from the HBU *bag* shared that:

> We had been told quite often to leave right away. They would chase our livestock away from there. Local officials would demand us to leave showing an official letter.... We managed to stay [there] for two months; persisted a lot, moving here and there and avoided seeing local officials etc...[41]

This indicates that the ministry's negotiation with other jurisdictional authorities was not, in practice, legitimate. Particularly in UU *bag* in Bayanjargalan *soum*, the ambiguity emerged in the arrangements made among the stakeholders at the Temporary Committee. The ministry blamed Bayanjargalan officials for breaching the ministry's policy of granting access,

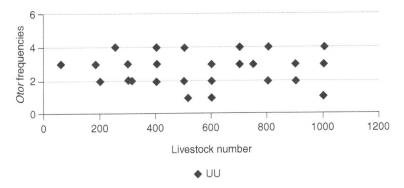

Figure 8.7 Ulaan Uhaa *otor* frequencies by livestock number 2000–2010.

220 *State territorial strategy*

which was based on a consensus among stakeholder officials. Bayanjargalan argued that the negotiation was limited to a verbal understanding between *aimag* officials at the committee meeting, rather than an actual contract to make it a legal act. Also, Bayanjargalan officials were concerned that visiting herders went against their policy by residing without permission[42] nearby local herders' spring pasture[43] that was left vacant for rehabilitation.[44] Moreover, Tuv *aimag* officials accused HBU *bag* herders of remaining close to HBU *bag* and letting their livestock graze in HBU *bag* territory across the river (MFA, 2009a). They suggested that the ministry send HBU *bag* herders elsewhere on distance *otor* or send them back to their own *bags*. Therefore, a lack of collaboration emerged between the state-based actors regarding their attempt to protect their herders' production and their interests. Fifth, the state failed to pursue exclusion and impose collaboration due to its conflicting legal environment and the pursuit of formal and informal rules/norms to regulate depleting pastoral resources. Bayanjargalan officials defended their position of forbidding visiting herders as legal under the land law. The *soum* acted in accordance with the *aimag* and *soum Hural* decree (MFA, 2009a) to avoid more land degradation, which arose partially from increasing numbers of legally possessed campsites and *otor* herders passing through their territory in previous years to come to HBU RPA. For a time, Bayanjargalan *soum* sent its own herders to other areas as they could not enter HBU RPA due to the two-year ban. Its officials stated, "We will comply with the decision of our *soum* and *aimag* administration and protect the interests of our herders" (MFA, 2009a, p. 4). Tuv *aimag* (Bayanjargalan *soum*) officials also disagreed with the ministry's proposal, stating that it was wrong to impose cross-territorial *otor* on an area, where there was no more room for additional grazing (MFA, 2009a). However, the ministry pointed out that the state must impose reciprocity among different jurisdictions in order to organize *otor* and incorporate flexibility into cross-boundary movement. The ministry insisted that Bayanjargalan reciprocate by accommodating HBU *bag* herders at this time, since, in future emergency situations, their herders may need to stay in HBU RPA on *otor* (MFA, 2009a). Thus, the ministry attempt to employ *ulamjlalt* reciprocal mechanisms which contradict with other regulations in the land law.

Sixth, the state struggled to deal with local officials as they had ignored the existence of individual herders' informal control. Although Bayanjargalan officials agreed to accept visiting herders, while levying some fines or pasture use fees,[45] their decision was dependent on dual control. Local herders partially controlled access to the pastoral resources, particularly through controlling production and legal possession of campsites (Chapters 5 and 6). When resources were scarce, they demanded local officials take action against visiting herders whose herds were grazing on their seasonal pasture.[46] A visiting herder from the HBU *bag* shared his experience in UU *bag*:

These days, there are no unoccupied areas; I even tell others to leave, especially to *otor* households and their horses [when they graze in our place]. In BJ, all winter and spring campsites belong to someone ... thus, it is the same everywhere, people will tell you to leave.[47]

Other herders, who are pursuing *otor*, experience the same pressure. A visiting herder from UU *bag* shared his experience elsewhere:

Last year, we went north to X *soum* early because HBU RPA was closing for two years. However, when we got there we were told to leave, I guess our *soum* did not have a contract with that *soum*. X *soum* was asking for a payment. Also, local households were not welcoming and were complaining that we were camping in their winter pasture areas.[48]

This indicates that conflicts of interest arose between stakeholders as they obtain benefits from the production of their herders, who still retained a measure of informal control over pastoral resources. Seventh, in this way, the state hardly acknowledged the herders' production strategy in the manner it did in the collective time, offering secure access to other pastoral resources when pursuing exclusion. Local officials and the RPA officer constantly pestered the HBU and DD herders to comply with the government decree, and made them depart no matter how challenging the pursuit of long-distance *otor* was. Both herders and the HBU *bag* officials believed that the committee arrangement was official in terms of granting herders access rights to pasture in host areas, and the rehabilitation policy can be beneficial for preserving HBU Mountain and protecting their production.[49] However, in a condition of depleting seasonal pastures, the herders were hardly able to avoid using other's seasonal pasture in other jurisdictions:

When we camp, we follow the water resource. Then, the locals would say that this was their seasonal pasture ...[50]

We left in June. Then we went to someone else's area, it was closer to the locals' winter and spring pasture areas ...[51]

As a result, herders tried to pursue frequent short summer *otor* moves through any available patchy pastures, responding to local herders' pressure. A herder from HBU *bag* recounted that, "We moved 30 km to X, Z, and Y [other jurisdictions]. Then we moved 4–5 times again out there."[52] Herders practice this short distance *otor* more often on quality summer pastures which are shared among local herding households. However, during this time, the strategy was not effective. According to a herder from HBU *bag*, "Whenever we go, our livestock cannot get used to the area easily[53] and we are not able to graze and stay."[54] Thus, the herders' ability to gain access to pastoral resources is not open access, but is shaped by both their herd size and the suitability and availability of quality pastoral resources.

222   *State territorial strategy*

Eighth, the state was incapable of imposing exclusion as it overlooked the fact that herders' seasonal movement has been developed to work under the existing climatic conditions. Many herders from HBU *bag* and neighboring *bags* and *soums* eventually broke the two-year rehabilitation policy and moved back to HBU Mountain due to the poor arrangement of the policy, which allowed some households or livestock to stay behind while expelling others. According to a herder from the HBU *bag*:

> Well, this policy was enforced, but people did not leave, which means their livestock did not leave.... But then the decree was cancelled by December. And yet, most households were actually on the mountain before that.[55]

Thus, under competitive conditions of resource access, herders often questioned the legitimacy of state policy to ensure that they were not disadvantaged thus leaving the state powerless to pursue exclusion. Ineffective policy enforcement, in fact, creates open access. The *dzud* in 2009 left herders all over Mongolia no other option but to pursue distance *otor*. In late autumn before snow blocks the way in the UU river valley, herders abruptly returned to the HBU RPA. This was more for securing access to natural shelters and reserve pastures as a risk management strategy than a deliberate infringement of state regulations. UU herders described this chaotic situation of moving to HBU Mountain:

> We used to stay in our own winter campsite. However, we needed to stay in HBU Mountain last year. If not, we would have lost everything...[56]
>
> Yes, those who managed to come back, saved some of their livestock and those who did not come to HBU Mountain lost all of their livestock...[57]

Although the state shifted its policy from the two-year rehabilitation to a seasonal reservation from spring to winter, the ministry still struggles to enforce this policy. The following spring and summer, a drought occurred in the HBU case area, affecting herders' seasonal mobility and the preservation of the mountain in 2009 and 2010 (Figure 8.8). According to a UU respondent:

> We recently went through HBU Mountain, B and C valleys in the mountain. There are households already staying there. At the same time, they milked their mares, built extra *gers* and livestock fences on almost every single *buuts* [for extra pasture]. They are very close to each other [those were not all real households]. They do it because they are looking at staying there for the winter.[58]

Although the ministry is an official stakeholder, it is unable to implement state territorial strategy effectively due to a lack of acknowledgement of herders' production management under unstable weather and a conflicting legal environment.

Figure 8.8 Households already built their *gers* in the RPA by September 2010.

Outcome and challenges

The ineffective implementation of the state territorial strategy through zoning and exclusion policies led to the disputed use of pasture and to overgrazing. During the 2009 *dzud* and chaotic *otor* movement in the HBU RPA, local herders, who managed to return earlier to the RPA, had already claimed many *buuts* as campsites. Hundreds of visiting herders, who eventually came later than usual, experienced difficulties in finding *buuts* or natural shelters. One of the *otor* herders said "We did not know if it was owned, but the owner showed up later."[59] Since the recognition of possession certificates was not observed on the ground,[60] the problem of accessing *buuts* particularly affected the visiting herders, who tried to gain access through *ulamjlalt* arrangements for *otor*. Another *otor* herder shared his experience,

> I guess it is their job [RPA administration] to [tell you to leave]. Yet, local people tell you to leave quite often because they claimed that we were staying on a campsite which belonged to them or their son or which was located next to their campsite, etc.[61]

This indicates that local herders take the chaotic condition for granted while securing access to multiple campsites to keep their flexibility in rotation at the expense of many *otor* herders. Also, these policies diminished herders' pastoral

224 *State territorial strategy*

production as these affected herders' access to *buuts*. During the chaos, some lost their livestock shelters (used by visiting herders or travelers) and struggled to secure livestock production. The following excerpt from a HBU *bag* herder, who lost his livestock shelter to fire, explains the importance of access to secure shelter for production,

> We used to stay really comfortable in our old campsite, which used to have a really nice shelter with black roofing [waterproof].... We could not fix it yet.... So last year, it was really hard for us to stay here and overcome the winter, which was really cold. We sheltered the livestock in our rock wall. Livestock kept urinating and the *buuts* kept freezing instantly, which was really bad for the sheep to lie down. So, we kept the sheep out and made them stay out in the open overnight. Then, I broke that frozen *buuts* and used it to build another *horoo* on that burned ash and sheltered our livestock on it. But then after a month, it was frozen again. So, then I built another little one. That is why we have these continuous long *buuts* tracks here. Otherwise, we used to have very neatly arranged *buuts*. And we built another shelter on it and that is how we managed to survive the winter.[62] ... It was very hard for our livestock that they got sick from ashes and their eyes got very bad...[63]

Moreover, the chaos of the *otor* led to the spread of livestock disease. In the risky weather conditions of the 2009 winter *dzud*, some visiting herders departed hurriedly, leaving their rubbish and/or carcasses from dead livestock behind[64] (Figure 8.9). This resulted in broken, unhygienic campsites and the spread of livestock disease. Herders were unable to use some of the affected *buuts* and pasture later. The RPA officers and the HBU *bag* officials were unable to enforce RPA rules to clean up the campsites. Besides, some herders lost their livestock. On their way out, some visiting herders (accidentally or not) departed keeping a few livestock, which separated from the local herds. Unlike previous systems, herders no longer bothered to separate them as they were rushing to move before the bad weather.[65]

In addition, the ineffective state territorial strategy also challenged the land law and the legitimacy of the HBU RPA. Although all participants do acknowledge the legitimacy of the ministry in the RPA management and organizing *otor* (Table 8.2), they are less convinced of its effectiveness

Table 8.2 Determining key actors in organizing *otor*

Key actor	Total participants (n = 97) multiple choices allowed by %
The department	40
Local administration	25
Individual herding households	54

Figure 8.9 Spring campsite tarnished and polluted with carcasses by visiting households (on the way out of the HBU Mountain) May, 2010.

226 *State territorial strategy*

(Table 8.3). Instead, they rely on their own arrangement, given the current circumstances of climatic, socio-economic and legal conditions for pursuing *otor*. For instance, herders from UU were reluctant to pay pasture use fees in the HBU RPA as they were skeptical that the fees would lead to better pasture management in the HBU RPA.[66] Simultaneously, the department lacked the human and financial capacity to enforce this policy, and failed to raise revenue from it and improve the reserve pastureland, whilst diminishing herders' access and production. Consequently, many of the research participants questioned the legitimacy of the RPA. On the one hand, visiting *otor* herders argue that there should be no local herders and/or legal campsite possession in the state RPA to enable *otor* herders' access to campsites. Visiting herders from UU claimed that they have use rights under both the state legal RPA policy and the informal *ulamjlalt* right to pursue *otor* in HBU RPA as they and their ancestors did in the pre-collective and collective periods. On the other hand, this challenges the rights of the local herders from HBU and DD *bags* to legally possess campsites. These herders often complained about the ineffectiveness of the HBU RPA and the local administration as the legal mechanism for regulating visiting herders' access in the RPA. Visiting households graze over DD herders' winter pasture in the mountain as they often arrive with the maximum number of livestock as one *hot*[67] in order to benefit as much as possible from their short stay. As a result, HBU *bag* suggests that the RPA should only control the mountain, and let HBU and DD *bags* control its other seasonal pastures. Yet, the ministry is interested in controlling both the mountain and the agrarian land in the seasonal pasture in HBU *bag*/village center.[68] Then, DD *bag* suggested canceling the policy of RPA establishment in HBU Mountain for good, and just make HBU Mountain the territory of HBU or DD *bags* (or cancel the existence of the whole HBU *bag* jurisdiction), so that Delgerhaan *soum* controls its own territory. It also suggested that instead of establishing the RPA within a fixed territory regardless of its grazing capacity,[69] the RPA should annually be selected from anywhere regardless of the jurisdiction, where the pasture has the potential to host visiting *otor* herders. Overall, these challenges to the legitimacy of the RPA indicate that the state overlooked the fact that relevant actors seek to gain benefits through various levels of formal and informal authority when managing pastoral production and pastureland.

Table 8.3 Satisfaction with current arrangement of *otor*

Rate	Total participants (n = 97) multiple choices allowed by %
Content	20
Neutral	43
Discontented	33

The relationship between territorial strategy and production management

In Mongolian pastoral production management, the state and the herders have been historically integrated into a single system as dual actors to interdependently control access to pastoral resources. Since privatization of the pastoral sector in 1990, the state created a legal environment to manage pastoral production in a compartmentalized approach; regulating herders' access to pastureland through exclusive individual/household rights to legal possession of campsites or *bag* community access to pastureland under state ownership. Simultaneously, the MFA supports herders' pastoral production whilst promoting intensive livestock production. Also, the labor aspect is absolutely liberalized. Ironically, such an approach has been counterproductive for the state's territorial strategy to support herders' production with the RPA policy. The failures of the previous policy initiatives led herders to continue their production as in the pre-collective *ulamjlalt* form. Herders remained dependent on the state regulating their access to the RPA, which reflects the state's historical complementary role in production management and the state's attempt to solidify its power over regulating access to pastoral resources. The state re-established the ministry RPA department, replacing an historical pastoral institution, which existed in parallel to the local administration. It becomes another state-based actor to enforce both exclusion and inclusion of visiting herders, following historical access patterns.

However, the state struggles in its implementation of the territorial strategy and de-railed its policies of preservation and rehabilitation to support herders' production due to the following reasons. First, the ministry employed the collective period RPA management approach. It did not fit the dramatically different transitional socio-economic conditions, where herders individually manage their private production, and where access to pastoral resources was regulated under a land-based legal environment rather than production. The state re-established RPAs as its territorial control over natural resources with zoning in order to both include and exclude herders. In this regard, it differs from other state territorial strategies; the state territorial administration, which has control over land only, and the protected areas for conservation. Similar to the protected areas, the RPA establishment affected the interests of different actors from its surrounding jurisdictions. For instance, re-drawing the HBU RPA boundary over the territories of HBU and DD *bags* in Delgerhaan *soum* was impractical for the local people's production as it went against the "social relationships and histories of their interactions with the land" (Vandergeest and Peluso, 1995, p. 389). This also created conflict among different state-based actors in controlling access to scarce campsites and seasonal pastures. Individual herders' production depends on their use rights to community pastoral resources. The social and resource boundary of a community is defined by the *bag* jurisdictional boundary. De facto, herders' use rights to pasture are legitimized by legal campsite possession. In other words, herders' legal campsite

228 *State territorial strategy*

possession now defines the once-fuzzy *bag* jurisdictional boundary. The RPA zoning, therefore, exposed the conflicting or sensitive border issues between DD and HBU *bags*, which emerged from the overlapping claims over the same campsites on the fuzzy border area. Unlike the collective (or even pre-collective) periods, the state did not compensate the local authorities for their lost jurisdictional territory, lost control over the production components, or support them with the necessary productive resources to avoid conflicting territorial interests. These changes led local officials to enter into disputes over border territory to maintain their economic and political (position offered by a political party) benefits derived from governing a jurisdiction.

Second, this conflict arose due to the fact that the ministry created the ambiguous status over the management of the HBU RPA territory. The ministry has the legal authority over the RPA territory in accordance with the land law provision to appropriate land for special needs[70] and it wanted to keep the HBU *bag* as its center. This inadvertently enhanced the status of the HBU *bag/* village officials, whilst diminishing the authority of others in controlling access to pastoral resources. *Otor* herders negotiated with HBU bag/village officials more than with any other *bag* or *soum* officials from the surrounding jurisdictions. The latter officials became concerned that the ministry uses *otor* as a justification to take over their territory. This creates disputes among different jurisdictions as each party claims their authority under the land law. Thus, the zoning of RPA opened up room for cross-level state-based actors to maneuver state regulations towards strengthening their own authority and maintaining their interests and benefits of governing pastoral resources.

Third, the state failed due to the assumption that it has exclusive management rights over the pastoral resources under the notion of modern state ownership. The ministry's pursuit of exclusion under this assumption contradicted herders' expectations that the ministry fulfils its complementary role of implementing state policy and organizing access. As a result, the two-year rehabilitation policy affected the authority of both informal and formal control over the resources. The ministry had failed not due to the top-down process as it once worked in the pre-transition period when the state controlled all aspects of production. Instead, it failed due to ignoring local actors' needs, as argued in Vandergeest and Peluso (1995). The ministry overlooked the contradictory exclusionary regulations under the land law. Under conditions of scarce pastoral resources, each actor has a legal right to protect their own pastoral resource within their jurisdiction from visiting herders. This contradicts the management model of the HBU RPA and discourages collaboration among different actors. The state ownership of pastoral resources and individual rights to legal possession of campsites are contradictory in the pastoral context, too. The ministry appropriating land from state-territorial units for the purpose of an RPA contradicts with the local government and its *Hural* to define and administer its own boundaries and individual households' legal possession of campsites with regard to its pastoral capacities. Moreover, the lack of collaboration among state-based actors in the conflicting legal environment resulted in challenging the legitimacy of the HBU RPA and creating insecurity of herders' rights to access either seasonal pastures elsewhere or in the HBU RPA during severe weather conditions. In other words, the RPA policy essentially failed to improve the quality of HBU RPA pasture management or to solidify state control over access through the zoning exercise and the two-year rehabilitation. For these reasons, the ministry perceived that it lacks adequate legal power to deal with these contradictory legislations. It proposed a separate law on pastureland to discuss exclusively the RPA jurisdiction in order to stop the herders' "sedentary" mode of production under fixed campsite possession.[71]

Furthermore, the ministry overlooked to incorporate herders' control over production management in its exclusionary policies as had been enforced in previous historical periods. When excluding herders, the ministry reached a rather mechanical solution. It let herders select only their *otor* area, instead of recognizing their legitimacy or their need for current production management under complicated formal and informal access conditions, coupled with the scarcity of pastoral resources. It also left herders in a dilemma in terms of protecting their private pastoral assets and legally possessed campsites, and gaining access to seasonal pastoral resources within their jurisdiction. The insecurity to access these resources forced herders to ignore the state policy of exclusion and arrange their own mobility. Moreover, the ministry hardly acknowledged the local herders' inexperience in pursuing distance *otor* in other localities. Besides, the ministry overlooked the herders' informal role in pursuing exclusion and inclusion based on production. Although the pastoral resource is migratory and large as argued by the CPR theorists (Dietz et al., 2003; Feeny et al., 1990), the use right is confined within and between specific social and resource boundaries, and enforced by state territorial units in Mongolia. Historically, in this boundary, the formal authority and herders exercised dual control through their separate complementary mechanisms to exclude and include outsiders, depending on the weather conditions. Currently, due to the weakness of local administrations, informal control over production and land use is strong. In UU *bag*, local herders controlled visiting HBU *bag* herders' access to convenient pastoral resources. They included them based on negotiation or excluded them if necessary due to scarce pastoral resources. This is according to the *ulamjlalt* rules and norms regarding their seasonal herding practices, strategies, herd size, availability of labor and pastoral resources. This pattern is quite different from an open access condition, in which everyone could come and overgraze the pasture, in the absence of any rules or norms. Thus, exclusion is not necessarily difficult in the pastureland context as long as *ulamjlalt* dual control over production is placed in context.

However, herders' informal control to impose exclusion/inclusion over visiting herders can also be diminished in a conflicting legal environment. The contradiction between the state RPA to secure visiting herders' access to RPA and the legal possession of campsites resulted in disputes as well as occasional "open access" conditions since herders pursue any mechanism or

230 *State territorial strategy*

strategies available to them to gain access to already competitive desirable *buuts*. This situation also increased herders' financial burden as they re-establish live-stock shelters in order to maintain their access to pastoral resources through legally possessed campsites. However, herders often fail in their efforts to maintain their access and benefits under depleting pastoral resources. Regard-less of herd size and herders' ability to use various mechanisms and strategies, they still face the loss of livestock. Thus, obscure territorial control between state-based actors resulted in neither improved land management, nor decreased the disputed resource use. The ministry's inability to resolve these complexities arose from the inadequate legal environment. This problem seems to be related to the regulation under the property regime concept, where in different regimes some actors are less likely to acknowledge one's exclusive individual, group/communal or state rights due to the overlapping claims under legal pluralism (Cellarius, 2004; Feeny et al., 1990). In this regard, current land-based policies, in which the state allocated resource man-agement rights to different levels of state-based actors without regulating the components of pastoral production, proved to be highly conflicting and impractical in the pastoral context. In this legal environment, it even seems unrealistic[72] that the state could solidify its legitimacy and ability to control resource access, because the state overlooks the fact that these actors pursue pastoral production for obtaining benefits to take advantage of the existing cli-matic conditions (Sneath, 2007). Therefore, it is essential to recognize that the state/public ownership of pastoral resources in Mongolia goes beyond the state introducing or claiming property rights to land. Regarding its functions, responsibilities and abilities, state/public ownership involves the interdepend-ent relationship between the state and the herders with their complementary historical mechanisms to control the components of the pastoral production.

Notes

1 Hunting was considered one of the supplementary sources for food security in times of the loss of livestock (see Lattimore, 1962).
2 http://whc.unesco.org/en/tentativelists/936/1996.
3 See also MNE, 1996, p. 31.
4 Two hundred years later UNESCO recognized *ulamjlalt* protection mechanisms, which involve local and national level pastoral institutions (territorial units or monasteries), and the worship of specific mountains and hills over many genera-tions. http://whc.unesco.org/en/tentativelists/936/1996.
5 1924 Constitution.
6 1940 and 1960 Constitution.
7 Constitution 1924 (Article, 2.10), 1940 (Article 2.17).
8 Author's 2000 fieldwork.
9 Mongol TV news broadcasts (2006).
10 HBU RPA is not for intensive livestock husbandry such as ranching or farming as it does not have the facilities to take care of livestock that have become adapted to sedentary farming. Also, this is for winter only and all livestock except horses will be allowed. A dedicated horse RPA area will be designated perhaps in Dornod steppe (Interview 16, Undargaa, 2013).

State territorial strategy 231

11 Article 1.5.5, Constitution of Mongolia, 1992.
12 Interview 19 (Undargaa, 2013). "Re-establish, re-enhance the protection of inter-provincial *otor* RPAs" was articulated in provision 10.3 of implementing the first stage (2003–2008) of the "State Food and Agriculture policy" approved by decree No. 245, 2003 of the Government of Mongolia.
13 www.otor.mn/ Department of Interprovincial RPA Management, MFA.
14 Exempting herders from tax, help from international organizations in providing aid such as forage and fodder and several micro-credit programs to help herders re-stock themselves.
15 Article 16.1.6, Law on Land, Mongolia 2003.
16 In accordance with decree No. 187, 2007 of the government of Mongolia.
17 De facto nine places (Interview 15, Undargaa, 2013).
18 Source: DIPRPU document, MFA, 2010.
19 Interview 25 (Undargaa, 2013).
20 Interview 16 and 25 (Undargaa, 2013). Until 2009, it was the decision of the ministry to keep the governor of HBU *bag* as the head of the HBU RPA. This was a favorable condition for the ministry to decide in collaboration with the HBU village governor independently of the *soum* for cultivating the agrarian plot in the HBU *bag* without permission from the *soum* administration. An amendment to the law on territorial administrative units in 2008 emphasized the authority of the *soum* administration over the *bag* administration and its power to decide on territorial matters (2009 Committee meeting protocol, DIPRPU document, MFA).
21 Interview 16 (Undargaa, 2013).
22 Interviews 5 and 16 (Undargaa, 2013). It is common for horses or non-milking cattle herds to cross the territorial boundary for grazing, until their owner collects them, as they mainly graze on their own with oversight from the owners. This grazing practice was common in UU or DD or other *bags* surrounding HBU Mountain. Thus, the officials in the collective and current periods assumed it was necessary to set wide and extensive boundaries around the HBU Mountain and to include other seasonal pastures.
23 Interview 25, (Undargaa, 2013).
24 Questionnaire 25, (Undargaa, 2013).
25 The discussion in Chapter 6 showed that regular *bag* officials also benefited from controlling pasture as most of them are herders or have wage-earning herders working for them.
26 *Soum Hural* and governors have the power to make decisions on territorial issues according to the land law.
27 Interview 22 (Undargaa, 2013).
28 Interview 25 (Undargaa, 2013).
29 Interview 24 and 25 (Undargaa, 2013).
30 Ministry decree No. 165, 167 issued March 1, 2009; Enforced in late spring after herders had finished delivering baby livestock, though movement began in June.
31 Interview 5 and 16 (Undargaa, 2013).
32 Interview 22 and 36 (Undargaa, 2013).
33 Questionnaire 35 (Undargaa, 2013).
34 These *bags* are within 20–80 km from HBU *bag*.
35 Interview 21 (Undargaa, 2013).
36 Article 20.2.5, The law on Land, Mongolia decreed that the state appropriate land for special needs after negotiation with the local governor and present the proposal to the respective level *Hural*.
37 The funding issue was rather blurred in the local *soum* administration. My inquiry about funding revealed a limited but interesting insight. HBU *bag* officials stated that they were not allocating any funds to their herders, because most returned

232   *State territorial strategy*

back after a month (the earliest arrived back on August 1st) (Interview 21). The *soum* had allocated funding for 4–5 DD households (each was given 100,000 MNT for transportation and petrol), which managed to leave on a major long-distance *otor*, but lost a large number of livestock.

38 Interview 6, 26 and 34 (Undargaa, 2013).
39 Questionnaire 35 (Undargaa, 2013).
40 In some areas, physical fighting and verbal attacks on visiting herders were reported. These were recorded not only in the committee meeting minutes (MFA, 2009b), but also stated by many participants during my fieldwork in 2010.
41 Interview 13 (Undargaa, 2013).
42 Interview 56 (Undargaa, 2013).
43 This is also because the locals' spring campsite is expanded to summer pasture, where visiting herders were staying to access water and labor resources.
44 Some UU herders left their area for elsewhere considering that HBU RPA would be closed for two years.
45 Interview 42 and 56, Questionnaire 8 and 14 (Undargaa, 2013).
46 Interview 56 (Undargaa 2013).
47 Questionnaire 35 (Undargaa, 2013).
48 Questionnaire 66 (Undargaa, 2013).
49 Interview 21 (Undargaa, 2013).
50 Questionnaire 30 (Undargaa, 2013).
51 Questionnaire 36 (Undargaa, 2013).
52 Questionnaire 27 (Undargaa, 2013).
53 Herders use the term *mal togtohgui* (the livestock movement is unstable), livestock move around often and cannot graze in a stable manner to get fat and maintain the fat.
54 Questionnaire 28 (Undargaa, 2013).
55 Interview 23 (Undargaa, 2013).
56 Questionnaire 65 (Undargaa, 2013).
57 Interview 7 (Undargaa, 2013).
58 Interview 55 (Undargaa, 2013).
59 Questionnaire 82 (Undargaa, 2013).
60 At the time of fieldwork, many respondents in HBU *bag* did not have their certificates with them as the local administration kept them all for several years with the excuse of changing them over to the new version of the certificates.
61 Interview 46 (Undargaa, 2013).
62 Interview 12 (Undargaa, 2013).
63 Questionnaire 32 (Undargaa, 2013).
64 Local herders and officials in HBU and Dolood *bags* were critical of the ministry department, because local and visiting herders lost many livestock in 2009 in the HBU RPA as their movements were blocked by *dzud*, but the ministry still reported to the nation that there was no *dzud* in the HBU RPA.
65 Livestock thievery also occurs at the same time. However, this act is not strictly conducted by only visiting herders.
66 Interview 5 (Undargaa, 2013).
67 Creating more *buuts* on pasture is actually not helpful for pasture growth. Many *otor* herders pool their resources of labor and mobility and camp together on the same *buuts*. This strategy often works well for short periods of *otor* movement.
68 The department has planted different forage vegetation and root vegetables as fodder crops for stock. Fieldwork note, October, 2010.
69 This is less realistic, because the HBU RPA is not just about pasture, but also related to good natural shelter for overcoming cold winters. Many local and *otor*

herders explained that regardless of pasture, they would move to the HBU Mountain to shelter and feed their livestock with fodder and forage if necessary.

70 Article 16.1.6, the Law on Land 2003.

71 This sedentary approach is often explained in relation to the experience of collective herders or new herders. This is a very simplistic argument when examining the impacts of more sedentary legal policies on diminishing herders' socio-economic situations. My research found that herders' mobility patterns depended more on weather conditions and their herd size than on their background.

72 This is a condition where the state is particularly shaped by societal actions. Because zoning relies on strict enforcement, it is not effective when it is not compatible with the local ways of using the resource.

References

Badarch, D, Zilinskas, R A and Palint, P J (2003) *Mongolia Today: Science, Culture, Environment, and Development*, Routledge Curzon, London, UK.

Bedunah, D J and Schmidt, S (2004) "Pastoralism and protected area management in Mongolia's Gobi Gurvansaikhan National Park," *Development and Change* 35:1, 167–191.

Bold, B (1996) "Socio-economic segmentation: khot-ail in nomadic livestock keeping of Mongolia," *Nomadic Peoples* 39, 69–86.

Bold, B (2001) *Mongolian Nomadic Society: A Reconstruction of the "Medieval" History of Mongolia*, The Nordic Institute of Asian Studies, Richmond, Surrey.

Cellarius, B (2004) "'Without co-ops there would be no forests': historical memory and the restitution of forests in post-socialist Bulgaria," *Conservation & Society* 2:1, 51–73.

Constitution (1992) *The Constitution of Mongolia*, Ulaanbaatar.

Dietz, T, Ostrom, E and Stern, P C (2003) "The struggle to govern the commons," *Science* 302, 1907–1912.

Endicott, E (2012) *A History of Land Use in Mongolia*, Palgrave Macmillan, New York.

Feeny, D, Berkes, F, McCay, B J and Acheson, J M (1990) "The tragedy of the commons: twenty-two years later," *Human Ecology* 18:1.

Fernandez-Gimenez, M E, Batkhishig, B and Batbuyan, B (2012) "Cross-boundary and cross-level dynamics increase vulnerability to severe winter disaster (*dzud*) in Mongolia," *Global Environmental Change* 22, 836–851.

Humphrey, C (1978) "Pastoral nomadism in Mongolia: the role of herdsmen's cooperatives in the national economy," *Development and Change* 9, 133–160.

Lattimore, O (1962) *Nomads and Commissars: Mongolia Revisited*, Oxford University Press, New York.

Mearns, R (2004) "Decentralisation, rural livelihoods and pasture-land management in post socialist Mongolia," *European Journal of Development Research* 16:1, 133–152.

MFA (2009a) "The meeting protocol from the Committee of Inter-Provincial Reserve Pasture Area," Vol. July 3 (ed., Department of the Inter-Provincial Reserve Pasture Area) Ministry of Food, Agriculture and Light Industry, Ulaanbaatar.

MFA (2009b) "The meeting protocol from the Committee of Inter-Provincial Reserve Pasture Area," Vol. December 28 (ed., Department of the Inter-Provincial Reserve Pasture Area) Ministry of Food, Agriculture and Light Industry, Ulaanbaatar.

MFA (2010) "Action plan for reserve pasture areas" (ed. Department of Inter-Provincial Reserve Pasture Area), Ulaanbaatar.

234 *State territorial strategy*

MNE (1996) *Biodiversity Conservation Action Plan for Mongolia*, GEF/UNDP/MNE, Ulaanbaatar.

Natsagdorj, Sh (1972) *Soum, khamjlaga, shavi, ard*, Academy of Science Publishing, Ulaanbaatar.

Rossabi, M (2005) *Modern Mongolia: From Khans to Commissars to Capitalists*, University of California Press, Berkeley.

SDC (2010) "Livelihood study of herders in Mongolia," Swiss Agency for Development and Cooperation (SDC), Ulaanbaatar.

Sneath, D (2007) *The Headless State*, Columbia University Press, New York.

Sokolov, V E, Neronov, V M and Lushchekina, A A (1991) "Modern state and prospects of protection of mammals in Mongolia" in J A McNeely and V M Neronov (eds.) *Mammals in the Palaearctic Desert: Status and Trends in the Sahara-Gobian Region,* The Russian Committee for the UNESCO Programme on "Man and the Biosphere," Moscow, 251–257.

Undargaa, S (2013) "Property 'owners' without rights? Exploring property relations and access in the Herlen Bayan-Ulaan Reserve Pasture Area of Mongolia," Crawford School of Public Policy, Australian National University, Canberra.

Vandergeest, P and Peluso, N L (1995) "Territorialization and state power in Thailand," *Theory and Society* 24, 385–426.

Vreeland, H H (1954) "Mongol community and kinship structure," Walter Hines Page School of International Relations, The Johns Hopkins University, New Haven.

Wingard, J R and Odgerel, P (2001) "Compendium of environmental law and practice in Mongolia," GTZ Commercial and Civil Law Reform Project, Ulaanbaatar, Mongolia.

9 Conclusion

Introduction to the problem

As introduced in Chapter 1, this study first set out to explore the underlying problems in pastureland management from a perspective of political ecology by examining the socio-economic, historical and institutional aspects of pastoralism in Mongolia. The current broader literature on CPR management emphasizes the significance of defining property rights institutions in managing CPR. However, I have found the literature limited in explaining mobile pastoralism and its long established and persisting historical institutional arrangements for regulating access to pastureland in Mongolia. Although mobile pastoralism and its property relations in Mongolia are self-evident for those who have long been exposed to this production system, it is certainly complex for others to systematically explain the historical logic of herders' settlement patterns and their social organization. This challenge has resulted in misleading interpretations of the problem as an absence of property rights in pastureland management in Mongolia. Thus, understanding these factors will situate the local notion of property relations in its place in Mongolia. Combining field research with a review of existing studies and archival materials, this book elucidates what constitutes the specific aspects of the fundamentals of Mongolian Pastoralism, and the ways in which the state dismantled this system, and how and why privatization and land reform affected herders' access to resources. In conclusion, this book presents several challenges that emerged from this transition.

Property relations emerge from the historical process of a society (Benda-Beckmann et al., 2006). They reflect socio-political relationships that are based on long historical experiences of environmental dependencies and vulnerabilities. In the Mongolian context, property relations are deeply embedded in the historical foundations of pastoralism (Undargaa and McCarthy, 2016). Land tenure evolved as an element of pastoralism that worked as a socio-technical system: here, the historical socio-political structure of pastoralists was integrated with the natural and material resources available in this environment (Sneath, 2004). Mongolian pastoralists developed the *ulamjlalt* system of pastoral production as a means of

236 Conclusion

allocating political and economic benefits from natural resources in the prevailing climatic and geographical conditions (Sneath, 2007). Here, those who controlled production also controlled access to pastoral resources (Chapter 3). Historically, until privatization, the state regulated access to pastoral resources based on two fundamentals of pastoral production management: a dual (formal and informal) system of controlling the production components to benefit from pastoral production within a jurisdiction. State formal control (jurisdictional residency and taxation of production under state territorial administration) worked to balance the number of households and livestock to match the availability of ecologically preferable land (EPL). The state's use of these jurisdictional mechanisms to extract benefits from pastoral production also depended upon herders' informal control. Herders employed jurisdictional mechanisms to claim their right to practice *ulamjlalt* pastoral production and use pastoral resources. The state allowed herders to micro-manage production components including daily pasture use informally based on *ulamjlalt* production principles. In doing so, herders exercised individual or community use rights. A common practice was to exercise locally recognized use rights; this practice was highly flexible and relational as herders reciprocated this right with others in exchange for use rights to access available pastoral resources within and beyond their jurisdictions. This enabled herders' freedom and flexibility of movement, in a territorial manner. Herders pursued *ulamjlalt* seasonal rotations and long/short distance *otor* movement based on a production strategy, which depended on coordinating access to, and the availability of, livestock, labor and pastoral resources. The flexibility that is an essential element of herders' mobility is beyond the capacity of de jure property rights to land that are allocated exclusively to different actors such as the state, state-based actors or herders. All these actors are dependent on each other through the production system and vice versa. In other words, dual control facilitated the principles of freedom of movement and reciprocity in pastoralism and functioned as exclusionary, as well as inclusionary, mechanisms for regulating access to pastoral resources. Thus, the property relations bequeathed by historical practices were embedded in the system of pastoral production. This system persisted through several socio-economic and political systems as long as the state maintained these fundamentals. Although the modern Mongolian state changed some aspects of the pastoral production management during the collective period, both the state and herders continued to obtain benefits from pastoralism whilst maintaining rangeland conditions (Chapter 4). However, the state dismantled these fundamentals, following the advice of international development organizations in order to adjust and/or transition Mongolian Pastoralism to a market economy and improve the efficiency of rural land management. They based their policy analysis on popular theoretical and policy discourses, which presented several issues in improving rangeland management.

Conclusion   237

Issues in CPR management approach

Issue 1: Overly prescriptive approach based on misreading

The transition policies reflected a particular interpretation of property theory. In order to control the benefits from natural resources, the government created a hybrid system of resource management. During privatization, the state dismantled dual control over integrated management of *ulamjlalt* pastoral production. It liberalized the labor and livestock aspects of production, whilst shifting its control exclusively to land under the notion of a state property regime. At the same time, the state continued to regulate access to pastoral resources through its territorial administrative units, but allowed herders to control production. This resulted in the collapse of formal pastoral institutions and created an ambiguity in terms of who actually had the power[1] to control herders' access to pasture. Herders de facto took control over access to land, because they controlled the production (livestock and labor), which enabled them to "mediate other's access" (Ribot and Peluso, 2003, p. 158). Local administrations' inability to control production components (e.g., incoming migration and the number of livestock in their territory) diminished their authority to control both pastoral production and the land. Analysts interpreted the system in accordance with a highly prescriptive reading of collective action theory that argued for addressing the problems of exclusion and subtractability inherent in CPR management (Undargaa and McCarthy, 2016). This policy narrative supported state recognition of historical forms of self-governance (Feeny et al., 1990). Accordingly, the state formalized co-management over pastureland involving the local government and its *Hurals* enforcing *ulamjlalt* pasture use rules and norms. However, this formalization process overlooked the historical co-management of production, which had previously balanced the components of production. *Ulamjlalt* production and pasture use rules and norms are pragmatic adaptations based on existing ecological conditions that the state is unable to enforce because it formalized these as land use rules and norms. Further, the state implemented land reform in 1994, derived from a policy narrative that called for clear property rights to land and pastoral resources. Applying this principle, the state formalized herders' rights to campsites with statutory exclusive possession rights, decoupling its tenure arrangement from once integrated use rights to pasture. However, this failed to allow for freedom of movement – an essential element of the herding system. The land policies blocked herders' ability to pursue their usual seasonal movement and rotation according to *ulamjlal* and exacerbated depleting pastoral resources between campsites and overgrazing. For these reasons, herders themselves changed their access patterns in order to adjust their seasonal mobility to the changing legal environment and climate conditions (Chapters 6–8). As in other cases (Cousins, 2009), this reform disembedded rights from their social functions towards supporting the development of a land market. In the process, it broke down pre-existing

238 *Conclusion*

arrangements that had protected herders from losing rights to pastureland. As in other cases (Meinzen-Dick and Mwangi, 2009, cited in Cousins, 2009), these reforms attempted to transform Mongolian land tenure in a way that fitted more closely with western ideals of property rights. However, Mongolian Pastoralism was a case where property rights were applied to the pastoral context without questioning the concept of property (Humphrey and Verdery, 2004). A property rights' approach is inadequate in defining the complex relationship between various herders (subjects) claiming rights to different campsites/pastures (objects) under the arrangement of locally recognized use rights (Chapter 3). Also, land reform emphasized land as the primary production resource, disregarding the labor and livestock components, which are crucial in managing production and pasture use. In particular, the ownership of livestock truly embodies exclusive property rights and shapes herders' ability to access pastoral resources (Chapter 3).

Although the collective action approach, with its emphasis on the "bundle of rights" concept and its preference for co-management of land resources, provides a sophisticated framework for analysis, those employing this approach inadequately interpreted the realities of Mongolian Pastoralism (Undargaa and McCarthy, 2016). Based on the collective action and co-management approach, which promotes CBNRM, national and international advisers promoted forming autonomous herder groups or self-governing property institutions to be nested in a state territorial administration. This was to engineer co-managed institutions and define herders' exclusive property rights to pastoral resources in order to solve the so-called open access problem to pastureland (Chapter 7). Forming herder groups may intend to mend historical self-governing institutions or craft a new community institution (Dietz et al., 2003; McCay and Jentoft, 1998), or perhaps to reflect traditional community (Schmidt, 2004). However, as discussed elsewhere (Addison et al., 2013; Fernandez-Gimenez et al., 2008; Upton et al., 2013), the HBU case revealed (Chapter 7) that experimental community-based natural resource management (CBNRM) projects struggled to define social and resource boundaries and to provide the reciprocity and flexibility of movement required by herders in all living conditions. In non-egalitarian pastoralism, herders have different herd sizes, mobility patterns and different needs to pool labor due to changing *hot ail* structures. The ideal fixed social boundary of a group herder is small and limits the members' social networking ability and collective action with others beyond their group. Herder groups are also unable to control fixed group membership based on seasonal pastures when migrant herders access their seasonal pastures with the legitimacy of the local administration under the mechanisms of residency and legal campsite possession. Besides, the failed attempt to establish herder groups also opened up room for conflicts of interest between different actors in terms of who represents the interests of *bag* herders in improving pasture management. Thus, it is an open ended question as to whether herder groups are able to pursue pasture management by excluding outsiders (Chapter 7). In fact, group formations from experimental projects are mainly limited to a paper registration, their positive outcomes limited to a few groups, which were dependent on major financial and technical support[2] (Chapter 7). Therefore, formalizing herder groups' possession of pastureland in the proposed pastureland law is questionable in terms of its broader application.

Attempting to apply CBNRM through design principles faced critical challenges elsewhere in terms of strengthening collective action (Nelson and Agrawal, 2008). In Mongolia, this attempt to apply a CBNRM approach became a blanket policy or a form of theoretical panacea that overlooked the socio-political, ecological and institutional aspects of rangeland governance in the past (Addison et al., 2013). This initiative provided for smaller nested jurisdictions that neither contain sufficient EPL nor are able to balance the increasing dynamics of labor and livestock under unstable weather conditions. Without making use of the well proven historical formal mechanisms to balance these production components and of production-based collective action within and beyond a jurisdictional community under conditions of a changing legal environment and climate (Chapter 7), this model conflicted with herders' insistent pursuit of flexibility or freedom of movement. In contrast, any traditional groups in the past, referred to territorial administrative units such as *aravt*, and functioned for governing the residency of pastoral people and their livestock production. These are local patterns of resource use, which the state and community-led interventions need to incorporate carefully in resource management (Sikor and Muller, 2009; Upton, 2009). Establishing a form of property institution has only focused on exclusion instead of addressing an inclusionary paradigm in pastureland management. Herding households in Mongolia often do not stay together with the same household and/or they may need to join other households, groups, kin, or communities in times of severe weather, livestock disease, a lack of labor or poor grazing (Erdenebaatar, 1996). Regarding herders' need to share and access pastoral resources, community membership is dynamic and subtractability becomes an issue that goes beyond specific community resource management. The production system involves different types of CPRs and community structures, which are defined by a larger socio-political system critical for managing CPRs in Mongolia. Hence, a puzzle emerges: to what extent can the collective action approach be used to explain the characteristics of Mongolian pastureland management? Can this framework provide a prescription for reforming pastoralism in Mongolia? In other words, is the co-management approach able to remedy problems in Mongolia's CPR resource management? Many analysts defined Mongolian land tenure in various ways from the perspective of the CPR property regimes theory (Chapters 1 and 5). In attempting to find a new nested relationship between state and customary institutions, co-management re-invented the wheel, whereas, in Mongolia, the state and customary forms had already been integrated into a single, historically tested and socially embedded form of pastoral production and resource management (Undargaa and McCarthy, 2016).

240 *Conclusion*

Misreading this historical system may be a reason why various actors dispute herders' membership to indigenous or traditional communities, and/or the ownership of community territory.[3] The Dana declaration's[4] use of the term "indigenous people" may be useful for protecting Mongolian herders' right to practice their lifestyle. However, defining who is a "native" or an "indigenous" "community" appears open to debate (Fratkin, 1997; Humphrey and Verdery, 2004; Meijl, 2006). Thus, these terms may not be a strong mechanism for protecting individual herders' rights to specific land due to the dynamic migration backgrounds of herders and their ancestors, changes in their jurisdictional residency, and changes in the state jurisdictional structures in the past. Instead, formal mechanisms of residency and livestock ownership have always been providing solid rights for any herder to produce and access pastoral resources in any jurisdiction as long as they practise *ulamjlalt* pastoral production. Beyond property rights to land, these mechanisms embody the rights to land or even ownership of natural resources under the emic notions of *nutag orondoo ezen ni baih, bolj turuh* (to be born as or to become master, authority[5] or owner,[6] and to be there for their *nutag* or take care of their *nutag*). In fact, Sneath emphasized the concept of *gazar* (land) in Mongolia:

> This ideation emphasizes land use rather than a common substance that can be owned or possessed.... The most widely used term for private land is *huviin gazar* ... [meaning] to divide or apportion. So, items of personal property are explicitly part of wider fields – be they domestic, district, or state political economies.
>
> (2004, p. 170)

Unlike in many other societies with native communities, herders did not claim formal rights to land through indigenous or traditional ancestral claims. Sneath (2004) argued further that "regimes of property and of citizenship were constituent elements of the pastoral socio-technical systems that provided the productive base of the rural economy" (Sneath, 2004, p. 178). Herders claimed their rights to pastureland through their jurisdictional membership and the ownership of livestock and the jurisdiction mobilized their entitlement to pursue pastoral production. In this regard, international and national development organizations could have advocated and invested in strengthening the authority and legitimacy of centralized and self-governing local institutions over an integrated management of production components as in the past. This would have contributed to natural resource governance and protection of local actors' territory from land grabs by other interested groups.

Issue 2: Misconstructing the natural resource challenge as "open access"

Application of the property rights approach rested on a narrow understanding of property in the Mongolian pastoral context (Undargaa and McCarthy, 2016).

Conclusion 241

This policy narrative promoted "a confused and confusing set of ideas that obfuscates the real problems and opportunities of rights-based approaches" (Cousins, 2009, p. 6). As a result, analysts diagnosed the underlying problem as "open access" that prevailed to pastureland (Fernandez-Gimenez and Batbuyan, 2004; Fernandez-Gimenez et al., 2008; Griffin, 2003; Ickowitz, 2003; Mearns, 2004a, 2004b). However, pastureland is not open access; access is regulated by co-existing formal and informal rules and norms (Klein et al., 2012; Upton, 2005). Upton (2009) employed the concept of "institutional bricolage" to explain the problems involved in adhering to these rules and norms. The author emphasized that where contests emerge over notions of customary use rules and norms, actors seek legitimacy for their use, and will re-invent customs. The HBU case presented the complex relationship between formal and informal mechanisms and the ways in which these mechanisms functioned and have changed during the transition. As I have argued, in the past the state territorial administration met a critical need of herders by coordinating the components of production, thereby shaping how herders practice pasture use rules and norms (Chapter 3). This understanding is critical in our analysis of institutional change and its impact on herders' ability to adhere to customary pasture use rules and norms (Undargaa and McCarthy, 2016). There are two issues regarding institutional bricolage, which affect herders in adhering to customary pasture use rules and norms. First, "institutional bricolage" emerged in the overall pastoral production system, which currently combines elements derived from different periods: the re-emergence of a pre-collective pattern of private livestock production; a socialist collective pattern of smaller jurisdictional boundaries; and a post-socialist market economy that prioritizes the application of property rights to land-based resources and liberalization of labor. Herders now needed to operate without the arrangements that had formally governed production components in the past, thus creating difficulties in practicing pre-collective *ulamjtlalt* pasture use rules and norms (Chapters 5–6). Second, herders re-invented the custom of using residency requirements and livestock ownership to facilitate their freedom of movement as in the past. The use of these mechanisms persists, because pre-collective *ulamjlalt* patterns of production are rooted in the logic of pastureland management and are still relevant (Chapter 6).

Issue 3: Increasing complexity of property institutions

In several other post-socialist countries such as Romania, Bulgaria, China and Vietnam, the process of specifying exclusive property rights exacerbated the "fuzzy" quality of property relations (Verdery, 1999, 2004). In other words, it intensified the gaps between "actual property arrangements with their complex interrelationships and multiple actors," and an "idealized image of exclusive private rights and obligations held by normative individuals" set out in the new land law (Yeh, 2004, p. 108). As in these other cases "within a single historical period" a government issued mutually contradictory laws, "allocating rights to the same resources to different parties" (Ribot and Peluso, 2003, pp. 162, 163).

242 *Conclusion*

In Mongolia, misdiagnosing the problem as one of open access, reformers introduced property rights instead of addressing the underlying problems generating disputes and overgrazing. This in turn broke down a historically proven system that provided legitimate secure access for herders in all living conditions (Undargaa and McCarthy, 2016). The transformation of historical (pre-collective and collective) state/public territorial ownership and control over production management to a state property regime, and formalization of exclusive landed-property rights and pasture use rules and norms reproduced "fuzziness" (Sturgeon and Sikor, 2004). It created ambiguity with respect to who really controls access to what resource through what mechanism. As in the HBU case, herders and local authorities employed competing legal and extra-legal mechanisms to extract benefits from pastoral resources. In fact, there is a thin line between formal and informal mechanisms and the ways in which different actors define and employ these mechanisms depend on the context that suited them. For the sake of recognizing customary institutions, the state formalized herders' rights along with some basic *ulamjlalt* rules and norms in the land law. These formalizations were also proposed in the draft pastureland law. However, "property rights are more complicated than just the state enforcing them from the top down" (Easterly, 2006, p. 90). The issue of whether the state, herder groups or individual herding households have the ability to regulate access to pastoral resources (campsites and pasture) through property mechanisms was hardly addressed. In fact, overestimating the capacity of formalized property rights obscures the importance of other mechanisms in strengthening the state and local community co-management and collective action institution. Additionally, the state did not clarify which actors could better make use of specific *ulamjlalt* rules and norms to access pastoral resources in various contexts (Chapters 6–8). The formalization of property rights and fuzzy property relations in fact create room for those representing the state or state-based agencies and individual actors to grab land under the guise of the state or a private/group property regime for the purpose of mining, tourism or some special use, etc. As in the HBU case, this resulted in the fact that various state-based agencies and jurisdictional governments had disputes over territory and contested each other's legitimacy in controlling access to pasture (Chapter 8).

Issue 4: Production components

Privatization and land reform policies in Mongolia ignored the fundamental logic underlying the integrated management of pastoral production and created difficulty in adjusting pastoral production to a market economy (Undargaa and McCarthy, 2016). As suggested by Peluso (1992) in another case, after de-collectivization, the state shifted its control over the components of production to control of land only, and its historical co-management approach from production to conservation oriented land management (Mearns, 2004b). Indeed, many studies of extensive pastoralism insufficiently provide a means of integrating all the components of production, insufficiently taking into account the

Conclusion 243

dynamic relations between these components under unstable weather conditions (Bazargur, 1998). By dismantling the management of the components of production, in a similar fashion to that described by Polanyi (1944), the state disembedded the pastoral economy from its social, political and ecological foundations. A long historical experience underlies private livestock ownership and production in Mongolia. However, by developing a system that lacked the proven, customary, mechanisms to control labor and livestock, these reforms discarded a long established understanding of what worked in the local environment (Undargaa and McCarthy, 2016). As collective action theory has emphasized, particular arrangements need to "fit" ecological and social-structures (Ostrom and Nagendra, 2006). In the past these mechanisms fitted with the fundamental logic of pastureland management. The healthy functioning of historically developed and resilient institutions remains critical to property relations: indeed the credibility of such institutions is more important than the form (state, communal or individual) they take (Ho, 2013). This study has argued that jurisdictional authorities provide several resource governance mechanisms for all actors which draw benefits from taxable pastoral production. This is why some herders support state involvement in the co-management of components of pastoral production (Chapters 6 and 7).

Issue 5: Access mechanisms – more sophisticated analysis of production

This analysis of the political economy of resources – principally exploring why some benefit irrespective of the property rights they hold – enables us to understand pastoralism in new ways (Ribot and Peluso, 2003, p. 155). It led us to shift our focus from the management of pastureland to the management of production and its marketing, exposing a whole range of mechanisms that pastoralists employ to access resources and draw benefits from production. Further, this critique of the application of property rights and CBNRM in this case raise theoretical and policy questions that need to be answered in order to improve understandings of production and resource practices. This requires a broader understanding of the context and abandonment of overly prescriptive institutional approaches (Undargaa and McCarthy, 2016). In other words, examining various mechanisms involved in producing and marketing livestock, and the ways in which these mechanisms affect resource management is critical in understanding pasture management practices. In terms of production, ambiguities in transition policies have led to different actors pursuing a variety of means of access to legitimize their claims to pastoral resources. These mechanisms were similar to what Ribot and Peluso (2003) argued, which were a complex set of rights-based or relational access mechanisms that the law is incapable of addressing (Ribot and Peluso, 2003). As the HBU case revealed, frustrated by conflicting authority among state-based actors, herders employed multiple structural and relational mechanisms simultaneously to gain, maintain and control access to pastoral resources. This caused alterations to the herders' way of pursuing seasonal mobility or long

244   *Conclusion*

distance *otor* movements. In fact, distinctions between rights-based or relational mechanisms are not as clear-cut as those observed in different property regimes (Verdery, 1999). Also, herders' use of different access mechanisms presents a way to gain access, while the ability to maintain or control access depends on the availability of pasture.

In terms of marketing, CPR management is often affected by multi-level cross-scale national and international markets and resource exploitation (Berkes, 2009; Ribot and Peluso, 2003). Particularly, where there are conflicting legal arrangements in the regulation of access to pastoral resources and in light of depleting pastoral resources, it is important to examine why herders focus solely on increasing the numbers of livestock, though they acknowledge the importance of quality over quantity. Thus, further research on production marketing is critical regarding (a) to what extent the commodity value chain operates; (b) how production marketing at the local, national and international levels shapes this chain; (c) how actors control the benefit mechanisms; and (d) how this affects herders' decisions to increase livestock numbers. Therefore, policy initiatives need to be built upon an analysis that "puts property in its place among the many other mechanisms that shape the distribution of benefits, landscape of incentives and the efficiency and equity of resource use" (Ribot and Peluso, 2003, p. 173). This involves understanding property relations in the larger socio-political context and in relation to the existence of diverse ecological systems (Sneath, 2004). To this effect, I argue that improvement in pastureland management requires the following.

Recommendations

Integrated management of production components and pastureland

Re-establish *ulamjlalt* production management or an integrated approach over managing all three production components under a production-oriented rather than conservation-oriented land management approach. Also, the regulation of pastureland and campsites needs to be integrated, perhaps under the same use rights. These integrations involve re-establishing historical jurisdictional mechanisms over herders' residential migration and livestock taxation. This is because, historically, these mechanisms are far better suited for state and local communities rather than formalized property rights to manage pastureland and obtain benefits from pastoralism. First, control herders' (population) residential migration based on their pursuit of pastoral production and the number of livestock they own since migrant herders with large numbers of livestock often affect local capacity. In other words, migrant herders would be allowed only if (a) their livestock numbers were compatible with the local capacity and (b) they register for residency without livestock ownership (e.g., wage herder or for non-herding settlement). Based on these conditions, their residency could be approved based on dual control: (a) legitimacy by local herders (recognized and accepted by local herders informally and at the *bag*

Hural) and (b) approved formally by the local administration based on "a." Second, integration involves re-establishing livestock taxation (*maliin huliin tatvar*), contingent upon improved incomes for herders. This requires (a) tax exemption of a certain number of livestock to reflect historical patterns of risk management and (b) herders' improved ability to market value added livestock products with the support of formal mechanisms. Under current conditions,[7] of open international markets and technological development, the government could develop laws and regulations to enhance benefits from pastoral production by devising adequate and necessary formal mechanisms: promoting the development of value added production as in the socialist period, reducing the number of middlemen in marketing raw and value added products, price control and control over the commodity chain, etc. This could contribute to improving herders' income and their ability to focus on quality of livestock and reduce burdens on pastureland. This production-oriented land management approach could potentially help transition Mongolian private livestock production into the market system. Devising these formal mechanisms requires comprehensive research to produce systematic knowledge about (a) how and why the current commodity chain works; (b) what should be addressed in improving the marketing mechanisms and how it should be reflected in specific laws and regulations; and (c) the historical taxation system. Also, the development of value added production requires careful consideration of the environmental impacts regarding the chemical wastes emitted from processing raw livestock products.

Pastoral institution

Many developing countries dismantled their historical institutions and are in the process of mending or designing new self-governing institutions under the CBNRM approach. In a similar fashion, national and international organizations in Mongolia have recognized the potential of herder groups for this purpose. However, unlike other countries, the historical institutions were based on the state territorial administration and dual control, which de facto, has not broken down as much as it has in other developing countries due to its geopolitical location/position. Here, the notion of "community" in Mongolia is problematic regarding its social and resource boundaries. Clear distinctions of what constitutes a community, in terms of its membership and territory, are more likely to be made at the *bag* level (the smallest local territorial administrative unit), because it contains the seasonal pastures. This is evident because *bag* level actors sanction pastoral resources within the *bag* jurisdictional boundary, and can employ either state legal or *ulamjlalt* mechanisms to balance production components and accommodate herders' flexibility in mobility and reciprocity with others. In other words, making use of historical territorial administrative units to integrate the management of production components is necessary.

Therefore, for CPR management to succeed, national and international policy advocates could promote and invest in devising formal mechanisms

246 *Conclusion*

towards strengthening historical territorial administrations for integrated management of production. In other words, it is critical to strengthen the authority of both the *soum* and *bag* governments and their *Hurals* in the following ways. First, territorial authority is their right to protect their territory along with local herders' rights to access pastureland, so they obtain benefits from taxing pastoral production as it was in the pre-collective period where local lords decided whether to give up territory for other uses (i.e., monastery jurisdiction). This can be done by involving them in national level decision making about the use of their territory in order to avoid land grabs by powerful groups and individuals backed by the national government under the guise of a state property regime. Second, local administrations could reach their residents and, if necessary, re-install historical *aravt* groups, e.g., using the formation of herder groups for the purpose of administering pastoral people and production. This is similar to an earlier experiment by a GTZ Nature Conservancy Project of forming "community organizations,"[8] but free of formalized group property rights to pastureland. These arrangements will allow integrated control of local administrations to extend across all three production components and involve it in the management of *bag* herders' pastoral production as a whole. It will also help give herders a better voice to express their concerns. Third, it will provide *bag* herders the ability to micromanage their access to pasture within and between different jurisdictional units as in historical periods. Fourth, such dual control over integrated management of production components facilitates herders' flexibility in mobility (right-based exclusion) and allows inclusion based on reciprocity (a highly relational aspect) with herders from other groups and jurisdictions. This is because *ulamjlalt* pasture use rules and norms confer a high degree of legitimacy upon all actors and they fit the ecological context, which has become increasingly unstable in terms of climate and geography. In other words, both exclusion and inclusion can be enforced within a jurisdictional context under the integrated system. The state's property relations that were based on the *ulamjlalt* pastoral production was integrated, combining all rights-based (use rights), structural (state support) and relational mechanisms (historical, kinship and neighborhood).

Whilst "putting property in its place," this is not to say that arrangements should remain the same as in the pre-collective and collective times due to absolutely different political and economic conditions. Nonetheless, in pre-collective times, rulers enjoyed private ownership of livestock under use rights to pasture within their jurisdiction. In the collective period, rulers adjusted this historical pastoral production management to the political and economic conditions existing at the time, in keeping with the existing ecological context. Thus, instead of eradicating pastoral production and imposing an alien concept of rangeland management, the current government needs to make use of the historical fundamentals of pastoral production management as they did in the collective period, but to fit the current economic situation (for example, an independent business entity based within a jurisdictional context).[9] In other words, it needs to allow private ownership of livestock by herders, as it existed in the pre-collective time, but also collaborate with the independent business entity on production management to avoid land degradation and increasing poverty in both urban and rural Mongolia.

Notes

1 In this case, I refer to power as the "capacity of some actors to affect the practices and ideas of others" (Weber, 1978 and Luke, 1986 cited in Ribot and Peluso 2003, p. 156).
2 This reflects almost a hundred years ago, when irregular pasture use patterns by individual herding households occurred due to the destruction of the previous aristocratic institution in Mongolia. The modern Mongolian government was forced to engineer new socio-economic units and socially constructed collective action with enormous political and financial support from the Soviet Russia (Chapter 4).
3 See http://bankwatch.org/sites/default/files/letter-EBRD-OT-15Feb2013.pdf, or www.theguardian.com/global-development-professionals-network/2015/mar/09/mongolian-nomads-displacement-mining-impact-development-projects.
4 Dana Declaration at www.danadeclaration.org/.
5 Sneath (2007) used *ejen* or *ezen* for master or main authority as "notions of order and authority," which is a

> central value, one that applied to series of social scales – from the imperial to the domestic.... Proprietary authority was so central to the notion of social order that to be "masterless" was to be wild or chaotic. The term *ejengui baidal* (literally, a situation without an *ejen*) means "anarchy."
>
> (Sneath, 2007, p. 194)

Those who define access to pastureland as open access, absence of property rights, almost assume there is this *ejengui baidal* or masterless anarchy occurring to the land. Sneath's argument is important for my argument. In Mongolia, there is a localized notion of *nutag orondoo ezen ni baih*, another way of using the word *ezed* (plural of *ezen*), which has been regulating Mongolian pastureland among different levels of *ezed* (state to domestic) through production. Thus, instead of "open access" the question is why do overgrazing and disputes occur in the presence of control of these *ezed*. The answer is related to how and why transition policies changed the mechanisms different actors use in managing pastoral production and pastoral resources, and affected the rights, authority and ability of or property relations among these actors and the objects in question.
6 Not in terms of bundle of rights or exclusive individual land ownership.
7 In the pre-collective period under private production, herders benefited from subsistent and yield-oriented pastoral production. However, the benefits from the yield-oriented production were limited due to the poor marketing mechanisms for raw materials, and the poor development and marketing of value added products nationally and internationally due to the restricted geo-political location/position and Mongolia's dependency on our two neighbors. Now, herders seek to be occupied in yield-oriented production.
8 See Schmidt (2004).
9 Sneath (2007) argued that in the pre-collective period, nobility ruled pastoral people and their production under the aristocratic order. Under socialism, the state entities and collectives controlled these. Today, re-establishing these historical formal institutions is impossible, thus the option could be a private business entity nested in state territorial administration.

248 *Conclusion*

References

Addison, J, Davies, J, Friedel, M and Brown, C (2013) "Do pasture user groups lead to improved rangeland condition in the Mongolian Gobi Desert?," *Journal of Arid Environments* 94, 37–46.

Bazargur, D (ed.) (1998) *Geography of Pastoral Animal Husbandry*, TTC Company, Mongolian Academy of Science, Ulaanbaatar.

Benda-Beckmann, F V, Benda-Beckmann, K V and Wiber, M G (2006) "The properties of property" in F V Benda-Beckmann, K V Benda-Beckmann and M G Wiber (eds.) *Changing Properties of Property*, Berghahn Books, New York, 1–40.

Berkes, F (2009) "Revisiting the commons paradigm," *Journal of Natural Resources Policy Research* 1:3, 261–264.

Cousins, B (2009) "Capitalism obscured: the limits of law and rights-based approaches to poverty reduction and development," *Journal of Peasant Studies* 36:4, 893–908.

Dietz, T, Ostrom, E and Stern, P C (2003) "The struggle to govern the commons," *Science* 302, 1907–1912.

Easterly, W (2006) *The White Man's Burden*, The Penguin Press, New York.

Erdenebaatar, B (1996) "Socio-economic aspects of the pastoral movement patterns of Mongolian herders" in Caroline Humphrey and David Sneath (eds.) *Culture and Environment: Inner Asia 1*, The White Horse Press, Cambridge.

Feeny, D, Berkes, F, McCay, B J and Acheson, J M (1990) "The tragedy of the commons: twenty-two years later," *Human Ecology* 18:1.

Fernandez-Gimenez, M E and Batbuyan, B (2004) "Law and disorder: local implementation of Mongolia's land law," *Development and Change* 35:1, 141–165.

Fernandez-Gimenez, M E, Kamimura, A and Batbuyan, B (2008) "Implementing Mongolia's land law: progress and issues," The Center for Asian Legal Exchange (CALE), Nagoya University, Japan.

Fratkin, E (1997) "Pastoralism: governance and development issues," *Annual Review of Anthropology* 26, 235–261.

Griffin, K (2003) "Urban-rural migration and involution in the livestock sector" in K Griffin (ed.) *Poverty Reduction in Mongolia*, Asia Pacific Press, Canberra, 56–71.

Ho, P (2013) "In defense of endogenous, spontaneously ordered development: institutional functionalism and Chinese property rights," *The Journal of Peasant Studies* 40:6, 1087–1118.

Humphrey, Caroline and Verdery, Katherine (2004) "Introduction: raising questions about property" in Katherine Verdery and Caroline Humphrey (eds.) *Property in Question: Value Transformation in the Global Economy*, Berg, Oxford, New York, 1–25.

Ickowitz, A (2003) "Poverty and the environment" in K Griffin (ed.) *Poverty Reduction in Mongolia*, Asia Pacific Press, Canberra, 95–112.

Klein, J A, Fernandez-Gimenez, M E, Wei, H, Changqing, Y, Ling, D, Dorligsuren, D and Reid R S (2012) "A participatory framework for building resilient social-ecological pastoral systems" in M Fernandez-Gimenez, Xiaoyi Wang, B Batkhishig, J A Klein and R S Reid (eds.) *Restoring Community Connections to the Land: Building Resilience Through Community-based Rangeland Management in China and Mongolia*, CABI International, Oxfordshire.

McCay, B J and Jentoft, S (1998) "Market or community failure? Critical perspectives on common property research," *Human Organization* 57:1, 21–29.

Mearns, R (2004a) "Sustaining livelihoods on Mongolia's pastoral commons: insights from a participatory poverty assessment," *Development and Change* 35:1, 107–139.

Mearns, R (2004b) "Decentralisation, rural livelihoods and pasture-land management in post socialist Mongolia," *European Journal of Development Research* 16:1, 133–152.

Meijl, T V (2006) "Who owns the fisheries? Changing views of property and its redistribution in post-colonial Maori society' in F V Benda-Beckmann, K V Benda-Beckmann and M G Wiber (eds.) *Changing Properties of Property*, Berghahn Books, New York, 170–.

Nelson, F and Agrawal, A (2008) "Patronage or participation? Community-based natural resource management reform in Sub-Saharan Africa," *Development and Change* 39:4, 557–585.

Ostrom, E and Nagendra, H (2006) "Insights on linking forests, trees, and people from the air, on the ground, and in the laboratory," *PNAS* 103:51, 19224–19231.

Peluso, N L (1992) *Rich Forests, Poor People: Resource Control and Resistance in Java*, University of California Press, Berkeley.

Polanyi, K (1944) *The Great Transformation*, Beacon Press, Boston, MA.

Ribot, J C and Peluso, N L (2003) "A theory of access," *Rural Sociology* 68:2, 153–181.

Schmidt, S M (2004) "Pastoral community organization, livelihoods and biodiversity conservation in Mongolia's Southern Gobi region," in *Annual Meeting of Society for Range Management*, Salt Lake City, USA.

Sikor, Th and Muller, D (2009) "The limits of state-led reform: an introduction," *World Development* 37:8, 1307–1316.

Sneath, D (2004) "Property regimes and sociotechnical systems: rights over land in Mongolia's 'Age of the Market'" in K Verdery and C Humphrey (eds.) *Property in Question: Value Transformation in the Global Economy*, Berg, Oxford, New York, 161–182.

Sneath, D (2007) *The Headless State*, Columbia University Press, New York.

Sturgeon, J C and Sikor, T (2004) "Post-socialist property in Asia and Europe: variations on 'fuzziness'," *Conservation & Society* 2:1, 2–17.

Undargaa, S and McCarthy, J F (2016) "Beyond property: co-management and pastoral resource access in Mongolia," *World Development* 77, 367–379.

Upton, C (2005) "Institutions in a pastoral society: processes of formation and transformation in post-socialist Mongolia," *Comparative Studies of South Asia, Africa and the Middle East* 25:3, 584–599.

Upton, C (2009) "'Custom' and contestation: land reform in post-socialist Mongolia," *World Development* 37:8, 1400–1410.

Upton, C, Moore, K, Nyamsuren, N and Batjargal, E (2013) "Community, place and pastoralism: nature and society in post-soviet Central Asia," University of Leicester, Mongolian State University of Agriculture, The Leverhulme Trust.

Verdery, K (1999) "Fuzzy property: rights, power, and identity in Transylvania's decollectivization" in M Burawoy and K Verdery (eds.) *Uncertain Transition: Ethnographies of Change in the Post-socialist World*, Rowman and Littlefield Publishers, Lanham, MD, 53–82.

Verdery, K (2004) "The property regime of socialism," *Conservation & Society* 2:1, 190–198.

Yeh, Emily T. (2004) "Property relations in Tibet since decollectivisation and the question of fuzziness," *Conservation and Society* 2:1, 107–131.

Glossary

aimag Province/the largest state territorial administrative division in the country (21 *aimags* in Mongolia)

aravt Grouping of ten households for administrative purpose

bag Subdistrict/the smallest state territorial administrative division

belcheer Pasture

buuts Camping spot with thick layers of livestock dung

buuts gazar Campsites

ders Broom grass

dundiin Communal or shared use among a *bag* community

dzud Heavy winter storm, snow blockage and pasture inaccessibility. The two types of *dzud* are white *dzud*, which is due to a heavy snow storm and black *dzud* due to a heavy winter storm which clears and blackens all the grass.

ecologiin zohistoi nutag Ecologically preferable land

ertnii zan zanshil Ancient or traditional customs

ezemshil Legal possession

ezen (s) ***ezed*** (pl) Owner or master

ezengui baidal Anarchy

gan drought

gazar Land

ger Mobile felt dwelling

***ger* district** Residential district composed of lines of individual family ger

havarjaa A spring campsite with buuts, which often has a livestock shelter or rock wall on it to shelter livestock

Glossary 251

hond   Camping spot with thin layers of livestock dung

horshoo   Collective enterprise

hoshuu   Formal territorial administrative unit known as a banner

hot ail   Camping group of more than one household

Hural   Self-governing assembly of public representatives for each territorial administrative level

hurzun   A wall made of frozen dung blocks usually on a winter campsite

huviin   Equivalent to "private"

neg nutag usniihan   People who are from the same jurisdiction, or share the same valley or pastoral resources

nutag   General term for a territory which someone utilizes in several different ways that represent one's belonging to a certain administrative territory. One of the major affiliations is one's birth land and another is one's seasonal pasture and grazing area.

nutag (belcheeriin)   One's selection of a specific area for grazing. Nutaglah, v. A place where someone lives. It is commonly used by herders in rural areas indicating their location of home or grazing area.

nutag orondoo ezen ni baih, bolj turuhj   To be born as master or authority, owner and to be there for their nutag as a local resident and represent and take care of their nutag. Nutag songoh v. Select an area to live or graze livestock.

nutag zaah   Sending someone to a specific place for settlement or exile

otog   A quasi-administrative unit that mobilizes a certain number of warriors. It consisted of a group of appr. 10,000 households that were related to one another, but not strictly descended from the same lineage as a union. Later, monastery jurisdictions also used this term for administrative purposes.

otor   Short- or long-term temporary movement out of the regular seasonal pastures

otor tejeeliin aj ahui   Reserve pasture and fodder enterprise

soum   District, the second level state territorial administration division

suuri   The smallest herding unit of a collective, which consists of one/two to four herding households, sometimes more in a milking suuri

tugrug   Mongolian currency

uhriin darsh   Silage for the cattle

ulamjlalt   Equivalent to 'customary,' which referred to practices inherited from or transferred by the ancestors and which are still adhered to and mainstream in the present

252 *Glossary*

unasan nutag Geographical area of one's birth place

uvuljuu A winter campsite with buuts. It sometimes has a livestock shelter or rock wall on it or is established on a sheltered mountain or in a valley to shelter livestock.

zuruulj ideh Passing by each other for grazing

Index

Page numbers in *italics* denote tables, those in **bold** denote figures.

access: open access 1, 4–5, 11–12, 16–17, 106–7, 111, 113–14, 118, 120, 122–3, 127, 138, 142, 148, 151, 157, 162–3, 166, 168, 191, 193, 221–2, 229, 238, 240, 242, 247; access approach (mechanisms and strategies) 7, 22, 33, 194, 243–4
agrarian-based poverty 36
agro-pastoral husbandry 27
aj ahui infrastructure 97–8, 122; collapse of 118
Amboseli ecosystem, in Kenya 29
aravt 55, 178, 195, 239, 246
Asian Development Bank (ADB) 135

Bayan-Erkhtii Mountain 83, 101n23
biodiversity, loss of 208
bio-mass 174
Bogd Khan Mountain 206
Bulgan *soum* 141
buuts (livestock shelters) 63, 69, 78, 91, 96, 137, 160, 162

campsites and pasture reserves: allocation of 107; decision making and use rights 137; family splitting strategies 148, 161; feudal ownership of 136; formal control of 142–6; herders' rights to 136, 146; informal control of 146–51; land law, implementation of 138; legal possession of 138–9, 142–51, 161; open access problem 162–3; pasture use rules and norms *156*; possession certificate, issue of 136; property rights to 160; rehabilitation and possession of 108; strategy of "reciprocity" 140; trespassing incidents 140

Chinese Empire 49
civil registration 55, 59, 71n21
commoditization of the land 3
commodity chain 245
common pool resources (CPR): access mechanisms 243–4; and complexity of property institutions 241–2; management of 1–5, 7, 16–22, 40, 107, 128, 237–44; pastoral institution 245–7; principle of exclusion 18; production components 242–3; self-governance of 17
communal management, of pastoral resources 163
community managed area (CMA) 200n5
community organizations 172, 176, 246
community-based natural resource management (CBNRM) 2–4, 16, 18, 32–3, 238, 243; approaches by donor organizations for 172–5; balance in power relations 173; community resource boundaries 187–91; development of 171; Green Gold program 173–4; group collective action and pasture management 175–7; group formation in HBU case area 177–81; group pasture management 192–9; herder groups, formation of 171; historical patterns of 5; institutional design principles for 172; institution of 195; micro-credit and project support 179; *otor* frequencies by households 189; social boundaries 181–7; Sustainable Livelihood Program (SLP) 173, 177, 181; territorial boundaries 195
corporate ownership, idea of 52

254 *Index*

crop cultivating 22, 50, 53, 58, 61
crop-cultivating societies 53, 61
cross-boundary mobility 91–2
custodianship, state territorial relations under 52
customary institution, notion of 19–20, 59, 172, 239, 242

dairy farms 89, 94–5
de-urbanization, issue of 117–18, 122
diseases, livestock 95; inspection records for 96
division of labor 39
dzud emergencies 8, 69, 85, 93, 111, 117–18, 124, 140, 143, 161, 177, 206, 209–10, 223

ecologically preferable land (EPL) 58, 136, 236; compensation for the loss of 85
environmental conservation, preservations for 206
environmental degradation 2–3
environmental equilibrium, concept of 22–3
European colonization 23–4, 33
ezemshil (legal possession) 135
ezemshliin gerchilgee (possession certificate) 137

family contribution, to household production **184**
feudal land relationships 51; under Manchu period 51
food production system 6, 32–4, 76, 79
food security 22, 27; risk management strategy for 205
forced settlement, on marginal land 26
freedom of movement 35, 38, 60, 62, 141, 158, 176, 187–8, 192, 236–7, 239, 241
free-market economy 106
free-range grazing, economic characteristic of 38
fundamentals, of production system: fundamental, 54, 59, 91, 116, 242–3; fundamentals 6–7, 10–11, 33, 40, 58, 69, 78, 86, 98, 163, 192, 235–6, 246
fuzzy, property rights: 5, 21, 22, 126, 208, 209, 241, 242; resource boundaries 52, 56, 214, 228

gazar (land), concept of 51, 240
global (market) economy 135

Gobi B Ecological Reserve 208
grazing, rights for 27
Green Gold program 173
group pasture management: conflicts with local norms and practices 179; herders' seasonal rotation and 193; idea of 175, 181; limitations of 192–9; seasonal camping and grazing 193; territory-based 192
GTZ Nature Conservancy Project 246

HBU Mountain 69, 88, 95, 119, 161, 183, 190, 192, 212, 215, 218, **222**; policy of RPA establishment in 226
herder group formation, by *bag 178*
herders' access to pastoral resources: legal mechanisms to control 2; property rights and 4, 135
herders' rights, to possess residential land 135
Herlen Bayan-Ulaan Reserve Pasture Area (HBU RPA) 8, 92–100; *aj ahui* assets 129n26; area administrative structure *10, 93–4*; *bag/*village administration 120; case study area, map of **9**; grazing for sheep and goats 97; group formation in 177–81; labor component of 94–5; land reform in 142–62; legal possession of campsites in 154–62; livestock production 95; management model of 228; pasture use fees in *212*; pastureland and its tenure 95–100; privatized management of pastoral production in 115–24; production management 93–4; reservation of 212–15; storage buildings from **119**; territorial boundaries of **213**; territoriality in natural resource management in 210–26; two-year rehabilitation policy 215–22; *ulamjlalt* herding strategies 95; winter and spring campsites 95; zoning of 214
Herlen River 69, 95, 121, **159**
horoo herders 95–6; seasonal pasture and campsites 96
hoshuu territorial administration 53, 76, 82, 88
hot ail 66–7, 85, 109, 135–7, 139, 144, 183, 185, 192–4, 238
hoton (camping and the production unit) 65–7
Household Responsibility System (HRS) 29, 31

Huh Serh National Park 207
hurals 79–80, 107–8, 112, 138; land management planning 153
Hustai Nature Reserve 208

Ikh Hural (Parliament) 211
income tax, for herders' livestock 62, 142
industrial development 26, 28, 79
institutional bricolage, concept of 125, 241
Inter-*Aimag* Cross-territorial Reserve Pasture Area (RPA) 92–3
International Monetary Fund (IMF) 106
"iron rush" 129n20

Khaan, Bogd 56
Khaan, Chinggis 50–2, 54, 56, 59, 69
Khan, Munkh 54
Kherlen River *see* Herlen River

labor control, notion of 50, 61
labor demand 185, 189, 194
labor market: liberalization of 107; privatization, impact of 110; regulation of 110
labor-intensive jobs 183
land degradation 1, 22, 24–31, 33, 208, 220, 247
land management 153; historical pattern of 207; market-based 135; practice of 40; regulation of 207; territorial-based 52
land ownership 32, 51, 53, 63, 127, 135
land ploughing 50
land reform, in HBU case area 142–62; institutional, social and environmental outcomes of 154–62; legal possession of campsites 142–51; pastureland management and 151–4
land reform, in Mongolia 135–42; open access problem 162–3; outcome of 139–41; possession conflicts 140; on right to use the surrounding pastures 139; social and environmental impacts on 139; *ulamjlalt* pasture use rules and norms 141–2
land rights 3, 6, 17
land stewardship 3
land tenure 138, 235; community-based 3; pastoral context of 52
land use 135; strategy of reciprocity 140; in wasteland 36

land-based resources: property rights to 241; public ownership of 75, 125
landholding systems 2
Law of Mongolia on Administrative and Territorial Units and their Governance (1993) 108
Law of Mongolia on Environmental Protection (1995) 108, 129n12
Law of Mongolia on Land (1994) 108, 129n11, 135
lease of land 135
"Left Deviation" political movement 76
liberalization of labor 241
livelihoods, herders' 205
livestock: cross-breeding 93; enclosure of 193; in HBU case area 115–16; husbandry 4, 27, 78, 85, 98; individual ownership of 109; inspection records, for infectious disease 96; as money 110; ownership 58, **183**; privately owned 86; privatization, impact of 108–10, 193; privatized management of 115–16; production system 86, 136; shelters (*buuts*) 63, 91, 137; taxes 50, 52, 60, 78, 142; village 26
livestock diseases 63, 91, 95, 224, 239
livestock grazing 31; free-range grazing 38; herding of mixed species 35; rotational grazing, concept of 35
livestock holdings, monopoly of 53

Maasai pastoralists 24, 26, 28
Manchu Qing dynasty, pastoralism under 25, 55–69; dual control 59–65; feudal relationship 58; governance structure, pre-collective 57; *hoshuu* territory 55–8; labor value regarding 67; livestock tax 60; primary production unit 65–9; production components 58–9; sale of land to outsiders 56; *Shavi Gazar* 56–8; state-based aristocracy and 59; state/ public ownership 60; territorial administration 55–8; *ulamjlalt* system of 56, 61, 64
market economy 1, 7, 11, 33, 100, 116, 136, 171, 236, 241
Marxist feudal class relations 51
mass unemployment, issue of 107
migration: policies on 142; rural to urban 110
Ministry of Food and Agriculture (MFA) 93, 111, 195, 207, 211
Ministry of Nature and Environment (MNE) 111

256   *Index*

mobile pastoralism 2, 23, 33–4, 98, 136, 235; agrarian lifestyle 49; challenges in pursuing of *158*; culture of 1; division of labor 39; economic production system 36; emergence of 36; Inner Asian 34–6, 39; with legal possession of campsites *157*; Marxist-Leninist-Maoist view of 37; in Mongolia 34–40; political and economic benefits 39; political structure of 39; risk-mitigation strategies 35; rotational grazing, concept of 35; socio-political structure of 40; techniques of 39; without campsite possession *157*

Mongol Empire 50; exclusive property ownership 52; livestock tax 50; *myangat* system 50; nomadic feudalism, notion of 51; pastoral production management in 50–5; property relations in pastoralism 51–2

Mongolia Revolution (1921) 75–8

Mongolian Pastoralism 5, 8, 64, 135, 236, 238; fundamentals of 40, 235; geo-political and geographical position 100; quasi-feudalism aspects of 51; socio-political context of 35; sociotechnical system of 33

Mongolian People's Revolutionary Party (MPRP) 106

mortgage, right to 137

myangat system 50

Namaqualand reserves, in South Africa 29

National Parks (NP) 208

Natural and Historical Monuments (NHM) 208

natural resource management (NRM) 2–4, 7, 16, 22; state territorial strategy for 205–10

natural resources: exploitation of 22; land-based 206; misconstructing 240–1; protection of 114; state/public ownership of 7, 107, 207; state territorial strategy for management of *see* state territorial strategy, for natural resource management

Nature Reserves (NR) 208

neg nutag usniihan 197; concept of 4, 171–2, 176, 181, 191–2; herders' collaboration as 183; herders' networking pattern 181; social boundary of 181

negdel collective institution 2, 78, 86–8, 106, 109–11; collapse of 111, 118

Ngorongoro Conservation Area Administration (NCAA) 28

nomadic feudalism, notion of 51

nomadism, idea of 35

nutag territory 52, 57; control over selection of 120–4; definition of 41n10

oil supply 111

otor herders 92, 96, 124, 145, 161, 186, 214, 223, 226, 228; campsites for 216, 220; temporary *otor* headquarters (TOH) 98; tenure system for 97

otriin aj ahui, collapse of 92–3, 115, 129

otriin shtab 98

overgrazing, problem of 113, 125, 141, 242

pastoral economy, collectivization of 27

pastoral institutions 1–2, 5, 7, 11, 19, 24–5, 33, 39, 55, 67, 77–8, 113–14, 163, 171, 176–7, 192, 198, 206, 210, 227, 237, 245–7

pastoral production system 2, 4–5, 54, 138, 207; and collective entity 84–92; collectivization of 78–92; components of 243; contributing to poverty 110; cross-boundary mobility and 91–2; emergency fodder fund 88; labor aspect of 87, 110; livestock production 86; management of 58, 244–5; in Mongol Empire 50–5; Mongolia Revolution (1921) and 75–8; *myangat* system 50; pastureland and tenure 87–92; principles of 125; privatization and its impact on 106–13; privatized management of 115–24; recommendations for 244–7; and reforms in state territorial administration 79–83; regulation of 114; relationship between territorial strategy and 227–30; *ulamjlalt* system 59; use rules and norms 127, 141

pastoral societies 2, 10, 23–5, 29, 31–2, 40, 49, 69, 98

pastoralism: historical foundations of 235; under Manchu Qing dynasty 55–69; non-egalitarian 238; property relations in 51–2; rangeland management in context of 22–34; significance of 3; and its tenure 110–13

pasture-user group (PUG) 173, 197

pastureland management 2, 4, 6, 35, 58, 136, 235; *bag* and *soum* 119; decision-making on 154; idea conflicts with local norms and practices 179; implementation of 151–4; laws and legislations governing 108; nature of property relations in 128; problem of 113–14; property relations in 51; rights to pasture 114; *see also* group pasture management

Pokot pastoralists, in Kenya 29, 38

predatory pastoralism 157, 197

price control 245

private ownership of land 51, 135

private property rights 135

privately owned livestock 86, 127

privatization, of pastoral production sector: administrative and territorial governance structure *108*; components of 106; guidelines for 109; in HBU case area 115–24; impact of 106–13; labor market and 110; livestock 108–10; as mechanism for rapid economic benefits 109; pastureland and its tenure 110–13; patron-client relationships 126; stages of 128n1; underground 109

privatized management, of pastoral production: control over seasonal mobility 123–4; control over selection of *nutag* 120–3; labor components 116–18; livestock ownership 115–16; pastureland and its tenure 118–24; property institution and 125–8

property, concept of 21

property institutions, in Mongolia 49, 125–8

property ownership: European concepts of 51; of livestock 51–2; Mongolian 51; by political unit 52; private 106

property relations, "fuzzy" quality of 241

property rights institutions 235

property rights, to pastureland 1; herders' 146; private 135; reallocating of 114

Przewalskii horse (wild horse) 208

public ownership of land 33, 53, 75

public sovereignty, notion of 107

Qing Dynasty 24–5

ranching, cash-based 31

rangeland degradation: ecological factors contributing to 29; in Mongolia 1

rangeland ecosystem 2, 158

rangeland management 6, 11, 106, 236; during colonial period 23–5; community rights 26; in context of pastoralism 22–34; grazing, rights for 27; group ranches 26; herders' access to pastoral resources and 33; during post-colonial or socialist period 25–8; property rights regimes 25, 37; sociotechnical system of 33; during twentieth-twenty-first century and post-socialist period 28–34

reserve pasture areas (RPA) 205, 210; herders' access to 207; implementation of 211–12; inter-provincial 211; map of **211**; reservation of 212–15; strategy for establishing 206; Temporary Committee for regulation of 212; zoning of 212, 228

residential registration system 144; legal notions of 148; process of 146

resource management 1–5, 7, 17–19, 21, 239

rights to land, types of 135

risk management 199; strategies for food security 205

Roman Empire 49

rural economy 85, 240

rural land, privatization of 3

rural to urban migration 110

sangiin aj ahui (state-owned enterprises) 85, 87–8, 92, 106

seasonal mobility, patterns of 67, 82–3, 89, 91, 114, 123–5, 127, 138, 141, 155, 157–8, 176, 197, 222, 237, 243

seasonal pasture, management of 138

Secret History of Mongolia 50

sedentarization, village-based 4, 29, 136

sedentary production system 136

Shavi Gazar 56–9

social capital 17, 179, 192–3

social networking 62, 88, 173, 176, 181, 192, 201n26, 238

social stratification 21

socialist competitions, for livestock products 87, 92

Society of Protection of the Environment and Nature 206

soum territories 84–5, 98, 107, 110, 138

Soviet Union, collapse of 106

state properties, privatization of 3

state/public ownership, of natural resources 7, 51, 53, 60

state special needs territory 211

258 *Index*

state territorial administration 52, 107; changes in *81*; reforms in 79–83

state territorial strategy, for natural resource management: collective period 206–7; in HBU case study area 210–26; pre-collective period 205–6; and relation with production management 227–30; transition period 207–10

stock exchange system 107

Strictly Protected Areas (SPA) 208

Structural Adjustment Program (SAP) 2, 106

Sustainable Livelihood Program (SLP) 173, 177, 181, 198

suuri herders 86, 90, 96

Swiss Development Cooperation (SDC) 173–4, 197

tax system, centralization of 77

temporary *otor* headquarters (TOH) 98

territorial-based land management 52

territoriality, in natural resource management: in HBU case study area 210–26; implementation of HBU RPA 211–12; outcome and challenges 223–6

"tragedy of the commons" 25, 113

tribal kinship society 38

Tsagaan Sar holiday 97

Tsarist Russia 25

Tuvan pastoralism 28

"*ujamaa*" (family hood) 26

ulamjlalt: family-splitting strategy 161; legal possession of campsites 161; livestock production 211; mobility strategies 141; *otor* movement 157, 161, 207, 209, 244; pastoral production 59, 61, 64, 77, 79, 86, 88–9, 95, 195, 237, 240; pasture use rules and norms 141–2, 162, 172, 197, 229, 237, 241; pattern in accessing cross-territorial mobility 162; practice of keeping livestock as money 110; rights to access pasture 161; seasonal movement 123, 125, 157; sharing pasture, norm of 161; structure of campsites 160; use rights, concept of 127

Union of Agricultural Cooperatives 109

uvuljuu havarjaa, allocation of 135–6, 138

value added production, development of 245

wildlife habitation 29

World Bank 2–3, 106; Sustainable Livelihood Program (SLP) 173

zoning of seasonal pastures 214